On the Ideological Front

STUART FINKEL

On the Ideological Front

THE RUSSIAN INTELLIGENTSIA AND THE MAKING OF THE SOVIET PUBLIC SPHERE

Yale University Press
New Haven &
London

Published with assistance fom the Louis Stern Memorial Fund.

Set in Sabon by IBT.

Printed in the United States of America.

Library of Congress Cataloging-in-Publication Data

Finkel, Stuart, 1970–
On the ideological front : the Russian intelligentsia and the making of the Soviet public sphere / Stuart Finkel.
p. cm.
Includes bibliographical references and index.
ISBN 978-0-300-12241-1 (cloth : alk. paper)
1. Intellectuals—Soviet Union—History. 2. Exile (Punishment)—Soviet Union—History. I. Title.
DK265.9.I55F56 2007
305.5'5209470904—dc22 2007017043

A catalogue record for this book is available from the British Library.

The paper in this book meets the guidelines for permanence and durability of the Committee on Production Guidelines for Book Longevity of the Council on Library Resources.

10 9 8 7 6 5 4 3 2 1

Contents

Acknowledgments

This book has been many years in production, if one considers when it began as a dissertation, and so I have received advice, counsel, guidance, and assistance from several institutions and many people along the way. Some of those whom I will thank below may not even remember reading early drafts or having discussed the project with me, but I assure them that they did, and I am grateful for their help. Needless to say, the customary caveat that any mistakes are mine certainly applies.

First and foremost I would like to thank my advisers: Terence Emmons, who helped foster my interest in the Russian intelligentsia and encouraged me to follow my academic instincts, and Amir Weiner, who challenged me throughout to remain focused on the larger, more substantial questions, not to lose the forest for the trees. Norman Naimark and Paul Robinson also provided sage counsel and insight. My fellow graduate students at Stanford, including Steve Barnes, Andy Jenks, Andrea Orzoff, Dusan Djordjevich, and Ann Livschiz, were subjected to numerous dissertation drafts, and they supplied both welcome camaraderie and enormously helpful advice. The research and writing that came to constitute this book were undertaken thanks to research grants from the American Council of Teachers of Russian, the Anatole Mazour Travel and Research Fund, and an Andrew Mellon Foundation grant by way of the Stanford Center for Russian and

East European Studies. I was able to write the dissertation on which this book was based thanks to generous support from the Stanford Humanities Center, the Spencer Foundation, and the Oakford fellowship fund.

I would also like to express my gratitude to all those colleagues and friends who have taken the time to look at my work-in-progress or to discuss my research with me and offer me their insight, including Randy Law, Bert Patenaude, Ronald Suny, Michael David-Fox, Peter Holquist, Lynne Viola, Ziva Galili, David Hoffmann, Jane Burbank, Douglas Weiner, Mark Johnson, Barbara Walker, Brian Kassof, Sharon Kowalski, and John Connelly. Marina Khlopaeva, Andrei Kvakin, and Mikhail Glavatskii offered expert advice on the expulsions of intellectuals and the Russian intelligentsia and emigration. My colleagues at the Davis Center at Harvard during my year there offered extremely useful guidance as I began to make the transition from dissertation to book. Joan Neuberger and Charters Wynn provided kindly encouragement while I was at the University of Texas, and my current colleagues at the University of Florida have welcomed me and offered wonderful support as I bring this book to its completion.

Special thanks go to Jonathan Brent and the other editors at Yale University Press with whom I have worked, to Ann Twombly for her scrupulous copyediting, and to Lisa Booth for her tireless work on the index and proofs, and to the two anonymous reviewers for their suggestions and improvements.

Some elements of this book have appeared previously in articles; these include "Purging the Public Intellectual: The 1922 Expulsions from Soviet Russia," *Russian Review* 62, no. 4 (October 2003): 589–613; "An Intensification of Vigilance: Recent Perspectives on the Institutional History of the Soviet Security Apparatus in the 1920s," *Kritika* 5, no. 2 (Spring 2004): 299–320; and "Sociology and Revolution: Pitirim Sorokin and Russia's National Degeneration," *Russian History/Histoire Russe* 32, no. 2 (Summer 2005): 155–69. I am grateful to the publishers of those journals for permission to use the material again in this book. In addition, portions of chapter 3 appeared in Russian in the conference proceedings *Vlast' i nauka, nauka i vlast'* (St. Petersburg: Dmitrii Bulanin, 2003).

Finally I would like to give thanks to those whose affection and support have guided me through this project: to my parents, for their love, encouragement, and understanding over so many years; to my brother Ed; to Max, who fills my daily life with joy, and to his little brother, Leo, who has just joined us, and to my wife, Lynn Patyk, for her counsel, her insight, and her love. This book is dedicated to all of them.

Introduction

I am that gadfly which God has attached to the state, and all day long and in all places am always fastening upon you, arousing and persuading and reproaching you. You will not easily find another like me, and therefore I would advise you to spare me.

• • •

And what a life should I lead, at my age, wandering from city to city, ever changing my place of exile, and always being driven out!

—*Socrates' Defense, from Plato, The Apology*

On 15 November 1922 seventeen intellectuals and their families prepared to board the German steamship *Preussen* off the shores of Petrograd, bound for Stettin, Germany. The members of this diverse group of professors, journalists, philosophers, writers, engineers, and agronomists were not departing voluntarily; they were leaving because Russia's new rulers, V. I. Lenin and his colleagues in the Bolshevik Party, had ordered their expulsion. On the docks Soviet secret policemen, called *chekisty,* carefully checked their documents and went through their belongings. The long and grueling day was complicated by the fact that no one on either side seemed to know exactly how much money or which possessions they could take. The process took some time, and the boat did not depart until the following morning. Only then did most of its passengers begin to relax.

Coincidentally, there were several other Russian intellectuals traveling under more normal circumstances on the same boat, including the theater director N. N. Evreinov. Evreinov's wife, Anna Aleksandrovna, recognizing the moment's historical import, wandered the deck with a notebook asking the deportees to record their thoughts. Those who obliged expressed a mixture of shock, relief, despair, resentment, and confusion. Some reflected on the bittersweet experience of leaving their tortured but much beloved homeland; others attempted to make sense of their expulsion. Such were the musings of the agronomist Boris Odintsov: "Among us are professors and litterateurs, but in vain will you search for politicians dangerous to the usurpers of power in Russia. Why did they deport us? What was it—stupidity or fear? I think that it was both. The rulers of Russia, despite their insolence, are sufficiently cowardly that they are afraid of any independently and honestly expressed opinion and out of stupidity send us to where we will have the full opportunity to speak those truths that they hope to hide from themselves and the entire world." The philosopher Nikolai Losskii also wondered what he was being deported for: "It was not for political activity, for I have not engaged in any over these past five years. Thus I am banished from Russia, as a year ago they banished me from Petrograd University, guilty only of my religious-philosophical ideology. This means that my opponents themselves secretly admit that the following thesis is true: being is determined by consciousness, the spirit rules over matter." Others angrily denied having done anything wrong. Losskii's colleague Ivan Lapshin defiantly proclaimed, "I am not a state criminal!" The journalist Boris Khariton simply threw up his hands, noting philosophically, "I look upon our deportation as one of the final revolutionary excesses, and in excesses there is never either any kind of logic or sense."[1]

In all, close to one hundred intellectuals and their families were expelled in fall 1922 and winter 1923, and dozens more were deported to various internal locations. The deportation of intellectuals was a critical moment in the unmaking of the old Russian intelligentsia; it greatly accelerated the process of removing prominent non-Communist intellectuals from positions of influence and prestige.[2] An integrated set of measures accompanying the expulsions—the consolidation of control over universities, periodic purges of students and professors, the erection of a surveillance apparatus over independent societies and organizations, the establishment of a central censorship organ, and the closure of nonofficial journals and publishing houses—sharply curtailed the autonomy of the intellectual public sphere.

Bolshevik polemicists spoke of this effort as the "struggle on the ideological front."[3] Most intellectuals did not experience the time of the New Economic Policy, or NEP (1921–28), as a time of relative permissiveness, as has sometimes been suggested in the historical literature, but as one of increasing state encroachment on their scholarly, professional, and artistic activities.[4] The 1920s were characterized by marked inconsistencies in Bolshevik policy toward intellectuals, but these inconsistencies were the result of indecision and limited resources rather than tolerance or a fondness for pluralism.

The making of the Soviet intelligentsia depended on a radically different understanding of its role. No longer were intellectuals to claim their time-honored place as the conscience of the nation, the defenders of the popular masses. This was now reserved for the advance guard of the Revolution, the Bolshevik Party. The Soviet definition of intelligentsia was at once broader and less elemental, including all those who performed "mental labor" (*umstvennyi trud*) but rejecting the idea that the intelligentsia had any unique historic mission. The intellectual was to be a leader by example, to whom the Soviet state would grant privileges in return for refraining from criticism and independent political action. Those willing to serve the new order would be rewarded for their contributions, and great efforts were made to attract "bourgeois" technical specialists, or *spetsy*, to work in Soviet institutions.[5] But the liberal ideal of the independent-minded, morally autonomous individual was not compatible with the Bolshevik vision of civil society.

This book will trace this shift in the composition and character of the intelligentsia, in the very definition of the place and function of intellectuals, between 1917 and the onset of the so-called cultural revolution in the late 1920s. I will argue that NEP featured the introduction of significant restraints on intellectuals and their academic, cultural, and professional institutions. Conflicts between the regime and the intelligentsia in the early 1920s went a long way toward determining the shape of *obshchestvennost'*, of the self-conscious public sphere, in early Soviet Russia. In the immediate postrevolutionary years that are the subject of this book, *obshchestvennost'* referred at once to a sense of civic involvement, or "public mindedness," to the network of public organizations (*obshchestvennye organizatsii*), and to the remaining nonaligned intelligentsia as a group.[6] The overwhelming consensus among leading Bolsheviks, despite important differences on how best to proceed, was that the public sphere in a socialist society should be unitary and univocal. They thus proceeded to establish a uniquely Soviet public sphere, one purged of the political heterogeneity, partitioning, and divisiveness that characterized the bourgeois public sphere. As Michael David-Fox has noted, "The Bolsheviks embraced the concept of a 'Soviet *obshchestvennost*'' after the

Revolution even as they moved swiftly to ban many societies and independent organizations."[7]

This concept was in fundamental opposition to the understanding of *obshchestvennost'* shared by most intellectuals. Many still hoped that autonomous public organizations could generate space outside the purview of the state, and even in potential opposition to it. The sociologist Pitirim Sorokin explicitly defended this notion of civil society, calling it the "Anglo-Saxon position."[8] Central to this conception of the public sphere was the existence of restricted voluntary organizations, which aroused the Bolsheviks' deep-seated antipathy toward what they termed "corporate," "caste," or "separatist" inclinations among the intelligentsia. Having dispensed with political rivals, the Communist leadership was determined not to allow them to arise again among purportedly apolitical intellectual groups. As Lenin and his colleagues adamantly insisted, there was no such thing as neutrality in the midst of an unfinished class struggle, and the public sphere was inherently political.[9]

Although most intellectuals may not have explicitly identified the principles that Sorokin espoused, their activities—the formation of societies, the publishing and writing, and the defense of university autonomy—all pointed to a general sharing of the values of *obshchestvennost'*. That they were often concerned as much with protecting collective self-interest as with serving the people or the nation does not diminish their significance as oases of autonomy in Soviet society. Professional unions and agricultural cooperatives had already been largely bolshevized during the Civil War, as had the soviets themselves. Independent press organs were prohibited, which made the brief appearance of unofficial journals at the beginning of NEP that much more remarkable. The publishing of these journals, together with the autonomous universities of the Civil War period and the independent societies that flourished briefly at this time, should be seen as among the final instances of civil society, of the "bourgeois" public sphere, in Soviet Russia.

Although some historians have suggested that, because of the endurance of certain autonomous organizations, the continued presence of "bourgeois" professors in the universities, and the existence of independent publishers, one may speak of civil society as lasting until the end of NEP, I would argue that this was so only in an external or formal sense.[10] As of 1923, strict limits had been placed on the formation, operation, and composition of voluntary societies, and the avenues for critical public speech had been sharply curtailed. Universities, though not under complete Bolshevik curricular control, were no longer administratively independent, and the professoriat as an independent corporate entity had been dismantled.

The Intelligentsia and the Public Sphere

Self-conscious introspection over what role intellectuals should or must play in society was a prominent topic of Russian public discourse. By the late nineteenth century, "What is the intelligentsia?" had become—along with "What is to be done?" and "Who is to blame?"—one of the eternal "accursed questions" for Russian thinkers.[11] Although the origins of the intelligentsia can be traced back to the end of the eighteenth century, it was an identity that existed in its classic form only between the great reforms of the 1860s and the October Revolution. The term originally referred to anyone who thought independently, more often than not opponents of the regime, with a deep sense of moral commitment.[12] Just as quickly as it had originated, however, the concept became hopelessly complicated. As industrialization, urbanization, and the rise of mass education led to a rapid growth of the professional classes in the last decades of the nineteenth century, *intelligent* came to designate any member of the educated public. In response, intellectuals from a variety of political backgrounds tried to revive the original, more exclusive, missionary sense of the word.[13]

A pervasive disappointment with the 1905 Revolution led some thinkers to criticize the purported failings of the intelligentsia and to question its proper role in civic life.[14] While the populist R. V. Ivanov-Razumnik led a defense of the intelligentsia, others believed that its single-minded self-righteousness and fanatical materialism had resulted in grave mistakes and could lead to disaster. The most famous articulation of this point of view was the 1909 set of essays entitled *Vekhi* (Signposts or Landmarks). The *Vekhi* authors, including Mikhail Gershenzon, Nikolai Berdiaev, Pëtr Struve, and Semën Frank, differed on a number of points, but they agreed that the intelligentsia had a dangerous obsession with external change at the expense of personal growth. They enjoined their fellow intellectuals to look first to their own internal spiritual and ethical state before claiming to speak for the people.[15] The vast majority of intellectuals, however, considered *Vekhi* to be a bitter betrayal and a thinly veiled apologia for the tsarist regime.[16]

At the same time, the dramatic expansion of the educated public had at last created an incipient civil society. There was a variety of newspapers representing multiple points of view; there were professions forming their own corporate societies and organizations; there were national movements constituting an ever-increasing set of imagined communities, each with its own newspapers and organizations; and there were political parties, elections, and a (limited and imperfect) parliamentary body. The growth of the educated public led to a corresponding increase in a sense of civic involvement, or *obshchestvennost'*, a concept of great significance at the time.[17] For revolutionaries, *obshchestvennost'* signified "both the qualities of social engagement and the sector of society most likely to manifest such qualities, the radical intelligentsia." For liberals, on the other hand, it came closer to matching the concept of the public sphere, "to concern with public duties and common deeds (*res publica,* in Russian *delo obshchestvennoe*), and also to 'public opinion' (*obshchestvennye mnenie*)."[18] A brittle but real civil society was developing via the growth and consolidation of voluntary associations, and serving the public good through this evolving civil society represented a more inclusive alternative to the traditional intellectual goal of revolution.[19] The burgeoning intellectual, cultural, and professional organizations inculcated in their members the value of autonomy, of a sense of public involvement independent of the state. Despite the predominance of statism, a belief that the state had a central role to play in fostering both economic and social development, engineers, agronomists, physicians, professors, and lawyers became increasingly frustrated by how a lack of political liberties under the tsars hampered their professional work.[20]

Members of the Bolshevik leadership harbored an overwhelming disdain for most of their fellow intellectuals. The fractious nature of prerevolutionary intellectual debate fostered a conviction that even their fellow socialists were not to be trusted, and the chorus of protest with which the overwhelming majority of the intelligentsia greeted the October Revolution only exacerbated these suspicions. The Manichaean divisions of the Civil War led to a determined hunt to root out the enemy, and the *intelligent* was often made to stand in for the increasingly elusive *burzhui* in revolutionary rhetoric.[21] Many intellectuals emigrated during the Civil War or after the downfall of the White forces, and many others perished in the conditions of deprivation, disease, and famine. Already by 1921, irrevocable changes had taken place in the makeup of the intelligentsia, and periodic arrests and a barrage of anti-intellectual propaganda had further alienated those who remained.

Under these conditions, intellectuals attached great significance to the introduction of the New Economic Policy in 1921, and many assumed that similar concessions would be introduced in the cultural sphere. The reintroduction of private publishing buoyed these hopes, and both the universities and literary societies showed signs of revival after seven difficult years of European war, revolution, and civil war. Alarmed by this "renaissance of bourgeois ideology," Lenin and his colleagues began to pay greater attention to the so-called third, or ideological, front. Their subsequent efforts to assert control over higher education, literary, scholarly, and professional societies, and private publishing were met with fierce resistance. Professors and litterateurs, publishers and publicists, physicians, engineers, and agronomists were determined to maintain or regain autonomy in their scientific, cultural, and professional activities.

The desire to maintain a sphere outside direct state control motivated a vigorous defense of university autonomy, a renewed interest in nongovernmental societies, and a revival of independent journals. There was at least one explicit theorist of the value of autonomous civil society, the sociologist Sorokin, who maintained that only a robust set of social institutions could instill the qualities of individualism, responsibility, and personal initiative necessary for a democratic citizenry.[22] Many of those who shared Sorokin's distaste for Bolshevism doubted that even this was possible. The authors of *Vekhi,* convinced that their dark prophecies had come to pass, compiled a sequel entitled *Iz glubiny* (Out of the Depths), in which they blamed the Bolshevik catastrophe once again on the unwillingness of the intelligentsia to recognize the dangers of revolutionary maximalism.[23] Aleksandr Izgoev rejected any hope of carving out a civic sphere as impractical under the current order, and he argued that substantial political change would be necessary before such "public action" was possible.[24]

The intelligentsia's vocal criticism redoubled the Bolsheviks' long-standing scorn for what they saw as a predominantly useless class of people. Those intellectuals who did not possess useful technical skills, or at least a productive approach to cultural development, were deemed (at best) superfluous. The cultivation of *spetsy* in no way indicated endorsement of an autonomous public sphere for higher educational institutions, associations, and publications. Lenin and his colleagues had seen enough opposition from the intelligentsia to assume that concerted "public action" independent of their direction was inherently inclined toward separatist, and, from there, counterrevolutionary tendencies. As Jane Burbank has observed, the Bolsheviks felt that "the discourse of civil, bourgeois society was unnecessary and dangerous, and thus the limited openings to a pluralistic, fluid politics in the decade before the revolution were closed off once again."[25] There was great pressure placed on intellectuals to become part of the greater collective.[26] The promotion of the autonomous citizen, the morally responsible individual, inherent in the liberal concept of *obshchestvennost'* was incompatible with the goals of the dictatorship of the proletariat. The Bolshevik leadership decided to send a powerful message regarding the limits of acceptable public behavior, which culminated in the deportation of scores of intellectuals from Soviet Russia and of dozens more to distant provincial locations in fall and winter 1922–23.

The Philosophers' Steamboat

For the leaders of the young Bolshevik regime, any feelings of triumph at the end of the Civil War were tempered with the realization that they remained isolated and weak, surrounded by external foes and threatened by internal unrest. In such circumstances, it was imperative to crack down on dissent, and Bolshevik leaders portrayed the expulsions as both necessary and merciful. Lev Trotsky declared, "In view of the fact that the professors and their ilk have not been able to make peace with the Soviet regime over the past five years, they must be regarded as enemies." In case of war, the Bolsheviks would be forced to shoot them, and the regime was thus acting with "farsighted humaneness." Grigorii Zinoviev, too, stressed the fact that they had "selected the most humane measure, deportation abroad."[27] While emphasizing the merciful nature of their actions, however, the Bolsheviks also meant to show that they dealt firmly with their foes. *Pravda* asserted that the deportations represented a "first warning": although the regime valued the skills and labor of those willing to work for it, it would use all means possible to uncover and eliminate hidden struggles.[28] Stalin proclaimed that "humanitarian" methods would not be in use long if this warning was not heeded, and he hinted at a return to the terror of the Civil War: "Let them remember that we carry out our promises. And how we follow up our warnings—this should be known by the experience of recent years."[29]

The expulsion of intellectuals has come to be known as the Philosophers' Steamboat (*filosofskii parokhod*), after the most famous group of deportees, including four of the seven contributors to *Vekhi:* Nikolai Berdiaev, Semën Frank, Aleksandr Izgoev, and Sergei Bulgakov. A number of other philosophers were also deported, including Ivan Lapshin, the Hegelian scholar Ivan Il'in, the logician Nikolai Losskii, and the medievalist Lev Karsavin. Similar ideological motivations dictated the expulsion of other humanities and social science scholars, including the literary critic Iul'ii Aikhenval'd, the historians Antonii Florovskii and Aleksandr Kizevetter, the economist Boris Brutskus, and the sociologist Sorokin. They were joined by publicists and litterateurs, including Mikhail Osorgin, Vladimir Rozenberg, Nikolai Volkovyskii, and Boris Khariton. Some of these writers were associated with newly revived independent journals and almanacs, whose editors and publishers, including Dalmat Lutokhin and Abram Kagan, were also among those banished from Russia. Some were also former members of other political parties, including the Popular Socialists (*Narodno-sotsialisty,* or NSs) Venedikt Miakotin, Aleksandr

Peshekhonov, and Sergei Mel'gunov, and the Kadets Kizevetter, Izgoev, and others. For these individuals, it was a combination of their recent political associations and current publicistic or scholarly activities that determined the decision to deport.

Several of those expelled had been leaders of professors' organizations or rectors and deans of leading higher educational institutions (or both) during the bitter struggle over university autonomy. These included the zoologist and former Moscow University (MGU) rector Mikhail Novikov, the astronomer and dean of the MGU Math-Physics Faculty Vsevolod Stratonov, the agronomist and Petrograd University (PGU) vice-rector Boris Odintsov, the Kazan University rector A. A. Ovchinnikov, and the Moscow Higher Technical School engineer Vsevolod Iasinskii, who had also been de facto leader of the Commission to Improve the Lot of Scholars, or KUBU. The publicist Ekaterina Kuskova, her husband, Sergei Prokopovich, and several others were deported for their leadership of the short-lived and ill-fated public famine relief committee formed in summer 1921. Bolshevik anxieties concerning the agricultural cooperative movement led to the expulsion of a dozen agronomists and cooperative leaders, including Brutskus, Aleksandr Ugrimov, M. D. Shishkin, and A. I. Sigirskii. Others were associated with "sectarian" religious and spiritual movements, including the prominent Tolstoyan Valentin Bulgakov, V. F. Martsinkovskii, a leader of the evangelical Christian student movement, and V. V. Abrikosov, head of a Moscow-based ecumenical movement aimed at Catholic-Orthodox unity.

The final tally of intellectuals expelled during fall and winter 1922–23 is difficult to determine precisely.[30] Certain individuals left after the primary group, and, though the vast majority of deportees originated in Moscow and Petrograd, a handful came from provincial cities, including Kazan and Odessa. In addition, a number of those originally consigned to expulsion had their sentences altered after submission of petitions and reconsideration. The number who were actually banished was far fewer than the "several hundred" originally ordered by Lenin and is closer to eighty, not including their wives and families.[31] Several very well-known intellectuals were originally scheduled for expulsion but set free (and even allowed to continue working in Soviet institutions) after appeals on their behalf, including the writer Evgenii Zamiatin, the Tolstoyan Vladimir Chertkov, the engineer Pëtr Pal'chinskii, and the agronomist Nikolai Kondrat'ev. Others were sent into internal exile, including more than a dozen physicians whose skills were needed in the struggle against famine and disease, and who were therefore deported to Turkistan and other remote locations. In Ukraine the party leadership's trepidation about augmenting the vocal nationalist emigration with prominent intellectuals resulted in the deportation of the vast majority of those designated for expulsion to places within Soviet Russia.

The Enemy and the Body Politic

The individuals selected for expulsion were considered to have overstepped the boundaries of permissible behavior by asserting for the intelligentsia a role to which it was no longer supposed to aspire. The Bolshevik leadership branded their efforts to maintain an autonomous public sphere in their societies, publications, and universities a danger to social harmony, to the unity of the socialist state. The selection of expulsion as the method of excision had much to do with the politics of the moment: encircled by hostile capitalist nations, with the world revolution evidently delayed, the Bolshevik leadership strove to present a more moderate face to the outside world.[32] Although exile abroad was used only in exceptional cases after 1923, the Soviet system of internal exile developed directly from the events discussed in this book.

The oft-repeated charges of "corporatism" and "caste separatism" leveled against intellectuals and professionals highlight the Bolshevik conviction that there was no place in their society for an independent public sphere. The French theorist Claude Lefort has argued that the logic of Soviet ideology denied the possibility of legitimate social partitions, so that "there can be no other division than between the people and its enemies."[33] The Bolshevik Party viewed itself as the sole legitimate representative of the people, making a distinct and separate public sphere anachronistic and a threat to the unity and harmony that had been (or would be) established. The image of the enemy, Lefort notes, became a critical component of social discourse; "the definition of the enemy is constitutive of the identity of the people. . . . The campaigns of exclusion, persecution and . . . terror reveal a new image of the social body. The enemy of the people is regarded as a parasite or a waste product to be eliminated. . . . The pursuit of the enemies of the people is carried out in the name of an ideal of social prophylaxis, and this has been the case since Lenin's time." That unions, organizations, and cultural groups, seemingly distinct "micro-bodies," were allowed to continue to exist was a matter of form; they were in fact "consubstantial" with the regime.[34]

Peter Holquist has shown how the techniques of the Soviet regime in identifying, observing, and eliminating its opponents developed into a holistic system for constructing a socialist society, such that "the project of fashioning society by excising particular 'elements' was an intrinsic aspect of Soviet power from the very first." What differentiated the Soviet Union from other modern states was that the principles of wartime mobilization were institutionalized as the basis of organizing society.[35] Excision was not simply a process of removal but one of societal formation; equally critical was the task of gathering information about and dividing and categorizing the population, and not just those who were enemies.[36] The development of the modern surveillance state was not unique to the Bolsheviks, but, as Holquist notes, the public sphere as they understood it was a significantly broader concept than it was elsewhere, and so the surveillance apparatus was that much more comprehensive.[37]

The presence of the enemy was a critical component of the Bolshevik Weltanschauung. This idea received one of its first thorough expositions from Berdiaev, who opined: "The communist is defined psychologically chiefly by the fact that for him the world is sharply divided into two opposed camps—Ormuzd and Ahriman, the kingdom of light and the kingdom of darkness, without any shading. . . . The fanaticism, intolerance, cruelty, and violence of the thorough-going type of communist is explained by the fact that he feels himself faced by the kingdom of Satan and he cannot endure that kingdom. But at the same time he depends negatively upon the kingdom of Satan, upon evil, upon capitalism, upon the bourgeoisie. He cannot live without an enemy, without the feeling of hostility to that enemy; he loses his *pathos* when that enemy does not exist, and if there is no enemy he must invent one."[38]

As the intelligentsia became identified with the natural enemy of the proletariat, the bourgeoisie, its various elements were categorized by a set of ever more elastic pejorative labels designed to clarify its true position vis-à-vis the unified people. The Manichaean vision of which Berdiaev speaks rejected the possibility of neutral or apolitical activity, a fact that would come to be a frequent point of contention in the conflicts between the regime and the intelligentsia.[39] It was at the basis of their fundamentally different understandings of the public sphere.

The use of the term *public sphere* in the context of Soviet history necessitates some explanation. In his groundbreaking and immensely influential work, Jürgen Habermas traced the development, and eventual decay, of the "bourgeois" public sphere in Western societies from the Enlightenment through the mid-twentieth century, but he was quite explicit in not intending for his analysis to be converted into an ideal-typical model.[40] As Philip Huang has noted, however, Habermas also used the idea of the public sphere in a broader sense, and historians of certain non-Western European regions have recognized the value of the general analysis and adapted it with extremely fruitful results to a number of national experiences.[41] One need not limit one's use of the concept to the type and particular historical circumstances that Habermas described. That is to say, one may investigate and analyze social formations that may share some but not all of the characteristics of the Habermasian public sphere.

I will employ the term in its broader sense, particularly as it serves as an appropriate and useful rendering of *obshchestvennost'*. The struggle depicted in the pages that follow—over the parameters of public discourse, professional organizations and universities, and the roles of "society" and of literary production—was precisely a debate over whether a public sphere in the Western model would be realized in Soviet Russia. As Habermas suggested, "Citizens behave as a public body when they confer in an unrestricted fashion—that is, with the guarantee of freedom of assembly and association and the freedom to express and publish their opinions—about matters of general interest."[42] The Bolsheviks viewed the insistence of Russian intellectuals that they be allowed to operate according to principles of public behavior quite self-consciously adopted from the West as tantamount to a political act. In place of bourgeois *obshchestvennost'*, the Bolsheviks strove to create a new public sphere, of a sort hinted at but never described fully by Habermas: a "plebiscitary-acclamatory form of regimented public sphere characterizing dictatorships in highly developed industrial societies."[43] The Soviet public sphere would, in form, be quite similar to the autonomous civil society it was intended to replace—replete with a variety of press organs, higher educational institutions, professional unions, voluntary organizations, and cultural societies. At the same time, however, it would be purged of the disturbing heterogeneity that characterized the bourgeois public sphere and infused instead with the enforced harmony and unity that was a central element of the Soviet utopian project. The new public sphere would enhance and amplify the comprehensive educative project that was, as Peter Kenez has suggested, intended to create the new *Homo sovieticus*, Soviet man.[44]

This book, a study of the structural transformation or, more accurately, formation of the Soviet public sphere, will thus follow several interrelated narratives. First, it is the very human account of how dozens of people were expelled from their homeland for ideological reasons. It is also a depiction of the kind of society that was being forged as Russia was at last emerging from the cataclysm of seven years of war, revolution, and civil war. It is the story of the debate over what kind of intelligentsia would now emerge in this new polity and over what role it would play; it is the story of the establishment of the institutions that would come to constitute a distinctly Soviet public sphere; and it is the story of the formation of many of the practices of power that would come to characterize the Soviet system.

1

The Russian Intelligentsia and the Bolsheviks at the End of the Civil War

The intellectuals, the lackeys of capital, . . . consider themselves the brains of the nation. In fact they are not its brains, but its shit.
—*Lenin to Gorky, 15 September 1919*

By the end of 1917 it was readily apparent, if it had not been previously, that a wide chasm separated the Bolsheviks from most of the rest of the intelligentsia. Dozens of intellectuals fled to join the embryonic counterrevolutionary forces, while many others denounced the Bolshevik coup d'état and called for the convocation of the Constituent Assembly. The professoriat reacted with almost universal opposition, as did most student groups. Those intellectuals who lived in Moscow and Petrograd under extremely difficult conditions during the Civil War remained overwhelmingly hostile toward the Soviet regime. Even the cautious Academy of Sciences described the October Revolution as "a great tragedy."[1] This criticism infuriated Lenin and other leading Bolsheviks, who already considered the intelligentsia a predominantly useless class of people. Even after many intellectuals came to accept the new regime, their intentions were always suspect. In addition to those who openly joined the Whites, underground anti-Bolshevik groups of varying size and seriousness of intention flourished in the two capitals during the Civil War. The party leadership directed the Cheka, the Soviet secret police, to increase its vigilance: "Having undergone defeat on the external front, the counterrevolution is directing all of its forces to shattering Soviet Russia from within."[2]

The constant threat of arrest was only one of many hardships intellectuals faced during the Civil War. Economic collapse, disease, and malnutrition led to a high premature death rate among scholars, and extensive emigration completed a massive brain drain.[3] Horrified at the decimation of Russia's educated forces, Maxim Gorky emerged as their most important patron, setting up a network of organizations led by the Committee to Improve the Lot of Scholars, or KUBU, to aid intellectuals and appeal for the release of those in prison.[4] In addition, the Political Red Cross, run by Gorky's first wife, E. P. Peshkova, interceded where it could on behalf of arrested political prisoners. Lenin was well aware of the Soviet state's dependence on intellectual expertise and warned his more zealous colleagues that "bourgeois" specialists must be attracted to work for the new order. He was, however, less than sympathetic to Gorky's appeals on their behalf, warning him not "to waste yourself on the whining of decaying intellectuals."[5]

The continued existence of underground organizations uniting opponents of varying political tendencies greatly troubled the conspiracy-minded Bolsheviks. The most prominent result was the trial of the so-called Tactical Center in fall 1920, at which a number of intellectuals were accused of establishing a vast umbrella organization of anti-Bolshevik forces. The fear of hidden enemies intensified considerably after the Kronstadt uprising in March 1921, and dozens of professors and other intellectuals were implicated in the so-called Petrograd Battle Organization affair and executed in August 1921. Although the Cheka (unlike its descendants in later years) did not invent these anti-Bolshevik conspiracies out of whole cloth, it had a considerable tendency to exaggerate their extent and import. This played off the fears of the Bolshevik leadership, which rightly saw itself as isolated and surrounded by enemies, but which tended to overstate its foes' cunning and organizational power. Nevertheless, its fixation on these conspiracies had important implications for the larger public sphere; it greatly enhanced the leadership's suspicion of intellectual groupings in general, especially those with ties to émigré groups.

Despite the mutual suspicion with which the regime and most of the educated elite regarded one another, and despite the enforcement of a one-party political monopoly, certain prominent intellectuals argued that public figures (*obshchestvennye deiateli*) could and should play a constructive role even under a Bolshevik dictatorship.[6] This was a logical continuation of the task moderate intellectuals had envisioned for themselves under tsarist rule: to do what was possible, even though the authoritarian regime made this difficult, to serve Russian society.[7] The Soviet regime and the intelligentsia thus had radically different views of the role of *obshchestvennost'*, of the character of "public work" in a socialist society.

This disagreement came to a head over the formation of a semi-autonomous famine relief organization in summer 1921. The All-Russian Committee to Aid the Starving (*Vserossiiskii komitet pomoshchi golodaiushchim,* or VKPG) brought together prominent public figures and high-ranking Bolsheviks in an effort to provide relief to the famine-stricken Volga region. Mutual suspicions soon doomed this attempt at cooperative public work, however, and Lenin ordered the Cheka to arrest most of the non-Communist participants. Ekaterina Kuskova, her husband, Sergei Prokopovich, and other committee leaders were then deported to internal provincial locations, and several were later expelled from the country. The ill-fated famine relief committee epitomized the conflict over the shaping of the Soviet public sphere. Although members of this group explicitly saw themselves as performing "public work" on behalf of the Russian people, just as they might have under the tsarist regime, the Bolsheviks strongly rejected the idea that such autonomous *obshchestvennost'* was either necessary or desirable under the dictatorship of the proletariat.

The Tactical Center, Kronstadt, and the Tagantsev Affair

The moderate socialist and liberal intelligentsia that had formed the core of the Provisional Government was understandably displeased by its overthrow and the establishment of the Bolshevik regime. Academic, cultural, and professional collectives reacted with vocal condemnation of the October Revolution and of the disbanding of the Constituent Assembly, which many viewed as the great last hope for Russian democracy. As the country moved toward civil war, many emigrated, while others joined the various White movements. A good number of those who remained in Bolshevik-controlled Moscow and Petrograd hoped for the downfall of the new order or actively schemed on behalf of its enemies, even while adapting to the difficult wartime conditions in their daily lives. Gradually, various past or current members of moderate socialist or liberal parties, the Kadets (Constitutional Democrats), SRs (Socialists-Revolutionaries), and NSs (Popular Socialists), began to gravitate toward several conspiratorial organizations that were established in the two capitals, in the Russian south and east, and in Ukraine.

One of the first prominent attempts to unite anti-Bolshevik forces was the National Center, formed in Moscow in spring 1918. Its activities centered on maintaining contacts with and advising both the White forces and other anti-Bolshevik groups inside Soviet Russia. Closely tied to Denikin's Volunteer Army, it was riven by divisions between its Kadet-dominated "all-Russian" organization and the Russian nationalists who controlled its Kiev branch, and it was discredited by its contacts with foreign agents. The Cheka uncovered the National Center in summer 1919 and quickly executed sixty-seven of its leading members.[8] The Union for the Regeneration of Russia arose at the same time, bringing together elements of various center-left parties, including right SRs, NSs, Kadets, and even Mensheviks. One of the group's founders, the historian and NS Venedikt Miakotin, explained, "We did not consider it possible to accept reconciling relations with people who had seized power by force, . . . destroyed the elementary basis of civil liberty, established their tyranny over an exhausted people, and planned to conduct monstrous social experiments on them."[9] During the hard Civil War years, many of its leaders left Moscow for provincial cities such as Kiev, Odessa, and Rostov, but it was soon apparent that the union enjoyed neither unity nor broad support in these places. After the Bolsheviks took Rostov in December 1919, some of the leaders of the Union for the Regeneration of Russia fled abroad; others, including Miakotin, awaited their fate in Soviet Russia.[10]

Before the dissolution of these conspiratorial organizations, their leaders met on several occasions in early 1919 to discuss the type of government that they hoped would succeed the collapse of the Bolsheviks in south Russia. Although these meetings were marked by sharp disagreement and did not generate any real substantive action, the authorities were convinced that a larger, even more conspiratorial association had arisen. In 1920 the Cheka announced it had exposed an organization called the Tactical Center, but what they in fact discovered is a matter of some dispute. At most, the Tactical Center was supposed to serve as an information source for its constituent member groups, and, as the accused insisted, it certainly had neither the size nor the structure to foment an armed uprising in Moscow.[11]

From the Cheka's point of view, it did not truly matter whether there was a real plot or simply gatherings at which hostility to the Soviet state had been expressed. In the arrests and trial of the leading "members" of the Tactical Center, one catches a glimpse of how the new order's vigilance in uncovering conspiracies would soon move from real to illusory targets. Sergei Mel'gunov later caustically observed, "For Bolshevik justice, founded on an extremely elastic understanding of 'revolutionary conscience,' the establishment of this or that concrete action by the accused is essentially a secondary question."[12] The Bolsheviks used the Tactical Center trial as a forum for expressing their suspicion of and contempt for the intelligentsia. "Comrade judges," declared the prosecutor N. Krylenko, "the details of this affair have shown with full clarity how the Russian intelligentsia, entering into the crucible of the Revolution with the slogan of popular power, exited it as allies of black generals, as obedient hired agents of European imperialism. The intelligentsia violated its own slogans and threw mud on them."[13] The prosecution repeatedly hurled generic epithets such as "enemies of Soviet power" and "counterrevolutionaries." Foreshadowing future show trial tactics, Krylenko utilized confessional denunciations extracted from several of the accused to tar the remainder. Several of the "leaders," including Mel'gunov and Sergei Trubetskoi, were sentenced to death, which was soon commuted to ten years' imprisonment.[14]

In March 1921 conspiracy turned to open resistance as the treasonous talk of intellectuals gave way to an armed insurrection of soldiers and sailors. The brutal and bloody Kronstadt rebellion shook the new regime to its core and prompted its leaders to intensify their efforts to eradicate opposition.[15] Mensheviks and SRs had become bolder in their agitation, calling for free elections, an end to terror, and the restoration of civil liberties, demands echoed in the proclamations of the Kronstadt rebels. The hopeful welcome with which the rebellion had been greeted in the émigré press convinced the always-suspicious Bolshevik leadership that its old enemies were masterminding these events. The Cheka, already on high alert to root out conspiratorial organizations, redoubled its efforts, arresting large numbers of Mensheviks and SRs and increasing its general surveillance of intellectual activity.[16] The "lessons of Kronstadt" were among the most critical factors in motivating Lenin and his colleagues to eliminate foes at the beginning of NEP.

Not all intellectuals arrested during 1921 were suspected of political conspiracy, but this did not necessarily mean that their predicament was less precarious. In May 1921 fifty engineers and technicians working for the Main Fuels Administration, or Glavtop, were put on trial, accused of mismanagement and incompetence, including the theft and black-market resale of kerosene and other products. In the aftermath of Kronstadt, at a time when fuel shortages posed grave difficulties for the faltering economy, seemingly minor charges such as these were greatly magnified. Krylenko demanded that the revolutionary tribunal find the leaders of this group guilty of sabotage and order their execution. In the end, however, most were sentenced to short terms in prison, and the few death sentences were quickly commuted to similar imprisonment. Still, the tone set was in sharp contrast to the official policy of encouraging rapprochement with "bourgeois specialists."[17]

The accusations and consequences in the case of the Petrograd Battle Organization (PBO), or Tagantsev affair, were far more serious. Uncovered by the Cheka in summer 1921, the PBO was a conspiratorial alliance of professors, other intellectuals, White military officers, former Kronstadt sailors, émigrés, and foreign spies coordinated in Finland. It was headed by the geographer V. N. Tagantsev and included the pro-rector of Petrograd University N. I. Lazarevskii, the chemist M. M. Tikhvinskii, and the poet Nikolai Gumilev. The official party and Cheka version of these events emphasized the enemy's capacity for shifting strategies and for consolidating their disparate forces to foment counterrevolution. Bolshevik propaganda explicitly linked the affair to Pavel Miliukov's call for "new tactics" in the wake of the Civil War.[18] The PBO was said to involve individuals with views ranging from Menshevik to monarchist. The prosecution, urged on by the zealous Petrograd party leader Grigorii Zinoviev, focused on how the intelligentsia was attempting to utilize the facade of apolitical "*bespartiinost'*" (nonpartisanship) to cover up nefarious anti-Bolshevik activity.

The Cheka conducted a short investigation and interrogated the alleged conspirators during summer 1921. Lenin, convinced by Feliks Dzerzhinskii and his deputy Iosif Unshlikht of the gravity of the affair, rejected Gorky's entreaties and several poignant appeals from Tagantsev's father, a well-known academician and professor of jurisprudence.[19] To Gorky and the Petrograd intellectual community's horror, Tagantsev, Lazarevskii, Gumilev, and fifty-eight others were executed in late August 1921.[20] As in the case of the Tactical Center, the degree to which the Petrograd Battle Organization constituted a real conspiracy was doubted at the time and has been hotly debated by historians. Though there were indeed active anti-Bolshevik discussions, and Tagantsev's own confession, extracted by the skillful *chekist* Iakov Agranov, did detail his ties to Russian émigrés, it is questionable whether the unified conspiratorial organization portrayed in Cheka reports truly existed. Rather, the participants focused on acting in concert *if* another Kronstadt-like uprising occurred, which they felt (and hoped) was quite likely.[21]

The executions produced a profound effect on Petrograd intellectuals. Zinoviev's virulent advocacy of a return to terror reconfirmed the community's belief that the Petrograd chief was a violent anti-intellectual demagogue and tyrant.[22] Many intellectuals claimed not to believe that a conspiracy existed at all. Most were no more than a few degrees of separation removed from one of the victims, and those who had been critical of the regime feared once again for their safety. Recounting the official charges against each man, Sorokin exclaimed: "Shot for adversely describing the state of the Soviet oil industry! . . . Shot for giving information about the museums! Shot for writing a project for a new electoral law! . . . Shot for his monarchist opinions! Not the fact that Goumileff was one of the greatest poets in Russia, not his bravery in the war, . . . not the discretion of his daily conduct was enough to save him. He had monarchist convictions."[23] Even A. P. Karpinskii, the president of the Academy of Sciences, which had carefully cultivated neutral relations with the new regime, expressed shock and despair to Lenin: "I have not been able to ignore the deep moral outrage these events have caused by their unjustifiable cruelty, with such weak motivation, so unnecessary and harmful for our country. . . . The execution of scientific citizens, . . . who were completely uninvolved in active political activity, is an irreparable blow not only to those close to them, but to their numerous current and former students, and will inevitably create hostile attitudes toward the new order."[24]

Bolshevik leaders faced a dilemma in dealing with intellectuals, in particular experts with rare and useful knowledge. The extremely difficult social and economic conditions with which the country's new rulers had to deal dictated that they recruit as many *spetsy* as they could. They did not, however, intend that their efforts to cultivate *spetsy* should overshadow their drive to eliminate opposition. In denying an appeal for clemency on behalf of Professor Tikhvinskii, Lenin dryly remarked that "chemistry and counterrevolution are not mutually exclusive."[25] The bloody end of the Tagantsev affair dashed the hopes of many intellectuals that NEP would usher in a "breathing space." It did not help that the executions occurred at the same time as the demise of the All-Russian Committee to Save the Starving and the arrest of its leading members. Political loyalty had to come first, and this included not only avoidance of active conspiracy, but also recognition of the limits of acceptable behavior within the Soviet public sphere.

The Formation of the All-Russian Committee to Aid the Starving

The Bolsheviks' anxieties concerning anti-Soviet conspiracy caused them to be suspicious of all intellectual organizations, and particularly those that openly advocated autonomous action. Intellectuals, even before the shock of the Tagantsev shootings, had become increasingly wary of activities that might draw undue attention from the authorities, but there were still some who believed that there was a place for "public figures" to perform socially useful work even in a politically closed society. The transition to NEP initially led to hopes that there might be new opportunities for involvement in the public sphere. Even Tagantsev, in his deposition to the Cheka three weeks before he was executed, believed that in the post–Civil War circumstances, a "moderation of the dictatorship" would be inevitable and held out hopes that "the new political conditions will bring the center of struggle out of the underground and into the practical sphere [*delovuiu oblast'*]."[26]

Ekaterina Kuskova and some other practically minded intellectuals were convinced of the possibility of doing "public work" under Bolshevik rule. Kuskova insisted that this did not mean that they had changed their convictions, but instead that they recognized that sabotage would harm the entire country. As she noted, "Because of the usual tendency of Russians toward 'unfounded dreams,'" they still awaited "changes in the sociopolitical sphere."[27] As news of the Volga famine began to reach the capitals in spring 1921, many intellectuals felt compelled to assume their customary place as helpmate to the Russian people, particularly in its hour of greatest need. Whereas others still believed that collaboration with the Bolsheviks could not lead to anything good, Kuskova and other politically moderate or apolitical intellectuals felt that something had to be done. As dire reports trickled in, they became convinced that foreign aid was necessary, and that it was more likely to be provided if public figures not associated with the Soviet regime appealed for help.[28]

On 22 June 1921 the agronomist A. A. Rybnikov and the cooperator M. I. Kukhovarenko described the desperate situation to a packed meeting of concerned public figures at the Moscow Agricultural Society. Kuskova's husband, the economist Sergei Prokopovich, declared to the hall: "We do not have the right to sit with our hands folded. We do not have the moral right. We must act. And if we are to act, then we cannot avoid those circumstances in which this action must be taken. *We cannot take a single action without the agreement of the Soviet regime, without its approval, without its cooperation.*" A delegation was selected to appeal to the authorities for the formation of a public famine relief committee.[29] This delegation was initially refused an audience not only with Lenin, but also with I. A. Teodorovich, a top official in the Commissariat of Agriculture. Kuskova and Prokopovich turned to Gorky, who, a bit reluctantly, contacted Lenin on their behalf.[30] On 28 June Lenin informed Teodorovich that he had no objections to "Gorky's project," and on the following day the Politburo assigned Lev Kamenev to meet with a delegation led by Kuskova, the Kadet N. M. Kishkin, and the cooperator P. A. Sadyrin.[31] The negotiations were brief and to the point; Kamenev agreed that external help was needed but made clear that the committee would include a handful of leading Bolsheviks along with the public figures. It was stressed that neither side should use the initiative for political purposes.[32]

After the committee had been sanctioned, but before its official convening, its Bolshevik faction gathered to determine how to conduct its business and to deal with the public figures.[33] They appointed Gorky as a "special representative" to send abroad for the purpose of garnering assistance, but he demurred, uncomfortable with being placed in this official role. He did, however, draft a petition with a poignant account of Russia's suffering, concluding with an animated plea for donations of bread and medicine. "The corn-growing steppes are smitten by crop failure caused by the drought," he lamented. "The calamity threatens starvation to millions of Russian people. . . . Gloomy days have come for the country of Tolstoy, Dostoevsky, Mendeleyev, Pavlov, Mussorgsky, Glinka, and other world-prized men." Patriarch Tikhon, the head of the Russian Orthodox Church, issued a similar entreaty to international religious figures.[34] These appeals and news of the creation of the famine relief committee caused quite a stir in the West, which, as we shall see, in turn reinforced the Bolsheviks' distrust of the public figures.

Lenin was not as uneasy as some of his colleagues about the famine relief committee. He replied cheerfully to anxious inquiries from Commissar of Health Nikolai Semashko, "Don't be so capricious, my dear! . . . Don't be jealous of Kuskova. There is a directive in the Politburo today: Render Kuskova completely harmless. You will be named to the "Communist cell": don't nap, *watch those people rigorously.*"[35] The Politburo directed that no more than two of the seven spots on the committee's presidium go to public figures, and the All-Russian Central Executive Committee (VTsIK) named the chair, deputy chair, and presidium. The Politburo broadened the authority of the parallel official relief organization, the VTsIK Central Commission to Aid the Starving (*Tsentral'naia komissiia pomoshchi golodaiushchim pri VTsIKe*), known as Pomgol.[36] The existence of the two parallel bodies led to much confusion and eventually made the public committee expendable.[37] Although the presence of Kamenev, Semashko, and other Bolsheviks on the committee was designed to ensure its amenability, its non-Communist members had something else in mind entirely. In conjunction with the growing excitement in the émigré press over the committee, the willfulness of the public figures soon caused Lenin and other leading Bolsheviks to adopt a much harsher tone vis-à-vis Kuskova and her partners.

Meanwhile, Kuskova and Prokopovich held council in their apartment in an alley off the Arbat debating under what conditions it would be possible to operate and involving more people in their work. The atmosphere of "uninterrupted commotion," activity, and engagement in this "corner of old Moscow" drew together many figures who had not participated in public work for the previous four years. The meetings here and at the impromptu offices of the committee's short-lived bulletin featured a who's who of former Duma deputies, provisional government ministers, *zemstvo* activists, venerable revolutionaries, literary and artistic giants, Tolstoyans, and others. A student member of the committee later described his awe at working together with a wizened but still vibrant Vera Figner, who declared that the students, as always, would be the backbone of this popular effort.[38] Many of the older public figures and *zemstvo* activists had been involved in the relief efforts at the time of the famine of 1891–92, and now, thirty years later, they saw their task in much the same light. Despite their antipathy toward the authorities (in fact, precisely because they felt the regime was not capable of resolving the problem), a sense of civic duty (*obshchestvennost'*) demanded that they set aside their differences and come to the aid of the Russian people in this time of national emergency.[39]

The full committee's first meeting took place in the hall of the Moscow soviet on 20 July 1921. A Red Army soldier checked credentials at the door, and the public figures were acutely aware of the potential risk. Kamenev declared that "the government regarded this initiative with full sympathy and is prepared to render it full support." Kishkin spoke for the public figures, noting, "For the first time in the past four years representatives of the regime are meeting with public workers [*obshchestvennye rabotniki*] in order to reach mutual agreement and embark on a public-state matter, to battle against a most grave popular calamity." He vowed that the committee would be apolitical and insisted that it be allowed to operate without state interference. Prokopovich added that because of the number of people in potential danger—he put the figure at thirty-five million—help would be needed from abroad, and because of the unsettled nature of relations between the new regime and foreign powers, it fell to society (*obshchestvennost'*) to make that appeal.[40] Kamenev concurred that the committee would be apolitical, acknowledged the need for help from abroad, and reassured the deputies that the authorities would not interfere with the committee's efforts and would offer every assistance. Kuskova later marveled that these "guarantees were given publicly, openly, not secretly, not in 'private negotiations' via intermediaries." She and the other public figures nevertheless left the meeting asking each other, "Do you believe Kamenev's promises?"[41]

VTsIK officially established the All-Russian Committee to Aid the Starving the following day. Most Bolshevik members of the public committee, including Kamenev, were also on the official Pomgol.[42] Although the VKPG was provided broad rights to acquire food and medicine from abroad, distribute it among the population, and organize local branches, Pomgol was always the ultimate arbiter of famine relief. The VKPG's public figures, however, saw themselves as empowered to make decisions, sign agreements, and promulgate their views. Its members represented a broad swath of society, including the venerable revolutionary Figner, the celebrated director Konstantin

Stanislavskii, Lev Tolstoy's daughter Aleksandra, the writers Boris Zaitsev and Mikhail Osorgin, the publicist and *Vekhist* Mikhail Gershenzon, the former Duma deputy F. A. Golovin, the economist N. N. Kutler, the agronomist A. V. Chaianov, the ethnographer N. Ia. Marr, the Tolstoyans Valentin Bulgakov and Pavel Biriukov, the president and permanent secretary of the Academy of Sciences, A. P. Karpinskii and S. F. Ol'denburg, and fifty other professors, writers, agronomists, and cooperators. There were a significant number of prominent Kadets among its members, including Kutler and Kishkin. Gorky convinced the writer and critic V. G. Korolenko, who was near the end of his life and at the height of his fame and popularity, to lend his name as honorary chair. The Bolshevik cell, in addition to Kamenev, included Aleksei Rykov, Teodorovich, Semashko, Anatolii Lunacharskii, M. M. Litvinov, and L. B. Krasin, most of whom were considered moderates and had relatively good relations with nonparty intellectuals.

The formation of the committee, ironically christened "Prokukish" after Prokopovich, Kuskova, and Kishkin, ushered in a brief truce between the public figures and these Bolshevik moderates. Kuskova noted that their "gracious chairman," Kamenev, "tried during meetings of the presidium to create a certain intimacy for exchange. . . . He did not practice the favorite Bolshevik jargon, so tiresome and importunate. No, this was an intellectual, just like all the rest," who even read them excerpts from the émigré press.[43] Both the Bolshevik and public committee members spent a great deal of energy attempting to ward off critics both within the regime and among its sworn enemies. Lunacharskii and Kamenev, on the one hand, and committee members such as Osorgin, Kuskova, and Figner, on the other, argued that at a time of such horrific need, it was necessary to unite under the banner of the (neutral) Red Cross.[44]

Both within the émigré community and among more resolutely anti-Soviet intellectuals in Russia, there was immediate suspicion of the VKPG. Korolenko had his misgivings, calling the famine "artificial," but he nonetheless agreed to write appeals for aid. The publisher M. V. Sabashnikov expressed doubts about the committee's efficacy but felt he had to try to help.[45] A number of public figures, led by Miakotin and Mel'gunov, considered it base appeasement.[46] The conservative MGU historian Iurii Got'e wrote in his diary. "What fools are those worn-out public activists who took part in the conference on hunger. And from whom is anything good to be expected? . . . No, let the bolsheviks disentangle what they have done!"[47]

The committee members defended their participation against such detractors. Kuskova argued fiercely that their activities had nothing to do with "appeasement," and that they were not nearly so naive as they were made out to be.[48] Osorgin similarly retorted, "We always knew how to separate Russia from the Bolsheviks."[49] Vera Figner asked the doubters, "Is it really possible to boycott a struggle with famine? to boycott a struggle with death from starvation?"[50] Sabashnikov, undoubtedly echoing the feelings of other public figures, agreed: "The skeptics have the right to say that nothing will come out of all of this. But what then is there to be done? It is impossible to refuse, not even having tried." He participated "with a heavy heart. To friends, who ask, why I am doing so, I reply: 'I don't believe in success, but duty calls.'"[51]

On the other side, Kamenev was forced to respond to more radical Communist comrades. The public committee, he explained, by agreeing to work with the regime without any conditions, had unmasked the base motives of the emigration and divided the bourgeoisie. The dictatorship of the proletariat, he argued, was not at all threatened by the involvement of "former ministers and members of the Kadet Party Central Committee, leaders of the petty bourgeois cooperatives and agronomist societies" in famine relief.[52] A secret Bolshevik Central Committee circular agreed, adding that "thanks to the Committee's activities we can count on receiving from foreign bourgeois and government circles a certain amount of material goods for supplying the suffering population," and echoing Kamenev's assertion that the committee would "cause disorganization and lead to vacillations in the emigration." At the same time, however, it reminded Communists that though they should allow a certain degree of autonomy, they must keep a careful eye on the local committees; the Cheka had therefore already been given "corresponding instructions on the intensification of vigilance."[53]

The Activities of the VKPG

It soon became clear, however, that the moderate Bolsheviks' and public figures' attempts to cooperate faced tremendous obstacles. As the famine relief committee began its work, the unbridgeable fissures between the Communist and liberal understandings of *obshchestvennost'*, of participation in the public sphere, soon became apparent. The public figures through the very process of autonomous activity threatened the Bolshevik monopoly on setting policy and hegemony over the public sphere. Neutrality, as Lenin and Zinoviev insisted, was a mirage, and this was true as much in social activity as in politics directly.

At its first formal meeting on 23 July, the members elected a presidium consisting of Prokopovich, Kishkin, and the cooperator D. S. Korobov, along with Kamenev and Rykov, the appointed chair and deputy. Kishkin noted that the committee needed to remain "manageable and flexible," and Kutler reported on its finances. During the next several meetings, Kishkin gathered donations from the committee members to the tune of 511,000 rubles (not a very large sum, given that American Relief Administration officials arriving in August found the effective exchange rate to be approximately 34,000 rubles to the dollar, although this fluctuated wildly).[54] Emphasis was placed on the need to send a delegation abroad to secure international assistance. Kamenev presented guidelines on the proposed delegation, noting that it must avoid political statements and, though autonomous, should coordinate its activities with Soviet representatives and send all donations back to Russia. After Kishkin declined because of poor health, the committee unanimously elected a delegation of Kuskova, Prokopovich, Golovin, the cooperator and banker M. P. Avsarkisov, and the professor and physician L. A. Tarasevich.[55] The committee also established local branches. Kukhovarenko and Rybnikov were named plenipotentiaries for Saratov region, and representatives were appointed in Kazan and elsewhere. From provincial representatives and a constant stream of telegrams the committee attempted to learn the real scope of the famine, of which the authorities had spoken only in carefully controlled disclosures.[56] Prokopovich, Kishkin, and other committee members openly disputed the accuracy of official figures and criticized the insufficiency of the government's measures. Kamenev replied pointedly to these charges, but the committee resolved nonetheless to form its own statistical bureau to determine the extent of the catastrophe.

Committee members divided into groups according to their expertise. The independent All-Russian Union of Writers, whose leadership was represented on the committee by Zaitsev, Osorgin, and others, pledged its full support and offered to organize lectures and issue additional appeals for international aid. A literary commission was formed within the VKPG, which included Osorgin, Zaitsev, Kuskova, Gershenzon, and the critic Iul'ii Aikhenval'd, to issue brochures, posters, and a collection of articles on the famine, and Osorgin was appointed editor of the committee's bulletin, *Pomoshch'* (Aid). It also issued a series of appeals, "To the Citizens of Moscow," "To Sectarians," "To the Youth," and others. Artists planned an exhibition to raise relief money and intended to appeal to a broad group of artistic professionals to issue slogans and posters. Actors under Stanislavskii's direction proposed benefit performances and the formation of theater-trains to aid the starving.[57]

The leadership of the central agricultural and industrial cooperative organs, including Prokopovich, Sadyrin, and I. P. Matveev, took energetic part in the work.[58] Convinced that only a changed approach to agriculture would prevent the low harvests endemic to Russia, Aleksandr Ugrimov issued a call to local "agronomic and public" forces to join the fight against the famine. He declared that "only the unimpeded autonomy [and] healthy initiative of the farming population" could resolve the nation's problems.[59] D. S. Korobov lamented that the agricultural cooperatives were a shadow of their former selves, but he urged them to serve as distribution points for the committee. A group of cooperative organizations published an appeal in the Berlin émigré paper *Golos Rossii* calling for international cooperatives of all sorts to assist the public committee. In the last weeks of August, when it had already roused the wrath of the regime, the VKPG was endorsed by the newly formed central agricultural cooperative body, Sel'skosoiuz, which itself would soon come under fire.[60]

In Petrograd the prominent engineer Pëtr Pal'chinskii led a number of public figures in organizing a local branch. Upon his return from Moscow, Gorky assumed the leadership of this group, which included Karpinskii, Ol'denburg, Marr, and members of the city's prominent literary and artistic societies, including Evgenii Zamiatin, N. M. Volkovyskii, and A. B. Petrishchev.[61] Headquartered in the White Hall of the House of Scholars, the Petrograd branch first aimed to organize the entry and dissemination of foodstuffs into Russia but before long served as a center for the entire northwestern region from Pskov to Archangel. Numerous offers of assistance and donations soon streamed in.[62] Gorky worried about conflict with the local authorities, warning Lenin that the Petrograd committee needed sufficient capacity to handle the massive numbers of refugees from the famine regions already heading north. Despite (or, given Zinoviev's antipathy toward him, because of) Gorky's presence, the Petrograd authorities were soon actively interfering in the committee's work and pressing for changes in its makeup.[63] Nevertheless, the committee began organizing for the influx of refugees; by one estimate there were already more than twenty thousand heading toward Petrograd. The committee formed a medical-sanitary department to organize children's homes and coordinate with Narkomzdrav (the Commissariat of Health) and other Soviet institutions.[64]

Branches arose in the provinces as well, maintaining contact with the committee in Moscow through the plenipotentiaries who had been appointed to coordinate work. In Vladimir the initiative for the committee's formation came from a group of students who turned to their elder public figures. Work focused on the collection of donations, the establishment of children's homes, and the organization of a way station for refugees from the famine regions. Similar actions were taken in Cherepovets, Simbirsk, Podol'sk, Vologda, and elsewhere. Although the Moscow organization attempted to guide its local affiliates, communication was extremely difficult and local initiative proceeded more or less independently.[65] As in other matters, the question of local networks of public figures was of deep concern to the authorities, who saw to it that they were balanced by local branches of the official Pomgol, which would then take over their duties. In the meantime, local Communists were instructed to permit and to assist both Pomgol and VKPG branches but to keep a very careful eye on the activities of the latter.[66]

The Moscow committee created student sections under the auspices of the all-city student bureau, including representatives from eleven of the capital's higher educational institutions. The students vowed to take part both in the Moscow organizational work and in distribution efforts in the provinces. Led by V. D. Golovachev, a student at the Polytechnic Institute, Iu. N. Maksimov, who studied at the Lazarevskii Institute of Oriental Languages, and the medical student G. L. Levin, it quickly attracted numerous volunteers.[67] *Pomoshch'* issued nationwide appeals asking students to set aside their political differences and bring their "youthful forces" to the work of famine relief. They appealed directly to the intellectual ideal of serving the people: "Only there, among the boundless human misfortune, suffering, and tears, in active struggle with the famine, can the brilliant flame of love for the people flare."[68] As the authorities became increasingly irritated with and suspicious of the famine relief committee, its appeals to a segment of society considered critical to the future of Soviet Russia further exacerbated the situation. Kamenev directed the Moscow party organization and its cells within higher educational institutions (VUZy) to form a student section within the official Pomgol. They were to urge students toward joining the work of *its* local branches, instead of the public committee's.[69] The parallel entities represented the two competing visions of the public sphere, official and autonomous, but many were not yet sure how to choose between them. At a meeting of Moscow VUZ representatives on 15 August, students listened to Semashko, representing Pomgol, as well as Kuskova, representing the VKPG, and resolved to join the work of both organizations.[70]

The first open conflict concerned the public figures' contacting the Church to assist in the relief effort. Patriarch Tikhon had already issued an appeal, but it was a different matter to have a semi-autonomous public committee colluding with what was regarded as the most reactionary of institutions. Kishkin and Prokopovich approached Tikhon, whose moral authority they hoped would help in securing foreign aid. Tikhon issued a call "in the name and for the sake of Christ" to assist "the distressed with hands full of the gifts of mercy, with hearts full of love and the desire to save a perishing brother." Although Kamenev expressed his dissatisfaction with this appeal to "forces of counterrevolution," and especially its openly declaring itself to be a "prayer before the throne of God," he agreed to have it published. The Church moved toward forming its own famine relief bodies, and a prayer service led by Tikhon on 5 August 1921 in the Church of Christ the Savior proved an immensely popular and emotional event for the Moscow public. As Kuskova later noted, this alliance of Church and society undoubtedly was a major cause of the Bolsheviks' growing conviction that their enemies were consolidating forces.[71]

The committee's bulletin, *Pomoshch',* also caused a stir. Even its design was controversial, mimicking that of the well-known prerevolutionary liberal newspaper *Russkie vedomosti,* to the great excitement of those awaiting *any* non-Soviet newspaper, and much to the irritation of the Bolsheviks.[72] Osorgin highlighted the significance of the rapprochement, noting that its initiators came from "a variety of social and political camps" that had joined the government to fight the famine. "Let him who can stand to the side. We, as much as our strength and opportunity allows, will fight this evil." They rejected the slogan "the worse, the better" for Russia and urged all "public forces" to join their lead. Kuskova defended the committee's neutrality. In a time of war and revolution, when all aspects of life were politicized, only under the auspices of an organization such as the Red Cross could differences be put aside and a starving child fed. Lower on the same page of the newspaper appeared a piece by Lunacharskii echoing this theme: "The Communist Party, a militant party, a party jealous of its ideals, . . . cannot at such a moment and in the face of such need refuse broad rights of initiative [*samodeiatel'nost'*] even to people who, approaching it, say, 'not any political reconciliation, but—the Red Cross.'"[73]

The common hope of Bolshevik moderates and the public figures that politics might be set aside did not, however, long grace the pages of *Pomoshch'.* Lunacharskii's article would be the last piece by a Soviet official, and the authorities became increasingly irritated by what they saw as more or less open criticism in what was the first non-Bolshevik newspaper to be permitted since the Civil War.[74] Although they continued to insist on their neutrality, Osorgin and the other committee members writing in *Pomoshch'* demanded full autonomy and the right to speak freely. Speculating on the true nature of a "freely acting public organization," Osorgin noted the necessity of open membership, free and open internal elections, and flexibility and the ability to initiate action. In countries used to free organization, the population had developed the ability to help itself, to fulfill the tasks it had set itself. "On the contrary, in countries with a weakly developed public sphere [*obshchestvennost'*], people consistently look to the government, expect help from it, scold it if help does not come in time." Russia, unfortunately, fell into this latter category, and it was something that it desperately needed to outgrow.[75] It was precisely such a growth of extra-governmental public activity that most concerned the Bolsheviks, and open theorizing about *obshchestvennost'* did not help the cause of this already suspect independent publication.

I. Stukov, a member of the Moscow party bureau, was soon complaining to the Orgburo that *Pomoshch'* was "unquestionably political, skillfully moving to discredit our political regime and the structure of Russia in various and, at first glance, completely loyal articles." He pointed in particular to the provincial correspondents, who more or less openly blamed Soviet policies for the famine.[76] The Orgburo asked Kamenev and Lev Sosnovskii, the *Pravda* contributor and future Trotskyist, to report on *Pomoshch'* only several days before the dissolution of the committee.[77] Sosnovskii had in fact already been keeping tabs on the bulletin. Although he insisted to Osorgin, "I am not a censor—there is no censorship," he nevertheless carefully examined the page proofs. "From the first issue," Osorgin recalled, "he didn't delete a single line. From the second also not a single line. From the third—he immediately deleted 1,400 lines."[78] Predictably, *Pomoshch'* would share the fate of its parent organization, and that third issue, dated two days after the arrest of Osorgin and his comrades, was confiscated before its dissemination.[79]

The Public Committee and the Eyes of the World

The Bolshevik leadership was also very much concerned with the possibility that foreign authorities would want to deal directly with members of the public committee. These fears were fanned when the British trade representative, R. M. Hodgson, arranged a meeting with Kishkin, Prokopovich, and other committee leaders.[80] In addition, the VKPG sent a radio address to Europe and America announcing its upcoming delegation abroad and pleading for assistance. At the same time, these increasing ties with foreign dignitaries caused more cautious committee members some concern. One skeptic remarked dourly that this "joining [*smychka*] with foreigners" represented the "Committee's first terrible crime."[81] Foreign officials and émigrés reacted with great interest to Gorky's plea and to the committee's formation, which some saw as a potential weapon against the Bolsheviks. Although opinions differed within the emigration over the appropriate response to the famine, in general a new hope percolated that the Soviet regime was in serious trouble.

Outlandish rumors began to circulate in Berlin and Paris, including the idea that the public committee in Moscow would somehow form the basis of a post-Bolshevik proto-government. At meetings of his faction of the Kadet Party in Paris, Pavel Miliukov cautioned against complicating the position of the members of the Moscow committee.[82] He tried more than once to downplay the unbridled optimism that often appeared elsewhere in his own newspaper: "The independence of the committee of public figures is a rare and magnificent flower, the first that has grown in the political desert of Soviet power. It must be guarded by all means from bad weather. And the first thing that is needed for this is not to assign it any tasks other than those that follow naturally from its primary appointment."[83] But others were not so restrained. Vladimir Burtsev's *Obshchee delo* gleefully welcomed the end of Soviet rule and saw in Kishkin's pronouncements hope that the committee members really would undertake political tasks.[84] This, of course, further exacerbated Bolshevik suspicions. As rumors continued to circulate, the VKPG found it necessary to publish a joint circular signed by public figures and Bolshevik moderates reiterating that the committee was "devoid of any political character, that it is an organization pursuing strictly practical matters."[85]

Those émigré groups willing to endorse the activities of the committee quickly formed local branches of it in London, Paris, Berlin, and other cities.[86] Bolshevik diplomats were undecided on how to react to philanthropic organizations consisting of their sworn enemies. Kamenev replied that branches of the official VTsIK Pomgol should be formed in their stead—specifying that these be called "commissions" and not "committees" to avoid confusion.[87] Meanwhile, émigré notables worked to convince Western dignitaries that they should deal only with the VKPG. Pavel Riabushinskii, who served as financial and economic advisor to the Russian Embassy-in-Exile in Washington, assured an American Relief Administration (ARA) representative that the famine relief committee was "entirely nonpolitical." He nonetheless expressed the hope that it "might in time grow to be the most powerful organization in Russia and might . . . finally become the actual governing body of Russia, whether the Soviets desired this or not."[88] Alexander Kerensky told French officials that the Bolshevik government was undergoing its "final agonies" and would be finished by the beginning of the following year.[89]

But the man who responded most directly to Gorky's appeal, Herbert Hoover, was not interested in working through the public committee.[90] As head of the privately funded American Relief Administration, Hoover declared that assistance could be provided if the Soviet regime officially asked for help. He wanted assurances that his organization would be able to operate autonomously, and he needed to hear this from the authorities, not some dubious public committee. Hoover warned his director of European operations of "the supreme importance of keeping entirely aloof not only from action but even from discussion of political and social questions."[91] During negotiations with Bolshevik representatives in Riga in mid-August

1921, the ARA made no mention whatsoever of the famine relief committee. As Litvinov, the deputy commissar for Foreign Affairs and diplomat extraordinaire, explained to his boss, G. V. Chicherin, "The Hoover organization insists on negotiations and agreement specifically with the Soviet government, and not with public organizations such as 'Kukish' (as the Kuskova-Kishkin committee is called here)." He added the following day that Hoover's representative, Walter Brown, "has not yet decided himself whether he will utilize the 'Kukish' committee or create new committees." In fact, the ARA mission to Russia would be instructed quite explicitly to ignore the VKPG and its local branches.[92] As the Bolsheviks became increasingly suspicious of the public committee's activities, the ARA's lack of interest would become a critical factor in its fate and that of its members.

For the committee members, the fact that the Bolshevik regime was financing their apparatus was a source of significant discomfort, and they made determined efforts to secure donations from other sources.[93] Kutler noted that it was their intention to use government funds only until they had reached a point at which they could be self-supporting. Although Soviet sources would claim that the VKPG managed to collect only 60 million rubles during its brief existence, it had in fact already collected 350 million by mid-August, according to one report, and another 39 million in contributions were received before the committee was dissolved.[94] But in those hyperinflationary times, even this was a pittance in the face of desperate need. The planned delegation abroad was intended to secure much more substantial funds from international sources, but this trip was a source of great tension between the public figures and their Bolshevik overseers. The Bolsheviks grew increasingly apprehensive at the prospect of the proposed VKPG delegation's coming into contact with Western and émigré notables. For the public figures, on the other hand, the trip had become a focal point. Unaware of the impending agreement with Hoover, they saw their ability to persuade potential benefactors as critical. They represented society, after all, and enjoyed far more sympathy in the West, not to mention the emigration, than did the Bolsheviks. In preparation they added to Gorky's their own direct appeal for help abroad, "with deep faith in the strength of the sacred value of human compassion."[95]

A joint session of public and Bolshevik committee members carefully spelled out the delegation's rights and responsibilities. It was to be allowed to operate independently, but in close contact with Soviet missions, which it would keep well informed of its work. Individual interviews would not be permitted, and, most important, it would deal only with matters relating to famine relief and strictly avoid political questions, "as befits its Red

Cross character." All monetary donations and foodstuffs given to the committee were to be sent back to Russia without delay, and it would accept no offers made with any political conditions. But, over the objections of even the moderate Krasin, it was to be allowed to consider itself a "foreign branch of the Committee," which could include both émigrés and foreigners as members.[96]

With this carefully structured plan, it seemed as if Kamenev, Rykov, and their colleagues would allow the delegation to proceed. One committee member, Pavel Biriukov, a prominent Tolstoyan, had already gone abroad in a separate capacity. Biriukov wore several diplomatic hats: that of a semi-official government representative; that of a Tolstoyan looking after Tolstoyan interests; and finally that of a VKPG member. In this capacity he spoke with the émigré press and reported to the public committee's local affiliates. He also represented the VKPG at the International Red Cross conference in Geneva, which appointed the Norwegian explorer and humanitarian Fridtjof Nansen as high commissioner of the newly formed International Committee for Russian Relief. In addition to describing the committee's activities, Biriukov repeatedly defended its neutrality against all attempts to depict it as a political organization.[97]

Biriukov's successes did not for a moment make his VKPG colleagues think their delegation was any less necessary. To receive their passports, the delegates filled out a Cheka form implying that the remaining committee members would serve as guarantors against any misbehavior. Visas were received from England, Sweden, and Germany, and an 18 August departure date was set.[98] But the progress made in the talks with Hoover and with Fridtjof Nansen led the Bolshevik leadership to reconsider. Several other plans to request relief already existed, including the formation of a rival delegation under the auspices of the official Pomgol.[99] The Bolshevik VKPG members appointed Gorky as a plenipotentiary, but he balked at the awkward position this would put him in. He wrote his son Maxim that this attempt to turn him into an official representative was "patently provocative," and he complained to Lenin that the naming of the two rival delegations made him uneasy. "I can do much more alone, by myself, as M. Gorky and not as a 'plenipotentiary.'" In fact, having already sent appeals all over the world, he didn't see much sense in going abroad at all.[100] When Gorky did leave the country several months later, it would be under very different circumstances.

After Soviet representatives signed an agreement with the ARA on 20 August 1921, the VKPG became expendable. The Bolsheviks were anxious that the delegation abroad would allow Kuskova, Prokopovich, and their colleagues to expand their network from a domestic to an international public sphere. At the same time, more cautious Bolsheviks advised that it would be a mistake to cancel the delegation at this point. Chicherin noted that its impending arrival had led to important gains for the Bolsheviks in the eyes of international opinion: "To forbid the foreign trip of the 'public figures' after all of the noise about it, . . . and even more to liquidate the committee of public figures, would mean the destruction of this impression. . . . The creation of the committee is seen as a sign of our flexibility, and in particular a demonstration of the fact that the Soviet government will lead Russia's revival, and that it is therefore profitable to invest capital in it."[101] Krasin agreed entirely with Chicherin's reasoning, adding that "the prohibition of an already permitted . . . trip abroad will compromise our entire new course—and all our initial successes in hoodwinking the entire world [*vtiranie ochkov vsemu svetu*]. . . . There is no danger at all that Prokukish will become some sort of danger abroad."[102] But Lenin and other leading Bolsheviks were no longer interested in such restraint.

On 18 August, the date of the delegation's planned departure, the Politburo "postponed" the trip and directed the committee members to travel to the affected provinces to assist in feeding the starving.[103] When it became clear that they would not be going abroad, Kuskova would recall, the news "brought the committee to its knees, ended its autonomous work, and paralyzed its will with a directive from above and a demand for absolute obedience." This was no exaggeration. Although Kamenev responded to the leaders' demand for an emergency presidium meeting, he informed them that their threat to cease operations would be considered "an insurrection against the highest organ of the republic!"[104] The VKPG protested to the Politburo that the committee's work would be impossible without more assistance from abroad: "Concerning the government's proposal on the intensification of the committee's work in the localities, such work would not render aid to the starving. No matter how many members of the committee went off now to the localities, it would not add to the foodstuffs there and would not in any way change the circumstances. Therefore the committee stands by its earlier decision—to immediately send a delegation abroad. If the obstacles to this departure are not removed, the committee will consider it necessary to cease its activity owing to the complete impossibility under the circumstances of fulfilling its duties."[105]

The Politburo was unmoved and ignored a final appeal from Lunacharskii and several others to allow the delegation.[106] Pëtr Smidovich made one last attempt to convince the public figures that they were making a mistake in refusing to go to the provinces, also to no avail. The VKPG insisted that their public organization would not be turned into just another Soviet-run institution.[107]

Meanwhile, the Petrograd branch of the committee rebuffed the authorities' demands that it purge certain unacceptable members. In response, as Gorky complained, "The Petrosovet, that is to say Zinoviev, ordered that it immediately cease its activities . . . 'until such time as . . . '—until what? I don't understand."[108] Exasperated, Gorky angrily informed Kamenev that he was quitting the committee. When called for an official chat by Zinoviev the next day, he announced that Ol'denburg, Marr, Karpinskii, and other committee leaders also no longer found it possible to work in these conditions. Gorky's frustration grew greater still with the arrests in Moscow several days later. "The motives for the dissolution of the committee," he wrote Korolenko, "are not sufficiently convincing for me to understand them; the motives for the arrests are even more incomprehensible. . . . My mood is abominable. Forgive me, if I end this letter,—I don't have the strength to write, my hands are shaking."[109] According to Vladislav Khodasevich, Gorky's "shame and vexation were boundless. Meeting Kamenev in the Kremlin cafeteria, he said to him through tears, 'You have made me into a provocateur. That has never happened to me before.'"[110] Korolenko also had no doubt that the supposed antigovernment conspiracy was a fiction, having recently received a letter from Kuskova in which she urged him publicly to support the notion that the Bolshevik regime posed no obstacle to famine relief work.[111] For Gorky, the dissolution of the famine relief committee represented the dramatic end of his efforts to reconcile the regime and the intelligentsia. Just days earlier, at the final full meeting of the Petrograd committee, he had overflowed with optimism. "In addition to this difficult task," he proclaimed, "which the committee must undertake in order to aid the starving," he hoped they might take on the even more ambitious task of "uniting all of the intellectual forces of the country."[112]

As Gorky would soon learn, the struggle in the political sphere was far from over. A Bolshevik informer reported that Prokopovich was delivering openly anti-Soviet speeches; the committee refused to accept the rejection of its foreign delegation; and Nansen, who had arrived to complete a separate aid agreement, had had conversations with one of the committee's prominent Kadets. After meeting with Dzerzhinskii, Lenin wrote to Stalin: "What more are we waiting for? . . . To wait longer would truly be an enormous mistake." He ordered the committee's dissolution and directed that the newspapers conduct a merciless propaganda campaign against these "Whiteguards" (counterrevolutionaries). Prokopovich was to be arrested immediately, while the rest of the committee should be deported from Moscow, "dispersing them singly among the district cities, if possible ones without railroads, *under surveillance*." With the foreign aid workers beginning to arrive, "Moscow must be cleansed of 'Kukish.'"[113] The Politburo agreed and quickly dispatched Unshlikht to arrest the entire committee "with maximum speed."[114]

In the late afternoon hours on Saturday, 27 August, the hall on Sobach'ia Square was crowded with nervous committee members, their guests, provincial delegates who had just arrived for this meeting, and foreign correspondents. The anxiety grew as Kamenev, who had always been punctual, did not show. Vsevolod Iasinskii, who had met with him just an hour earlier concerning a dispute over an independent professors' union, said that Kamenev had assured him he would be there. A call was made, and it was reported that the "gracious chairman" was on his way and would arrive in ten minutes. There was little conversation as the mood grew ever more tense. Those who did speak wondered aloud whether this would be their final meeting; Osorgin turned to Figner and remarked that they were about to be arrested. And then, as Kuskova recalled, "We saw this picture: a black snake writhed along the walkway—one after another people in jackets with revolvers on their belts . . . and so many of them! Now they moved to the entrance. The door opened and—into the rooms literally burst this army, the leather-wearing guard of the Soviet state."[115] The Chekists streamed in, shouting, "Don't move! Get away from the window!" As they were patted down, Kuskova whispered to Osorgin, "Do you think they are going to shoot us?" They agreed they probably would. The committee members were separated from the guests and staff members, and Figner, Tarasevich, and several other prominent figures were let go. The rest were placed under arrest and taken to the Lubianka, the prison at Cheka headquarters—even the foreign journalists were detained for a time, which they protested bitterly. The committee's accounts and files were confiscated.[116]

Prison, Interrogation, and Exile

Most of the arrested committee members were held at the Lubianka for only a few days. At first, they were kept in two chambers, divided by gender, and the assemblage in these cells was once again a who's who of former VIPs. Osorgin recalled that the ever-proper Golovin, displaying typical "Kadet lack of foresight," had shown up for the final meeting in an extravagant outfit, white pants with a fine crease and a formal blue jacket with a high, stiff collar. He refused to take this off even in the sweltering prison cell—when in society, this was not appropriate. The elderly Kutler asked patiently if he could lie down. "For the former deputy former minister of former finances there was not space on the planks," until someone finally made way for him. "Former provisional government minister" Prokopovich with his pince-nez held forth doggedly on the statistical verities of the current situation. Valentin Bulgakov and his comrades particularly impressed Osorgin with their dignity under dreadful conditions and in the face of the coarse behavior of the *chekisty.* "The Tolstoyans are good people, although terribly inconvenient, always trying to do the right thing." Soon a cycle of lectures had been organized; the cooperators from the provinces in particular were eager to hear the eminent scholars of Moscow and Petrograd. There were to be talks on economics, art, theater, the natural sciences, and even on refrigeration; Kutler held forth on finances and E. L. Gurevich on recent archival discoveries. Zaitsev started to lecture on contemporary literature, only to be interrupted by a Red Army soldier; to his dismay, he was not allowed to finish because of his release.[117]

The case brought against these men and women was familiar; only the evidence was scantier. The formerly amenable Kamenev accused them of "playing political games" and of trying "under the guise of aiding the starving to set up a political strike at the Soviet regime."[118] The Cheka gave as proof a plan in Kishkin's handwriting for the formation of a new government (which turned out to have been written in 1907), a note from a local delegate that the committee was engaged in "interesting business," and an excerpt from Bulgakov's diary, seized during a search, that noted, "We and the famine—are the means for a political struggle." (Bulgakov responded indignantly that his diary entry on the politicization of relief work was meant to apply to the Bolsheviks and not to the committee members.) It was explained that the enemies of the Revolution had now turned to using legal means in their never-ending struggle against the dictatorship of the proletariat.[119] Despite the fabrications and twisting of words, the Cheka very much believed that the arrests were justified and that the VKPG was a genuine threat. Unshlikht reported to the Politburo that émigrés and British officials had developed plans for utilizing the committee as a stepping-stone to overthrowing the government. Foreigners would have been able to make contacts and work in Russia independent of the Soviet authorities—that is, via Russian public organizations—strengthening and expanding the domestic public sphere. Lenin had no doubts that the committee had outlived its usefulness and that its leaders must be punished.[120]

Rumors quickly circulated that the Cheka was planning to execute the leaders of the dispersed committee. Although there is no direct evidence that this was the case, in light of the concurrent mass shootings in the Tagantsev affair, it certainly seemed plausible. After the arrests, émigré notables turned to Nansen and Hoover to request their intercession. Chicherin swiftly replied that the rumors were "absolutely false" and that there was never any intention of executing Prokopovich, Kuskova, or Kishkin.[121] Even Hoover, who had shown little interest in the committee during negotiations and even now considered its fate "a political matter in which private relief organizations can take no interest," directed his deputy to warn the Soviet authorities that such an action would undermine the aid effort. The London ARA office believed that its appeal might "be instrumental in saving the lives of the persons in question in addition to establishing our own position which we may need for our own protection."[122] William Haskell, the director of its Russian unit, turned to Kamenev concerning "a very delicate matter." American public opinion, he wrote, would not tolerate executions of members of the famine relief committee, and this would be disastrous to ARA efforts in Russia.[123] Kamenev replied directly, as Chicherin had to Nansen, that these reports were utterly unfounded and a complete fabrication; nothing more severe than expulsion from Moscow was planned for the few committee members who were still in prison.[124]

There is little question that the committee itself would have been doomed whether or not the foreign relief agencies took any interest in it. Hoover's indifference had made clear that international aid was not dependent on the existence of the committee, and Nansen's contact with prominent committee members exacerbated suspicions. Neither the ARA nor Nansen was discouraged from aid efforts by the arrest of the committee members. The short experiment of cooperation in public work with prominent non-Bolshevik figures would not be repeated, particularly with foreign organizations entering the picture. When an ARA official met with several of the public figures shortly after their release in early September, he found that "every one of the men interviewed has refused to sit on the [ARA] committee, either on account of time or illness, or similar reason; we believe, however, that the root of the matter is deeper: that the intelligentsia and intellectuals in Russia have been so intimidated that they are not willing to subject themselves to any further arrest or other humiliation."[125]

Some groups, especially the Tolstoyans, continued relief efforts, and their autonomous (if limited) relief organization was allowed to remain in operation. When Valentin Bulgakov wrote to Kalinin and Emelian Iaroslavskii proposing participation in the work of the official Pomgol, however, it was clear that he had missed the point. Bulgakov claimed that more public involvement was necessary to reinstate trust in Pomgol, particularly after the unpopular state seizures of Church valuables to finance famine relief. But his plea that the Bolsheviks should make use of all "public figures loyal (from a political standpoint) to the Soviet regime" fell on deaf ears.[126] Such participation, even from "loyal" public figures, was no longer welcome. Indeed, the Bolsheviks were even more cautious because of the presence of foreign aid workers, whose activities were closely monitored.[127] The Bolshevik leadership and Cheka wished strictly to delimit the manifestation of both the Russian public sphere and especially its cosmopolitan variant.

Kamenev directed Smidovich to organize the seized files, finances, and other materials of the VKPG to be turned over to the official Pomgol.[128] All except a few former members were released from prison within a couple of days. By mid-October the Politburo had directed Unshlikht to exile the six still in prison to remote provincial locations. The Cheka presidium decided to deport Osorgin and Kishkin to Kostroma, Kuskova and Prokopovich to Vologda, and the cooperators Korobov and I. A. Cherkasov to Mariiskaia. They would be allowed to receive goods from their relatives, and then a Cheka convoy would escort them into exile.[129] Kuskova and Prokopovich were moved about several times before being among the first intellectuals expelled from Russia in late May 1922.[130] Osorgin was briefly allowed to return to Moscow before joining the larger group of deportees in the fall. Kishkin, perhaps owing to his advanced age, was not included in this group. Rykov and L. M. Khinchuk petitioned to permit Korobov and Cherkasov to return from internal exile in summer 1922, swearing that they were apolitical and useful specialists. The GPU, the Cheka's successor, demurred, claiming that they would foment anti-Soviet activity; but they were in the end allowed to return to Moscow.[131]

The famine relief committee affair catalyzed the campaign against "anti-Soviet groups among the intelligentsia," which culminated with mass deportations in 1922. The GPU planned to expel a number of those who had been involved in the work of the VKPG: agronomists and cooperators such as I. P. Matveev, A. A. Rybnikov, and A. I. Ugrimov, the student leader V. D. Golovachev, Professors V. Iasinskii and P. A. Velikhov, litterateurs such as Osorgin, Aikhenval'd, Zamiatin and Volkovyskii, Valentin Bulgakov, and the engineer Pal'chinskii.[132] Other committee members had already emigrated, most famously Gorky, whose (not entirely voluntary) departure was closely linked to his frustration over the continued persecution of intellectuals.[133] At the Twelfth Party Conference in August 1922, Zinoviev depicted the dispersal of the famine relief committee as a critical turning point in the activities of the anti-Soviet intelligentsia. It signaled a move toward using legal opportunities within the public sphere to mask their ceaseless struggle against the Revolution. "'Prokukish,'" Zinoviev explained, "was the first sign of this 'public' spring. . . . But we knew how to get from them all we could to help the starving, and when it became apparent that part of this organization stubbornly wanted to continue counterrevolutionary tactics, we employed our measures."[134]

Intellectuals unsympathetic to the regime had hoped that the NEP reforms might breathe new life into public institutions, if not into politics. They believed, or wished to believe, that a space remained for an independent public sphere even under the proletarian dictatorship. After the experience of the famine relief committee, however, many intellectuals were far more reluctant to work with the regime in a state-run organization. Efforts to preserve an autonomous public sphere subsequently centered on professional, cultural, and academic organizations, on agricultural cooperatives, on private publishing and journals, and first and foremost on the country's higher educational institutions. The struggle over university autonomy and control of higher education proved to be a critical skirmish in the battle the Bolsheviks saw themselves as fighting against those who refused to accept the hegemony of the Soviet state.

2

Bolsheviks and Professors: The Struggle over University Autonomy

> *Almost five years after the conquest of political power by the proletariat, in its, the proletariat's, state schools and universities the old bourgeois scholars teach the youth (or rather, defile it with) the old bourgeois rubbish.*
>
> —*Lenin, Pravda, March 1922*

Before 1921 the Soviet regime, enmeshed in a brutal struggle for survival, did not have the luxury of devoting significant resources to reforming higher education. As the sociologist Pitirim Sorokin wryly remarked, "Busy with Civil War, the Bolsheviki had not yet annihilated all University Life."[1] The changes introduced were piecemeal, often contradictory, and had little practical effect. The situation changed considerably, however, at the end of the Civil War. With the external enemy vanquished, the Bolsheviks felt ready to turn their attention to the "ideological front." The autonomous professoriat was seen as a major obstacle to ensuring hegemony over the broader public sphere, and so between 1921 and 1923, a series of measures was taken to establish preliminary control over Russia's higher educational institutions, or VUZy (*vysshie uchebnye zavedeniia*).[2] The regime introduced reforms to create small, reliable administrative bodies and to end the dominion of the professors' councils, whose "corporate" interests the regime saw as separate from and hostile to those of the Soviet state. Like all other public entities in Russia, higher educational institutions were to be made to serve the interests of society as a whole, as interpreted by its vanguard, the Bolshevik Party.[3]

The professoriat fiercely resisted these changes. Most professors believed strongly in the ideal of university autonomy, that scholarship was inherently apolitical, and that teachers could and must strive for objectivity.[4] The Bolsheviks, on the other hand, had no sympathy for such "bourgeois" relics. Marxism taught that the intelligentsia's protestations on behalf of unfettered scholarship were disingenuous, that "free science" was itself a value, and one that was used to sustain the educational—and therefore economic—status quo. As Lenin proclaimed, "The very term 'apolitical' or 'nonpolitical' education is a piece of bourgeois hypocrisy, nothing but a deception of the masses. . . . We must put the matter frankly, and openly declare, despite all the old lies, that education cannot help being connected with politics."[5] The Bolshevik project depended on reforming political consciousness, on shaping and reshaping minds. The primary weapon in their propaganda arsenal was education, the enlightenment of members of the working class to their true interests. To allow those whose philosophical viewpoints differed from their own to influence and corrupt university students was unacceptable.[6]

Despite the consensus within the party about the need to bolshevize higher education, there was disagreement over the most suitable tactics for achieving this goal. Hard-liners such as E. A. Preobrazhenskii, who briefly headed Glavprofobr, the Narkompros organ in charge of higher education, maintained that the regime should not compromise with recalcitrant professors. Pragmatists like Lunacharskii agreed in principle, but they recognized that the battle would of necessity be a protracted one. The Bolsheviks did not have the manpower to change everything immediately, and they therefore needed to assert control over higher educational institutions without antagonizing the professoriat. One of higher education's primary functions was the training of technical specialists, and it was imperative not to interrupt their production. At the same time, the teaching of non-Marxist or, at the very least, starkly "anti-Soviet" courses in the humanities and social sciences had to be eradicated as quickly as possible.

By mid-1923 major changes had been wrought in how universities were organized and in what was taught. Although the Bolsheviks had not yet completely taken over higher education, they had by and large achieved administrative control. Major steps had been taken in breaking the so-called caste spirit among professors by banning their most important organizations, vastly reducing the role of faculty councils, and removing the most notorious dissident voices. The autonomous university would no longer be one of the principal constituent parts of the intellectual public sphere. Bolshevik intervention in higher education had had its emphatic debut, and its proponents would grow ever more fervent over the course of the decade.

Background: Higher Education in Revolution and Civil War

The university's role in society was highly contested in late imperial Russia.[7] Government officials were caught between the need to educate productive servants of the autocratic state and the knowledge that institutions of higher education were bastions of political unrest. Therefore, it was entirely natural that the state should control these institutions, both to make sure that they were properly fulfilling their functions and to limit the political damage that the unruly, radical studentry and dangerously corporate-minded professoriat might cause. The professoriat had a very different understanding of higher education and insisted that it could and should remain politically neutral. Their "ideology of *nauka* (science)," based on the German Humboldtian ideal, held that the main purpose of the university was to serve as a forum for individual personal, intellectual, and moral cultivation through a broad classical liberal arts education.[8] In the Russian context, however, the professoriat packaged their calls for university autonomy within the general discourse of the intelligentsia. Thus, they also emphasized the utilitarian values of the university, although, unlike tsarist officials, they promoted serving the nation rather than the state. In addition, although Russian professors argued that they represented the "above-class" ideology of academic freedom, many of them were active members of political parties after 1905, especially the liberal Constitutional Democratic (Kadet) Party.

The professoriat's central aim was to overturn the authoritarian 1884 statute on higher education and to establish university autonomy. During the 1905 Revolution, the professors' collectives became more openly political, declaring that autocratic government was incompatible with scholarly ideals and pressing for liberal democratic freedoms.[9] The professoriat was briefly able to achieve some of its corporate goals, while resisting the more radical urges of younger instructors and the studentry.[10] Soon, however, new limits were established on professorial decision making and on the rights of student organizations. The resulting tensions climaxed at Moscow University (MGU) in 1911 with mass faculty resignations and student expulsions. Although the situation improved under the moderate wartime minister of Education, Count Pavel Ignatiev, the 1884 University Statute remained in force until February 1917.

The vast majority of professors and students heartily welcomed the February Revolution. Normal academic activity halted, as teachers and pupils alike spent more time attending meetings and demonstrations than in the classroom, and a number of professors participated in the Provisional Government.[11] Liberal professors looked forward to the opportunity at last to reform higher education on the basis of the "ideology of *nauka*." The Commission for the Reform of Higher Schools was formed and chaired by the zoologist Mikhail Novikov, a Kadet and former Duma deputy. Despite the political tempest that was a distraction from the quiet work of educational reform, Novikov looked to eliminate obstacles to autonomy.[12] At the same time, even liberal advocates of free science did not deny that the state had an inherent interest in overseeing higher educational institutions. Although old rivalries among professors, instructors, and students occasionally resurfaced, relations were remarkably even, and conflict was limited mostly to small groups of radicals. This relative lack of division would hinder Bolshevik attempts to create a wedge between the "reactionary" professoriat and other groups within the VUZy.[13]

The predominantly liberal or moderate socialist professoriat reacted in almost unanimous opposition to the October coup, and a majority of student groups did likewise. The academic council of Petrograd University (PGU) was one of several professors' groups to issue an open condemnation of the coup and a call for the convening of the Constituent Assembly. A number of academic groups in Petrograd, as well as in important provincial cities such as Kharkov, Kazan, and Tomsk, refused to recognize the new government, and most student groups, which were led by SRs, Mensheviks, and Kadets, did likewise. When the new regime began to arrest professors, the protests became even louder.[14]

The thrust of the opposition rested on the radical disagreement between Bolsheviks and professors over the question of university autonomy. A May 1918 letter to Narkompros signed by a number of PGU professors held that the state "has neither the power nor the right to determine the nature of science and art, or to forge a path toward its 'true form.'" Even the regime's few allies supported some degree of autonomy and were uneasy over the fate of academic freedom.[15] In general, the VUZ academic councils tended just to ignore the new government and to continue administering the universities on their own terms. The Bolshevik leadership, from Lenin to Lunacharskii, did not bend in its belief that the philosophy of academic freedom and university autonomy was but a mask for professorial corporatism and Kadet values in the classroom. At the same time, few Central Committee members and Narkompros officials harbored illusions about their ability to replace the old professoriat immediately. As the Civil War advanced, the young and unstable regime was much more concerned with its survival than with reforming the universities. What followed was a series of half measures and uneasy negotiations between the regime and the professoriat over the future of higher education.[16]

At first, Lunacharskii, his deputy, the Communist historian Mikhail Pokrovskii, and other Narkompros leaders faced little intraregime competition in directing higher educational policy. Their initial reform efforts focused on "democratization": expanding working-class access by removing admissions and tuition requirements, and changing the composition of the teaching staff by requiring reelections of professors and instructors.[17] The professoriat was not against democratization on principle; it strongly supported the expansion of higher education, and during the Civil War, a staggering number of new VUZy were established in spite of a singular lack of funding.[18] At the same time, professors were reluctant to lower admissions standards, and they were particularly opposed to the introduction of party- or class-based affirmative action. The professoriat was also extremely protective of tenure, and younger instructors were not as easily swayed by promises of advancement and hints of "class struggle" as Soviet officials had hoped.

In summer 1918 Soviet officials drafted a charter that, while mandating open admissions and abolishing tuition, also contained concessions to the professoriat. Further negotiations with professors' representatives, however, soon broke down. The MGU council, led by the Kadet historian Aleksandr Kizevetter, was sharply critical of the proposed reforms, and Narkompros soon stopped asking professors for input.[19] A new statute was put on hold in favor of piecemeal legislation, which included requiring professors to undergo reelection; replacing juridical faculties with "faculties of social science," or FONy (*fakul'tety obshchestvennykh nauk*); installing commissars in problematic VUZy; and creating "workers' faculties," or *rabfaki* (*rabochie fakul'tety*), designed to prepare proletarians for full entrance. These regulations had little initial effect, however, beyond further alienating the professoriat. The same professors were reappointed (where elections were held at all), the commissars had little power, and the FONy effected few substantial curricular changes. University administration remained in the hands of professors' councils, except in the ever-increasing number of newly opened VUZy, where the regime strove to install reliable directorates from the start.[20]

The professoriat thus effectively retained the autonomy it had attained in 1917, but this did not lessen its displeasure with the regime. Some professors openly supported the White governments that briefly ruled important academic centers such as Kazan and Kiev. Others were members of short-lived conspiratorial organizations like the National Center. Those who did not flee when the tide turned against the White Generals Kolchak and Denikin were offered amnesty, but this lessened neither Soviet suspicion nor their own opposition.[21] The regime continued to search, interrogate, and arrest professors on a regular basis; the material deprivations of instructors, students, and staff were severe; and a significant number of older professors perished.[22]

The Utility of Higher Education and the Teaching of Social Science

Very few Russians had a higher education in 1921, and the regime was fully cognizant of the pressing need to extract knowledge from those who did. To stem the brain drain, due both to emigration and mortality, Lenin allowed Gorky to establish the Central Commission to Improve the Lot of Scholars, or TsKUBU (*Tsentral'naia komissiia dlia uluchsheniia byta uchenykh*), in December 1919. TsKUBU worked to ensure that professors, scientists, and other intellectuals received special consideration from the state. Rations were increased and, although professors continued to suffer from malnutrition and disease, their position was somewhat better than that of other groups, in particular the studentry.[23] Organizations such as TsKUBU would come to serve an important function in the government's efforts to win the support of valued specialists.

While Gorky looked to the intelligentsia's material needs, many Bolsheviks believed that Trotsky's ideas on the militarization of labor should be applied to educational policy. VUZy were seen as a critical part of economic production, whose purpose was to create suitable labor resources.[24] The Main Committee for Professional-Technical Education, or Glavprofobr (*Glavnyi Komitet professional'no-tekhnicheskogo obrazovaniia*), was therefore established, formally subordinate to Narkompros but often, as it turned out, at odds with its parent institution.[25] Its leaders, Otto Shmidt and then E. A. Preobrazhenskii, "envisioned their committee as a production organ *par excellence*. Its job was to produce trained human specialists."[26]

In order to make VUZy more productive, open admission was partially abandoned, and exams, which had been abolished in theory if not practice, were reintroduced as "knowledge checks." Though only a minority were Marxists, technical professors tended to be supportive both of vocationalization and of state economic planning, sharing the belief that rational decision makers could vastly improve on the unruly market.[27] Even many of those who recoiled at changes in VUZ administration actively assisted state economic organs such as VSNKh (the Supreme Council of the People's Economy).[28] The utilitarian turn in higher education reached its zenith in Ukraine. Under the leadership of G. F. Grinko, the Ukrainian Narkompros remolded VUZy into a production network that would respond directly to the state's need for specialists. Universities were abolished and replaced with "institutes of popular education," which would have the primary goal of teacher training.[29] Grinko's deputy, Ia. P. Riappo, contended that "the higher school must in all ways serve the multifaceted demands of life and be restructured on the basis of the economy and state building; knowledge and science must be made means, and not self-contained ends in themselves."[30]

Although reforms in Russia were never taken this far, Glavprofobr's utilitarian accent continued under Preobrazhenskii, who clashed openly with Lunacharskii. Preobrazhenskii, an economist and not a pedagogue, believed that Narkompros's resources should be directed at practical professional schools rather than wasteful universities.[31] Lunacharskii retorted that "it is not only inadmissible for us to reduce our higher educational institutions, we need to set ourselves the task of expanding their work."[32] Over the next year and a half, the utilitarian principle would be enshrined in the VUZ charter, but the maximalists did not achieve all their goals, and universities remained the foremost centers of higher learning in Soviet Russia.

Although pragmatists recognized the need to implement gradual reforms, Soviet educator-bureaucrats up to and including Lunacharskii looked forward to the eventual replacement of the old professorial cadre. This was particularly true in the humanities and social sciences, subjects crucial to the acculturation of a new generation of Soviet elites. The replacement of the juridical and historico-philological faculties with social science faculties (FONy) had little initial effect, and the Communists assigned to teach courses in historical materialism and Marxism were often too busy to do so.[33] This situation changed in fits and starts. Although a number of "bourgeois" instructors remained in their positions until the end of the decade, the regime did manage to effect a significant shift in the makeup of the professoriat at the start of NEP, as well as to institute a system for the surveillance of university teaching.

In fall 1920 the State Academic Council, or GUS (*Gosudarstvennyi uchenyi sovet*), under the direction of Mikhail Pokrovskii, began to purge particularly unacceptable instructors, in spite of fierce resistance. The abolition of law faculties removed a number of professors, despite the vigorous opposition of Sergei Prokopovich, the last dean of MGU's Juridical Faculty.[34] The regime abolished historico-philological faculties in March 1921, and the FONy were expanded to include most of their former departments.[35] The Petrograd University rector V. M. Shimkevich informed Lenin that the professors' council "considered the abolition of the faculty and even certain departments as incomprehensible both from an instructional and from the government's point of view. This mistake has been brought about by a narrow party perspective."[36]

This and similar protests fell on deaf ears, and in July 1921 GUS's scientific-political section was given jurisdiction over social science teaching. Within a year, the FONy at major universities introduced required courses in Marxism, Bolshevik thought, and Soviet politics and had instituted end-of-the-year exams in "the history of materialism," "the development of social formations and law in the RSFSR [Russian Soviet Federated Socialist Republic]," and "the history of socialism."[37] Students in the other faculties also had a dose of mandatory Marxism introduced.[38] Though professors opposed these requirements, and the courses suffered from a shortage of qualified teachers and textbooks, they nevertheless established a foundation in Marxist learning for the nation's future elite. In addition, the Institute of Red Professors was created in response to the dearth of Communist scholars, and the Socialist Academy was expanded to help develop a social science orthodoxy.[39]

While planning for the future, GUS tried to get rid of the worst of the old. First on the list were the philosophy departments, where the popularity of courses taught by neo-idealist thinkers was a particular irritation. At the end of the 1920–21 school year, owing partially to the requests of D. N. Bogolepov, the rigid Communist rector at MGU, philosophy was disbanded and its professors either removed or shuffled to other departments. Nikolai Berdiaev and Ivan Il'in were prohibited from teaching.[40] The PGU philosophy department was dismantled in fall 1921, and the same processes occurred at provincial VUZy.[41] Semën Frank had to cease teaching at Saratov, and Kazan purged several social science and philosophy instructors.[42] Humanists and social scientists were often, as Pitirim Sorokin noted, "removed to the Research Institute, where they would not be harmful to students."[43] Thus, when GUS abolished philosophy at Petrograd University, it assigned Ivan Lapshin and Nikolai Losskii to its scientific research institute.[44] And so philosophy found itself forced to the margins. The Moscow University Institute of Scientific Philosophy, which included Il'in and Frank, organized temporary courses for continuing majors in fall 1921. Scholars in Moscow and Petrograd lectured in conjunction with independent philosophical societies such as Berdiaev's Free Academy of Spiritual Culture.[45]

In 1921 GUS began reviewing social science course programs, very few of which were truly Bolshevik. Although a prescribed set of courses in Marxist thought and the Soviet state was now required at all major VUZy, the regime could not yet manage what was taught.[46] With the exception of MGU, PGU, and two other universities, the social science faculties were dissolved in

1922, and, despite continued modifications, no FONy survived to the end of the decade.[47] The Soviet achievement in restructuring the social science curriculum in the early 1920s was more negative than positive: certain old ways of teaching were proscribed, but what was to replace them had not yet been fully developed. Nevertheless, Marxist subjects had been introduced for the first time, and some manner of requirements had been instituted.

There was also a significant change in the FON teaching staffs at both Moscow and Petrograd universities. Despite the small number of Bolshevik professors, fellow-traveler groups such as the Left Professors in Petrograd grew rapidly, and more and more liberal or moderate socialist professors were banned from the classroom. Over the next several years, GUS's scientific-political section conducted background reviews and developed a system to weed out suspect professors and instructors.[48] GUS and Glavprofobr often appointed proregime professors over the protests of their colleagues, and there were bitter disagreements over appointments not only in the FONy, but in the natural sciences and at technical schools as well.[49] These changes to the composition of the professoriat would help to eliminate one of the primary manifestations of the autonomous public sphere.

Professors and Students: The Minds of Tomorrow

The regime's removal of politically unreliable scholars was driven by a concern that alien ideas would infect the next generation of educated citizens.[50] Bolsheviks repeatedly grumbled that unrepentant anti-Soviet forces were defiling and seducing the nation's youth. To Communist educators, altering the composition of the student body was at least as critical as overhauling the faculty. Efforts at "democratization" during and after the Civil War focused, first, on flooding the traditional faculties with *rabfak* (workers' faculty) graduates and, second, on placing Communists and Komsomol (Communist Youth League) members in the VUZy. Though historians disagree over the extent to which the regime's early efforts at proletarianization succeeded, this is only part of the story.[51] More crucial than immediate proletarianization was replacing politically suspect students with Communists and "nonparty Bolsheviks." These loyalists would assist in the process of reforming VUZy and would have a salutary effect on the broader ranks of uncommitted, impressionable youths. The result was a "dual policy of repressing non-Communist student movements and co-opting 'neutral' or 'apolitical' students."[52]

The first critical step toward reconfiguring the student body was the formation of *rabfaki.* The *rabfakovtsy* were older and more working class than the student body as a whole, and they were well aware of their indebtedness to the regime. While professors and student activists claimed openly to welcome the *rabfakovtsy*, many instructors expressed scorn or frustration concerning the poorly prepared newcomers.[53] As the *rabfakovtsy* began to enter the traditional faculties, and Narkompros altered admission to favor Communists and proletarians, the student body began to acquire a very different character.[54] The first Bolshevik student cells were established at the end of the Civil War; they were initially small and isolated, and their efforts to influence the critical "nonparty student masses" were of limited consequence. Often, the majority of Communists were *rabfakovtsy*.[55] Gradually, however, the alliance between the student body and the liberal professoriat began to fray. The most vocal opposition to professors came from Communist student cells, which (with the party's support) managed to gain control over student assemblies and drive out Mensheviks and SRs. In the meantime, the regime cracked down on traditional student groups and began to arrest opposition-minded student leaders.[56]

Older student organizations had been highly critical of state policies and, when VUZ reforms were introduced in fall 1921, had joined the professoriat in support of university autonomy. Students' living conditions were, by all accounts, absolutely catastrophic: many were near starvation, there was little light, and they had no heat in winter.[57] The students' protests led to further repressions, and as of fall 1921 all student groups required Glavprofobr's approval. Arrests of student leaders increased, and the GPU grew more vigilant in weeding out "anti-Soviet" groups. Glavprofobr announced that student interests would thenceforth be represented by two sanctioned "sections" in each VUZ.[58] Replacing independent organizations with officially authorized ones was a central tactic in bolshevizing the public sphere, but it did not always work right away. At PGU student leaders welcomed the new groups as an opportunity to resume control over their own affairs. At Moscow Higher Technical School (MVTU) old student leaders dominated the sections, which were soon disbanded and their leaders arrested. At the start of 1923 the Party Secretariat directed Glavprofobr to establish a new set of more controllable student organs.[59]

Still, the balance of power had already shifted.[60] Older student leaders and professors complained bitterly that the Communist minority was able to gerrymander the student assembly elections for candidates to new VUZ administrative boards. The Communist students also managed to dominate meetings at MVTU, in Kazan, and elsewhere in the wake of professorial protests in February 1922; for the first time since the Bolshevik takeover, the studentry came out highly critical of their teachers' fight for autonomy. While active Communists and members of the working class were still minorities, their numbers were growing rapidly, furthered by admissions changes and purges of the student body. Most students remained politically uncommitted, and opposition to the regime simmered through the NEP period,[61] but the studentry was now led not by pro-professor elements but by fire-breathing supporters of the regime. Communist students might, on occasion, have been rebuked for overzealousness, but the party did not renounce them, and the GPU enlisted many of them as informants in the VUZy.[62]

Toward State Control of Higher Educational Institutions

At the end of the Civil War, Narkompros did not yet fully control the nation's higher educational institutions. Efforts were made to ensure that newly opened VUZy were under state direction, but even this was not always workable. A more concerted takeover started in fall 1920 by overhauling the administrations of the nation's oldest and most prestigious universities and technical schools. At this time, MGU, PGU, and MVTU received new charters containing the basic ingredients of the later nationwide reforms.[63] These schools were to be placed under the single-person control of a rector, himself part of a broadened board (*pravlenie*) that included not only younger instructors and students, but also representatives of "interested organizations" outside the university, such as official professional unions and other Soviet organs.[64]

Real reform was slow to materialize in Petrograd, but the changes made at MGU led to open conflict. The nation's oldest and most prestigious university would thenceforth have Communist-controlled governing bodies, but the old professoriat did not accept this calmly. Mikhail Novikov, the outgoing rector, bitterly dated the "catastrophe" that befell MGU to the fall 1920 formation of a new presidium, with D. N. Bogolepov as rector.[65] At the time, Pokrovskii declared triumphantly, "It is necessary to put an end to autonomy, which is nothing but an ideological remnant."[66] Novikov, in response, angrily compared Narkompros leaders with reviled tsarist officials: "If, despite all of our arguments, this new charter goes into effect, then I am of the opinion that history will have to note that where Pobedonostsev and Kasso did not succeed in bringing about the destruction of higher education, Lunacharskii and Pokrovskii did."[67]

The new rector, Bogolepov, who also served in GUS, proved a vigorous proponent of rapid proletarianization, and he quickly alienated his colleagues. His authoritarian methods and open sympathy with the Communist students on the administrative board led the professoriat to complain loudly and often to Sovnarkom (the Council of People's Commissars) and other high government organs.[68] As Narkompros and party organs began to discuss more comprehensive plans for national higher educational reform, Bogolepov left no doubt on his views. Striking a more strident tone than most party leaders, he called for replacing "bourgeois" specialists in all fields as quickly as possible, and he suggested that Communist methods be introduced not only in the social sciences, but in the hard sciences as well. "We need decisively to terminate university autonomy and freedom of teaching," he declared. "All administration should be put in the hands of a small collegium, predominantly made up of Communists, and all the faculties' business should also be in the hands of small collegiums of Communists, or of individuals close to communism."[69]

Bogolepov deeply antagonized the astronomer Vsevolod Stratonov, dean of the Physics-Math Faculty, who would play a large role in the struggle over university autonomy. Bogolepov's attempts to control faculty appointments exacerbated tensions and led Stratonov to complain to Narkompros.[70] Even Pokrovskii realized that the situation was untenable and that Bogolepov was making things worse. Bogolepov was replaced, although Pokrovskii noted that the presidium did have the final right to confirm appointments.[71] Despite the concessions, the majority of professors refused to vote in the election of a new presidium, which once again acquired a proregime slant. The new Communist rector, V. P. Volgin, was, however, more conciliatory than his predecessor, and the professoriat found his approach far more tolerable.

In the meantime, Narkompros moved forward with plans for comprehensive reforms at the First All-Russian Party Conference on Education in early 1921.[72] Even Lunacharskii affirmed that higher education must always have production as its end goal, asserting, "It is necessary to put an end to the idea of autonomy for higher educational institutions. . . . The subordination of the higher schools to a general plan for economic and cultural socialist construction is a most urgent task."[73] Such rhetoric was indicative of the prevalence of utilitarianism among party educators, and it would have an influence on how higher education was reformed. Glavprofobr's purview was expanded to all VUZy, and in March 1921 the Narkompros Collegium approved a draft charter on higher education that gave Glavprofobr the ability to appoint rectors.[74] Lunacharskii had his doubts, writing to Lenin that "this charter goes somewhat against that policy that you had recommended to us, against the policy of a certain reconciliation with the professoriat; on the other hand, in its favor is the extreme counterrevolutionary mood among the professoriat, at the very least in Moscow." Lunacharskii, joined on this occasion by Pokrovskii, ordered that the new charter not be immediately implemented in order to avoid conflict.[75] But its supporters refused to back down, and the ensuing conflict at MVTU, the nation's most important technical school, marked the formal entrance of Lenin and the Politburo into higher educational reform.

The conflict at Moscow Higher Technical School began in early 1920, when professors demanded the removal of a Communist student from the VUZ council and briefly went on strike. A temporary, compromise charter for MVTU was enacted, but tensions between the professors and the vocal Communist student minority increased. The city Komsomol student cell heartily welcomed the March 1921 VUZ draft regulations, insisting that no concessions be made to "Kadet-Blackhundred [reactionary] professors."[76] Preobrazhenskii, the new head of Glavprofobr, agreed, and in April 1921 he replaced the old, recalcitrant MVTU administration. The professors again went on strike, and although the MVTU Communist student cell demanded an all-Bolshevik board, most students supported their professors. Lunacharskii, who wished to delay matters, rescinded the new appointments, to the dismay of Communist student activists. Preobrazhenskii not only defended the changes but told Lunacharskii to rethink his order. The frustrated commissar wrote to Lenin that Preobrazhenskii had made a major mistake, but that the new troika would now have to be installed in order not to damage further Glavprofobr's prestige. At the same time, he had little sympathy for the MVTU professoriat, whose inclinations he considered "disgusting."[77]

The professors protested to Lenin and the Politburo, which agreed that Glavprofobr had overstepped its bounds. It installed a temporary troika headed by the old rector, I. A. Kalinnikov. At the same time, the Politburo directed Lunacharskii to issue a declaration that, while chiding Glavprofobr and the overzealous Communist students, offered a sharp warning that further professorial insubordination would not be tolerated.[78] Lunacharskii made clear that he had no sympathies for the striking professors, who "are experienced enough to understand that such an act is a manifestation of struggle against the government as such, a crude attempt to pressure it, and an expression of mistrust in the ability of the government to deal with the matter objectively and without such pressure."[79] The higher leadership's direct involvement changed the dynamics of VUZ reform. Lenin had no patience for those who represented the educational equivalent of "infantile leftism," who wanted to throw out all that was old, even what was useful. But he despised the old professoriat and its attempts to resist the regime's control of higher education, and he was more frustrated with Lunacharskii's caution than with Preobrazhenskii's rashness.[80]

The MVTU strike led Narkompros officials and party leaders to take stock of higher educational policy. Lunacharskii advised Lenin that the Party Central Committee needed to signal more strongly whether repression or concession was to be the rule. Though a "proponent of this second, soft cultural policy," Lunacharskii understood the rationale behind the "harsh line." His suggestion that he himself might be removed from the process displayed the commissar's frustration with the challenges to his authority.[81] The Politburo in turn directed Narkompros to elaborate the proper relationship between itself, the VUZ Communist Party cells, the nonparty studentry, and the professoriat; to revise the draft charter; and to convene a conference to discuss the reforms. A commission headed by Pokrovskii reworked the charter and submitted it to the Central Committee in May 1921. The process for fundamentally reforming the administration of higher education had commenced.[82]

Battling the "Caste" Organizations of the Professoriat

During 1921 the regime became increasingly annoyed with the various professors' associations that were coordinating resistance to the new VUZ order. These groups were held to evince the professoriat's "caste" or "corporate" spirit, its tendency to look out for its own group interests rather than those of the people. This was precisely what the Bolshevik leadership most despised about bourgeois *obshchestvennost'*: the supposedly divisive and selfish nature of the various elements that constituted the intellectual public sphere. The most important professors' societies, the Moscow Union of Scientific Actors and the United Council of Higher Educational Institutions in Petrograd, soon came under the scrutiny of Pokrovskii and of the official educational workers' union, Rabpros. The unwillingness of most professors to enter into Rabpros, even when offered a separate "scientific workers' section," irritated those who believed that all organized representation should be done within the official union system. The issue was not to prevent professors from obtaining special privileges, as the continued functioning of KUBU demonstrated, but rather to make sure that these organizations adjusted their collective action to the framework of official interests.[83] That is, the bolshevization or elimination and replacement of such organizations was meant to effect their absorption into a significantly more unified—and hence more Soviet—public sphere.

Lev Kamenev, as chairman of the city soviet, not only did not object to the Moscow Union of Scientific Actors, but, according to Vsevolod Stratonov, was fairly supportive. The Mossovet (the Moscow soviet) agreed to participate in a lecture series proposed by the union and asked the Moscow

Department of Public Education, or MONO, to help organize it.[84] MONO, however, insisted that professors instead join Rabpros, complaining that the union was "in fact a private organization" of suspect political orientation, aimed primarily at guarding its members' privileges.[85] Rabpros and the Narkompros Academic Center, headed by Pokrovskii, both agreed. Pokrovskii moved to eliminate the union and other groups like it and to merge them with Rabpros. The union's chief, the MVTU professor Vsevolod Iasinskii, insisted that it was a purely scientific association that had organized a lecture series and looked after its members' needs. He noted that professors were reluctant to join Rabpros in view of its statements of explicit support for "the dictatorship of the proletariat." Pokrovskii and his colleagues responded that "the union is an exclusive caste organization," since only professors elected by their colleagues could join.[86] The decision was therefore made in April 1921 to abolish the union as "an institution having anti-Soviet tendencies" and to form a "section of scientific workers" within Rabpros in its place. Rabpros urged all professors to join and warned that "any separatism is uncommonly harmful in our particularly critical times, especially if it is demonstrated by people of such high qualification. . . . Science can never be neutral, cannot stand to the side of that sociopolitical struggle that is the most fundamental fact of modern human society."[87]

Here the fundamental dispute over the ideology of *nauka* was displayed. Iasinskii and his colleagues protested that the union's closure and the pending VUZ reforms would "culminate in the complete abolition of freedom of scholarly teaching and even research. . . . The freedom of science is not only an ideal that might be relegated to the distant future, but an inseparable quality of science as such." Intelligent students, they added, would recognize that the artificial imposition of a single party line would prevent real learning. "Such a simplified mechanization of things will strike university scholarship at its very core and can create only sickly castrati of thought, incapable of autonomous creative activity." The union's opponents were hardly swayed by these arguments, maintaining that there never had been nor could be freedom of teaching. At that time, in particular, there were certain subjects that could not be taught, and that the Union of Scientific Actors denied this fact clearly showed its political colorings.[88]

Pokrovskii and Rabpros agreed that the new "scientific workers' section" should replace all such professorial unions, and queries went out as to whether there were such societies in the provinces.[89] In particular, Pokrovskii had his eye on the Petrograd United Council of Scientific and Higher Educational Institutions (also known as the United Council of Professors). He wrote to Lenin that it unnecessarily paralleled existing Soviet organs and warned that "the council is attempting to broaden university autonomy in Russia beyond all bounds that it has heretofore crossed." Lunacharskii, however, while referring to the United Council as "a citadel for the right professoriat," added, "I don't want to irritate the Petersburg professors now and start a new conflict with them, when the upcoming conference opens the possibility of tolerable cooperation. It would be better to hold off for now."[90] But the council proved to be an even more inveterate critic than the Moscow Union had been, and Lunacharskii's hopes for cooperation were dashed. In addition, the corporate professors' councils at particular VUZy revived the accusations made by the Union of Scientific Actors, as the professoriat made one more attempt to resist what it saw as an assault on academic freedom. The regime soon made sure that all such independent-minded associations were silenced. Organizations looking after particular interests in Soviet society thenceforth had to do so within a narrow network of officially sanctioned institutions, within a tightly controlled public sphere.

Finalizing the Regulations on VUZ Reform

A summer 1921 all-Russian conference on VUZ reform represented a final, unsuccessful effort at collaboration. Despite Lunacharskii's assurance that the Bolsheviks would work with everyone who discussed the matter in a "loyal" manner, the professors' delegates were deeply suspicious. They were fiercely protective of university autonomy, and they felt that the deck was stacked in favor of pro-Bolshevik elements.[91] It was clear that the regime would brook no protest to the main elements of the proposed regulations. Lunacharskii and Pokrovskii stressed that VUZy must be made to serve the interests of the state, and to accomplish this they intended to replace the unwieldy professors' councils with small, centralized boards answering directly to Narkompros.[92] By including instructors, students, and even representatives of unions and local government organs, the plan was to dilute these bodies with more sympathetic elements. The conference ratified the basic plan, and even most of the details, without significant change. A professors' group led by the Petrograd medievalist Lev Karsavin, at times allied with a block of "nonparty students," tried to alter almost every objectionable element in the regulations, but their amendments were roundly defeated.[93] For their efforts, they were denounced and threatened with arrest in the official press, while on the other hand a group of Moscow professors who had boycotted the conference accused them of appeasement.[94]

The September 1921 charter and its subsequent revisions attempted to balance the regime's dissatisfaction with the fact that most VUZy remained under professorial control with its recognition that heavy-handed actions would result in further disruption. It was made clear that Narkompros and, within Narkompros, Glavprofobr had ultimate say over higher education. VUZy were to have as their chief goals: (1) preparing specialists for the Soviet state economy, (2) preparing "scientific workers," and (3) disseminating "scientific knowledge among workers and peasants."[95] The regulations focused on the critical question of administration, taking power away from "corporate" professors' councils and centralizing it in easier-to-control, more efficient boards (*pravleniia*) reporting directly to Glavprofobr. The system of designation to the boards was a compromise between election and appointment, with the assumption that there would be several candidates sympathetic to the regime.[96] The board was to have complete control over ratifying faculty resolutions, appointment of instructors, and consultation with GUS concerning professorial appointments. The rector was given ultimate veto power. In addition, the faculty councils were to cede power in several directions: to the board, to the faculty deans' offices, and to "subject commissions," newly created bodies that were to "unite related disciplines." Upon their formation, the subject commissions quickly turned into contentious bodies in which Communist students battled scornful professors over what to teach and how it should be taught.[97]

The primary goal of the regulations was thus to place control of each VUZ in the hands of a small group of people closely tied to the government. Whatever their tactical disagreements, Bolshevik leaders from Lenin and Preobrazhenskii to Lunacharskii and Pokrovskii agreed on the necessity of breaking the system of corporate university governance by professors' councils. Their attempts at reconstructing VUZ administration, however, would meet massive resistance in fall 1921 and winter 1922, which would lead first to attempts at conciliation, but soon to more drastic methods of dealing with the "caste-like" professoriat.

The core of the new VUZ charter was the establishment of central government control through the formation of administrative boards. It would take well over a year to complete the process: boards were selected and reselected until a tenable equilibrium was reached. The direct result was confusion and highly politicized conflicts, as the professoriat attempted to hold on to its dominant role while vocal Communist students demanded radical change. The local Soviet institutions usually did not know or care much about VUZ affairs; where they did intervene, it was usually to assert their prerogative to do so. The professors did not hide their condescension toward radical students and local bureaucrats, nor did the latter hide their antipathy toward the old intellectuals. Mutual accusations of misconduct marred candidate elections, which led professors to protest directly to the highest organs of government. The professoriat found to its dismay, however, that simply ignoring Soviet laws and regulations was no longer feasible.

In October 1921 Glavprofobr's Council on VUZ Affairs, led by the MGU rector V. P. Volgin, established an electoral procedure, stressing the urgency of implementing the reforms. The critical first step was selecting a new board at each VUZ that could then oversee the rest of the reforms. Each of the electoral "curiae"—professors and teachers; researchers and "scientific workers"; students; local government organs, unions, and other "interested institutions"; and other VUZ employees (*sluzhashchie*)—were to make lists of candidates for the boards, which would then be sent to the Council on VUZ Affairs for confirmation. Elections at most VUZy were scheduled to take place in November and December, after which the lists of candidates were presented to the Council on VUZ Affairs.[98]

The actual implementation of these reforms proved to be an enormous headache. Both militant Communist students and opposition-minded professors spoke of an atmosphere of "open struggle." The Communist cell at the Moscow Institute of Transportation Engineers noted that everything boiled down to "us against them"—on one side was the "professoriat, defenders of bourgeois ideology and the bourgeois order," and on the other was the Red studentry and its defenders in the *rabfak* and among the *sluzhashchie*. The radicals complained that the "nonparty, cowardly mass" of students continued to be swayed by a few White leaders, and that they had had to push their list of candidates through to achieve a Communist majority. Frustrated that their peers retained a "backward" mentality, they also hinted at a need to purge the studentry of undesirable elements.[99]

Communists were determined to control the election process within the student curia, which, despite its lackluster political outlook, they hoped would present alternatives to the professors' candidates. At a meeting of Moscow Communist student cells, it was disclosed that conflicts had been acute at five local VUZy where the "counterrevolutionary" studentry was particularly combative. At MGU the Communists lamented the growing "reactionary mood among students," which they blamed on the pernicious influence of the professors; the leniency of Glavprofobr, which they characterized as "an ineffective [*ne trudosposobnoi*] organ"; and the Bolshevik rector Volgin, whom they viewed as weak and too conciliatory. Dissatisfied with the MGU student elections, the Bureau of VUZ Communist Cells sent Glavprofobr its own list of candidates—which did not originally even include Volgin—but this list was largely ignored.[100] When Glavprofobr confirmed the board, however, it consisted almost entirely of Bolsheviks or sympathizers, and it was highly supportive of the regime during the protests that followed. Glavprofobr confirmed boards for all Moscow VUZy in late December. Although it could not fill all positions with Bolsheviks, its efforts to appoint persons it perceived as loyal were largely successful.[101]

The Petrograd office of Glavprofobr delayed implementation of the decree, and the professoriat protested what changes were made.[102] The faculty at Petrograd Technology Institute warned that "if the regulations are strictly enforced, the VUZ will quickly move toward disorder and dissolution," and that in the nation's interest, those most immediately concerned (i.e., the professors) should be allowed to administer all aspects of VUZ life.[103] Even where the professors followed instructions, the process did not run smoothly. The PGU board received little response to its attempts to gather input from local institutions such as the Petrograd branch of Rabpros, the official medical workers' union, the Petrograd regional Executive Committee, and the local department of education.[104] In addition, the Petrograd Glavprofobr branch organized a student meeting only at the very last minute, so that the vast majority present were *rabfakovtsy.*[105]

In early 1922 resistance took on a more comprehensive character and was linked to complaints of material hardship. The regime was accused of not having taken sufficient care of the nation's VUZy, of bringing them to the edge of ruin, and thus of jeopardizing the country's future. Fuel shortages led to stoppages at several Petrograd VUZy in January 1922.[106] Though most soon resumed, many problems endured, and protests grew ever more vociferous. The Petrograd United Council of Professors openly criticized not only the reforms but also Narkompros itself. The regulations, the council complained, were based on bureaucracy and appointment, an "unreal [*nezhiznennyi*], artificial principle," which "will lead the VUZy to complete destruction." In practice, it added, the process had been hijacked by a small number of Communist students, and the Petrograd authorities had broken their own rules. The professors agreed to submit candidates for the VUZ board only under the conditions that the rector and most of the board be chosen from the their list, and that the board be allowed to function without interference from local officials. Otherwise, the council would direct its members to refuse to accept their posts. Finally, it insisted on the right of its members to decide voluntarily whether to join the official union and rejected the forced inclusion of all professors in Rabpros. In so doing, it reaffirmed its own right to exist as an independent voice in the public sphere.[107]

Professors' collectives at particular VUZy made similar complaints. The PGU council complained of unheated buildings, unprepared students, and unwanted interference from Soviet officials. It sharply questioned the propriety of having party cells in the university and opined that affirmative action based on class and political affiliation would "turn the university into a privileged school of one class." Even worse was the "principle of supplementing the teaching staff with those named for party-political reasons, rather than for their scientific qualifications. In the university there are now two categories of instructors—the privileged and the tolerated." The *real* danger of corporatism, the council contended, would occur when Bolshevik appointments turned the teaching staff into a "narrow, intolerant caste, doomed to severe vegetation in terms of scholarship." Scholars were under increasing pressure not to pursue the truth, but to confirm imposed theories. "Under the new university charter, and in spite of all the efforts of its teaching staff, the university's future activities do not promise any sort of fruitful results for science, the motherland, or the studying youth."[108]

The pro-rector Boris Odintsov told the PGU faculty council in February that the lack of funds might "even lead to the closure of the university, if monetary resources are not granted to us immediately." When administrative elections occurred later that month, the instructors nominated the rector Shimkevich, the agronomist and pro-rector Odintsov, the medievalist Lev Karsavin, and the jurist and former pro-rector A. A. Bogolepov, whereas local Soviet authorities put forth pro-Bolshevik candidates headed by N. S. Derzhavin.[109] Glavprofobr's attempted compromise did not satisfy the professors' council, which insisted on a board made up entirely of their candidates. This demand was considered incontrovertible, but a delegation was sent to Moscow to negotiate with the new Glavprofobr head, Varvara Iakovleva, and Volgin.[110] They were ready to make concessions, but ominous evidence of conflict remained. The delegates reiterated that the United Council required that professors nominate the board. While refusing to recognize the very existence of the United Council, Iakovleva conceded that Lunacharskii had instructed her to reach agreements with individual VUZy on the makeup of their boards; she promised to pay all back wages and to form a commission to discuss the financial crisis.

Although the negotiations displayed a certain give and take, they failed to resolve the crisis. The professors' demand that they choose all board members was unacceptable, as was their choice of rector, V. M. Shimkevich. Iakovleva proposed that the delegates put forth a different candidate, and the PGU council defiantly selected the equally unacceptable Odintsov. The matter was at last settled by Glavprofobr's appointment in May of Derzhavin, the founder of the solidly proregime "group of left professoriat." The professors' representatives, including Odintsov, refused to have anything to do with the Derzhavin-led board. The next round of elections in September would be supervised directly by the Petrograd regional party committee in the presence of Pokrovskii and Zinoviev and result in a securely Communist board.[111]

Matters were no better at MGU. On 27 January 1922 the Physics-Math Faculty, dismayed at the appalling material conditions, refused to teach classes until a general instructors' assembly could be held. As the dean Vsevolod Stratonov noted, such a gathering was itself illegal, as the regime had prohibited the convening of the university council.[112] The MGU board, already in the hands of regime appointees, condemned the action and demanded that classes resume; the Bolshevik rector Volgin angrily rebuked Stratonov for not exploring other solutions. A. V. Kubitskii, a Bolshevik board member, denounced the strike as illegal and impermissible. The board not only refused to join the protest but pronounced the faculty's declaration null and void.[113] Stratonov and his colleagues paid little attention and sent a declaration to Sovnarkom blaming the regime for the catastrophic material degradation, and in particular the high rates of illness and mortality.[114] Although government assistance had improved matters for more famous scholars, even they were not receiving sufficient relief. "How paradoxical it is," the MGU council noted, "that a professor at a higher technical institute—a specialist on light transport, unique in Russia, receives five times less than the chauffeur who drives him." Noting that specialists employed by VSNKh and other economic organs were treated much better, the professors contended that Glavprofobr grossly underestimated "the significance of science for the economic and cultural life of the country." For students, many of whom were starving and hardly had the means to study, things were even worse. The general MGU assembly therefore concurred with the Math Faculty and resolved not to resume classes until steps were taken to improve the situation.[115]

The authorities reacted swiftly. The Politburo, which discussed the matter five times in the first half of February, instructed Narkompros to end the strike quickly "without employing repression," to find a way to pay the professors, and to form a commission with professors' delegates. It directed Glavprofobr to give preference to professors' candidates to the boards, an important concession that would be included in the subsequent revised version of the VUZ charter. Preobrazhenskii's angry protests against this conciliation were overruled, and the Politburo accepted his resignation as head of Glavprofobr on 13 February. A. D. Tsiurupa, the deputy chair of Sovnarkom, hastily arranged a meeting with a delegation of MGU professors. When the delegates demanded a resolution to the financial crisis, Tsiurupa replied that none of this was news and that steps had already been taken to pay professors their back wages. He announced the formation of a commission to discuss salaries and VUZ budgets, and he noted that steps would be taken to hasten the closure of insolvent VUZy, a measure supported by MGU professors, who saw it as a way of concentrating funds in the older, more important, and more viable institutions.[116] At the same time, Tsiurupa angrily rejected the idea that the regime had neglected higher education. He reiterated that it was wrong for the professors to have taken action before going through proper channels, ominously suggested that going on strike had been a serious misstep, and demanded that classes resume promptly. Despite the concessions, the MGU council complained to Sovnarkom several days later that a strike had been their only option, since repeated attempts "to draw the attention of those in positions of high power to the threatening catastrophe" had been fruitless.[117] Nevertheless, they had at last been heard, meetings with Lunacharskii were scheduled, and the strike was ended directly.

In the meantime, controversy was again brewing at Moscow Higher Technical School. In December 1921 Glavprofobr named I. A. Tishchenko, a new instructor with little standing in the professors' council, as rector, and two Communists, the engineer V. L. Tsudek and the student D. A. Epshtein, to the new VUZ board. The professors rejected these appointments, declaring that the rector and board must "enjoy the trust of the instructors' collegium."[118] Through January, both the old and new boards claimed authority, while several instructors named to the new board refused to serve, having been "recalled" by the professors' collegium. Preobrazhenskii rejected out of hand the professors' choice for rector, I. A. Kalinnikov, because of his involvement in the April 1921 protests. On 26 January 1922 the deans and secretaries of all four faculties resigned in protest. Preobrazhenskii ordered the new board installed, and Kalinnikov was forced to hand over the rectorship.[119] When the professors' collegium hinted at an imminent strike, the regime moved swiftly, and Tsiurupa, joined by Stalin, met with an MVTU delegation on 14 February. The delegates demanded the formation of a compromise board and budgetary allotments favoring the older, established VUZy. They declared that Glavprofobr was "an empty space" and the cause of most of the problems, and that only the instructors knew how to run MVTU. They denied having called a strike, since they had no "political colorings," while complaining that the Communist cells were ruining everything. Although objecting to the professors' methods, Tsiurupa and Stalin hinted at potential compromise and alluded to the coming changes in Glavprofobr.[120]

Varvara Iakovleva soon replaced Preobrazhenskii at Glavprofobr, but the professors' meeting with Tsiurupa and Stalin occurred too late to avert a delay in the start of spring classes. Although a Communist-dominated student assembly denounced the professors' "methods of struggle" and condemned the strike, the Cheka informed Iakovleva that the students as a whole "are behaving passively; only about a third are studying."[121] Tsiurupa angrily declared that the strike took away from the progress that had been made, demanded that the deans resume their responsibilities, and proposed that the professoriat again nominate candidates to the board. A compromise board of three professors and two Communists was finally confirmed several weeks later.[122] But the truce did not assuage the professors' concerns.

If the party leadership had indeed paid insufficient attention to higher education, this was certainly not true after this round of turbulence. Though Lenin chided the professors, he set forth a policy of conceding to some of their economic demands and even certain board nominations. Preobrazhenskii, whose intransigence was held largely responsible for inflaming the professors' indignation, was driven to resign and was chastised by Lenin at the Eleventh Party Congress in March.[123] Lunacharskii and Pokrovskii met with representatives of the Moscow and Petrograd professoriat and concurrently with other Soviet officials in a desperate effort to obtain budgetary assistance. At the same time, Lunacharskii, who began to take a more active role, denounced the "extreme disorderliness" of the strikes, expressing "the sternest condemnation." He angrily noted, as Tsiurupa had, that the professors should have gone through official channels and called on them to resume teaching immediately.[124]

Narkompros leaders and professors' delegates met several times in February and March to discuss the material crisis and funding issues, including the payment of back wages. The commissariat entertained detailed discussion of how it might obtain resources, but all questions concerning the new charter were put off until the final meeting. At this point, the professors were allowed to read their prescriptions for altering the reforms, which had been agreed on at a gathering of elected representatives the day before. They emphasized returning authority to the professors' councils, eliminating the subject commissions, and devolving rights from the board back to the faculty councils. Lunacharskii and Pokrovskii responded evasively that they needed time to muddle over these suggestions.[125] At several concurrent meetings with other Soviet officials, Lunacharskii explained the dire crisis, argued that the dearth of trained specialists threatened economic production, and begged the other commissariats to help support those VUZy most critical to their own functioning. The mostly unsympathetic officials replied that they would do so only if given jurisdiction over the VUZy they funded (a proposal that Lunacharskii categorically rejected), but they did produce lists of institutions most important to the nation's economy.[126] To restore financial viability,

VUZ closures continued rapidly through 1922, despite anxious petitioning from the instructors and students affected.

Compromise and Repression

The window for compromise closed quickly. Hard-line forces in the Soviet educational establishment regrouped, while the professoriat's complaints did not abate, even after steps were taken to satisfy their material demands.[127] Bolshevik leaders flatly rejected the professors' insistence that their resistance was strictly apolitical. Preobrazhenskii had been stripped of his post at Glavprofobr, but he was still editor of *Pravda*, which charged that the faculty strikes had come on the direct orders of the Kadet émigré leader Pavel Miliukov.[128] The notion that the strikes had resulted from a Kadet conspiracy greatly agitated Lenin. In a memo to Kamenev and Stalin, he urged that if this was true, they needed to get rid of dozens of professors, and that the time had come to "strike hard."[129] When protests and an aborted strike also broke out at Kazan University, a Bolshevik student made similar accusations against the leaders of the local professoriat.[130] Lenin began to see evidence of such treason frequently; his article "On the Meaning of Militant Marxism" in *Pod znamenem marksizma* suggested that professors who yearned for "bourgeois freedoms" had no place in Soviet Russia.[131]

It was evident that economic concessions alone would not satisfy the dissident professors, and the criticism was indeed relentless. MVTU professors declared that despite positive steps since meeting with Tsiurupa, "peaceful instructional work has been made extremely difficult by the political harassment that is systematically conducted against the instructors' collegium." They feared that the vituperative articles in *Pravda* indicated more arrests and naively suggested that the time had come to set aside animosity and work together to save Russia from utter destruction.[132] The all-Moscow professors' delegation was less conciliatory. It demanded alterations to the VUZ charter, declared that the professors would never accept Glavprofobr-appointed boards, and accused GUS of consistently mishandling the appointment process. Lunacharskii and Pokrovskii's meetings with professors, they had soon realized, had been "created only for the appearance that they were seriously concerned with the given matters."[133]

Despite these harsh reproofs, Lunacharskii at first tried to remain conciliatory. He and Pokrovskii gathered Communists to discuss potential changes to the charter after the Eleventh Party Congress. They encountered opposition, however, not only from the radical students, but also from Red professors and even Iakovleva, who, Lunacharskii noted angrily, did not consider herself bound by "collegial discipline."[134] Even Lunacharskii, however, grew irritated with the professors' relentless criticism. He passionately defended himself at a 10 May 1922 Sovnarkom meeting to which professors and Narkompros officials were invited. According to Stratonov, the professors refused to respond to Lunacharskii's and Pokrovskii's attacks, while Dzerzhinskii hysterically accused them of anti-Soviet activities, reiterating the charge that the strikes had come on direct orders from Miliukov in Paris. Soviet leaders made clear that enough was enough. Sovnarkom exonerated Narkompros, noted that it had made "maximal amendments to the charter in the direction of the professoriat's wishes," and warned the professors that it was time to stop opposing the reforms.[135] In fact, the revised charter would broaden the rights of GUS and Glavprofobr to intervene directly in VUZ affairs. While it seemingly made concessions to the professors, the provision that Narkompros could name a rector if none of the professors' candidates was acceptable provided a critical loophole through which Iakovleva and her successors at Glavprofobr could continue to control the appointment of administrative boards.[136]

In May, as Lenin and Dzerzhinskii began to plan the expulsion of hundreds of professors, Narkompros put an end to the remaining institutional homes of the corporate professoriat. First and foremost, it shut down the United Council of Professors in Petrograd, and Iakovleva sent word to all VUZy that such organizations would no longer be tolerated. Glavprofobr also banned the meetings of Moscow professors' delegates, warning that it could not protect them from the consequences of their illegal assemblies.[137] At the same time, Glavprofobr convened a series of rectors' conferences, chaired first by Volgin and later by Iakovleva herself, as an official substitute for these professors' gatherings. At these meetings, rectors and carefully selected professors discussed VUZ matters, in particular the financial situation, with Glavprofobr officials.[138] In this way, the regime was able to eliminate the private, "corporate" professors' meetings while providing an official forum for nonpoliticized feedback, thus effectively replacing their heterodox public discussions with a more controlled, Soviet public sphere.

In June 1922 party leaders discussed how to punish their most vocal critics among the professoriat. On the Politburo's direction, the GPU drafted a memo on "anti-Soviet activities among the intelligentsia," hinting at evidence of more planned strikes and warning that the professors' openly political behavior would continue to corrupt the studentry.[139] Dzerzhinskii's deputy, Iosif Unshlikht, outlined a series of measures to cleanse the VUZy of "rotten" elements, and a commission of Unshlikht, Iakovleva, and the Agitprop leader A. S. Bubnov was assigned the task of purging the studentry.

The recruitment of proletarian students was to be intensified and a system of weeding out politically unreliable students established. This same commission was to set strict limits on how and when professor and student groups could meet, to prevent autonomous "corporate" groups like the United Council from reemerging.[140] These efforts had some clear immediate successes; resistance to the government's VUZ reforms was far more muted, and the professors' councils at the individual VUZy rarely spoke out of line.

The Politburo simultaneously began planning the deportations of intellectuals, not least among whom were professors who had actively defended the ideology of *nauka* and opposed the state's VUZ reforms. Those targeted would include Vsevolod Stratonov and the former MGU rector Mikhail Novikov; several MVTU professors, including two of the deans, P. A. Velikhov and I. I. Kukolevskii; Vsevolod Iasinskii, who had headed the Moscow Union of Scientific Actors and was the effective leader of KUBU; leaders of the Petrograd professoriat, such as Boris Odintsov, Lev Karsavin, and A. A. Bogolepov; three of the more outspoken Kazan professors, including the rector, A. A. Ovchinnikov; and a significant number of PGU and MGU humanities and social science professors, including Pitirim Sorokin, Nikolai Losskii, Ivan Il'in, and Aleksandr Kizevetter.

By summer 1922 a significant number of VUZ boards had been appointed according to the new regulations. Moving two steps forward and one step back, the Bolsheviks were able to place reliable people at the helm. The revised charter promulgated in July 1922, despite limited concessions, retained the central principles of Glavprofobr appointment of rectors and GUS approval of professors. Only a few dissenting voices could be heard in the formerly opposition-minded MGU professors' council, now under Volgin's firm control.[141] Over the following year, Glavprofobr conducted a thorough review of the implementation of the reforms, in particular how successful they had been in establishing Communist, or at least "loyal" administrations. Although troubled by isolated instances of persistent anti-Soviet attitudes in certain localities, Iakovleva and her colleagues were by and large extremely pleased with the overhaul they had managed to effect in less than two years.[142] By mid-1923 she could confidently proclaim, "We have rebuilt the administration of the higher school in such a manner that we can already dictate to it its tasks, watch over their fulfillment, and take measures against their perversion."[143] Most administrative boards now more-or-less faithfully implemented the remaining elements of the VUZ charter. In more than one school, Communist students even managed briefly to run affairs until Glavprofobr reined them in.

A major reregistration of students took place during the 1922 summer break to purge those deemed politically unreliable, and a number were arrested. Although the proletarianization of the student body would take time, significant changes had already occurred. Communists dominated student organizations, and dissident voices had been silenced. The student public sphere, like the professorial public sphere, was already well on its way to the elimination of heterodoxy and to bolshevization. The danger that the student body would be corrupted from within did not disappear, since the enemy was envisioned as relentless, and several more student purges were ordered in 1923–24, targeting the brand-new heresy of Trotskyism.[144]

Russia's higher educational institutions remained alien to the regime in certain critical ways, most notably in the continued shortage of Bolshevik scholars. But a major step had been taken to ensure that VUZy were administered in the government's interests. The professoriat would never again be effectively organized in opposition to the regime; independent associations were banned; all VUZ teachers were forcibly inducted into Rabpros; and dissent in the faculty councils was silenced. Although the FONy failed to replace all "bourgeois" subjects, officially oriented courses had been successfully introduced. In addition, a significant number of bourgeois subjects departed along with their teachers into exile or to research institutes, most prominently philosophy and the fledgling discipline of sociology. While a number of "old" professors continued to teach into the late 1920s, it is simply not the case that the universities went through NEP unchanged and unhindered.[145] The Bolsheviks rejected the ideology of *nauka,* the professorial vision of the autonomous university playing a central role in the intellectual public sphere, and they replaced it with the tenet that higher education had to serve the interests of the state, within the harmonious, unitary, Soviet public sphere.

3

Exposing the Caste Spirit in Professional and Scientific Organizations

The matter of constructing the state—this is an important, necessary matter . . . but it is only one of many, no less important matters of the organization of public life. The organization of . . . healthy—non-governmental—economic, professional, scholarly, educational, artistic, etc., associations and unions are of no less critical significance.

—Pitirim Sorokin, "On the 'Anglo-Saxon' Position," in Utrenniki (Petrograd), 1922

When Narkompros leaders eliminated autonomous professors' organizations, they were implementing in the academic realm what was fast becoming general policy toward independent intellectual and professional associations. Engineers, agronomists, physicians, and teachers were all welcome to organize, but such groups would be closely monitored for anti-Soviet activity, construed to mean something much broader than direct political opposition. Any indication that group interests might be distinct from or in conflict with those of the proletarian dictatorship was viewed as a manifestation of corporate, or "caste" (*kastovoi*), exclusivism. Societies could lobby on behalf of their members' material interests, but the party-state reserved the right to set the scope of their activities. Because leading members of these associations were loath to relinquish autonomy, the early 1920s featured a series of skirmishes over the fate of their organizations. The result was a series of measures that required all public groups to receive official sanction from the Soviet security apparatus.

Intellectuals were not altogether opposed to state intercession in the public sphere. Statism, the conviction that the state had an important role in shaping economic and social development, was particularly pronounced among *spetsy.* In the final years of the old regime, and especially during the Great War, intellectuals became intimately involved in what Peter Holquist has called a "parastatal complex" of semiofficial organizations.[1] This pattern of involvement was replicated after the Revolution despite general suspicion of the Bolsheviks. It soon became apparent, however, that this was often a devil's bargain, and many saw the dissolution of the famine relief committee as an example of the perils of such participation.

On the other hand, despite this proclivity for statism, professionals and other intellectuals were overwhelmingly reluctant to allow the regime to dictate their collective endeavors. Their predominating conception of *obshchestvennost'* may have allowed for and even encouraged state involvement, but it nevertheless retained a strong attachment to organizational autonomy. This inclination conflicted directly with the Bolshevik understanding of how the socialist public sphere should function, by which any separatist inclinations were seen as inherently harmful to society in general. Hence, Soviet leaders found alarming the tendency of intellectual societies to suggest that their interests might not always coincide with the state's. Moreover, spokesmen often expressed these sentiments in ways or in forums that the Bolshevik leadership found unacceptable—through work stoppages, such as the professors' strikes; or during professional congresses, at which this "corporatist" outlook might be disseminated; or in independent publications, which might transmit these anti-Soviet views still further.

The professoriat pushed actively for "pure science" and university autonomy, and it extended this effort to a defense of traditional professors' councils. Similar attitudes prevailed among many different groups within the intelligentsia, even where accompanied by what the actors involved considered loyalty toward the new regime. This strong sense of professional identity was soon causing a number of professional organizations to come into conflict with the new regime—much to the bewilderment of many of those involved. The Bolshevik leadership, however, was determined to set limits on the warp and woof of *obshchestvennost',* even and especially at the beginning of NEP. Although some practically oriented *spets* groups, such as engineers and agronomists, maintained semi-autonomous organizations after 1922, those that did survive were thenceforth under the careful watch of the

GPU (the State Political Administration) and the NKVD (the Commissariat of Internal Affairs).

It was, perhaps unexpectedly, a congress of the physicians' section of the official medical workers' union that galvanized the Politburo to place all such organizations under tighter control. Immediately after the physicians' congress in May 1922, the Bolshevik leadership outlined an interconnected series of measures concerning "anti-Soviet groups among the intelligentsia," of which the surveillance of cultural, professional, and other intellectual organizations formed a central component. Two specialized NKVD commissions were created: one to evaluate, register, and provide surveillance of all intellectual, professional, and other not-for-profit organizations, and the other to do the same for their national congresses, which were viewed as particularly dangerous points for the dissemination of "corporate" separatism.[2]

After the disbanding, or bolshevization, of those associations and societies deemed particularly insidious in late 1922 and early 1923, the NKVD commissions set about establishing a regime to sharply define the parameters of public organizational activity in Soviet Russia. These new surveillance institutions had ultimate control over which groups were legally allowed to exist through obligatory registration and periodic reregistration. The registration process required societies to submit a charter, or bylaws, that the NKVD then edited to its satisfaction. All organizations were required to have open membership—thus eliminating the caste nature of private associations, which, the authorities felt, excluded outsiders, and Communists in particular. Early NEP thus featured a strong drive to rein in separatist or "caste" organizations and to ensure that their activities did not go outside acceptable bounds of limited autonomy.

The Assault on Unions during the Civil War

During the Civil War, most trade unions and cooperative societies were not yet under the direct control of the regime. Union and cooperative leaders, many of whom were Mensheviks and SRs, tended to view their primary goal as defending their members' interests rather than promoting the Soviet productivist aim of rebuilding the economy. The Bolsheviks responded with a frontal assault on the autonomy of unions and cooperatives. Their tactics included creating rival Red unions or cooperatives and dissolving the original groups; refusing to recognize organizational elections; installing Bolsheviks in leadership positions; and, when necessary, forcibly seizing property and offices. By 1920 very few independent-minded unions remained, and the bolshevization process was nearly complete.[3]

Still, the conflict over how much freedom to allow unions was far from over. Although the fiercely independent-minded Mensheviks had been ousted, a number of leading Communists, including Mikhail Tomskii, the sometime head of the official central trade union organ, VTsSPS, were uncomfortable with a complete Bolshevik takeover. Trotsky and his allies, on the other hand, saw unions as instruments for aiding in the militarization of labor in the interests of the state. The resulting rift nearly tore the party apart, and the conflict among the Workers' Opposition, Trotsky, and the middle line pursued by Lenin and Zinoviev has been reconstructed many times in the historical literature.[4] A rash of strikes at the beginning of 1921 and the series of rebellions that led to the introduction of NEP also convinced Lenin, despite his denunciation of the Workers' Opposition, of the need to resolve this problem.

The ambiguous resolution defined the position not just of unions but of many semi-autonomous organizations during the 1920s. Although they were not officially incorporated into the state, as Trotsky had desired, unions were nevertheless supposed to serve the economic goals of the Soviet state and the educative aims of the Communist Party. The Bolshevik leadership installed commissars within the unions and closely controlled high-level appointments. Through 1921 and 1922 any remaining Mensheviks were sought out and purged.[5] At the same time, in conditions of partial free enterprise, the role unions could play in defending the interests of their members was recognized as important. Thus, unions came to serve the often-contradictory goals of advancing the interests of the ruling party and those of their membership. As a result of this tension, they were widely distrusted by their worker members.

Bolshevik leaders were still less accommodating of independent professional organizations. These groups, it was believed, would have a much greater tendency than the proletariat to put their own corporate interests ahead of those of the state and the national economy. This fear led the party to dissolve rival groups and to place professionals and intellectuals within more broadly based, industry-wide unions, often within a special division. I have documented one such instance in describing the battle over the existence of autonomous professors' associations and their forcible inclusion within the educational union, Rabpros, as a section of scientific workers. At the same time, the state's dependence on *spetsy* in reconstructing the economy led the Bolsheviks to permit the creation of mutual aid societies to protect particular classes of intellectuals. In the early 1920s the party leadership and its security apparatus began to separate out which of these organizations, such as KUBU, could be retained once purged of dissent and which, on the other hand, represented dangerous separatist tendencies and had to be eliminated.

The forced inclusion of a "specialists' section" within an official trade union, however, did not necessarily mean that this section would submit to the imperatives of the state. The dynamics of professional organization is clearly evident in the intertwined fates of the physicians' section of the official medical workers' union, Vsemediksantrud, and of the venerable independent doctors' organization, the Pirogov Society.

The Doctors' Section of Vsemediksantrud and the Pirogov Society

Physicians, like other professionals under the tsarist regime, became important social actors in the late nineteenth century in conjunction with the development of the local organs of self-government known as *zemstva*. Activist doctors began to push for greater professional autonomy while they remained economically dependent on a state that was famously leery of independent corporate bodies. Nevertheless, physicians were one of the first groups to be allowed to form such an organization, the Pirogov Society, which became a prominent exponent of medical professionalism and of establishing professional control of public health.[6]

Pirogovites and other leading physicians welcomed the February Revolution as an opportunity to implement their conceptions of how public health should be directed. Though they differed over the degree of trust they were willing to place in any administration, many doctors invested great hope in the provisional government—with the assumption that they themselves would now be active in policy making. The Pirogov Society issued a quick condemnation of the Bolshevik seizure of power, for which it was ever after viewed with great suspicion.[7] Like other *spetsy*, physicians did not deny the importance of the role of state guidance, and many worked in Soviet organs. We should not, however, underestimate either the level of their commitment to professional autonomy or the degree of animosity that existed. While the Pirogov Society itself was no longer seen as representative of Russian physicians, other collective bodies voiced similar critiques of the regime and concerns over losing autonomous collegial forums.[8]

After 1917 the proliferating medical workers' unions were united in an official organ, Vsemediksantrud, which, like other *profsoiuzy (professional unions)*, brought various types of employees into a single, industry-wide union.[9] The most important doctors' group, the All-Russian Union of Professional Associations of Physicians (VSPOV), founded by leaders of the

Pirogov, remained unaffiliated. Bolshevik sympathizers complained that it was an offshoot of the Pirogov and held the same "liberal" views, favored the professional caste interests of its members over the greater good, and had proved its attitude to the regime through a series of work stoppages after the October Revolution. They dismissed its supposed neutrality as "a disguised rejection of the Soviet regime and an adherence to bourgeois-democratic forms of social construction."[10] Hence, VSPOV was liquidated in 1920, and its leaders reluctantly agreed to the formation of a physicians' section within Vsemediksantrud, provided that it remain a "nonparty" organization.[11]

The creation of the Vsemediksantrud doctors' section did not, however, erase the squabbles between its leaders and Soviet public health officials. With the abolition of VSPOV, activist doctors placed their hopes on the physicians' section, taking Tomskii at his word that unions would be able to operate independent of state interference. Vsemediksantrud's pro-Bolshevik Central Committee, however, was deeply suspicious of these "elitist" doctors, and relations within the union were poisoned from the start. In addition, with the introduction of NEP, physicians believed that the regime had opened a space for "public actors," and many quickly grew frustrated with the state health organs' inefficiency and bureaucratism, particularly in dealing with the famine.

In early 1922 Ia. Iu. Kats, a leading figure in the Pirogov Society, VSPOV, and the physicians' section, and N. A. Vigdorchik, who was also prominent in these groups, hinted at their growing disenchantment. They noted that although "Soviet medicine strives toward what we earlier called 'social medicine,'" this "has nowhere and not at any point been realized to its full extent." At the same time, they feared that NEP-inspired decentralization, moving toward local payment for health care, would lead to a chaotic and uncoordinated misuse of the nation's resources. Their prescription was a mix of central coordination and local initiative, but one based on the work of the physicians' collectives rather than the government. "The Soviet regime has erected new signposts [*vekhi*] in all spheres of life," they wrote. "It is unavoidable that there will also be a 'change of signposts' [*smena vekh*] in the sphere of public health."[12]

That these views might lead to conflict became increasingly clear at several convenings of the Petrograd branch of the physicians' section in late winter 1922. Dr. M. M. Magula declared at a February plenum that Vsemediksantrud "must avoid . . . suffocating its sections. The sections should be granted broad autonomy; the physicians' section should cease being the unloved, always suspected stepchild."[13] At a conference in March, Vigdorchik reiterated his and Kats's concerns, arguing, "For the successful renaissance of social medicine it is necessary among other things that physicians be granted . . . full freedom of professional associations." A. Aluf, the Vsemediksantrud Central Committee representative, bitterly objected, but the majority overruled him. Still, the doctors decided to remain, at least temporarily, within the union; G. I. Dembo and other speakers expressed the hope that their concerns might be addressed more fully at the national meeting in May.[14]

Leading Bolsheviks saw the May 1922 convention of the Pirogov Society, as well as the subsequent national congress of the physicians' section, as egregious demonstrations of how doctors were giving priority to professional and collegial contacts at the expense of service to the state. The clear ties between the Pirogov, with its roots in the liberal traditions of *zemstvo* medicine, and the most important section of the official medical workers' union were deeply troubling. Assertions that the famine demonstrated the need for medical work outside state organs recalled the anxieties of Semashko and other leading Bolsheviks concerning the disbanded famine relief committee. The physicians' perceived resistance was therefore met with resolute measures directed against the most recalcitrant leaders and their organizations.

In his keynote address to the Pirogov congress, the venerable doctor L. A. Tarasevich remarked that physicians across the country were becoming ever more interested in the society's activities. Its journal *Obshchestvennyi vrach* (Public Physician), which was explicitly intended to create an imagined national community of doctors and to maintain contacts between the center and the provinces, had resumed publication. Plans were made for expanding the Pirogov Society into other cities, and D. N. Zhbankov regretted that it had been kept from assisting in the famine relief effort. The congress was clearly the work of an organization that saw itself having a large role in protecting the interests of its members for years to come, and it confirmed Bolshevik suspicions of those who defended corporate professional autonomy.[15]

Because the "treasonous" declarations at the ensuing physicians' section congress occurred within an official organ, they were that much more alarming. The delegates complained bitterly about relations with the union's central body; some went so far as to suggest that it was no longer capable of functioning. To this Tomskii, one of several high-level Bolsheviks present, angrily replied that the regime would not allow "independent advocacy," including economic demands, strikes, and direct supplication. "We reject the possibility of caste unions. Perhaps we will rethink things in a year, but for now a union of physicians or engineers is impossible." He then summarized the Bolshevik conception of how the Soviet public sphere should function: "We believe that the relationship of professional unions to the state is twofold: under a bourgeois state it should struggle with the regime, but in a worker-peasant state it should support the regime." He warned the physicians that if they wanted to continue to maintain union rights and privileges, they had better remain within Vsemediksantrud.[16]

Tomskii's pointed statements failed to sway most of the physicians present, despite the efforts by Kats, the conference chair, to avoid confrontation. Vigdorchik openly declared, "The main defect of the existing professional movement is its dependence on the state and in particular on the ruling party. . . . Physicians have gone forth hand in hand with the proletariat, but this does not mean that they agree on everything with the Communist Party. We have given much to the union: a voice of sober criticism, which it otherwise would not have heard." Other delegates made similar criticisms. Dr. Livin of Ekaterinburg noted that "Comrade Tomskii contradicts himself: on the one hand, there is to be a voluntary professional movement, on the other, such unions have no rights, that is, voluntary unions are not permitted." Dr. Kogan of Kharkov indignantly asserted that physicians had long worked and starved with the workers and peasants, and he suggested provocatively that physicians understood "the people" better than did the Bolsheviks.[17]

Tomskii and Semashko sternly rebuffed these criticisms. Tomskii warned that the "signposts that had been changed" could be changed back and that "a union outside of VTsSPS would be a competing union, and would unavoidably come into conflict [*bor'ba*] with us." He noted that "Dr. Vigdorchik has said that the physicians have performed a service with their criticism, but in the conditions of an unfinished Civil War this is a superfluous thing; right now we are not in the mood for criticism [*nam seichas ne do kritiki*]." Tomskii hastened to add, however, that there was no generalized mistrust of doctors, and he assured them that VTsSPS listened to its members' ideas. The problem was that the doctors had not done so. He suggested as a final compromise "a section with broad rights within Vsemediksantrud." Semashko agreed that the section's rights could be broadened, but, he warned, "This cannot approach anarchy. . . . This organization must be within the general norms of the professional movement."[18]

Kats's attempts to mediate did not succeed, and the conference resolutions reflected a deep disenchantment. They proclaimed that "Soviet medicine . . . is currently undergoing a deep crisis, which will unavoidably lead to the liquidation of a significant portion of existing medical institutions." The government's recent decision to shift the burden of public health expenditures to the localities came under particular fire. The best solution, it was argued, was to create collectives made up of physicians and popularly chosen representatives to reorganize medical planning. Under this scenario, Narkomzdrav would retain only general functions such as setting legislative norms and supervising the legality of medical organizations.[19] The doctors also expressed displeasure with the status of the physicians' section within Vsemediksantrud, and they criticized the union for having advanced "party politics to the detriment of purely professional work."[20] At the same time, it was noted that the physicians needed "to take into account all the difficulties of an autonomous organization in current conditions, the absence of the civil rights necessary for this, and, most important, the mistakenness of isolation from [other] medical personnel." Because of this, they recognized that they had best remain within the official union as a section "with broad autonomy," "unhindered in the freedom of association and organization of its members," and "with the right of extra-union representation."[21]

The Bolshevik leadership responded promptly to these declarations. Infuriated at what he saw as an attack on the very foundations of Soviet public health, Semashko warned the Politburo about "*important* and *dangerous* tendencies . . . widespread not only among physicians, but also *spetsy* from other specialties (agronomists, engineers, technicians, and lawyers)." He asserted that the physicians' efforts to stand outside the *profsoiuz* framework represented a Kadet-, Menshevik-, and SR-led rejection of Soviet medicine. VTsSPS should be extremely careful in granting autonomy to professional sections within official unions, and Gosizdat, the state publishing house, should stop *spets* organizations from issuing periodicals of a "sociopolitical (nonscientific) character." "For otherwise these journals and newspapers, like the currently permitted journal of the PIROGOV SOCIETY, will objectively evolve into organs of anti-Soviet propaganda." He suggested that the GPU deal with the most outspoken physicians.[22]

Lenin and the Politburo agreed. Within weeks, a dozen members of the physicians' section had been arrested, and more would follow. Narkomzdrav warned its local organs that the congress's resolutions had "an overtly anti-Soviet political content" and that they should not be influenced by the anti-Soviet agenda of these doctors.[23] The Vsemediksantrud Central Committee chairman, Aluf, also derided the section's calls for greater freedom, declaring that the physicians "have thrown from themselves the fig leaf of public mindedness [*obshchestvennost'*], baring themselves before the world 'in the clothes they were born in' and proclaiming the rights of 'the individual,' the rights of 'the person'—of the 'free' doctor."[24]

Kats and the rest of the physicians' section Central Bureau petitioned on behalf of their arrested colleagues repeatedly in summer 1922.[25] They protested that physicians were being persecuted for professional activity, rejecting the official GPU explanation that the arrests were for counterrevolutionary actions.[26] The bureau failed to obtain the help of VTsSPS in freeing those arrested, and it lamented its ever-worsening relationship with the Vsemediksantrud Central Committee (CC).[27] After sharp limits were placed on the section's autonomy at a Vsemediksantrud congress in late fall 1922, even Kats admitted that reconciliation did not seem possible. He noted that "new elements" with very different viewpoints had begun to infiltrate the section and doubted that it was still a viable entity.[28] Indeed, Soviet officials were determined to root out its separatist inclinations. At the end of the year, the leadership of the physicians' section was entirely replaced, and the section's former bête noire, A. Aluf, appeared as its chairman. The first item on the agenda was to create tighter ties between the section and the union's Central Committee.[29]

Meanwhile, Aluf and Semashko led an effort to abolish the Pirogov Society, which they viewed as the ultimate source of the physicians' "counterrevolutionary" mood. The newly formed NKVD commission on the reregistration of societies solicited opinions from the GPU, Narkomzdrav, and Vsemediksantrud, all of which opposed the Pirogov's continued existence.[30] The Vsemediksantrud CC argued that the Pirogov Society had consistently resisted cooperation with the Soviet regime. The Pirogovites were accused of adhering to a "liberal-populist spirit" and engaging in "caste politics," in opposition to Narkomzdrav and the union as a whole. The Pirogov was also unnecessary, the CC argued, in view of the existence of the physicians' section. "Such an organization at the current time is not only not useful, but also harmful, both from a political and from a professional-union point of view." Not surprisingly, Unshlikht, writing on behalf of the GPU, agreed with these assessments.[31]

On the basis of the unanimous opposition of the GPU, Narkomzdrav, and Vsemediksantrud, the NKVD commission refused to sanction the Pirogov Society, making it unlawful for it to continue to operate. An appeal of this decision, possibly supported by Tomskii, was rejected a few months later.[32] The Pirogov managed to limp along illegally for several more years. As one of its longtime leaders, D. N. Zhbankov, recalled, "From 1922 it became completely impossible to call Pirogov congresses and conferences without prior authorization; they began to demand official permission, and requesting permission for a society that did not possess a confirmed charter and was in a state of anabiosis was not going to be successful." Deprived of its journal, the Moscow-based board kept in touch with its members via ten "large letters" (newsletters) during 1922–24, and it held a series of eight scientific meetings in Moscow despite the ban on activities.[33] In fall 1924 the security organs turned their attention to shutting it down for good. OGPU operatives informed a September 1924 gathering of the Pirogov board that it was meeting illegally. The GPU Secret Branch (*sekretnyi otdel*, or SO) then notified the NKVD that "with the goal of the final liquidation of the already closed Pirogov Society, the SO OGPU has sealed the office of the society's secretary, Zhbankov." The GPU directed that all properties be given to Narkompros; in fact, when the liquidation was completed in February 1925, the books and property were turned over to Narkomzdrav and the Moscow soviet.[34]

The campaign against autonomous or caste-oriented physicians' organizations did not translate into significant long-term repression of doctors or the elimination of all nonofficial medical organizations. At least some of those arrested were allowed to return from their places of exile within several years and occupy important positions within Soviet medical institutions. Medical conferences continued after a careful review of requests for permission (and with the presence of OGPU observers, who would thenceforth surveil all *spets* gatherings). Doctors who had been part of the physicians' section and the Pirogov continued to work within Narkomzdrav, and Semashko's foray into repression did not appear to damage his relationship with them.[35]

But the elimination of the Pirogov and the bolshevization of the physicians' section had ensured that there would be no organizational criticism of Soviet medicine. In suggesting that decisions on public health should be made through a system of collegial contacts existing *outside* Soviet organs, the physicians' section had taken a stand that, from the regime's point of view, was tantamount to advocating an alternative system. This was why it was seen as a political and counterrevolutionary act. That most physicians viewed the maintenance of professional contacts outside official structures as entirely apolitical shows that they did not understand, much less share, the Bolshevik belief in fusing the interests of all groups with that of the state.

Engineers and Scientists

A tendency toward statism among engineers and other practical scientists and support for state intervention in the economy also could not mask a general distrust of the new regime, and the fate of independent engineering unions mirrored that of other autonomous bodies in the period following the Revolution. The All-Russian Union of Engineers, or VSI (*Vserossiiskii soiuz inzhenerov*), was disbanded in 1918, and engineers were encouraged instead to form sections within official unions. As in the case of the physicians' section, a great deal of mutual mistrust needed to be overcome before a conglomeration of engineering sections under VTsSPS met in 1921.[36] Several independent bodies were still permitted to function, as long as they were not considered unions, although the distinction between scientific-technical and professional organizations was easier to establish in theory than in practice. These groups included the venerable Russian Technical Society, or RTO (*Rossiiskoe tekhnicheskoe obshchestvo*), and the newly formed All-Russian Association of Engineers, or VAI (*Vserossiiskaia assotsiatsiia inzhenerov*). Significant numbers of scientists and engineers also worked within state structures, in particular VSNKh's Scientific-Technical Department, or NTO (*Nauchno-tekhnicheskii otdel*), and its pure science wing, the Scientific Commission.

Unlike Semashko, the leaders of VSNKh, Gosplan (the State Planning Committee), and other state bodies that worked closely with engineers and scientists were willing to overlook occasional political differences. These "practical Bolsheviks," in particular the VSNKh chief Pëtr Bogdanov, the head of Gosplan, Gleb Krzhizhanovskii, and even at times Dzerzhinskii, faithfully carried out Lenin's policy of courting *spetsy.* When their nonparty colleagues came under fire during the 1922 anti-intellectual campaigns, practical Bolsheviks came to the defense of those engineers and scientists on whose expertise they depended. While the GPU and NKVD did not trust *spets* organizations, and on several occasions they tried to eliminate them, the support of the practical Bolsheviks, and most crucially of Dzerzhinskii, allowed some of them to continue to function.

Despite early disputes over the October Revolution, many engineers and scientists took up work in state bodies, and in particular the VSNKh Scientific-Technical Department (NTO). Headed by the young Bolshevik engineer N. P. Gorbunov, and later by the non-Bolshevik chemist V. N. Ipatieff, the NTO would, for a brief time, become a bastion of bourgeois *spets* activity within the Soviet government. Though its aim during the Civil War years was primarily to secure funding for particular scientific-technical bodies, it became a model for involving nonparty *spetsy* in collaboration with the state.[37] In addition, the NTO formed a Scientific Commission to attract major scholars, including natural scientists, to serve within the state structure.[38] The MGU rector Novikov, who had little sympathy for the new regime, chaired this commission, which became a leading forum for scientific exchange and member support. It met many times during the difficult Civil War years, and Novikov remembered it as "one of the islands on which the flame of scientific thought burned during the stormy times of early Bolshevik rule."[39] By 1920 there were more than two hundred members in its Moscow and Petrograd branches. The autonomy the commission retained, as one VSNKh inspector recognized, was the chief reason that nonparty scientists were involved in the NTO.[40] The Scientific Commission was nevertheless soon accused of having overly "theoretical" leanings, and the Scientific-Technical Council (TsNTS) was formed in 1921 with the aim of better directing science to the service of industry. In summer 1922, while Novikov and several other members of the Scientific Commission awaited deportation, VSNKh cut off its funding, and efforts to maintain it as a private association faltered. TsNTS also proved unsatisfactory in the view of the regime; it was dissolved in September 1923 and replaced with a number of scientific councils, which, it was hoped, would better address specific needs.[41]

In addition to the NTO, engineers and scientists served in several other important state organs. The Academy of Science's Commission on the Study of Natural Productive Resources (KEPS) had been founded by V. I. Vernadskii during the Great War to coordinate scientific activities in the service of national industrial production. During the Civil War, it worked with the NTO, and Lenin and other Bolsheviks welcomed this as a sign of the academy's cooperation with the new order.[42] The State Commission for the Electrification of Russia (GOELRO), formed under the auspices of VSNKh by Krzhizhanovskii, also became a center of *spets* activity and was accorded great importance because of Lenin's increasing obsession with electrification. And, finally, out of GOELRO came Gosplan, which aimed to unite engineers, economists, and other *spetsy* in planning the state's economic reconstruction.[43] Although Gosplan and GOELRO soon came under fire for their "alien" composition, they were defended not only by Krzhizhanovskii and other practical Bolsheviks, but also by Lenin. In their first years in power, leading Bolsheviks thus welcomed "alien elements" deep into the heart of the Soviet state, though not without grave misgivings.

The growing disenchantment among scholars, as well as the energetic opposition of the Workers' and Peasants' Inspectorate (Rabkrin) to the predominance of nonproletarian elements, destabilized the uneasy equilibrium.[44] In February 1922 the Academy of Sciences denounced the disastrous material conditions scientists faced, and it proposed the creation of a special temporary committee on science to address the crisis. The Bolsheviks agreed to form such a committee under the auspices of Rykov, already familiar to scientists through his role in the NTO.[45] Working with major figures from the Academy of Sciences, the committee, like Iakovleva's rectors' conferences, afforded scholars direct access in order to prevent further complaint outside official forums. Rykov stressed the committee's potential utility for the Bolsheviks, explaining to Karl Radek that "the main motive of the organization is political: to give an outlet for the 'businesslike dissatisfaction' of the scholars and to create a government-scholar organ as a counterweight to the malicious information abroad about the Soviet regime's war on science." So far it had not been used sufficiently, he believed, and "it is necessary to use something, especially with the foreign press, which has been screeching [*podnimaet vizg*] about the recent expulsions."[46]

While the party-state thus formed official forums to simultaneously control and placate scientists and engineers, it pursued a policy of limited tolerance toward autonomous societies. Engineers' organizations were not, however, exempt from charges of caste separatism, and their gatherings, like the physicians' congress, featured expressions of dissatisfaction with Soviet power. A 1922 conference of the All-Russian Association of Engineers held to the generically statist position of "struggl[ing] for the development of the productive forces of Russia" but refused to endorse any political program. The presence of such independent sentiments, as well as the strikes at Moscow Higher Technical School,[47] led to the deportations of several individuals prominent in VAI, including I. I. Iushtim and N. P. Kozlov. In the end, however, the intervention of practical Bolsheviks such as Krzhizhanovskii and Pëtr Bogdanov would "rescue" most of the engineers arrested and slated for expulsion, including VAI members Pëtr Pal'chinskii and N. E. Parshin.

VAI, despite its semi-autonomous status, was spared the wrath of the NKVD commission during the reregistrations of organizations in fall 1922 and winter 1923. In December 1922 a carefully orchestrated congress of the engineering sections within the official *profsoiuzy* made clear that the regime welcomed the participation of VAI in the reconstruction of the economy as long as it remained a scientific-technical and not a union organization.[48] This tentative support mitigated the disappointment that VAI delegates expressed at not being able to form a union per se. In a speech to the congress, Pal'chinskii, without directly supporting the regime, called on all engineers to work together for the good of the national economy, and he expressed satisfaction with the fact that the highest organs of the Soviet state had sanctioned VAI's existence.[49]

VAI nevertheless refused to endorse the regime explicitly, and its chair, M. G. Evreinov, insisted that it retain its neutrality. "Our task," he averred, "is to remove the association from political declarations and not to make it an arena for political struggle."[50] VAI's official journal echoed that "the first" of its "guiding ideas and catchwords . . . is 'apolitical'—being apolitical in the sense that the Association of Engineers does not adhere to the ideology or tactics of any political party."[51] Although the regime welcomed the willingness of engineers to cooperate, it was uneasy with such ideological agnosticism. Still, when the NKVD commission on registration discussed VAI's fate in fall 1922, even the GPU did not at first object to VSNKh's support for its continued existence.[52] It is clear here that for a *spets* organization, the backing of the corresponding commissariat (which had been notably absent in the case of the Pirogov Society) was a critical factor in its continued existence.

At the same time, the NKVD commission insisted on several changes to the VAI charter designed to limit its rights and circumscribe its activities, which was to become standard practice in its assertion of control over societies. Among these amendments was striking the clause that stated that VAI had the rights of a full juridical individual; altering how members could be excluded, so that Communists could not be prevented from joining; and stipulating that all VAI congresses, conferences, and meetings be open to the public. The NKVD also prohibited several suspect individuals from participating in VAI, including N. K. Mekk and N. E. Parshin, who, although his deportation had been averted, remained persona non grata.[53] The VAI presidium objected that neither had committed a crime, and it eventually secured Mekk's (but not Parshin's) reinstatement.[54] The delay in registration caused by the changes to VAI's charter meant that for a time it could not convene. This, VAI's chair, S. Khrennikov, complained, "manifests itself extremely harmfully on VAI's work in the provinces," but his efforts to repeal the changes to the charter were in vain.[55] When a VAI congress was at last permitted, the NKVD, following now-standard practice, made sure there would be several GPU observers.[56]

The Russian Technical Society (RTO), which brought engineers and technicians together with economists, came under even more scrutiny, particularly as the affiliated journal *Ekonomist* openly criticized the regime.[57] RTO's registration was held up by the NKVD for more than three years, and it came under increasing pressure to merge with VAI. Twice the NKVD commission denied RTO registration on the grounds of "parallelism."[58] At the same time, Glavnauka (the Main Scientific Administration within Narkompros) cut RTO's budget and gradually took away its laboratories, buildings, and other property. Although Pal'chinskii succeeded in delaying its closure, he relayed in frustration to the RTO council that "it has become clear that they want to close all unclosed societies." The NKVD rejected a proposal to switch the RTO from the jurisdiction of Glavnauka to VSNKh, and by 1925 it had had its property expropriated and been forced into a semi-underground existence.[59]

VAI, on the other hand, continued to receive official backing, but its drift toward more openly endorsing the regime angered those who fiercely guarded its autonomy. The installing of a more regime-friendly VAI leadership in 1924 led Pal'chinskii to quit, expressing his disappointment with "VAI's having abandoned the ways of an independent public organization."[60] He refused to rejoin as long as the Soviet state controlled its activities and appointed its leadership. "There can be no talk of my return . . . so long as the association does not feel that it is again a free engineering organization and does not divest itself of those leaders who have been thrust upon it and who have deprived it of its character."[61]

The NKVD chief A. G. Beloborodov, on the other hand, forcefully demanded the abolition of all organizations like VAI and RTO. The NKVD shelved its efforts to combine the two groups and decided that *both* were exclusivist holdouts that needed to be merged into the official union structure.[62] In a 1924 memo to the official trade union center VTsSPS, Beloborodov warned, "In the recent period there has appeared a striving toward the creation of organizations uniting qualified workers of certain branches of mental labor (for instance, the All-Russian Association of Engineers, the Russian Theatrical Society, etc.). These organizations have a tendency to attain a caste character, fully detached from the corresponding professional organizations." He argued that these caste organizations should be replaced by sections within the *profsoiuzy,* "on the example of the existing section of scientific workers in the union of educational workers or the physicians' section within the union Vsemediksantrud."[63] But the mid-1920s represented the height of the *smychka* between *spetsy* and the regime, and Rykov had openly endorsed VAI at its recent congress. In its reply to the NKVD, VTsSPS asserted that societies that focused exclusively on scientific matters, "and not on defending their members' economic interests, are permissible."[64] It was only at the time of the Shakhty and Industrial Party trials in 1928–30 that these accusations of caste and separatist activity found more general resonance, and that VAI and the RTO were therefore shut down.[65]

Cooperatives and Agronomists

Like the engineers' societies, the All-Russian Society of Agronomists, or VOA (*Vserossiiskoe obshchestvo agronomistov*), and the Moscow Agricultural Society, or MOSKh (*Moskovskoe obshchestvo sel'skogo khoziaistva*), seemed to offer little direct challenge to the regime. Many non-Marxist members of these groups had come to terms with the Soviet state, and some served in high positions in the Commissariat of Agriculture (Narkomzem). Though they had been overwhelmingly critical of the forced grain requisitioning under War Communism (as the Bolsheviks' Civil War–era economic policy was known), agronomists saw the New Economic Policy as an opportunity to revive Russian farming. Despite these promising signs, however, agricultural and cooperative congresses in 1921–22 manifested the same tensions between the regime and agronomists as had occurred with other *spetsy.*

Equally contentious was the continued prominence of "alien" experts within the agricultural cooperative movement. Bolshevik leaders recognized that cooperatives would be critical in restoring agricultural production, but they worried over their ability to control them. Despite a concentrated and largely successful effort to replace the leadership of national cooperative bodies during the Civil War,[66] SRs and other non-Bolshevik experts remained prominent within the local cooperatives. The prospect that SRs might continue to influence the peasantry was at least as alarming to Lenin and his colleagues as the specter of Menshevik-led unions. As a result, the campaign to cleanse cooperatives in 1921–22 was particularly fierce. Although, like unions, they were not directly incorporated into the state structure, cooperatives were bolshevized and purged of prominent critics. They were important enough to be discussed at the Twelfth Party Conference both within the general context of attacks on "anti-Soviet groups among the intelligentsia" and as a separate item on the agenda. Like their colleagues in Narkomzem, however, most Bolshevik cooperative leaders did not fully share the Politburo or GPU's fears concerning the corrupting influence of their non-Bolshevik peers. This may have prevented the intended deportation of several (but not all) prominent agronomists-*cooperators,* but it did not stop a major shake-up in these organizations and the sending of a strong message about how agricultural *spetsy* were to serve as useful Soviet citizens.

The Third All-Russian Agronomist Congress of February–March 1922 was a joint production of Narkomzem and several agronomist groups, notably the All-Russian Society of Agronomists and the Moscow Agricultural Society (MOSKh). Unlike the Commissariat of Health, Narkomzem rarely campaigned against its experts and often spoke up on their behalf. The Agronomist Congress initially offered both non-Marxist *spetsy* and officials such as Deputy Commissar of Agriculture V. V. Osinskii reasons to be encouraged. Ossinskii gave the keynote address, outlining NEP policies in agriculture and calling for cooperation between the state and public organizations.[67] The non-Bolshevik delegates by and large hailed his remarks as confirmation that NEP represented an opportunity for real collaboration. As the editors of the nonparty *Vestnik sel'skogo khoziaistva* (Bulletin of Agriculture) noted with surprise and satisfaction, the official report responded quite directly to the questions that agricultural *spetsy* had posed, and it "unexpectedly turned out to be for the most part acceptable to the congress."[68]

Even with these indications of rapprochement, however, frictions resurfaced. At a post-congress dispute in the House of Unions, Boris Brutskus and Nikolai Oganovskii openly quarreled with Osinskii and other Narkomzem leaders.[69] This debate made clear that there were in fact three points of view on agricultural policy—the Bolshevik one, that of conciliatory agronomists, and that of those who still doubted the possibility of cooperation with the regime.[70] This last group, including Brutskus, A. I. Ugrimov, and A. A. Rybnikov, pressed for land ownership as a necessary component of NEP reforms. Osinskii and other Narkomzem Bolsheviks, although reaffirming the right of peasants to retain the land they worked indefinitely, flatly rejected denationalization. The differences on this key issue reflected a broader dispute over government regulation of agriculture; Brutskus and others openly blamed Civil War requisitioning for the current famine, an inflammatory accusation that Osinskii hotly denied.[71]

There were also important differences concerning the degree to which nongovernmental organizations should be involved in mobilizing the population. At an all-Russian conference of local agricultural societies held in January 1922, delegates agreed that the state should have a more limited role in the reinvigoration of agriculture, and that public societies were more knowledgeable of local conditions.[72] While recognizing the need for close collaboration between the government and society, they maintained a distinction between the two that most Bolsheviks refused to recognize. In his speech to the March agronomist congress, Osinskii carefully refuted the idea that private organizations, in particular cooperatives, could better serve the needs of the general population. "A cooperative . . . stands in defense of private interests, the interests of particular groups of the population," he asserted. "The state union, on the other hand, answers to everyone's interests and renders assistance to all sectors of the economy."[73]

Bolshevik publicists were soon denouncing the March agronomist congress for having "turned into an indictment of the Soviet regime's land policies and into a self-styled parliament, which not so much discussed as condemned the Soviet state's economic policies and remarked on desirable changes to these policies."[74] Certain experts, in particular Brutskus, openly blamed the famine on War Communism, and even conciliatory agronomists such as Nikolai Kondrat'ev suggested that state intervention had gone too far. That high state officials—Kondrat'ev was a member of Zemplan, the planning agency within Narkomzem—were implicitly criticizing policy caused some high officials to complain that Narkomzem was becoming a reservoir of "alien" specialists.[75] Kondrat'ev, A. V. Chaianov, and other neopopulist agronomists nevertheless remained supportive of a statist approach to agriculture and downplayed their differences with Osinskii and Narkomzem. Even as Bolshevik criticism of Brutskus intensified, these conciliatory figures remained in high-level positions within the commissariat. At the same time, Bolshevik leaders outside

Narkomzem, in the midst of planning the SR show trial, became uneasy with having former SRs in positions of authority. When Lenin angrily rebuked Osinskii for having allowed articles critical of Soviet policy in the official weekly *Sel'skokhoziaistvennaia zhizn'*, a decade-long debate began over the Commissariat of Agriculture's employing so many "aliens" in high-level posts.[76] The opening round in this struggle was a series of arrests of Zemplan specialists in fall 1922 in connection with the deportations of intellectuals.

Even more contentious than the dissent evinced at the March agronomist congress was the position of these same populist experts within the cooperative movement. Although during the Civil War the Bolsheviks had managed to replace the leadership of previously autonomous cooperatives in much the same way that they had in unions, they remained afraid of the holdover influence of prominent SRs and Kadets. This was particularly true after the declaration of NEP, when the regime purposefully released cooperatives from earlier constraints in the hopes that they would become more productive. While the leading organs of consumer cooperatives remained for the most part obedient organs (although this was more true on the central than local level), the newly formed central organs of agricultural and industrial cooperatives were dominated by old cooperators, many of whom had been Kadets or SRs.[77] Given the importance that leading Bolsheviks, and especially Lenin, foresaw for cooperatives, such a situation was quite galling. As leading Bolsheviks made clear, the reestablishment of cooperatives partially separate from the state economic apparatus was meant to increase peasant and producer initiative (*samodeiatel'nost'*) but by no means to promote autonomy (*samostoiatel'nost'*).

The August 1921 All-Russian Congress of Agricultural Cooperatives (Sel'skosoiuz) was a particularly controversial event. According to available data, there were thirty-two former SRs, twenty-five former Kadets, and only two Communists among the eighty-four delegates.[78] Though they agreed that resolving national economic problems should be a central goal, the delegates openly insisted on an organization free of state control and rejected placing government representatives in its leadership. The congress also openly supported the suspect social famine relief committee, which would be shut down in disgrace several days later.[79] The central conflict at this gathering focused on Narkomzem's effort to appoint two representatives to the board. Also problematic was the suggestion that Narkomzem might reject the candidacies of other potential board members for political reasons. Whereas some delegates refused to negotiate, others, including Chaianov, recognized that compromise would be necessary for Sel'skosoiuz to be allowed to function.

Eventually, on Chaianov's suggestion, it was agreed that two Narkomzem representatives would be allowed in the Sel'skosoiuz council, but not on the smaller board. A similar founding congress of craft-industrial cooperatives led to even greater conflict. While Narkomzem had managed to salvage a compromise out of the Sel'skosoiuz congress, the regime was so displeased with the results of the industrial cooperative congress that VTsIK shortly thereafter declared the congress unlawful, its board dismissed, and its resolutions null and void.[80]

On Lenin's orders, Cheka deputy chairman Iosif Unshlikht developed a plan to cleanse cooperatives in mid-1921. He warned that they were "becoming organs of political association," which the SRs hoped to use for insidious purposes. The Communist Party, Unshlikht argued, must "struggle for ideological predominance . . . and organizational leadership of cooperative organs," and the Cheka must undertake the "systematic and unceasing removal of all SRs and Mensheviks."[81] During 1921–22, while the party began the process of more effectively exerting control over cooperatives, the Cheka (and, later, the GPU) arrested dozens of regional leaders of Sel'skosoiuz, to the consternation of Narkomzem.[82] In his critical June 1922 memo to the Politburo on anti-Soviet groups among the intelligentsia, Iakov Agranov claimed that SRs had used the Sel'skosoiuz and craft cooperative congresses as pretexts for partisan gatherings. Cooperatives, he warned, remained "a most advantageous place for the association of anti-Soviet elements," at which, ominously, they came into contact with "a broad strata of the Republic's laboring elements."[83]

At the August 1922 Twelfth Party Conference, cooperatives were given special scrutiny in addition to being included in Zinoviev's declamation on the anti-Soviet intelligentsia. The conference acknowledged the utility of cooperatives in economic reconstruction but emphasized the need to remove "hostile elements" and to increase party control quickly and systematically. V. V. Kuibyshev remarked in his keynote address that cooperatives continued to be a dangerous seedbed of SR and Kadet influence, "in precisely that place where they can interact with the petty bourgeois class." Iaroslavskii, Kuibyshev, and other leading Bolsheviks derided Osinskii's lonely objection that the SR threat in agricultural cooperatives was being greatly exaggerated. For these "political groupings," Kuibyshev pronounced, cooperatives served as a basis for association "where they might prepare their attack against us."[84]

A number of leading *kooperatory* were arrested during the deportation campaigns, including several prominent members of Sel'skosoiuz and of the agronomist societies, such as Kondrat'ev, Ugrimov, N. I. Liubimov, I. P.

Matveev, and A. I. Sigirskii; and of the industrial cooperative board, including Rybnikov and A. A. Bulatov.[85] Brutskus was arrested in Petrograd, as were at least seven members of the Northern Union of Craft Cooperatives (Severokustar'), whose journal *Artel'noe delo* (Artel Affairs) had published a series of articles sharply critical of the regime. Both the cooperative organs and Narkomzem made great efforts to defend their prized *spetsy*, and in some cases, as we shall see, they were successful. Kondrat'ev was back at work in Zemplan by early October, and others had their sentences rescinded shortly thereafter.[86]

Both the cooperative organs and agricultural societies survived these events, but the former were integrated ever more closely with the state, and the latter faced increasing surveillance and harassment from the security apparatus. It was clear, particularly after the early 1923 publication of Lenin's article "On Cooperatives," that Bolshevik leaders considered them a critical component of the mixed NEP system. But the fact that they were to be cultivated only heightened the importance of establishing control over their central leadership. Some of the original leaders of Sel'skosouiz remained in prominent positions, but there were no more rebellions like those at its founding congress. GPU reports point toward a gradual eradication of the much-feared SR influence in provincial cooperative bodies.[87] Because of the Bolsheviks' mixed feelings toward *spets* organizations, there was some indecision about how to deal with the major agronomist societies. When the NKVD commission on registration began its consideration of the Moscow Agricultural Society (MOSKh) in fall 1922, Narkomzem and other government agencies that depended on agricultural experts proposed only to limit its scope of activity. The NKVD and GPU initially ratified these suggestions but did edit its charter and ban several suspect individuals from participating. The MOSKh presidium especially objected to a clause mandating its liquidation in the case of the arrest of a majority of board members, which seemed to them superfluous. Within two years (and over the objections of the Moscow soviet), the NKVD ordered the MOSKh closed for having refused to alter its charter.[88] Despite this, however, this venerable institution—minus certain individuals—managed to survive until the end of the decade.

The All-Russian Society of Agronomists, as a relative newcomer, faced even tougher hurdles. Narkomzem, while striving for more direct control, defended the VOA, but the NKVD commission denied its registration, "in view of the fact that chapters I, III, and IV of your charter sharply contradict the RSFSR constitution." The GPU concurred, noting that two of the VOA board members, Sigirskii and N. V. Maloletenkov, had been deported for anti-Soviet activity and that there was "compromising material" concerning a number of others. If the group was to continue to exist, at least six or seven of its leaders needed to be removed.[89] The VOA survived for several years, but by proscribing certain members and prescribing changes to its charter, the NKVD made certain that it could no longer exist as an "exclusivist organization, depriving interested institutions of infusing into the given society a desirable element that might oversee the society's activities."[90] Even after the deportations, five of the six remaining board members were rejected, and when they nevertheless continued to meet, the NKVD refused to allow a VOA congress, until in March 1924 the entire board resigned in frustration. One month later, the NKVD ordered the Moscow authorities to shut down the society.[91]

Thus agronomist *spets* organizations, even more than their engineering counterparts, faced constant harassment from the authorities. Although bourgeois agronomists remained in positions of prominence through the 1920s, their ability to work within autonomous structures external to the state was sharply limited. Cooperatives were increasingly assimilated, and though they continued to provide refuge for those who sought to promote individual agricultural initiative—as long as NEP remained in force—there was no longer a place within them for individuals critical of the regime. The GPU and NKVD became ever more vigilant in their hunt for hostile elements in these and other *spets* bodies. Such was the nature of the deal that *spetsy* were offered during the 1920s: the regime welcomed all who were willing to serve the interests of the socialist state, as long as they remained loyal. This meant not only refraining from openly political comments, but also avoiding any ambitions within the public sphere, any indication that *obshchestvennost'* entailed separateness. Organizations in Soviet Russia—even and especially *spets* organizations—were to bring together professionals and scholars to serve the state, and not to compete with it.

4

Cultural, Literary, Philosophical, and Spiritual Societies

When one thinks back, in the peace and comfort even of the agitated Europe of today, to Soviet Russia in the first years, it seems hard to believe that half-starving men could assemble in great numbers several times a week in badly lighted and unheated rooms, to debate philosophical problems for three or four hours and listen to poems.

—*Fëdor Stepun, philosopher and sociologist, Dresden, 1934*

Unlike agricultural cooperatives and *spets* professional societies, autonomous cultural, literary, philosophical, and spiritual groupings did not have any definite utility. Despite the difficult conditions in Moscow and Petrograd at the end of the Civil War, writers, litterateurs, translators, and artists had gathered in an increasingly vibrant set of societies and *kruzhki,* or literary circles.[1] During 1920–22 these institutions, particularly the House of Litterateurs and the House of Arts, provided a central focus for much of literary and cultural Petrograd, while the All-Russian Union of Writers and the Free Academy for Spiritual Culture fulfilled a similar function in Moscow. Maxim Gorky was the premier patron of writers and artists in Petrograd; the formalist writer Viktor Shklovskii dubbed him the "Noah of the Russian intelligentsia," for his role in establishing institutions that provided both material and cerebral sustenance.[2]

The revival of philosophical, spiritual, and sectarian religious groups was even more suspect, even while they proved useful as wedges in the regime's larger war against the Orthodox Church. Heterodox thinkers from Christian idealists to Tolstoyans to theosophists to Protestant evangelicals all found themselves under the closer scrutiny of a Communist Party leadership increasingly jealous of its ideological hegemony. The proliferation of such groups and their association with a renaissance of publishing enterprises fostered Bolshevik fears that they would serve as seedbeds of enemy ideology. At the end of the Civil War, the Bolshevik leadership eliminated a number of these autonomous literary, artistic, philosophical, and spiritual groups in conjunction with the deportations of intellectuals and the tightening of censorship. Despite the uncertainty over what constituted party policy in cultural affairs, the leadership began to pay closer attention to and provide support for loyal organizations so that they might eventually replace those outside its control.

Cultural and Literary Societies

Like professors and *spetsy,* writers and artists formed unionlike organizations and mutual aid societies after 1917. In December 1918, under the guidance of A. E. Kaufman, B. O. Khariton, N. M. Volkovyskii, and L. M. Kliachko, a group of Petrograd journalists and writers banded together to establish the House of Litterateurs (*Dom literatorov*).[3] N. A. Kotliarevskii was appointed chairperson, and the indefatigable Khariton and Volkovyskii were its daily administrators. The House of Litterateurs' early activities centered on material assistance such as food, shelter, and provisions, since "need among litterateurs was at that time unbelievable. Many were dying from famine."[4] A cafeteria provided high-quality meals, and there were plans for a dormitory.[5] Only after conditions had improved somewhat did the House begin to set up literary and cultural events; the first was an evening in January 1920 in memory of Herzen and the victims of Bloody Sunday, the start of the 1905 Revolution.

The founders of the House of Litterateurs were determined to avoid becoming dependent on state support. At first, it was able to get along with minimal government involvement, thanks in particular to the cafeteria revenue, but this proved insufficient. When the Bolsheviks ordered the House to provide its meals free of charge, the literary critic A. V. Amfiteatrov noted bitterly that "it appeared that the House would avoid destruction only through capitulation, bowing before the Soviet state and being kept on its budget like the philanthropic-enslaving [*kabal'nyi*] institutions of M. Gorky." Ties to Narkompros of necessity became more intimate. Against the wishes of some members, and with the assistance of the prominent Bolshevik V. D. Bonch-Bruevich, the House of Litterateurs began to receive more substantial funding from Narkompros in summer 1921. As the state became ever more displeased with the House's activities and as cost cutting in connection with NEP became a priority, however, the support dried up.[6]

Gorky was a member of the House of Litterateurs but was not particularly close to its leadership, which he considered too Kadet, and which in turn was suspicious of his ties to the Bolshevik leadership. There were several similar organizations, such as the Union of Belletrists (*Soiuz deiatelei khudozhestvennoi literatury*), formed on the initiative of Fëdor Sologub in 1918. Together with Gorky's publishing effort, "World Literature," the Union of Belletrists fostered a series of literary studios during the difficult Civil War years. But despite the presence of such luminaries as Aleksandr Blok, Gumilev, and Zamiatin, it had an extremely tumultuous existence and lasted less than two years.[7] In 1919, in an effort to maintain and expand the activities of the literary studios, Gorky, along with Kornei Chukovskii and other leading literary figures, established the House of Arts (*Dom iskusstv*).[8] Although it was founded on the example of the Palace of Arts (*Dvorets iskusstv*) in Moscow, the House of Arts was an autonomous (and more significant) organization. It aimed to unite writers, artists, and musicians, and it provided, like the House of Litterateurs, a cafeteria where the meals were known for their high quality, as well as a dormitory.[9]

Many writers were affiliated with both Houses; the Litterateurs attempted to be more universal, whereas the Arts limited itself to the "best" artists through a careful selection process. Although the House of Arts was thus more exclusive, the attention of Bolshevik critics focused more on the House of Litterateurs for its greater concentration of *byvshie liudi* ("people of the past").[10] These two Houses were not the only literary and cultural groups resurfacing at this time. The House of Scholars, which Gorky had helped to organize in conjunction with KUBU, also provided assistance to some writers, and its lectures and evenings—including among their topics philosophy, literature, and art—featured many of the same speakers as did the Houses of Litterateurs and Arts.[11]

The difficult material conditions proved enough to bring together writers and artists of widely different inclinations. Viktor Shklovskii recalled, "Futurists and academicians, Kadets and Mensheviks, the talented and the untalented sat together in the studios at World Literature and stood in line at the House of Writers."[12] But the Houses evolved into much more than mutual aid societies: they provided a meeting ground, a place to find meals, discussion groups, public lectures, library materials, and, for some, a place to live. A number of prominent writers, including Osip Mandelstam, Shklovskii, and Khodasevich, lived at the House of Arts, and a dormitory opened at the House of Litterateurs as well.[13] Those who later wrote of their experiences in the Houses often presented them through a nostalgic prism as the swan song of literary Petrograd.[14] Such reminiscences tended to focus on the luminaries who spent their final years in the Houses, including Gumilev, who was shot as part of the Tagantsev affair; Korolenko, whom opponents of the regime and Bolsheviks alike canonized after his death in late 1921; and in particular Blok, who passed away in August 1921 despite Gorky's and Lunacharskii's desperate appeals to the Politburo on his behalf.[15] Blok's death had an enormous influence, and the more pessimistically inclined saw in it the symbolic demise of the old literary world.[16] Katerina Clark notes that for many, Blok's death, together with Gumilev's execution, the mass emigration of writers after Gorky's departure at the end of 1921, and the deportations a year later, marked the period "as 'the end of Petersburg,' or the end of the cultural flowering, or the end of any kind of normalcy for intellectuals."[17]

The presence of famous literati and animated discussions made the Houses centers of constant activity. The House of Litterateurs soon turned its focus from material assistance to being a literary club and a vehicle for public education. Under the direction of the writer and journalist Viktor Iretskii, it amassed an impressive library of almost seventy thousand volumes, including hard-to-find journals from the prerevolutionary period. It was also one of the few places receiving, with the help of official friends, new publications from abroad. The House leaders instituted "Living Almanacs," evenings dedicated to the reading of as yet unpublished poetry, stories, and critical articles—Belyi, Blok, Zamiatin, Mikhail Kuzmin, and Nikolai Remizov were among the eminent speakers. A series of weekly "literary Wednesdays" featured readings from up-and-coming younger writers such as Mikhail Zoshchenko and Konstantin Fedin. In addition, there were scholarly lectures on such luminaries as Tolstoy, Gorky, Mayakovskii, Akhmatova; open discussions on current events; plays and concerts, including several "evenings of poetry in music"; and two literary competitions, one for belletristic prose and one for criticism.[18] These events, many of which were open to the public, were organized with the knowledge and often even the assistance of the Petrograd city administration.[19] The House of Litterateurs, together with other cultural institutions in Petrograd and Moscow, also commemorated a series of jubilees: in particular for Dostoevsky, for the historian Vasilii Kliuchevskii, for the poet Nikolai Nekrasov, even for Dante (the six hundredth anniversary of his death), and for Pushkin, for whom no special date was needed to celebrate.[20]

The themes of these public lectures and meetings, and their dissemination in journals and booklets, brought the wrath of the regime onto the House of Litterateurs and its leaders. The talks included not only innocuous literary topics, in particular those honoring Blok and Korolenko after their respective deaths in August and December 1921, but also a number of more controversial subjects. Dostoevsky, for example, who was openly celebrated in these literary jubilees, aroused very mixed emotions among Bolshevik intellectuals, some of whom saw him as an irredeemable reactionary and hopeless critic of revolution. The House became ever more open in its advocacy of freedom and independence of the press, and in particular the right to publish publicistic articles.[21] And some of the talks came dangerously close to open political discussion. The historian E. V. Tarle lectured on international politics and current German affairs to a rapt audience; A. N. Bukolevskii dissected the "contemporary state budget"; and V. V. Vodobozov spoke on the financial state of postwar Europe and America.[22] These well-attended events in the House of Litterateurs reflected a general mood of rebellion. As Katerina Clark notes, 1921 "saw an unusual concentration of literary works and intelligentsia rallies where the regime of the 'bosses,' of the 'tutor' (*guverner*), was denounced. Akhmatova herself contributed a poem fittingly titled 'All is Plundered, Betrayed, Sold Out.'"[23]

Perhaps most contentious were a series of disputes critiquing *Smena vekh* (A Change of Signposts). *Smena vekh,* a collection of articles by leading Russian émigrés, called on intellectuals to make their peace with the Bolshevik regime, as the sole legitimate defender of the Russian state, and to work within it so as to contribute to its moderation.[24] The debates at the House of Litterateurs, at which Aleksandr Izgoev, one of the original *vekhovtsy* (*Vekhi* authors), played a pivotal role, were by and large quite critical of *smenovekhovstvo,* much to the consternation of leading Bolsheviks. While deeply suspicious of *smenovekhovstvo,* Lenin and his colleagues believed that it might prove useful in their efforts to win over vacillating *spetsy* and provided its proponents with provisional support.[25] The Izgoev-led critique of *smenovekhovstvo* was seen as potentially quite damaging to these efforts.

The House of Arts was also a center for lectures, readings, and concerts, as well as a place for writers to work, a lively center for exchange, and the home of a number of Petrograd's leading writers and artists. The literary studio provided courses (often sparsely attended because of the lack of light and heat) on writing, theory, and technique by the likes of Zamiatin, Shklovskii, Chukovskii, and Gumilev. Despite the hunger and privation, those who lived there managed to create an intense and at times boisterous atmosphere. The House of Arts became the center of activity for the Serapion Brothers, a group of young writers that included Zoshchenko, Lev Lunts, and Fedin.[26] Despite the differences between the two Houses, many of the well-known literary figures, including Zamiatin, Gumilev, and Akhmatova, were very much involved in both. Though the House of Arts may not have had disputes as controversial as the *Smena vekh* debates, the cross-fertilization no doubt contributed to the trouble that it too soon encountered. Even Lunacharskii expressed displeasure with the House of Arts, which, he noted with irritation, did not publish "proletarian" writers in its journal, and he made clear his attitude toward all these representatives of the past: "Prerevolutionary literature, truly speaking, begins to resemble antediluvian literature: Some sort of cataclysm occurred, and this old flora and fauna remaining from the good old times and ending up clustered on some kind of island, looks with hostility at its surroundings, greatly suffering from the alien [*nerodnoi*] atmosphere; it strives, of course, to assert its right to existence, and, naturally, harbors a firm belief that in general and as a whole, the old time, when it flowered [*raspukalas'*] so magnificently, was undoubtedly better than the new, in which it withers." At the same time, he did see that "fresh vegetation and wondrous red flowers" were growing in these very spots, and he cautioned against those Communists who tended to see counterrevolution in all works of literature.[27]

As always, what most concerned leading Bolsheviks was the dissemination of so-called anti-Soviet ideas. Most irritating about the critique of the Changing Signposts movement, the publicistic lectures, and provocative literary criticism, was that these opinions were recorded in the publications associated with the Houses: the *Letopis' doma literatorov, Literaturnye zapiski, Dom iskusstv,* and also booklets on the *Smena vekh* debates, on Pushkin and Dostoevsky, and on other topics.[28] The limited public literary and artistic sphere that these organizations represented was problematic enough, but the possibility that a more comprehensive community of intellectuals could be established around these heterodox ideas was that much more threatening. It was not an accident, as we shall see in the next chapter, that as the Bolshevik leadership moved to eliminate these organizations, it shut down their journals as well.

Similar groups had also developed in Moscow. In spring 1919 a group of writers and scholars formed the Moscow Professional Union of Writers, which soon became the All-Russian Union of Writers (*Vserossiiskii soiuz pisatelei*).[29] This organization, like the House of Litterateurs, included not only belletristic writers but also philosophers, critics, and publicists. The leadership of its Petrograd branch, formed in July 1920 and essentially independent of the Moscow organization, overlapped to a great extent with the active members of the two Houses; by mid-1921 it had approximately two hundred members.[30] Though the VTsSPS made the union drop the word "professional" from its name and refused to register it as a *profsoiuz*,[31] the situation in regard to literature was murkier than it was in regard to other unions, so the Union of Writers was able to survive for a time while its counterparts ran into difficulties.

The Moscow branch of the Union of Writers established itself as the center of literary activity in the capital, particularly after it was given full rights to the Herzen House on Tverskoi Boulevard. It expanded its library, organized a cafeteria, and opened several auditoriums for meetings, evenings, and lectures, and it also planned for a small dormitory (this, complained one sympathizer, was delayed by the presence of inhabitants in the Herzen House who had nothing to do with literature).[32] On Mondays, at the so-called executive meetings, members read their latest works and reports; on other days there were public literary evenings and debates. The union also provided a meeting ground for some of the smaller literary *kruzhki* that had surfaced or resurfaced at the end of the Civil War.[33] Like the Petrograd Houses, it looked after the material interests of its members—as one sympathetic report noted, "Despite the removal from its name of the word 'professional,' the union in fact carries out the familiar professional functions, deciding tariff questions, providing aid to needy members, defending their material interests, and also maintaining representatives in the Commissariat of Enlightenment and in the State Publisher [Gosizdat]."[34]

Associated with the union was the Writers' Book Shop (*knizhnaia lavka pisatelei*), a cooperative bookstore organized several years earlier under the leadership of Mikhail Osorgin, Pavel Muratov, and Vladislav Khodasevich, designed originally to help support its proprietors. It purchased ("for the maximum price") the private libraries of numerous writers and scholars desperate for income. To supplement this it also sold "handwritten publications," a sort of *samizdat* in one or several copies of collections of articles and stories that could not be published elsewhere. The shop, which its founders proudly considered the "first purely commercial intellectual enterprise" in Soviet Russia, soon became a popular gathering place. Osorgin recalled: "For literary Moscow, the 'Shop' was not only a bookstore where it was possible to buy books at a discount and to sell them at advantageous prices, but also for a time the only living social center of literary association. The union for quite some time did not have a building, the 'Writers' Club' . . . met very rarely, but everyone ran daily to the 'Shop' on business, and to talk, and to look at books, and to arrange meetings. . . . We conducted philosophical and literary debates at the shop in which the client-habitués also took part. One felt crowded, smoky from the small stove [*pechurka*], warm from the felt boots, with fingers cold from the books, happy from the presence of lively people, and pleasant from the awareness that our business was curious, and useful, and the only one that was nongovernmental, that was alive, its own."[35]

As Boris Zaitsev recalled, literary lights such as Blok stopped in to buy books. The shop avoided the municipalization and later nationalization of bookshops during the Civil War. When other stores opened in Moscow and Petrograd, the Writers' Shop established close contact with them, and it began to sell not only to individuals, but to libraries, universities, workers' clubs, and museums. In 1921 the Writers' Shop became fully integrated with the Union of Writers, and Zaitsev, the union's chair, and Nikolai Berdiaev, a vice-chair, joined Osorgin (who was also a vice-chair) on the Writers' Shop's board. As a part of the union, the shop again avoided nationalization; it helped to support its new parent organization and to provide for both its needier members and its proprietors. In the end, however, increasing taxation and competition put it in dire financial straits, particularly after it was forced out of its premises on Leont'evskii Alley by the Comintern, which needed the building for a hotel. The shop would not survive the departure of its proprietors in 1922.[36]

The Union of Writers and the House of Litterateurs found themselves fulfilling another familiar function: petitioning the authorities when one of their members was arrested. Zaitsev and Berdiaev both had multiple meetings with Bolshevik officials, on a number of cases appealing directly to Kamenev, the Moscow soviet chief and Politburo member with whom a number of Writers' Union leaders also interacted on the famine relief committee. Both confirmed his reputation as a solicitous Bolshevik who more often than not came to the aid of imprisoned intellectuals.[37] In Petrograd, the situation was quite different. Zinoviev, unlike his once and future comrade Kamenev, was known for precisely the opposite stance and was rarely approached. When Aleksandr Izgoev was arrested for the third time, the House of Litterateurs, the Union of Writers, and several other organizations petitioned in February 1921 for his release to almost everyone but Zinoviev: to Kalinin, Lenin, Kamenev, Dzerzhinskii, D. I. Kurskii (the commissar of Justice), Lunacharskii, Pokrovskii, and Gorky. Using a not uncommon tack, they petitioned on humanitarian grounds; Izgoev's eighteen-year-old daughter had died while he was in prison, and his wife and elder daughter were both seriously ill: "He is extremely distressed by all he has lived through, especially having been separated from his family for a year and a half and by the news of its demise and ruin. He is now close to unalterable despair. In the name of humanity we ask you to bring an end to his suffering during such a tragic part of his life and free him entirely from further containment in the camp. The organizations listed below vouch for Lande-Izgoev, his loyal behavior in relation to the government, and, in particular, that he will not change where he is living without the permission of the regime."[38] The powers that be did indeed take pity on Izgoev, who was released at this time, although he would find himself among those deported the following year.[39]

Though unlike the House of Litterateurs, whose disputes often verged on open criticism of the new regime, the Union of Writers steered clearer of politics, this did not mean that they were quietist. The union had no Communist members, and, as Zaitsev suggested, it was only "by a paradox of the Revolution"—the fact that leading Bolsheviks still respected the prestige of literature—that they remained untouched for a time, although he adds that perhaps the real reason they were left alone was that the regime was too much concerned with the Civil War and uprisings to pay close attention to what was said at their readings and lectures.[40] At the start of NEP, the union did occasionally stray into dangerous territory, now that the Bolsheviks were paying more attention to them, as when Iul'ii Aikhenval'd gave a "rapturous" lecture on Akhmatova and Gumilev soon after the execution of the latter.[41] Berdiaev disdained participation in the short-lived famine relief committee, but Osorgin, Zaitsev, and many other union members became actively involved in it and were soon arrested for their troubles.

The Union of Writers also viewed with trepidation the activities and slogans of the All-Russian Proletarian Writers' Association (VAPP) and chafed under what they felt to be the reimposition of censorship soon after private publishing was permitted as of summer 1921. In a letter to Lunacharskii, leading writers and scholars protested in the name of the Writers' Union against both the control exercised by the Gosizdat Politotdel (Political Department) and by its leaders, N. L. Meshcheriakov and P. I. Lebedev-Polianskii, and the catastrophic state of literature in Soviet Russia. Although—to the great consternation of the censors—Lunacharskii sided more with the writers than with his underlings, the Politotdel would in the end receive the support of the Politburo (which elevated this body and rechristened it Glavlit). It is not accidental that several of those who signed the protest letter were later expelled.[42]

At the beginning of 1922, Lenin and the leaders of Agitprop began to formulate the principles that would increase the tempo of ideological warfare.[43] They also used the usual tactic of replacing suspect organizations with ones created by or beholden to the party, part of the larger project of reshaping the

Soviet public sphere. The major concern for Bolshevik leaders who turned their attention to belletrists was that younger writers who sympathized with the Revolution would be drawn to the organizations of the *byvshie liudi.* Most notably, the progressive-thinking Serapion Brothers gathered and lived at the House of Arts and were promoted by the House of Litterateurs, where their mentor, Zamiatin, was an active elder statesman.

A. K. Voronskii, the editor of the Bolshevik thick journal *Krasnaia nov'* (Red Virgin Soil), fervently promoted the creation of an arena where the "young" writers could be brought over to the Bolshevik cause and separated from the "old" writers who, as a whole, were irredeemable, not to mention a dangerous influence on their younger colleagues. Voronskii first promulgated the idea of establishing a *kruzhok* to Glavpolitprosvet (the Main Political Enlightenment Committee) in February 1922, and he warned Agitprop that recent literary publications had conveyed "various counterrevolutionary and petty bourgeois ideas and have not let pass a single complimentary word for Soviet Russia and the Bolsheviks." In such hostile circumstances, "the rallying of writers standing close to us is necessary, because only by such a path can we conduct the ideological struggle on the book market."[44] Agitprop and its deputy chair, Iakov Iakovlev, warmly embraced the idea, and the Orgburo passed a resolution, "On the Struggle with Petty Bourgeois Ideology in the Literary-Publishing Sphere," which also led to the creation of Glavlit and the establishment of several Bolshevik ideological journals.[45]

The Bolsheviks were uneasy with the existing groups claiming to represent the proletarian line in literature but operating independently; it is not accidental that the evisceration of Proletkult (the Proletarian Culture organization) occurred precisely at this time.[46] Though the party did not create a unified, directly controlled union of writers until the end of the decade, it was deemed imperative to attract as many different writers as possible to a Bolshevik-run organization. In the Politburo the proposal received the energetic support of Trotsky, who proposed an even broader program to reach out to potentially sympathetic writers, poets, and artists in order that they "don't end up tomorrow in a camp hostile or half-hostile to us."[47] To prepare a forum for potential non-Communist allies, for whom Trotsky would coin the term *fellow traveler* (*poputchik*) precisely at this moment, the Politburo directed Agitprop to create a society similar in form to the Houses and Union of Writers but guided by Voronskii and Iakovlev. This tactic mimicked the simultaneous abolition of independent professors' organizations and their replacement with the Glavprofobr-directed "rectors' conferences," and it also resembled the half-secret official support of the *smenovekhovtsy.* All these efforts were designed to create alternative forums for intellectuals within an officially sanctioned structure that would, Bolshevik leaders hoped, make obsolete what they most feared—the specter of "corporate" separatism.

A Politburo-organized commission drew up a list of both prominent and "up-and-coming" writers whom they hoped to bring within the auspices of this group. The list was extensive; at its core was to be the coterie of writers that Voronskii had already begun to group around *Krasnaia nov'*—in particular the Serapion Brothers—but it also included not a few writers whose relationship to the regime was in greater doubt.[48] Among the latter were Mandelstam; Belyi, who would soon return from his brief stint abroad; Aleksei Tolstoi, who was drawn back to the motherland by Smenovekhovite sentiments; and Boris Pil'niak, who, although his stories were already being read, debated, and criticized in the Politburo, was still warily deemed a potential ally.[49] Several even more questionable names—including Khodasevich and Marina Tsvetaeva, both of whom would soon emigrate—were appended to the list with a question mark.

The society was to be supported by a newly formed publishing house, subsidized by the Central Committee and headed by a diverse group potentially including Voronskii, Vsevolod Ivanov, Pil'niak, and Valerii Briusov.[50] The Politburo wisely limited the overt participation of Lebedev-Polianskii, whose association with censorship had already made him many enemies, and favored instead those such as Voronskii, who despite his frequent criticism of certain famous figures managed to maintain collegial relationships. This circle, formed as directed around the publisher Krug, did indeed become a forum for fellow travelers and Communists to join together in open support of the new order, as evidenced by the group's 1927 declaration.[51] Although it succeeded in drawing younger writers away from the organizations of "old men," however, it did not become as central in this process as the more informal association around *Krasnaia nov'*. It would also come to be overshadowed by the Union of Writers, which, after the removal of its most pernicious "old" leaders in 1922, would also serve as a focal point of fellow-traveler and official interchange into the mid-1920s.[52] In 1922 the party did not yet have either the desire or the means to establish a single official organization that would provide uncontested direction for writers in Soviet Russia.

Meanwhile, the independent groups found themselves under increasing fire. Of the House of Litterateurs' original directing committee, Blok and A. E. Kaufman had died, Gumilev had been executed, and Amfiteatrov, Remizov, and others had emigrated.[53] The *Letopis' doma literatorov* and *Vestnik literatury* were both prohibited in March 1922, and their replacements, *Literaturnye zapiski* and *Utrenniki,* an almanac edited by Dalmat Lutokhin, were quickly banned as well.[54] Petrograd Bolsheviks began to grumble that these "old men," many of whom weren't real literary figures, were receiving support, and they wondered, "Will this House of the Dead give anything practical and interesting to proletarian Russia? . . . One regrets money [spent on] the House of the Dead."[55] Government funding for the Houses ceased, and they found themselves under increasing financial difficulties. In spring 1922 the House of Litterateurs was forced to curtail its activities drastically and close the cafeteria that had previously offered free meals for destitute writers.[56] Auctions were held to raise money, and membership fees were introduced.[57]

Soon after the institution of these desperate measures, several prominent members of the House of Litterateurs were expelled from Russia, including Volkovyskii and Khariton, who were board members and the editors of its journals, as well as Iretskii, Izgoev, and the publicist A. B. Petrishchev. Zamiatin was arrested and spared deportation only through the intervention of Pil'niak and Voronskii. The leadership of the House of Arts (with the exception of Zamiatin) was not decimated in the same way, but this did not mean it escaped official disfavor, and several prominent members had also left Russia.[58] The Writers' Union, like its counterpart, KUBU, outlived both the Houses, but also like KUBU, it was decapitated: its chair, Boris Zaitsev, fled the country in summer 1922, and its two deputy chairmen, Osorgin and Berdiaev, were deported, along with Aikhenval'd and Iosif Matusevich; Volkovyskii and Iretskii had been among the leaders of its Petrograd branch.

The expulsions and journal closures were the death knell for the House of Litterateurs and, in Gorky's absence, the House of Arts as well. During a series of speeches at the Petrograd soviet haranguing the disloyal intelligentsia on the eve of the deportations, Zinoviev's deputy G. I. Safarov claimed that the House of Litterateurs not only was insufficiently open to the public but also "mocked the working class."[59] The recently emigrated Khodasevich saw the writing on the wall, and he bitterly proclaimed in an unsigned article in the Berlin newspaper *Golos Rossii:* "Zinoviev was long ago sick of writers. He was sick of the 'Petrograd House of Litterateurs,' that base nest . . . where they did a most seditious thing: they did not allow writers to die from famine. This House of Litterateurs existed in practice thanks to the efforts of B. O. Khariton and N. M. Volkovyskii. Both have been deported abroad. A proper accounting [*raschet*]: you will not transplant [*ne peresazhaesh'*] every single last writer, but the closure of the 'House of Litterateurs' (the unavoidable consequence of this deportation)—is if not a fatal then a heavy blow on all of Petrograd literature immediately. Indeed, for all the Petrograd intelligentsia, for whom the House of Litterateurs was a singular cultural refuge."[60] The move to close the Houses, which, as Khodasevich and others assumed, was ordered by Zinoviev, came swiftly.[61] The Workers' and Peasants' Inspectorate (Rabkrin) faulted the House of Arts for having sold art at speculative prices, and it was shut down shortly thereafter.[62] Despite its claims to a broader base and its connections to Gorky, its critics perceived it to be an exclusivist club and attacked it on a number of occasions for its connection to the old world of silk stockings, evening dress, and French conversation.[63]

Although the Narkompros officials in the Petrograd Academic Center did not object to the existence of the House of Litterateurs as long as it no longer received official funding, the local security organs overruled them.[64] On 27 October the Petrograd interdepartmental commission for registering societies refused to authorize the House of Litterateurs, "in view of the fact that the majority of the members of the 'House of Litterateurs' are personally politically unreliable."[65] Within a week, before any appeal could be made, the premises were occupied, the press, official stamp, and paperwork seized, and the doors padlocked on order of the local arm of the NKVD. District officials let the cafeteria stay open until further clarification, but the Petrograd Academic Center considered the property under its jurisdiction. Leaders of the House of Litterateurs protested that only they could decide to dissolve it, and that the disposal of property—including its library and the materials of the literary museum—should be handled "according to the charter, and not by way of confiscation."[66] Their efforts to control the liquidation failed; so, too, did an effort by the Petrograd branch of the Union of Writers to establish a House of Writers on the premises of the House of Litterateurs. In the end, Zinoviev and the Petrograd soviet handed the building and most of its property over to a group called the House of Red Journalists; the library and literary museum were eventually put at the disposal of the Academy of Sciences.[67]

In Moscow the NKVD commission edited the All-Russian Union of Writers' charter on the request of the official artists' union, Vserabis, to keep it from infringing on the activities of the professional union, and it ordered that certain individuals be banned from participating in the Union of Writers. With its composition and constitution thus altered, the Union of Writers escaped further harassment at this time, but the similarly organized Union of Poets did not. Set up at roughly the same time and with overlapping membership (Blok and Gumilev were among the founders), the Union of Poets—which had not produced anything openly anti-Bolshevik—was among those organizations that the NKVD commission refused to register during its initial meetings in November 1922. The proffered explanation, based on the

GPU's counsel, was that the Union of Poets was to be eliminated "in view of the overtly unreliable makeup of its founders." Kamenev's Moscow soviet protested, however, and in February 1923, in a rare reversal, the NKVD commission allowed it to reopen, and it continued to operate until the end of the decade.[68]

The Union of Writers, the worst of the "old men" removed, was transformed primarily into a forum for fellow travelers. Voronskii, despite expressing uneasiness with broad-based writers' organizations, eventually became its deputy chair.[69] An analysis of the leadership of the Leningrad branch in 1926 reveals that it was almost entirely different from that of four years earlier, with regime sympathizers like Fedin in prominent positions, although there were still some anomalies—most notably the fact that Sologub, that infamous "pornographer," was its chair.[70] Voronskii continued to press forcefully—and, through the mid-1920s, successfully—for inclusivity toward fellow travelers, arguing that the main goal of party policy in literature should be to bring all who might be useful to the side of the Revolution. The radical exclusionism of those around the journal *Na Postu* and other hardliners, Voronskii maintained, mistakenly carried the old anti-*spets* sentiment into the literary sphere.[71] But although the Central Committee more or less endorsed his accommodationist sentiments in 1925, Voronskii's star was already falling. With *Krasnaia nov'* in decline, the Union of Writers joined together with rival organizations to form the Federation of Associations of Soviet Writers (FOSP) in fall 1926, and the radicals quickly dominated Voronskii and his fellow travelers. As Robert Maguire argues, FOSP, the first real attempt to unite all the country's writers, "provided the prototype of the Union of Soviet Writers: the mass organization under tight Party control."[72] Herein lies the genealogy of the controlled and unitary Soviet literary public sphere.

The party's goals were significantly more modest at the start of NEP. The danger to the Revolution, it was believed, came from a select group of "old" literary and publicistic figures who were annoyingly adept at forming organizations and publishing journals. They represented the "corporate" literati, outside official channels. The Bolshevik leadership did not reject the possibility of organs looking after group interests but insisted that they be more sympathetic to the regime. As it was, these *byvshie liudi* were training and influencing a talented group of younger writers; the potential flower of Soviet culture was being brought up in the seedbed of bourgeois ideological reaction, and, if not separated from these influences, it would be lost to the proletarian cause. The idea was not to revile prospective fellow travelers, but to convince them, like the *spetsy,* to serve openly and loyally within official institutions.

As long as the loudly independent voices of the past were silenced and their organizations eliminated, some heterodoxy on issues other than unequivocal support for the Soviet regime could be tolerated.

Philosophical and Spiritual Organizations

The Bolsheviks' loudest opprobrium during the 1922 anti-intellectual campaigns focused on the revival of idealist philosophy and "mystical" spirituality. Publications from the time featured a wide variety of thought representing a brief renaissance of the Silver Age (as the cultural efflorescence in the decades before the Revolution was known), and a number of more or less formal groupings emerged. The most famous of these were the Free Philosophical Association, or Vol'fila (Vol'naia filosofskaia assotsiatsiia), in Petrograd, initiated by Belyi and the critic Ivanov-Razumnik, and Berdiaev's Free Academy of Spiritual Culture (Vol'naia akademiia dukhovnoi kul'tury) in Moscow. Vol'fila provided a forum for not only philosophical, but also cultural, artistic, and literary topics, whereas the Free Academy presented a series of wildly popular lectures on neo-idealist philosophy and related themes. In addition, the Moscow University Institute of Scientific Philosophy, the Petrograd University Philosophical Society, and the venerable Moscow Psychological Society provided more scholarly, but to the Bolsheviks no less pernicious, settings for philosophical debate.

Spiritual circles such as the Anthroposophical and Theosophical societies also experienced a brief revival, and religious sectarian groups blossomed. So, too, did the ecumenical movement, including the *kruzhok* organized by the Catholic priest V. V. Abrikosov dedicated to the unification of the Catholic and Orthodox churches, and Valentin Bulgakov's proposed Free Association of Spiritual Tendencies, which had an almost new-age resonance. The burgeoning Tolstoyan movement, of which Bulgakov was a key leader, and the still vital student Christian movement led by V. F. Martsinkovskii presented potentially even greater threats to Bolshevik ideological hegemony.

Unlike the larger writers' and *spets* organizations, the philosophical societies rarely ventured too far into the realm of professional protection or material provision. They were more narrowly focused on intellectual or spiritual matters and so were not in the same sense potential sources of "corporate" professional separatism. But no one else so clearly and directly flaunted opposition to the basic principles of scientific Marxism—only Christian theology itself was equally irreconcilable with atheist materialism. While a full history of the early attacks on the Orthodox Church is outside the scope of this study, we should note that in fomenting a schism and supporting the loyalist "Living Church," the Bolsheviks once again made use of the tactic of replacing an old, hostile organization with a newly formed, docile one. On the other hand, there could be no acceptable Theosophical or Anthroposophical societies, which were simply disbanded, and societies of Red scholars dedicated to scientific Marxism took the place of the independent philosophical organizations. Theology and philosophy were the first subjects whose formal teaching was eradicated at Moscow and Petrograd universities, and the Bolsheviks did not intend to allow them to exist in informal settings either.

There was significant cross-fertilization among the philosophical and spiritual organizations and with the literary societies discussed above. Bolshevik leaders found this networking quite disturbing: small *kruzhki* discussing esoteric topics was one thing, a wide circle of intellectuals in an interconnected set of groups was another. Vol'fila, founded in 1919 by Belyi, Blok, and Ivanov-Razumnik, was a perfect example of such an interconnected group. Although Belyi hoped to establish an organization that would "differ from the usual type of philosophical and religious-philosophical society, tied to tradition and often cut off from life," many of the older religious philosophers openly participated.[73] Vol'fila became a forum for discussion that was as often literary and cultural as it was strictly philosophical. Blok lectured on the "Collapse of Humanism," Belyi on "The Philosophy of Culture," and debates were held on Herzen, Lavrov, and, controversially, "Proletarian Culture." There was a lengthy tribute to Blok after his death. Like the Houses of Litterateurs and Arts, Vol'fila alternated between lectures open to the public and closed sessions, for more intimate discussion among its members. Idealist philosophers also gave talks at Vol'fila: Nikolai Losskii spoke on "God in the System of Organic World-Perception," and A. S. Aksol'dov on "Wonder." October 1921 was dedicated to Dostoevsky, with reports on his life and work at seventeen different meetings. Vol'fila also became one of the central spaces for anthroposophical discussions, thanks to Belyi's connections.[74] As Losskii recalled, the contradictions within Vol'fila became apparent to him when he was asked to join the board and was told it had the goal of "working out the ideals of socialism and assisting in the dissemination of them."[75]

Belyi, along with professors G. G. Shpet and M. P. Stoliarov, founded a Moscow branch of Vol'fila in fall 1921; soon after, branches were formed in several other cities.[76] The Free Academy of Spiritual Culture, however, overshadowed the Moscow Vol'fila. The Free Academy had grown out of a lively *kruzhok* at the Berdiaev house, which included Stepun, Pavel Muratov, Gershenzon,

Aikhenval'd, the young economist Ia. Bukshpan, the legal scholar M. S. Fel'dshtein, Belyi when he was in Moscow, and, on his arrival from Saratov, Frank.[77] Founded in fall 1919 by Berdiaev with the goal of "maintaining and developing spiritual culture in Russia," the Free Academy provided an opportunity for scholars who could no longer teach at MGU to lecture to a broader public.[78] Berdiaev explained, "I intended the circle to be as wide as possible and to include representatives of the most varied trends of thought united in a common recognition of the independence and primacy of spiritual values."[79]

The Free Academy existed without official support, on small contributions from its constituents. Although it repeatedly ran into trouble with the authorities, Berdiaev pointed out that Kamenev, the head of the Moscow soviet, had sanctioned its existence.[80] Like Vol'fila's, its lectures covered subjects ranging from theology to culture, but the religious idealism for which Berdiaev and his colleagues were well known predominated. It featured a series of courses, including Belyi's "Philosophy of Spiritual Culture," Muratov's "Art of the Renaissance," Frank's "Introduction to Philosophy," Stepun's "Life and Creativity," Father Abrikosov's "The Stages of the Mystical Path," and Berdiaev's "Philosophy of History," "Philosophy of Religion," and one on Dostoevsky. Lectures by Frank, Berdiaev, Stepun, Boris Vysheslavtsev, Aikhenval'd, and others covered the "crisis of culture," the "crisis of philosophy," Christian freedom, the ideal Greece, theosophy and Christianity, Russia and Europe, and Hindu mysticism. Perhaps most controversial was a cycle of lectures examining Oswald Spengler's recently translated *Decline of the West,* out of which came a collection of articles directly responsible for motivating Lenin to deport the philosophers.[81]

The lectures became extremely popular with workers, Red soldiers, sailors, and a loyal contingent of student disciples, whose interest greatly alarmed the Bolsheviks. (Berdiaev also recalled that among the regular attendees there was "what looked like a young Cheka agent, invariably sitting in the front row and looking at me with a blank gaze.") Soon the large auditorium of the building of the Higher Women's Courses (then the second MGU, formed after the Revolution) was insufficient for the crowds. Some lectures had to be repeated; others were given at the Polytechnic Museum, which was able to accommodate over one thousand people.[82] Berdiaev recalled wistfully: "These were people searching, thirsting, striving to find a new path. . . . Thus, there was an unusual, passionate intensity to the atmosphere at the presentations and lectures."[83] Berdiaev and Frank even organized a Philosophical-Humanitarian Faculty in spring 1922 for students who were "thirsting for serious systematic work."

A related group was the venerable Moscow Psychological Society. Led until his death in 1920 by L. M. Lopatin, it had witnessed the most famous philosophical debates of the late imperial period, and its journal, *Voprosy filosofii i psikhologii,* was one of the premier forums for publication.[84] Though its activities were curtailed during the Civil War, and its publishing activities ceased, it briefly revived in the early 1920s to become a forum for lectures and debates on both psychological and philosophical topics, although the latter became more predominant under the direction of Ivan Il'in.[85] Several lectures explored the question of understanding the psyche in light of evolution; Il'in spoke on "the fundaments of normal religious experience"; and Frank discussed "the logical nature of social phenomena." Revered figures such as Lopatin, Vladimir Solov'ev, and E. N. Trubetskoi were honored in talks by Berdiaev, Il'in, and others.[86]

The MGU Institute of Scientific Philosophy, headed by Gustav Shpet, provided a more formal setting for debate during its brief existence. Its courses, designed to replace the abolished Philosophical Faculty, were more strictly traditional and academic, as well as more systematic, than those at the Free Academy or Psychological Society. Its claim to "scientific" philosophy was meant to mark its neutrality and to distance itself from the "mystical" philosophy that the new order found most pernicious, and Shpet was briefly able to bring together people with antagonistic worldviews. Still, there was significant overlap with the Free Academy and Psychological Society: Il'in and Frank were among the institute's active members, and Vysheslavtsev was brought in as well.[87] Moscow's idealist philosophers had thus found three different forums in which to keep an active and public discussion of their subject alive into 1922.

In Petrograd the academic counterpart to Vol'fila was the PGU Philosophical Society, founded in 1897 and revived in 1921 after three years of inactivity. Its founder, A. I. Vvedenskii, having fallen ill, Losskii and E. L. Radlov headed the new incarnation of this group, whose lectures and discussions also featured idealist and religious themes. They also began to publish some of these presentations in the revived journal *Mysl'* and to prepare a series of other publications. Until 1922 the Philosophical Society, like other scholarly associations, was under the relatively benign jurisdiction of the Petrograd Glavnauka, the Narkompros body in charge of scientific organizations.[88] Its lectures at the public library featured Losskii on "Abstract and Concrete Ideal-Realism," Vvedenskii on "The Fate of Belief in God," Lev Karsavin on "The Freedom of Will" and on "The Mirage of Progress," and Ivan Lapshin on "Overcoming Solipsism," among other speakers and subjects. A philosophy *kruzhok* at PGU formed in 1921 provided a forum for talks and discussions, especially for younger scholars and students, and it kept close relations with both Vol'fila and the Philosophical Society.[89] That both the Philosophical Society and the *kruzhok* continued to provide fertile ground for idealist and religious themes within the university walls despite their leaders having been banned from teaching was a source of great irritation to the Bolsheviks.

Vol'fila and the Philosophical Society, like their Moscow counterparts, had significant overlap, despite their different aims. They shared a general sense that a revival of spiritual or philosophical conversation was imperative in the new Russia. These organizations would be remembered for their intensity and popularity; even allowing for nostalgic hyperbole, it is clear they were invested with great energy and significance. They covered a wide variety of topics, which linked them not only with one another but also both with cultural groups such as the Houses of Litterateurs and Arts and with social-scientific societies such as the Eleventh (Economic) Branch of the Russian Technical Society, the Petrograd M. M. Kovalevskii Sociology Society, and the Social-Bibliographical Institute. Such ties confirmed Bolshevik fears that an intimate network of scholars and artists was relentlessly spreading views hostile to Marxism.[90]

It certainly did not help that Belyi, Berdiaev, Losskii, and others had ties to the occult and new religious groups that had found a new lease on life in the immediate postrevolutionary years. Belyi had very close ties to the Anthroposophical Society; both it and the similar Theosophical Society survived the Revolution and, after the Civil War, again attracted the attention of the authorities. The Petrograd Administrative-Organizational Department, the local arm of the NKVD, looked into liquidating both groups in March 1922, and the Petrograd Political Enlightenment Department warned that their activities were "in sharp contradiction with the ideas put forward in [our] primary political enlightenment work."[91] These two groups were not alone in attracting what appears to have been a large number of seekers looking outside the bounds of traditional Orthodoxy for spiritual sustenance.

There was much interchange among nontraditional spiritual groups. For example, Vladimir Martsinkovskii, a leader of the interconfessional Christian Student Union who traveled the country evangelizing, had ties to Baptists, other Evangelicals, Salvation Army missionaries, Tolstoyans, anthroposophists, and even Messianic Jews, while (a bit disingenuously) maintaining that he continued to consider himself a faithful Orthodox. His ideal Christianity brought together Protestantism and Orthodoxy, "a synthesis uniting the masculine activity of the Western world with the feminine tenderness and contemplativeness of the East."[92] The Christian Student Union, which had branches in a number of cities, not only aimed to form *kruzhki* of devout students and to establish ties between these circles, but also emphasized the need to attract students to evangelical activities.[93] The Bolshevik leadership, very much concerned with how alien ideologies were corrupting the studentry, soon put it out of business.

Catholicism also experienced a brief postrevolutionary revival, embodied in the person of Father Vladimir Abrikosov, who with his ex-wife, Anna Ivanovna, had founded a Dominican community and a devotional center for young women.[94] The ascetic Abrikosov attracted to his Moscow apartment a diverse *kruzhok* devoted to the reunification of Catholicism and Eastern Orthodoxy. Abrikosov attracted a number of prominent intellectuals, including the jurist D. V. Kuzmin-Karavaev, the scion of a well-connected family, a former Social Democrat with close ties to Petrograd literary circles, and the ex-husband of E. Iu. Kuzmina-Karavaeva, who would achieve émigré fame as "Mother Maria." Berdiaev's wife, Lidiia, was also a convert (Berdiaev himself admired the group's spiritual and ascetic life), and Abrikosov lectured at the Free Academy of Spiritual Culture.[95] In April 1922 several Orthodox attendees to the Abrikosov *kruzhok* were arrested during the first wave of church trials. As the Abrikosov circle became ever more serious in its ecumenical mission, the GPU, which was particularly concerned with such efforts to bring different factions of the enemy camp together, paid increasing attention. A Chekist infiltrator attended these sessions in spring 1922, and when the list of deportees was drawn up, he pointed to not only Abrikosov and Kuzmin-Karavaev, but also the former senator A. D. Arbuzov and Professor A. L. Baikov, as particularly enthusiastic Church unifiers.[96]

The Tolstoyans occupied the other end of the spiritual spectrum, achieving remarkable success in forming peasant communes in the postrevolutionary era. They cultivated vegetarianism and pacifism while promulgating the memory of their late spiritual leader. Tolstoy's close friend Vladimir Chertkov prepared to publish his collected works, and Valentin Bulgakov, the author's last secretary, founded the Tolstoy home museum in Khamovniki and worked at the Iasnaia Poliana estate. Both were active members of the Society of True Freedom in Memory of L. N. Tolstoy (*Obshchestvo istinnoi svobody v pamiat' L. N. Tolstogo*), the center of Tolstoyan activity at the time, which stood against war, the death penalty, and cruelty to animals.[97] As the regime began to suppress the Tolstoyans and other cults, Bulgakov appealed to the antireligious activist Emelian Iaroslavskii, arguing that, unlike the Living Church, Tolstoyanism represented a progressive spiritual trend emphasizing "equality, brotherhood, and freedom."[98] He expressed great frustration that the Cheka had sealed off their building on Gazetnyi

Alley, banned the Tolstoyan-led United Council of Religious Communes and Groups (*Ob"edinennyi sovet religioznykh obshchin i grupp*), and subjected peasant Tolstoyans to arbitrary arrests in the provinces.[99]

Iaroslavskii replied candidly that the Bolsheviks were under no illusions about the "Blackhundred" churchmen, and they were more interested in their followers, whom they hoped to win over. But they were also under no illusions concerning the various sectarian and cult groups. In particular he saw ties between Tolstoyanism and SR populism. "You and your confederates," Iaroslavskii darkly noted, "are hardly the ideological voices of the poorest, but of the more affluent, more individualistic, and therefore more anarchically motivated layers of the petty bourgeois [*meshchanskoi*] intelligentsia, . . . hostile to Communism. . . . Hence our disagreements, hence—our struggle."[100] Iaroslavskii saw the Tolstoyans not as allies but as dangerous separatists who were more likely to join the regime's enemies.[101]

Valentin Bulgakov's next project was equally unwelcome. The United Council of Religious Groups having been outlawed, the Tolstoyans and other sectarians began to promote the Free Association of Spiritual Tendencies (*Vol'noe sodruzhestvo dukhovnykh techenii*) in fall 1922. This ambitious undertaking, led by Bulgakov and the anthroposophist V. O. Anisimova-Stanevich, envisioned a worldwide spiritual renaissance based on tolerance and religious pluralism. Preliminary meetings included Tolstoyans, theosophists, anthroposophists, representatives of the Student Christian Union, anarchist mystics, the Baha'i, and other free-religious groups. Bulgakov's mission statement gave it the goal of "bringing together representatives of various religious, philosophical, humanistic, and other spiritual tendencies." The association aimed to disseminate these ideas through discussions, public lectures, journals, bulletins, and books, as well as to participate in humanitarian activities such as famine relief.[102] It was precisely the uniting of already suspect groups that most upset the Bolsheviks, who quickly eliminated the Free Association of Spiritual Tendencies.

The NKVD dissolved several of these philosophical and spiritual organizations straight away in fall 1922, and most of the rest were disbanded by the mid-1920s. Few of these groups had pretensions toward protecting professional or group material interests, but they evoked in the Bolsheviks an almost visceral ideological distaste. The philosophers expelled included Berdiaev, Frank, Stepun, and Il'in from Moscow; Losskii, Karsavin, and Lapshin from Petrograd; and Sergei Bulgakov a few months later from his residence in the Crimea.[103] With these men gone, the Psychological Society and Petrograd Philosophical Society ceased to function. The acting chair of the Free

Academy, B. A. Griftsov, boldly submitted its application to the NKVD, but, unsurprisingly, it was among the first refused registration and dissolved. Even Narkompros, which on occasion protected cultural institutions, considered its existence "absolutely undesirable."[104] Vol'fila, on the other hand, managed to continue for several more years despite Belyi's absence, but it was much less vibrant than it had been, and the NKVD closed it down in 1924.[105]

The procedure regarding explicitly religious organizations was more complex. Although the GPU urged abolition of the United Council of Religious Communes and Groups and the Tolstoyan Society of True Freedom, a final resolution was deferred until the establishment of rules governing the registration of religious organizations. Other groups, however, were banned immediately—including the Free Association of Spiritual Tendencies and the Tolstoyan-affiliated Moscow Vegetarian Society, whose goals, the NKVD commission remarked, contradicted the constitution of the RSFSR.[106] A different procedure was soon put in place for religious societies, and the initial reticence to deal with these groups was overcome. The Theosophical Society, which the Petrograd authorities had already been attempting to eliminate for some time, was abolished on the admonition of the GPU and of Narkompros, which considered it "an undoubtedly mystico-clerical enterprise, and as a consequence of this, harmful." Its cousin, the Anthroposophical Society, lasted several months before it, too, was rejected "in view of the unclearness of its goals." The NKVD saw Martsinkovskii's Christian Student Union as particularly pernicious, and it was eliminated as well. The Samara-based evangelical group Lighthouse and the Salvation Army rounded out the initial group of sectarian spiritual groups shut down.[107] Several months after the mass deportations, three spiritual-intellectual leaders were informed that they too had to depart: Martsinkovskii and the Tolstoyans Bulgakov and Chertkov. The GPU operative who questioned Martsinkovskii explained: "Your line of work is dangerous for us at the current time. The intelligentsia, Whiteguards, gather around you. . . . All of them hide under the flag of your religious ideas." Chertkov was able to use his connections to overturn this ruling; the others left in April 1923.[108]

The distinction between the spiritual groups and other intellectual societies was rarely clear-cut. To resolve the impasse, a separate NKVD-Narkomiust commission was established to register religious organizations.[109] The regime began to see the usefulness of using sectarian groups as allies in its campaign against the Orthodox Church. Some of the larger groups, including Baptists and other evangelicals, welcomed the reform agenda of the loyalist Living Church. Although the Bolsheviks always considered them provisional allies at best, and the NKVD commissions inhibited their ability to form national organizations, a select number of these groups were allowed to flourish in the 1920s.[110] The Tolstoyans' usefulness as a sectarian wedge allowed them to make a comeback, and Chertkov still had important patrons. Though the appeals of Kamenev's Moscow soviet to the NKVD commission to reexamine its prohibition of the Moscow Vegetarian Society were at first rejected,[111] it did not stay closed for long. The Vegetarian Society was the only central Tolstoyan organization during NEP, and it even managed to disseminate a newsletter.[112]

Catholics, on the other hand, continued to face persecution. Although Abrikosov's departure ended his *kruzhok*, Exarch Leonid Fëdorov, the head of the Russian Catholic community, and Abrikosov's ex-wife continued to work for unification. Campaigns against Catholics intensified, and in December 1922 all Catholic churches in Moscow and Petrograd were shut down. Soon after, the GPU initiated a comprehensive anti-Catholic campaign that resulted in the trial and imprisonment of Fëdorov, Abrikosova, and at least sixty other activists. These efforts effectively curtailed the ecumenical effort, not to mention, for a time, legal Catholic activity in Russia.[113]

The campaign against idealist and mystical organizations was separate from, even when coincidental with, general antireligious efforts. It was directed at groups of intellectuals promoting ideas that the Marxist regime considered antithetical to its own guiding ideology. Unlike most of the other groups discussed in this and the preceding chapter, the philosophical societies were not unionlike organizations promoting group identity, potentially fostering the caste separatism that alarmed the Bolsheviks. Still, ties between these often disparate groups suggested the possibility of new intellectual alliances, of cross-fertilization, a prospect against which the party-state was determined to maintain its vigilance. Even more centrally, the Bolshevik leadership considered the philosopher's word more than academic; it was, as Lenin angrily declared, "a literary cover for a Whiteguard organization."[114]

When dealing with the physicians,' professors,' or even writers' organizations, the regime reacted to perceived separatist tendencies by purging specific individuals and establishing parallel loyalist groups. The methodology was not so very different when replacing philosophical organizations and related social science groups such as the Kovalevskii Sociology Society and the Archaeological Society in Moscow, which were also abolished.[115] Their successors, of course, had an entirely different scholarly and ideological cast. The rapid growth of groups such as the Scientific Society of Marxists (*nauchnoe obshchestvo marksistov*), despite the noted paucity of Marxist scholars, attests to the efforts of the regime and of loyal scholars (not all of whom were

Communists) to serve this purpose.[116] The intellectualized spiritual groups such as the Anthroposophical Society had no Marxist equivalent and were simply abolished. On the other hand, loyalist sectarian groups, including, provisionally, the Tolstoyans, were used as wedges against the Orthodox Church. Along with the Living Church, they were the religious *smenovekhovtsy.* This tactical alliance did not, however, mean that the atheist revolutionary regime ever forgot that spiritual groups remained implacable foes.

The NKVD Commissions on Registration

Despite the closures of a significant number of Moscow and Petrograd societies in fall and winter 1922–23, most organizations whose applications the NKVD commission examined were permitted to register, and most congresses were eventually given permission to meet. Control could, however, be exercised in other ways. Through a careful and often picayune editing of charters (with an emphasis on limiting autonomy), through prohibiting the participation of particular individuals, and through the sort of general harassing and delaying tactics employed against groups such as the All-Russian Association of Engineers, the NKVD and GPU could ensure that these societies were kept in check and not allowed to constitute a genuinely independent public sphere. The NKVD commission on registration quickly disseminated a set of rules explaining what the general restrictions on charters should be.[117]

One of the most critical tasks was to ensure that all societies had open membership so that Communists could not be excluded. Societies were made subject to outside scrutiny to ensure that they could no longer retain a separatist or caste nature. In effect, organizations could no longer fully decide their own composition. The NKVD commission's instructions also dictated open voting, most issues being decided by a clear majority, so that a small clique could not control the society through secret machinations. In addition, representatives of the GPU were granted a handful of passes to every professional congress.[118] The registration of societies and their congresses thus provided an important weapon in the arsenal of the surveillance state, even if it did not mean shutting all of them down.

Although this and the previous chapter have focused on organizations in the two capitals, which were by far the most active centers of intellectual activity, many of the national societies had branches in the provinces or connections with regional organizations, and the registration process took place (albeit in a somewhat disorganized manner) at the local level as well. The Petrograd Philosophical Society had connections with similar groups in Kostroma, at Don University, and at Perm University, and philosophical societies also existed in

Kiev, Saratov, and other cities.[119] The House of Litterateurs looked into setting up debates in provincial locations and even received invitations from several regional soviets.[120] Scholars at most local universities grouped in organizations of at least scientific if not more general professional interest; societies of regional studies (*kraevedenie*) began to proliferate. National professional societies such as VAI, the RTO, and the Pirogov Society had branches in many cities, as did religious associations like the Student Christian Union, and the Vsemediksantrud physicians' section brought together doctors from across the nation. It was out of concern over how imagined professional and cultural communities would develop on a national level that the regime paid particular attention to the convening of all-Russian congresses.

The NKVD explained to local administrative bodies that surveillance over these societies was a vital task for verifying that each organization's "activity would strictly conform . . . to the tasks and character of the society's charter."[121] Initially, however, registration in the provinces was uneven. Regional bureaus often informed the NKVD that none or very few of the societies that had been abolished in the capitals had branches in their area; sometimes they even asked the center for help in locating them. There was often confusion over whether religious organizations or for-profit artels (craft cooperatives) were to be registered under the same guidelines. The NKVD sent out numerous circulars and direct replies to guide its provincial organs. The Rostov bureau, for instance, inquired whether the local branch of the Vegetarian Society, which claimed that the Moscow branch was still open, should be refused registration (the answer was yes, it should be shut down). The Voronezh administration was not sure whether the local "Medical Society of Doctors named after Pirogov" was related to the liquidated "Society of Russian Doctors in Memory of Pirogov" (the answer was no, it could remain open). Iaroslavl, having followed NKVD orders and liquidated the local branch of the Union of Poets, was unsure of what to do, having read in *Izvestia* that it had since been registered (it was explained that the original decision had been reconsidered). The town of Ivanovo-Voznesensk was chided for having decided to abolish the local branch of VAI before a final decision on the national organization had been reached, whereas the Orlov soviet was rebuked for the opposite sin of having registered a society whose central body had not yet been approved.[122] Clearly, the process of registration and control in the provinces was at best a work in progress. As in many other areas of administration, the Soviet government remained relatively weak outside Moscow and Petrograd in the 1920s.[123]

The gradual and uneven establishment of a system of surveillance and control was not the only consequence of the Bolshevik confrontation with civil society. The closure of a number of important societies and organizations was not without profound and immediate effect on the cultural and professional landscape. The elimination of the bastions of the "old" writers and journalists significantly changed the face, in particular, of literary Petrograd. While private *kruzhki* continued to operate for five more years, many of the leading figures began to fade from view, and the larger public forums were limited to fellow-traveler- and Marxist-dominated institutions.[124] Although a few idealist philosophers survived the deportations of 1922, they were shunted to the side, their publications ceased, and the golden age of neo-idealist religious philosophy had been brought to an end. The elimination of independent professors' organs had profoundly altered the debate over university autonomy. Loyal *spetsy* continued to receive privileges, but even their organizations were not exempt from this clamping down on the public sphere. Although only a minority, such as the Pirogov, were abolished, all professional organizations remained subject to the constant scrutiny and frequent harassment of the NKVD.

In conjunction with the circumscription of the public sphere, the beginning of NEP featured an expansion of censorship and of controls over private and cooperative publishers. The ideological heresies that found their way into print were combated both on a particular basis and, increasingly, in a holistic propaganda campaign coordinated by Bolshevik leaders such as Zinoviev, Trotsky, and the Agitprop chief, Andrei Bubnov. It is thus to the independent publishers and their books and journals and, conversely, to the regime's efforts to contend with the resurgence of "counterrevolutionary ideology" that we turn in the following chapter.

5

Publishing, Censorship, and Ideological Struggles

Words are weapons, and just as the revolutionary regime cannot allow revolvers and machine guns to be in the hands of just anybody, since he might be the most malicious enemy, so too the state cannot allow freedom of the press and propaganda.

—A. Lunacharskii, "Freedom of the Book and the Revolution," May 1921

The perceived resurgence of bourgeois ideology at the beginning of NEP catalyzed the Bolshevik campaign against the intelligentsia. The re-emergence of "public figures," the obduracy of the organized professoriat, and the proliferation of autonomous societies were all of great concern, but the advent of unofficial journals, books, and almanacs constituted the central battleground on the cultural front. The persistence of alien view-points distressed, even enraged, Soviet leaders, who had taken great care to eliminate opposition newspapers. "Freedom of press in the RSFSR, surrounded by an entire world of bourgeois enemies, is a freedom of *political organization* for the bourgeoisie," Lenin declared. The readership of the publications emerging at the end of the Civil War, although small in number, constituted an elite with a dangerous level of influence on students and other critical audiences. The producers and consumers of these books and journals were the potential architects and builders of the autonomous public sphere.[1]

These new or resurgent publications presented an array of cultural, philosophical, political, and economic outlooks. Many of those involved would remember the years 1920–22 as the swan song of the independent intelligentsia, the period of its final articulations before a lengthy silence. Even though fellow-traveler artistic literature flourished during NEP, the early 1920s featured the final expression of journalistic and scholarly commentary and criticism.[2] Publicistic, literary, and academic writing flooded *Vestnik literatury, Letopis' doma literatorov, Mysl', Ekonomist, Utrenniki,* and other journals and almanacs, as well as books and pamphlets issued by Zadruga, Bereg, Academia, A. S. Kagan, and other private and cooperative publishers. They covered topics as diverse as Oswald Spengler's *Decline of the West,* Dostoevsky's place as prophet of the Revolution, the Changing Signposts movement (*smenovekhovstvo*), and the socioeconomic prospects of the Soviet state. For a number of contributors, editors, and publishers, participating in this discourse would lead directly to their sudden expulsion from Soviet Russia.

The regime's response was multifaceted: the creation of a network of official journals to counter these "bourgeois" writings; the consolidation of censorship within a newly created body, Glavlit, led by P. I. Lebedev-Polianskii; the immediate banning of a number of journals; and the closure of certain private and cooperative publishers. The campaign, initiated at Lenin's exhortations, was shaped first by a GPU report to the Politburo, "Anti-Soviet Groups among the Intelligentsia," and then by Zinoviev's vitriolic speech at the August 1922 Party Conference directly before the arrests and expulsions. A thorough propaganda campaign, orchestrated by the Agitprop chief, Andrei Bubnov, supplemented Zinoviev's call for vigilant action.

The formation of Glavlit was a critical moment in erecting a network of Soviet institutions, which also included the NKVD commissions on the registration of societies, the installation of loyalist VUZ administrations, and the establishment of administrative exile, for the surveillance of the cultural, academic, and professional intelligentsia. During the 1920s control did not mean the full abolition of heterodoxy as much as circumscribing its manifestations. Glavlit, like the NKVD registration commissions, was geared toward eliminating the most pernicious, hostile viewpoints, preventing their reemergence, and punctiliously tracking the carefully delimited public sphere that still existed. The ideological campaign accompanying the creation of these institutions was meant to be a shot across the bow, to clarify (if not once and for all) the boundaries of public discourse.

The Soviet Regime and Private Publishing

Notwithstanding the 1918 ban on unofficial publishing, a handful of private and cooperative publishers (most located in the two capitals) managed to stumble precariously through the difficult Civil War years.[3] Though the Moscow and Petrograd soviets ordered the municipalization of all publishers, Narkompros leaders recognized that private publishing could supplement the meager output of Gosizdat and other official organs. Unofficial publishing was nevertheless difficult, owing not only to the hostility of the local authorities, but also to the fact that the government controlled all means of production—including access to the nationalized printing presses and to the country's extremely scarce supply of paper.[4] In addition, Gosizdat was supposed to approve all manuscripts, although this censorship was still not strictly enforced. Still, the installation of Gosizdat as a supervisory organ represented a step toward greater control, formalized in 1921, which led to the banning of certain books, much to the consternation of unofficial publishers.[5]

The onset of NEP changed publishing as it did many other industries. Print production was thenceforth to be self-supporting and not dependent on state subsidies, and the free distribution of books was declared to be unsustainable. In reality, continued subsidization of Gosizdat publications was found to be necessary, given the party's desire to keep the price of books low enough to be accessible to a mass audience. The more permissive attitude toward partial free enterprise had its effect here too, and the authorities officially sanctioned the existence of private and cooperative publishers in August 1921. These decrees signaled recognition of unofficial publishing and abrogated the state monopoly on printing presses and the book trade. The Moscow soviet noted that publications should not be rejected unless they were "directed against the Soviet state or of clearly antisocial content." The Writers' Book Shop, which had been unique in escaping the earlier municipalization, was soon joined by a number of other bookstores in the two capitals.[6]

Lunacharskii tried to strike a balance between what he called the "ideals" of liberty and the necessity of control. On the one hand, he criticized Communists who wished to abolish freedom of speech and the press entirely. "Genuine art," he wrote, "that which carries in itself the stamp of genius or talent, cannot sing in a cage. A talent that has adapted to a cage turns from a nightingale into a finch, from an eagle into a chicken." At the same time, he held that such freedoms were not feasible at the moment; the regime was still battling myriad enemies and facing grave material shortages. Those who flinched before this reality were philistines and babblers, not genuine revolutionaries. "We are not at all afraid of the necessity of censoring even belletristic literature, for its banner, its elegant exterior, might hide a poison for the still naive and benighted spirit of the great masses." Thus, while promising freedom of speech eventually, the Soviet state could not allow it at the present. "What else is there to do? A time of transition is a time of transition," he concluded.[7]

Even with the introduction of NEP, private and cooperative publishers faced serious difficulties. Once Gosizdat acquired oversight over all publishing, interference became increasingly frequent and capricious.[8] At the end of 1921, the bookmakers began to speak out in defense of their collective interests. P. N. Vitiazev (F. I. Sedenko), a prominent and activist publisher, issued a pamphlet entitled *Private Publishers in Russia,* which offered a blistering indictment of the near extinction of book production. "The question of private publishers is now extremely acute," he began. "The Soviet regime . . . has apparently set down the path to their complete rout and destruction." He lamented the growing hostility of Gosizdat toward private publishers, the value of whose contributions to the starved book market it did not seem to appreciate.[9]

Vitiazev was far from alone in his dismay with Gosizdat, and he organized and coordinated a growing association of private and cooperative publishers. In December 1920 the All-Russian Union of Writers and a coalition of Moscow cooperative publishers both appealed to Lunacharskii, and the ailing legendary anarchist Pëtr Kropotkin and even Gorky addressed the Eighth All-Russian Congress of Soviets with concerns over the potential abolition of independent publishing in Russia. The coalition of cooperative publishers protested the consolidation of publishing within Gosizdat, since productive creative work depended on freedom of the press: "Every time that a society, some influential part of it, or a government has tried to tell artists and scholars what they should do, art and science have either disappeared entirely, become formulaic, or degenerated into crude craft," they declared. "The path to artistic and scientific development must be sought out by the writers themselves in their free and independent [*samodeiatel'nyi*] associations." The Union of Writers complained that conditions were steadily worsening; even as the country was emerging from crisis, Gosizdat was hindering the renaissance of literary production. If this continued, they warned, "Russian literature will cease to exist."[10]

Despite the market liberalizations of 1921, many writers and publishers continued to experience frustration. Evgenii Zamiatin, who had recently completed the anti-utopian novel *We,* expressed his foreboding in an essay entitled "I Am Afraid." It was increasingly clear, he noted bitterly, that only the "nimble" writers, those quick to learn to serve a new master, would survive:

"A writer who cannot become nimble must go to work with a briefcase if he wants to live. In our time, Gogol would have gone to work with his briefcase in the theatrical department; Turgenev, undoubtedly, would have worked for All-World Literature translating Balzac and Flaubert; Herzen would have read lectures for the Baltic Fleet; and Chekhov would have served in Narkomzdrav." Even more disturbing to Zamiatin than the material hardships was the evolution of a new orthodoxy, which he felt had already begun to smother true art. "Authentic literature can exist only where it is produced not by efficient and reliable functionaries, but by lunatics, hermits, heretics, dreamers, rebels, and skeptics," he wrote. "I am afraid that there will be no authentic literature until we are cured of this new kind of catholicism, which no less than the old one fears any heretical word. And if this disease is incurable, I am afraid that Russian literature has only one future: its past."[11]

Zamiatin's open attack on the new cultural order received several sharp replies and led to the rapid deterioration of his own position. Lunacharskii retorted that while certain Communists had "a tendency to extreme touchiness, to suspecting counterrevolution behind every page," Zamiatin was grossly exaggerating. "There isn't any new catholicism; instead, there isn't any paper—and this is much worse. The Soviet regime, if the means of production were sufficient, would print any neutral literature quite freely."[12] Voronskii, the editor of *Krasnaia nov'*, also asserted that the lack of books was due to poor material conditions and paper shortages, but he added that "ideological obscurantism" and "misunderstanding" exacerbated the situation. Still, though he agreed that "the striving to unite all or almost all publishing in the hands of Gosizdat is hardly correct," he had little use for Zamiatin's hermits, lunatics, and rebels. "Whom are they rebelling against now? We are involved with lunatics of a certain type. This is not a lunacy of the brave, but a madness of hate, malice, and impotence. . . . People who are physically ill, infected with disease, are isolated from the healthy. The same should be done with those who have rotted morally and ideologically."[13]

Zamiatin's fears were no doubt stoked by the censorship of a periodical the Petrograd branch of the Union of Writers tried to launch in spring 1921, called *Literaturnaia gazeta* (Literary Gazette) after a famous short-lived paper from the 1830s. Khodasevich's unsigned lead article cited Pushkin's famous reaction to literary censorship, "This silence is a public calamity," and added, "It is a law of history, similar to a law of physics: 'The silence of literature in Russia always marks a deeply reactionary epoch.'" Zamiatin, in a piece entitled "It Is Time," added, "An intellectual worker's hammer is thought, and for this hammer it is necessary to have free, completely uninhibited scope: only then will thought be forged and not just carelessly banged out." The journal was readied for publication, but the authorities stopped it before distribution for "not corresponding with the demands of the political moment"; Khodasevich and others assumed that it was the despised lord mayor of Petrograd, Zinoviev, who ordered the seizure of the page proofs.[14]

The banning of *Literaturnaia gazeta* reinforced the concerns of those writers, publicists, and publishers who foresaw the institution of official controls over speech. The Petrograd Union of Cooperative Publishers, led by Vitiazev and Abram Kagan, continued to press for liberalization, including allowing cooperative publishers to own or rent printing presses, ending the state monopoly on the paper supply, and dispensing with preliminary censorship.[15] While some of these economic proposals, in particular the permitting of private printing presses, were realized during 1921, they were accompanied by ever-stricter control over publications on the part of Gosizdat.

In the meantime, the publisher Vitiazev disseminated a questionnaire on censorship to leading intellectuals, many of whom responded with ominous predictions for the future free exchange of ideas. Pitirim Sorokin declared, "The closure of private book publishers and their final nationalization, from my point of view, will have completely predictable consequences for both science and art, and for all of public life." The book crisis would worsen, "for there will be nothing to replace the loss caused by the destruction of the publishers." Moreover, it would lead to "the growth 'of religious orthodoxy and dogmatism' (in this case Communist) to the detriment of science, for science cannot exist without free thought, criticism, and the struggle of ideas." Like medieval kingdoms, "all will depend on state 'inquisitors.' The *approbatio* of the pope will be replaced by the *approbatio* of the state functionary. . . . His opinion will be the law."[16]

The Gosizdat Politotdel

Although these protests may seem prophetic in hindsight, at the time they might have appeared somewhat alarmist. Although some Bolsheviks wanted to quash independent publishing, it was nonetheless permitted, if within tightly circumscribed parameters. In Petrograd several independent cultural publications, most notably *Vestnik literatury,* operated with relatively little hindrance.[17] There was no official consensus as to how much leeway to allow. Lunacharskii agreed with Gorky that given the state's inability to fulfill all of the country's book needs, private and cooperative publishing should be recruited just as private industry under NEP served broader economic interests. Gosizdat's new chairman, N. L. Meshcheriakov, however, stressed that it was incumbent on the state to make sure that "the enemies of the Revolution are not given the opportunity to use these publishers for counterrevolutionary goals."[18] Gosizdat's overview was solidified through the formation of the Politotdel (Political Department), headed by Meshcheriakov and P. I. Lebedev-Polianskii, which was to examine all materials intended for publication. In November 1921 the Politburo decreed that the Politotdel "should not permit obviously reactionary publications, including religious, mystical, antiscientific, politically harmful, etc., books."[19]

Those in charge of the Politotdel, especially Lebedev-Polianskii, held far stricter views on censorship than did Lunacharskii. The Politotdel's local branches were ordered not to permit "obviously reactionary publications." It was explained that "the goal of organizing the Politotdels is the surveillance of private and cooperative publishers and the struggle with literature flooding the market that is politically harmful to the Soviet regime—religious, mystical, and in general harmful to our construction of a new life." The Politotdel censors were to operate in conjunction with other Soviet organs of control, most notably the Cheka. In addition, the regional political-enlightenment committees (*gubpolitprosvety*) were to form political commissions to aid in oversight of private and cooperative publishing and to advise and assist the local Politotdels.[20]

In response to the Politotdel's activities, the journals *Vestnik literatury* and *Letopis' doma literatorov* passionately defended freedom of the press and publishing.[21] In a December 1921 letter to Lunacharskii, leaders of the All-Russian Union of Writers, including Zaitsev, Berdiaev, and Aikhenval'd, cataloged the Politotdel's increasingly capricious offenses. The growth of censorship, they argued, had little to do with political struggle and seemed to target the arts and humanities: "It is already impossible to indicate the borders of censorious examination. There are no norms that can be placed between the permissible and the impermissible. Therefore censorship evaluates even such weightless qualities as mood, reading between the lines and forbidding short stories and poems whose mood does not please the censor." The protest cited a number of examples of picayune interference in fiction and academic prose, complaining that censorship was delving into literary criticism and scholarship. The historian Aleksandr Kizevetter's review of S. F. Platonov's book *Boris Godunov* had been forbidden because it differed from a review by Pokrovskii. Two short works by Berdiaev, *Dostoevsky's Worldview* and *The End of the Renaissance,* were rejected, as was a story by Zaitsev said to have an "absence of foundation [*otsutstvie osnovatel'nosti*]."[22]

Meshcheriakov and Lebedev-Polianskii upbraided Lunacharskii indignantly for taking these complaints seriously and not recognizing that "they have a manifestly preposterous character with a significant share of deliberate lies." They angrily chided the commissar for giving any credence to the base charges against the sophisticated Bolshevik leaders of the Politotdel, who were faithfully carrying out the directives of the Politburo on the prohibition of anti-Soviet literature. It was their duty to allow nothing harmful to the Soviet state, and if they had erred, they asserted, it was on the side of permissiveness—in allowing, for example, the publication of a collection of articles on Oswald Spengler's *Decline of the West* (which would soon be the object of Lenin's special wrath), Semën Frank's *Methodology of Social Sciences,* "and several other manuscripts that we could have forbidden without any qualms." The instances of censorship enumerated in the writers' protest were exceptional and had all been directed at tendentious or idealist literature.[23]

Lunacharskii reprimanded his subordinates for their heavy-handedness. He and his deputies, Pokrovskii and E. A. Litkens, insisted that it was the role of the Politotdel to accept or reject an entire publication and not to outline specific corrections.[24] The Politotdel leaders, however, sharply rejected this rebuke. "You reproach me for the fact that in examining manuscripts we 'delve into literary criticism,'" Meshcheriakov responded irritably. "To a certain extent this is true. But such criticism is necessary, because we must judge a manuscript by its spirit, by the ideas permeating the book, and not by specific expressions. . . . It is possible to spread counterrevolutionary ideas without using a single counterrevolutionary expression."[25] The acute disagreement led to several acrimonious exchanges between Lunacharskii and Lebedev-Polianskii.[26] The Politburo agreed that the censors had overstepped their bounds and instructed the Politotdel to limit its efforts to material directly hostile to the Soviet regime.[27] At the same time, however, party leaders began to take steps that would greatly increase the scope and institutional base of censorship.

The fulminations against the objectionable publications took two diametrically opposed tacks. On the one hand, they were said to be pointless and insignificant and, on the other, extremely pernicious and on the verge of causing serious harm. Meshcheriakov maintained that private publishers had produced nothing of value and that their sudden abundance in the two capitals was due only to coarse profit seeking and a futile effort to resuscitate a bankrupt "bourgeois-intellectual" ideology.[28] And yet Lebedev-Polianskii, Voronskii, and others—including Meshcheriakov—continued to insist that the enemy ideologues had gotten the upper hand. In this they received the adamant support of Lenin, who demanded a much more forceful response. On reading in *Izvestiia* on 5 February 1922 that more than 143 private publishers were registered in Moscow, he ordered an urgent review of the state of the surveillance apparatus, especially on the part of Narkomiust, the Cheka, and the Workers' and Peasants' Inspectorate.[29]

The Politotdel was deemed an insufficient bulwark against the proliferation of heterodoxy, and the Central Committee looked for a more comprehensive solution. At a 21 February 1922 Agitprop meeting, Voronskii, the editor of *Krasnaia nov'*, gave a particularly drastic account of the current dangers: "Private publishers have been issuing belles-lettres, poetry collections, etc., conveying various counterrevolutionary and petty bourgeois ideas, without a single word favorable to Soviet Russia and the Bolsheviks. . . . Mysticism, negativity [*upadochnoe nastroenie*], and isolation from life all find a place in a series of collections, almanacs, etc. White-guard literature has already strolled right by us and built itself a nest in Petrograd (e.g., *Vestnik literatury,* the almanac *Severnye dni,* and similar publications hostile to us). . . . We must realize that when petty bourgeois, philistine, and hostile literature blossoms sumptuously, we must rally those writers who stand close to us, because only thus can we conduct an ideological struggle on the book market."[30] Meshcheriakov added that the Politotdel needed more qualified workers and firmer direction from the Central Committee. In an allusion to his and Lebedev-Polianskii's recent disagreements with Lunacharskii, he complained: "The orders of the Politburo are contradictory. There are rightward and leftward inclinations. Clarity is necessary—as also is the general organization of censorship." The Politotdel needed to be given broader capacities, including the ability not only to prohibit but also to urge private publishers in a particular direction. Despite its efforts to set up local branches, censorship was largely nonexistent in the provinces. He added that the time had come to unite the work of military and political censorship, which still operated more or less independently despite efforts to coordinate. And he echoed Voronskii on the need to wage ideological battle by patronizing sympathetic publishers, favoring those loyal to the regime through economic incentives such as reduced taxes, credit, and more paper.[31]

Agitprop moved toward augmenting intellectual propaganda and providing greater support for Gosizdat and Glavpolitprosvet. In addition to *Pechat' i revoliutsiia* and *Krasnaia nov',* both initiated in 1921, a new thick journal entitled *Pod znamenem marksizma* (Under the Banner of Marxism) appeared in early 1922 to help provide a more comprehensive critique of "bourgeois" ideology.[32] In an introductory letter fervently supporting the endeavor, Trotsky warned that in this "transitory epoch . . . it is extremely likely that idealist and half-idealist philosophical schools and sects will make attempts to control the consciousness of the working youth." Agitprop's task was to mount a multifaceted counteroffensive. Publishers and literary groups deemed close to the party should be supported and encouraged, including the *smenovekhovtsy,* insofar as they were "struggling with the counterrevolutionary mood of the leaders of the Russian intelligentsia."[33]

Lebedev-Polianskii, a Cheka representative, and several others were named to a commission to consolidate censorship, a process that would culminate in the formation of Glavlit several months later. In the meantime, the Politotdel was given more specific directions on stemming the tide of "ideological, mystical, and similar harmful literature" not only in directly political publications, "but also in the spheres of art, culture, theater, etc." (It was noted, however, that this did not mean prohibiting all fiction portraying the "dark side of contemporary Soviet existence," as long as it wasn't hostile to the regime.) Finally, Voronskii and the Proletkult leader Valerian Pletnev were to draft a detailed explication of the character of literature issued by Petrograd private publishers along with a proposal on exercising greater control over them. The Orgburo confirmed the measures on press and censorship proposed by Agitprop and urged their rapid implementation.[34]

The first step in this process, along with forming *Pod znamenem marksizma,* was to look at the most offensive publications. Meshcheriakov was directed to peruse the two most prominent Petrograd literary journals, *Vestnik literatury* and *Letopis' doma literatorov.* His report was rather measured; while noting that certain pieces should not have been printed and advocating the intensification of censorship, he added, "Most of the articles are politically and ideologically neutral. It is therefore my opinion that it is not worth closing either journal. . . . Banning them would evoke the discontent of almost all Petrograd litterateurs, and this would be politically disadvantageous to us." The Orgburo, however, while agreeing with his proposal to strengthen the Politotdel, did not share his concerns about alienating Petrograd literary society and ordered the immediate closure of both journals. The Petrograd Politotdel wasted no time in implementing this decision. In response, the journals' editors resorted to the venerable tactic of rechristening their publications; the House of Litterateurs put forth a new organ named *Literaturnye zapiski* (Literary Notes), and Lutokhin issued an almanac entitled *Utrenniki* (Morning Performers).[35]

In late March 1922 the Politburo authorized uniting all censorship in a single organ, officially within Narkompros but closely linked to the GPU.[36] As the regime thus moved toward the creation of Glavlit, the next stage of the ideological struggle played out in the pages of the new party thick journals. At the Eleventh Party Congress, the Agitprop deputy chief Iakov Iakovlev exhorted his comrades to beware the bourgeois onslaught on the ideological front and to take stock of the weapons at their disposal.[37] A full frontal assault was launched on both criticism of the regime and patently non-Marxist scholarship, explicit and implicit, intentionally combative and naively neutral. Particular venom was reserved for idealist philosophy. The eventual result was predictable, but for a short time the pages of Russian intellectual publications did indeed resound with the wild differences of viewpoint that the authorities found so intolerable.

The Ideological Struggle: Idealist Philosophers and Prophets of Doom

Party leaders targeted a number of arenas in their attacks on the "renaissance of bourgeois ideology," but it was the proliferation of decidedly non-Marxist philosophical ideas, of "religious-mystical" or idealist writings, that brought the most direct response. The Silver Age of Russian philosophy had its final flowering in these years, with the revival of the Petrograd philosophical journal *Mysl'* (Thought) and the publication of a number of important volumes—most famously, the sequel to *Vekhi* entitled *Iz glubiny* (Out of the Depths). In 1922 alone, publishers such as the Petrograd-based Academia and Nauka i Shkola and the Moscow-based Bereg issued several monographs, including Frank's *Study in the Methodology of Social Sciences,* Losskii's *Logic,* and Lev Karsavin's *Noctes Petropolitanae.*[38] Bolshevik publicists responded to these publications with a series of irate reviews in *Pod znamenem marksizma* and other official journals.[39]

Of the works that appeared, none provoked more furor than a collection of articles entitled *Osval'd Shpengler i Zakat Evropy,* reviewing Oswald Spengler's controversial masterpiece, *The Decline of the West.* The first volume of this massive project, published in 1918, had caused a stir in his homeland and was immediately immensely popular within Russian philosophical circles.[40] The *kruzhki* resounded with debates on its prophecies of doom, and Fëdor Stepun gave a series of well-attended lectures at the Free Spiritual Academy.[41] Spengler, at once synthesizing and critiquing the German philosophical legacy, heralded the end of the thousand-year reign of Western civilization, which, as the Great War had proven beyond any conceivable doubt, had entered the winter of its life.[42] To apocalyptic-minded Russian thinkers, this dark pessimism had the ring of prophetic truth.

A similar despair had permeated *Iz glubiny* as well. In Semën Frank's titular essay, "*De Profundis,*" he lamented "the suicide of a great nation," Russia's complete destruction. "If even a few years ago anyone had predicted the depths of degradation into which we have now fallen, and in which we flounder helplessly, no one would have believed him. The gloomiest pessimists never went so far in their predictions, nor approached in their imaginations that final limit of hopelessness to which fate has led us." Frank and his colleagues again concurred that the intelligentsia's spiritual emptiness was to blame. Positivism and materialism were false gods, the chasing of which had undone the moorings not just of socialists, but of liberals and conservatives as well.[43]

Frank, Berdiaev, Stepun, and the economist Iakov Bukshpan saw in Spengler a fellow traveler who shared their distrust of overemphasizing matter over spirit, "civilization" over "culture." And yet, just as several of the gloomiest essays in *Iz glubiny* had concluded with the hope that out of complete destruction would come rebirth and renewal, so, too, the Russian review of Spengler added an optimistic coda to his grim prophecy, a hope that out of the ashes the phoenix would rise. Russia, the ultimate realization of Spengler's apocalyptic warnings of what awaited Europe, could therefore also be the site of its resurrection.[44] Berdiaev, in his essay "Faust's Last Thoughts before Death," noted that while Spengler may have caused a sensation in Europe, it was in Russia that his ideas rang truest. It was there that excessive materialism had reached its logical apocalyptic conclusion, had made itself most evident, and so it had, he optimistically concluded, cleared the way for the longed-for rebirth. Berdiaev declared, "That which we now are living through should at last lead us out of our secluded existence. . . . In Russia there is hidden a secret, at which we ourselves cannot fully guess. . . . Our hour has not yet come."[45]

Stepun's article "Oswald Spengler and the Decline of Europe" provided the most direct critical response to *The Decline of the West,* at once measured and awestruck. "It is the creation if not of a great artist, then at least of a fine craftsman," he gushed, but he added that an annoying inconsistency and "personal haughtiness, almost arrogance," detracted from its overall effect. The contradictions with which it was littered were at once confusing and the center of its originality and significance. He remained transfixed in particular by one of the critical oppositions of Spengler's schema, that of culture and civilization, the former representing the powerful creative spirit, the latter its decline into mechanized and routinized practicality. Spengler brilliantly argued for the inevitable circular motion of the history of specific cultures, "from spring to winter, from culture to civilization, from life to death." Stepun concluded that Spengler's prophetic insight more than made up for any lack of specific philosophical originality or logical contradictions.[46]

Frank, in "The Crisis of Western Culture," seized upon the mantra that Western secular civilization was in the process of decaying, and he fervently agreed with Spengler's firm rejection of universal history, "with its vapid rationalistic optimism expressed in the theory of 'progress.'" Spengler shared with the Russian Slavophiles an abhorrence of contemporary secular European civilization and, Frank felt, had shown just how decrepit it had become. On the other hand, Frank criticized Spengler's failure to appreciate the central role of Christianity in Western culture and looked to the purer spirituality of pre-Renaissance Europe. Noting that threads of this spirituality had survived into modern times, he suggested that a religious reawakening could somehow save Europe (and Russia) from the current catastrophe.[47]

Zakat Evropy deeply upset Bolshevik leaders, despite their fundamental concurrence with the notion that bourgeois European civilization was bankrupt.[48] Lenin furiously denounced the volume as a "literary cover for a Whiteguard organization."[49] Its seemingly esoteric discussions challenged Marxism's core teleology; in place of dialectical materialism, predicated on the march of universal history, of science, progress, and the perfectibility of man, Spengler wrote of circular motion, decay, decline, and reincarnation. Party publicists quickly condemned the book, declaring that Berdiaev and Frank had found nothing new to say in the dozen years since the publication of *Vekhi* and seemed "to want to make the same mistakes and turn out to be false prophets all over again." Their unempirical dismissal of historical progress had been proven entirely incorrect by history itself, by the triumph of the worker-peasant forces and the establishment of the world's first socialist state. It was unsurprising that Berdiaev and company, who had long babbled about a "crisis of consciousness," had found in Spengler a kindred spirit. The Russia these mystics read into Spengler was rooted in "the most harmful aesthetically perceived gloom of Dostoevsky, an exotic, benighted Russia, having only with difficulty survived the burden of the Asiatic."[50]

The Bolsheviks found utterly unacceptable the Russian Spenglerites' contention that what had been born in the fire of war and revolution represented the last stages of decline and not the start of the final, golden historical age. Georgii Piatakov denounced Spengler's thinking as "vapid idealistic muddle, utterly unscientific pretentious-mystical rubbish," a pseudophilosophical defense of modern imperialism, which no real Marxist could engage in at any level. Spengler and his Russian advocates were mistaken; it was not Europe and its culture that were about to perish, but the world of the bourgeoisie. Their affinity for Spengler, the Bolshevik writer V. Vaganian noted, was due to a misunderstanding of the laws of history. Although "we also think that 'the West' is entering its dusk, its twilight," the proletariat knew that it was precisely bourgeois culture, and most of all the mysticism so revered by Berdiaev, Frank, and Stepun, that had proven bankrupt.[51]

The Ideological Struggle: Reinventing Dostoevsky at One Hundred

While the furor over *The Decline of the West* and its Russian reviewers reached the Kremlin itself and directly contributed to Lenin's decision to exile these inveterate ideological foes, it was in the memorialization of a native genius, Dostoevsky, that a more protracted and nuanced debate spilled forth.[52] Spengler referred to Russia only obliquely, and his Russian commentators differed with him on several critical matters, most notably the role of religion.[53] Dostoevsky, on the other hand, spoke directly to the accursed questions with which the intelligentsia occupied itself. From the time of *Vekhi,* the current generation of idealist intellectuals had seen his scathing portraits of the revolutionary intelligentsia, and in particular *The Demons,* as their primal source; he was heralded as the unquestioned prophet of the Russian tragedy that they had the misfortune to witness.

The years 1921 and 1922 were replete with literary jubilees. There were reminiscences in honor of Pushkin, Nekrasov, and other literary giants, as well as memorials for the recently deceased Blok and Korolenko. The question whether Blok and Korolenko were revolutionary martyrs or disappointed and conscientious critics of its failings was hotly debated; such also was the case with the legacy of Pushkin, whose caché continued to be used to promote a variety of points of view.[54] Perhaps most controversial, however, was the proliferation of Dostoevskiana, which was more immediately divisive and fraught with weighty symbolic baggage.

The portrayal of Dostoevsky as genius-Cassandra of the rotten Russian positivist ethos predated the Revolution, of course,[55] but it became particularly pronounced after 1917, as his admirers tried to make sense of the tragedy that they believed had befallen the motherland. "It is impossible not to see Dostoevskii as the prophet of the Russian revolution," Berdiaev asserted in "Specters of the Russian Revolution," his essay in *Iz glubiny.* "Dostoevskii showed that Russian revolutionism is a metaphysical and religious phenomenon, and not a political and social one. Thus, religiously, he was able to grasp the nature of Russian socialism. Russian socialism is occupied with the question of whether or not there is a God, and Dostoevskii foresaw how bitter the fruits of Russian socialism would be."[56] During his short time at MGU in 1920–21, Berdiaev led a seminar on the amoralism, maximalism, and apocalypticism of characters such as Pëtr Verkhovenskii and Ivan

Karamazov. From these seminars he compiled a book, which the Politotdel quickly banned.[57] Dostoevsky, Berdiaev held, had depicted the inner nature of revolutionaries with prophetic foresight, having seen "in them a mighty spirit of the Antichrist, the ambition to make a god of man." This diabolical striving to perfect the material world was at the heart of Dostoevsky's (and Berdiaev's) criticism of the Revolution. Berdiaev argued that Dostoevsky had shown brilliantly how socialism would lead to a nightmarish anti-utopia, particularly in *The Demons* and in "The Legend of the Grand Inquisitor" in *Brothers Karamazov.* "Dostoevsky foresaw the fatal process that in a revolution leads to loss of liberty in unbelievable slavery and prophesied even the details of its windings."[58]

It is of little surprise that Berdiaev's writings on Dostoevsky were prohibited in Soviet Russia. He made no attempt to appease the censor in his effusive accounts of Dostoevsky's devastatingly accurate hostility to socialism: "The revolution is by nature 'amoral,' placing itself above any consideration of good and evil (and in this respect the counterrevolution is outwardly very much like it). Dostoievsky opposed the revolution and its morality on behalf of the dignity of human personality and its moral value. Revolution is madness, an obsession that attacks the personality, paralyses its freedom, and subjects it completely to an impersonal and inhuman force."[59] Although Berdiaev's views were not allowed in print, they were well known through his lectures and shared by a significant portion of the cultural intelligentsia. Not all of the commentary adopted his openly political tone, but there was much that the Bolsheviks nevertheless found displeasing.

The critic and literary historian Iul'ii Aikhenval'd also emphasized Dostoevsky's current resonance. "Despite the passing of many decades, he remains a contemporary of our excruciating times—precisely because he was its precursor and forecaster." Aikhenval'd described Dostoevsky as the "celebrated novelist-psychologist of tumult, the painter of catastrophes." In tune with the chaos and rebelliousness of the human spirit, Dostoevsky understood that the Revolution was predicated most of all on man's internal, psychological turmoil: "*The Demons* is the living, animated epigraph of the current bloody chronicle; we live today as if intensely and tormentedly rereading this novel as it turns into reality. We compose it all over again along with the author; we see dreams carried out while we are awake, and we are stunned by the clairvoyance and premonition of an agonized dreamer. Like a kind of sorcerer, Dostoevsky augured the Russian Revolution." For all Dostoevsky's complex literary genius, Aikhenval'd held, his political views were clear and unambiguous; revolution and socialism could bring nothing but sorrow and chaos to Russia. Dostoevsky, he wryly concluded, had no place in a socialist republic, and he found it inappropriate that such a state would officially celebrate his jubilee.[60]

A number of thinkers focused on Dostoevsky's religious worldview. Nikolai Losskii argued that Dostoevsky demonstrated how "Satanic natures" are an inevitable consequence of a rejection of God. The path to evil resulted even and especially when this rejection arose out of moral outrage and a desire to improve upon God's works, as shown most famously in Ivan Karamazov. The Antichrist hid himself in the guise of just such an atheistic humanism.[61] Lev Karsavin added that in Dostoevsky's writings, one sensed "our entire Russian life—wild and burdensome, but profound; all of our tortuous questions, all of our unwashedness and all of our idealism. . . . Forty years have passed since Dostoevsky's death, one hundred since the day of his birth, and the content of his thoughts and observations is all the closer to us, continues to live in us, poses our contemporary questions." Dostoevsky had shown that the only solution to these questions was through (Christian) love and a religious worldview. He had fervently rejected both socialist and "Catholic" aspirations to realize an ideal life on Earth, which inevitably led to despotism and slavery.[62]

Pitirim Sorokin, who often disagreed with the idealist philosophers on other matters, reached a similar conclusion in his "Dostoevsky's Testaments." The moral he distilled from Dostoevsky was very much akin to the Vekhists' exhortation that Russia could be saved only through individual moral improvement and not external changes. Dostoevsky, Sorokin explained, had argued persuasively that only an internally produced "religious-moral energetic love," not excluding love for one's enemies, could guide a people to a healthy collective life. "*Authentic freedom* consists not in unrestrained license [*raznuzdannost'*], as they suggest nowadays, but 'rather in the conquering of oneself and one's will, in order always to be your own genuine master.'" The purveyors of the socialist idea believed that "injustice would disappear and an earthly paradise could be established" simply "by using violence to change laws and social institutions," but they were false prophets who would produce "neither brotherhood, nor liberty, nor equality. . . . It is impossible," Sorokin insisted, "to save people with violence."[63]

The Bolsheviks at the time did not quite know what to do with Dostoevsky, taking their cues in large part from Gorky's lifelong ambivalence toward Russia's "evil genius," whose portraits of depravity he saw as utterly reactionary. According to Bonch-Bruevich, Lenin fully shared this blend of virulent dislike for Dostoevsky's politics with recognition of his indisputable talent.[64] As the jubilees and publications proliferated in 1921, party cultural leaders felt the need to rebut the popular portrayal of Dostoevsky. One Bolshevik critic warned: "The enemies of the Russian Revolution . . . are attempting to make Dostoevsky into the prophet of the Russian Revolution—more precisely, of the counterrevolution—who several decades ago perspicaciously indicated that the Russian Revolution would usher in the reign of the Antichrist, bloody chaos, boorishness, etc. 'Read Dostoevsky!' they proclaim, so that the reader of Dostoevsky's works will find a condemnation of Bolshevism, internationalism, and other things hateful to the counterrevolution."[65] Official literary commentators, including Lunacharskii himself, were unwilling to accept the idea that this unquestioned genius might be the intractable enemy of the Revolution and religious mystic that the contemporary counterrevolutionary held him to be.

What emerged might be termed the soft line on Dostoevsky, an effort to rescue him for the Bolsheviks. The first two prominent salvos in this reinterpretation were Lunacharskii's essay "Dostoevsky as an Artist and Thinker" and the Marxist critic Valerian Pereverzev's "Dostoevsky and Revolution." Pereverzev was keenly aware of Dostoevsky's contemporary resonance: "To speak of Dostoevsky still means to speak of the most burning and profound questions of our current life. Seized by the whirlwind of the mighty Revolution, spinning amid the problems it poses, passionately and painfully aware of all the vicissitudes of the revolutionary tragedy, we find ourselves in Dostoevsky, we find in him such a painfully passionate treatment of the problems of revolution that it is as if the writer were living through the revolutionary storm with us." Pereverzev asserted that the rebellious spirit was a fundamental aspect of Dostoevsky's ethos and that the writer expressed a deep ambivalence toward revolution. "Read Dostoevsky, and you will understand much more of the drama experienced in the Russian Revolution than previously; you will condone and accept many things as necessary, which previously you neither understood nor condoned." While agreeing that Dostoevsky had depicted the revolutionary underground with "hysterical malice," he had no problem with Dostoevsky's grim portrayal of how events would unfold. He decried the efforts of "Blackhundred publicists" to "present Dostoevsky as their ally in the struggle against the revolutionary movement," asserting that despite appearances, the writer had more in common and even sympathized with the revolutionaries whom he seemed to condemn. Pereverzev was not above integrating Dostoevsky's disapproval, suggesting that the writer's cautions concerning revolutionary excess might be salutary for committed Communists who found their unfamiliar power too intoxicating. "He who is afraid of despotism, terror, blood, and corpses is not a revolutionary and in vain appeals in the name of Revolution. . . . The Revolution has in all of its horror, in all of its immoralism, an undoubted cleansing fire of liberty."[66]

Lunacharskii was not quite so bold in his interpretation, but he also argued that Dostoevsky was as much fascinated as repulsed by socialism. The commissar claimed that even Ivan Karamazov and the fanatics in *The Demons* were representative of one aspect of Dostoevsky's own multivocal psyche, sympathizing with the revolutionary cause despite the author's best intentions. He was all too aware of the injustices of the autocracy; even his Christianity carried in it the "maximum revolutionariness." Lunacharskii assigned Dostoevsky the exact inverse of the position posited for him by Berdiaev and his colleagues: that of prophet, not of doom but of Russia as world missionary, leading to a higher historical stage despite the unavoidable suffering. "The Russian people, according to Dostoevsky, precisely out of its forsakenness, its torment, its chains, could bring forth all of the necessary highest spiritual qualities, which the West, having become philistine [*omeshchanivshiisia*], would never obtain."[67]

Not all pro-Soviet commentators subscribed to this reinterpretation. The critic V. M. Friche remarked dryly in the Narkompros weekly *Narodnoe prosveshchenie,* "Dostoevsky is a writer whom the working class can hardly consider 'its own.'" While acknowledging his indisputable genius, he argued that Dostoevsky represented the class interest of the urban petty bourgeoisie, and that, disappointingly, "the workers' democracy has, in fact, nothing to learn from him."[68] Others shared this reluctance to accept Dostoyevsky as a rebel in disguise; Friche's point of view was certainly closer to what Gorky had been arguing in the years before the Revolution.

But the reinvention of Dostoevsky as revolutionary, the sanction of Lunacharskii and other leading cultural Bolsheviks, provided the cover for a continued proliferation of Dostoevskiana. During the 1921 jubilees, it was not uncommon for Lunacharskii and Pereverzev to lecture at the same gatherings as Aikhenval'd and other "bourgeois" litterateurs.[69] Two volumes of Dostoevsky studies, the first of which included numerous articles by the soon-to-be deported philosophers, appeared in 1922 and 1924. Pereverzev continued to expand his analyses, and the previously unpublished chapter from *The Demons* with Stavrogin's infamous confession was published in two different journals in 1922.[70] Still, the Bolshevik "soft line" on Dostoevsky coexisted with a persistent hostility toward the man who seemed so hostile to revolution and sympathetic to conservative Orthodoxy. By the time of Stalin's Great Break at the end of the decade,

Pereverzev found himself under fire, and Dostoevsky became once again persona non grata among the Bolshevik cultural elite.[71]

The Ideological Struggle: Changing Signposts

Apprehension that Russia might not recover from the recent catastrophic events played a significant role in the doomsayers' auguries. As it became clear that the Whites would lose the Civil War, patriotic concerns over the future of the motherland led some conservative émigrés to reassess their opposition to Bolshevism. In 1921 a group led by N. V. Ustrialov and Iu. V. Kliuchnikov put forth a volume entitled *Smena vekh* (A Change of Signposts). The book's title was an unambiguous homage to *Vekhi* (Signposts), the prerevolutionary clarion call for intellectuals to abandon their hostility to the regime and look to their own internal moral development.[72] The Bolsheviks, though wary of its nationalist overtones and predictions of a Bonapartist Thermidor, cautiously welcomed *smenovekhovstvo* as a way to further divide the emigration and convince the intelligentsia to give up its futile and destructive opposition. "Beginning in 1921," one historian has noted, "the Soviet leaders took great pains to legitimize their rule by portraying themselves as heirs to Russian national traditions and defenders of Russian soil against foreign intervention." While always suspicious of the authors' motivations, the Politburo, hoping to convert more of the technical and professional intelligentsia to serve the Soviet state, for a time supported the Smenovekhovite newspaper *Nakanune* (On the Eve) and invited Kliuchnikov and Iu. N. Potekhin to Moscow.[73]

Several of the original *Vekhi* authors, joined by other like-minded intellectuals, categorically rejected *smenovekhovstvo*, especially its attempt to link itself to the Vekhist legacy. The House of Litterateurs held a series of debates on *Smena vekh* chaired by N. M. Volkovyskii. Intellectuals who had come to support the regime, including S. A. Adrionov, N. A. Gredeskul, and V. G. Tan (Bogoraz), dominated the first two debates. Still, most participants seemed to sympathize with P. K. Guber, who was skeptical of these exhortations to support the Soviet regime.[74] The next two debates, which took place in early 1922, featured speakers who scorned *Smena vekh*, including the Vekhist and former Kadet Aleksandr Izgoev and the publicist J. Clemens (I. A. Kleinman). Izgoev, Clemens, and Guber then repeated their talks at several public events held at Petrograd University, in which, significantly, students of the city's VUZy actively participated.[75]

Criticism of *smenovekhovstvo* began to appear in the already suspect Petrograd literary periodicals such as *Vestnik literatury*. In his December

1921 article "'*Smena Vekh*' as a Social Symptom," Pitirim Sorokin asserted that the *smenovekhovtsy* were interested only in a strong government and did not care what form it took. "Today," he wrote caustically, these unprincipled opportunists "are prepared to shout, 'All hail Caesar!' and tomorrow, 'All hail Brutus!' if this Brutus will be a strong and supported power." *Smena vekh* expressed the ideology of those interested in a secure and stable state, particularly *spetsy* and those vying for commercial concessions (whom he called "*gosklienty*," or state clients). As often happened, this social group had taken its own interests for those of the entire nation. On the other hand, *smenovekhovstvo* would not win over the independent intelligentsia (a category from which Sorokin definitively excluded the *spetsy*), much less the peasantry or the proletariat. He hoped that there might still be room for the intelligentsia to operate in a semi-autonomous public sphere, a standpoint that he referred to as the Anglo-Saxon position.[76]

Whatever their suspicions of the *smenovekhovtsy*, the Bolshevik leadership was far more distrustful of those who repudiated reconciliation. Criticism of *smenovekhovstvo* was both a threat to its recruitment of *spetsy* and a clear indication of the obstacles it still had to overcome to win over the intelligentsia. Those who spoke against *Smena vekh* were clearly unwilling to reconcile with the new regime and could only do it harm. Indeed, the non-Communist intelligentsia had few good things to say about *smenovekhovstvo*. Izgoev even disagreed with Sorokin's contention that there remained room for autonomous public action. True liberty, he argued, lay only in complete moral and spiritual independence from the current regime.[77] Izgoev and several other publicists issued a collection of essays based on the earlier debates entitled O *smene vekh* (On the Change of Signposts), which reviewed their primary reasons for rejecting reconciliation with the new order.

Smena vekh, in Izgoev's opinion, was "to a very large extent a purely political declaration," far more so than its supposed precursor, *Vekhi*. Izgoev rejected the claim to intellectual lineage: "Beneath some external resemblances, there is an enormous difference in principles between the old and new 'Vekhists.'" Although the Vekhists had advised intellectuals to rethink their categorical opposition to the old regime, "they were far from deifying the state. Their God was commensurate neither with social institutions nor with human establishments." The *smenovekhovtsy*, on the other hand, effected precisely such a deification of the state, and they subordinated the "moral and spiritual character of the intelligentsia" to it. In so doing, they altered what for Izgoev was the fundamental task of the intelligentsia. "The intelligentsia did not, does not, and will not have physical, material power. . . . The power of the intelligentsia is only moral, and spiritual. When a country does not sense this moral power of the intelligentsia, the harmony of life is drastically disturbed." Such was the tragedy of the moment: the intelligentsia had lost its moral authority. Furthermore, Izgoev wrote, the authors of *Smena vekh* had not only missed what was most central in *Vekhi,* but also misunderstood the nature of the current regime. Their conviction that the dictatorship of the proletariat would gradually fade into an ideologically nationalist state was hopelessly naive and not shared, he grimly noted, by the Bolsheviks themselves.[78]

The critic A. B. Petrishchev wryly remarked that the debate over *Smena vekh* was more interesting than the book. He wondered why its authors had gone to such length to justify their desire to return to Russia, adding that if they wanted to change their signposts, it was their own personal business. Like Izgoev, he found their reverence of the state above all else problematic. "And so, our faith in the absolute is supposed to become relative, and what is relative in life should be absolute (property, for example?); we must deify the state (recognize what is mystical in the police?) and, it seems, debase the Divine." But Petrishchev, unlike his Vekhist colleague, saw a substantial similarity between the two collections; both claimed to look inward while in fact criticizing others. For Petrishchev, the appearance of and reaction to *Smena vekh* was primarily interesting as a symptom of the personal inclinations (and naïveté) of the emigration. He found all the references to the coming Russian Thermidor to be vacuous nonsense, and he dismissed any notion that the Russian Revolution was already turning into a "nationalist" phenomenon.[79]

J. Clemens saw nothing either new or particularly noteworthy in the collection. Indeed, General Brusilov had called on Russian officers to back the Soviet state out of patriotic motives during the Polish invasion, a far more pivotal moment. The attempt to unite great power nationalism with socialist internationalism, religious messianism with revolutionary maximalism, Clemens found inconsistent, "hermaphroditic," irreconcilable. Their claim that Russia had somehow leapt ahead of the rest of Europe, when in fact its economy, culture, and so on were centuries behind, was pure fantasy. In the end the "ecstatic outburst" of the *smenovekhovtsy* was but a projection of their own desires. "The *smenovekhovtsy* believe in the sorcery of words, but only *their own words.* They want to convey, to introduce, not only into the general consciousness, but into the consciousness of their enemies of not so long ago, their magic incantations, their messianic prayers."[80]

O smene vekh received less direct reaction than the Spengler volume or other philosophical works from Bolshevik literati, who were more occupied with responding to the *smenovekhovtsy* themselves. The Bolshevik allies present at the House of Litterateurs' debates did immediately raise objections. Gredeskul retorted that Izgoev had gotten it exactly wrong: whereas *Vekhi* was an example of a reactionary, individualistic mood, *Smena vekh* was full of belief in the victorious Revolution.[81] The most prominent party leaders to review *O smene vekh* were Preobrazhenskii and Voronskii. Voronskii highlighted the damage that might be done by Izgoev's vocal opposition to intellectuals' "coming over" to the new order. "*Smena vekh* summons the intelligentsia to active support of the Soviet regime. Izgoev answers: that is not the point; one needn't support the Soviet regime, one should be filled with religious consciousness and come to believe in an absolute," Voronskii noted. "Izgoev counsels that one should [refuse to] cooperate with the Soviet regime not only in the political sphere, but also in the economic sphere." This so-called independent public opinion would in reality serve the "new filth," the NEP men. The prophecies of the *Vekhisty* had already been tried and failed, Voronskii added; the intelligentsia had blundered in its overwhelming rejection of socialism. There was no reason to think that they would succeed this time.[82]

Like Voronskii, Preobrazhenskii recalled Izgoev's participation in the "renegade group" of Vekhists who had deserted the people after 1905. Despite the utter defeat of the bourgeoisie, Izgoev and his comrades remained loyal to their "old master." Preobrazhenskii mocked their mystical turn and elevation of man's relationship with God. Izgoev, as was the habit of these intellectual lackeys, hid his bourgeois allegiances under pretty phrases and a specious claim to absolute eternal truth. Especially suspect was his advocacy of an independent, classless intelligentsia that would never bow to any state power—when what he really meant was that it should reject the Soviet regime. Although Preobrazhenskii also disaffirmed the Smenovekhovite claim that Communist internationalism would give way to Russian nationalism, he nevertheless held to the party line that whatever their motives, the *smenovekhovtsy* were helping the Soviet cause.[83]

Those associated with *O smene vekh* did not escape notice. By the time the volume was issued in spring 1922, the fate of the House of Litterateurs was already in doubt, the Central Committee had banned its *Letopis'*, and Izgoev, Petrishchev, and Kleinman would soon be included on the list of deportees.[84] At the same time, the official tolerance of *smenovekhovstvo* gave way to more open disapproval, particularly after Lenin's stroke in May 1922, when Zinoviev and Bubnov began to direct the ideological attack. At the Twelfth Party Conference, in August 1922, Zinoviev allowed that the *smenovekhovtsy* had been useful, but he warned that they were not true friends of the regime.[85] Yet even as relations with Kliuchnikov and his colleagues deteriorated, those who openly opposed reconciliation were still seen as far more pernicious foes, as the party continued to woo *spetsy* (and other intellectuals) to work for the construction of the socialist state.[86]

The Ideological Struggle: Sociological and Economic Critiques of Socialism

Not all intellectuals who expressed anxiety over Russia's impending doom did so in the metaphysical or religious tone typical of Berdiaev, Stepun, and Frank. Some analyzed Russia's fate in the language of scientific analysis. Their criticism, with its empirical, positivist veneer, was all the more irritating to the Marxist leaders of the new order, who claimed a monopoly on objective scientific truth. The premier forum for the writings of Pitirim Sorokin, Boris Brutskus, and like-minded social scientists was the journal *Ekonomist,* the organ of the eleventh (economic) division of the Russian Technical Society. Its editor was Dalmat Lutokhin, who also ran *Vestnik literatury* and later the controversial almanac *Utrenniki.* The journals *Ekonomicheskoe vozrozhdenie* (Economic Revival) and the iconoclastic *Artel'noe delo* also published articles that tended to criticize official social, economic, agronomic, and cooperative policies.[87]

Sorokin wrote on a variety of cultural, social, and other matters, but his expertise lay in the science of sociology. One of the first in his field, he depicted in a positivist, scientific manner a postrevolutionary Russia very different from the official Marxist prognosis. He theorized that the preceding catastrophic years of war, revolution, civil war, and famine had led to the utter destruction of Russian society. While explicitly differentiating his pessimism from that of the Spenglerites, he saw the cumulative effects of these horrific events as having terrible consequences not just for individuals, but also for the collective mental health and vitality of the Russian people. "The war and a series of catastrophic events in recent years cannot but have destroyed the psychic balance of all cultured humankind, and most of all Russian society," he wrote. He strongly disagreed, however, with the Spenglerites' conclusion that Europe was in its final crisis; he scoffed at the budding Eurasianist belief that salvation would come from the East; and he adamantly defended "scientifism,"[88] which was not in the least to blame for the crisis but would in fact be instrumental in resolving it and was not at all incompatible with a religious view of the world.[89]

In a series of articles in *Ekonomist* and *Artel'noe delo,* Sorokin drew a sociological portrait of a nation brutally decimated, deprived of its vital forces, and unlikely to recover soon from eight years of prolonged catastrophe.

"One of the many consequences of a long and exhausting war is the change of the social organization of the warring group in the direction of a military-socialist type society," featuring unlimited government power and few individual rights. "An ideal-typical military-socialist society is one in which: 1) the degree of the regime's interference, tutelage, and regulation of life, behavior, and the interactions of citizens is unlimited, 2) the degree of autonomous 'self-determination' of its members in their behavior and their interrelations is destroyed, made close to nil. . . . People [in such a society] are not autonomous individuals, but directed and administered by the regime; they are not anything inherently valuable, but simply the property of the latter. Speaking in juridical terms, there are no completely private-legal relations; rather, all relations are legally public, regulated from above." Sorokin's prediction of a totalitarian regime, where the "regime is higher than the law," affords no civil rights, is completely centralized, and allows no private property (or any private sphere), was based on the theory that such was the result of militarization, of the marshaling of resources for total war. In addition, the population of such countries was made more suitable for such a government by the loss of its best and most useful members, the decline of the general "quality" of the population.[90]

War, he argued, reduced not only the total population, but also its health, energy, morality, and intellectual forces by disproportionately affecting its best elements. Nations thus continued to pay the price for wars well after they ended because of the overall "degradation" of the population. War did not "give birth to heroes," but in fact killed them off. And those who survived would be morally deformed by their experience; "*function creates the organ: every action has a ricochet effect on the spirit and organism of the actor.*" The murder, violence, cruelty, deception, theft, and spying necessary to the conduct of war left their mark on the society and led to a decline in respect for life, freedom, and the rights and property of the individual. These effects were especially pronounced after a civil war. Sorokin framed his theory in scientific terms and used examples from throughout history, but the real object of his analysis was patently obvious. Russia, which had always toiled under despotic governments, had become, owing to its recent cataclysms, a prime target for military socialism. Still, he did express some optimism about the potential for NEP, contending that with the end of the Civil War there were already hopeful signs of a decline in this trend.[91]

Sorokin had recently traveled to the Volga region to observe the effects of the famine.[92] Horror-stricken by what he saw, he analyzed the influence of hunger in human affairs; the book, to have been published by Vitiazev's Kolos press, was immediately banned by the censors, but several extracts from it managed to appear in *Ekonomist.*[93] His conclusions dovetailed with what he had previously written concerning war; he focused again on how catastrophic events inevitably lead to national decline. The economic effects of a massive famine, he argued, would soon manifest themselves as degradations of the entire sociopolitical structure. Like war, famine could hasten a state's movement toward greater authoritarianism and coercion, the result being the loss of autonomy and individual freedoms and government involvement in all spheres of life.[94] The collective social consciousness became deformed in situations of great distress such as famine, favoring those elements concerned with matters of basic survival. And among the ideologies most suited to this situation, Sorokin claimed, was socialism (communism), which in its redistributionary goals and coercive methods resonated with the needs of the moment. "It is important only that the *ideology gives its blessing to these acts of seizure, partitioning,* [and] *equalization.*"[95]

Sorokin's theories, in suggesting that the Soviet victory had been the result of war and famine suffered by a devastated population, and not due to the triumph of historical inevitability of which the Bolsheviks were the vanguard, were already infuriating enough to party leaders. The claim that their regime was neither new nor progressive, but rather represented ancient authoritarianism in a new "sauce" (as Sorokin put it), contradicted every tenet of Marxist ideology. Moreover, in concluding each one of his pieces with a faint note of optimism, Sorokin indicated that the new order's prospects for continued success depended entirely on the artificial continuation of the catastrophe.

Having advanced his scientific sociological explanation of the Revolution, Sorokin then took his argument several steps further and proved himself as plaintive a prophet of doom as Spengler. In a lament entitled "I Believe, O Lord, Help Me in My Disbelief!" he conveyed unadulterated pessimism: "I don't know . . . I want to believe that the history of the Russian people is not finished . . . But 'God help me in my disbelief' . . . The losses which have been incurred are too great and irreparable, the contemporary condition of the Russian people is too bleak." The population decrease, both biological and due to the loss of territory, had been enormous, but "far more terrible are the consequences of the *qualitative damage to the population,* which we have suffered over these years." Russia had been deprived of its most gifted citizens, and the remaining "second-class" people, he alleged, would pass their inferior abilities on to their offspring ("bad seeds," he explained, would reap a "bad harvest"), which would lead to a process of "biological degradation." His harsh words, Sorokin claimed, were called forth by his deep love and sorrow for Russia, and by the belief that the first step toward surmounting these enormous obstacles was to recognize reality.[96]

Most of the articles in *Ekonomist* and similar journals took a more strictly economic look at conditions. Of those critical of the new order, the most thorough was an analysis by the economist Boris Brutskus entitled "Problems of National Economy in a Socialist System."[97] In lectures at the Petrograd Agricultural Academy, Brutskus had emphasized that "quite apart from the conditions produced by the [civil] war," the Communist system was "intrinsically unsound and must inevitably break down."[98] Brutskus was unusual in questioning the statist principles that had led even many non-Communist intellectuals to advocate centralized economic planning.[99] He argued that Marxism failed to explain how the value of labor could be properly calculated. As a result, the labor theory of value did not provide a way for the state to make accurate estimates necessary for economic planning. He maintained that rent and capital must be retained even in a socialist system. True value was inherently subjective, was based on intangible social needs, and could be determined only by the market. "Thus the socialist state," he concluded, "is not in a position, even with the help of all its scientific theory and immense statistical apparatus, to measure the needs of its citizens or to reduce these needs to one level; for this reason it is unable to provide production with the guidance it needs." In addition, without the capitalist entrepreneurial spirit, initiative and innovation would suffer, and the result would be "immense indolence and conservatism." Socialism in practice—that is, War Communism—had already demonstrated the abysmal failure of the command system to reinvigorate any sphere of the economy, and it had ended with the admission by the Communists themselves that a partial return to market relations was necessary.[100]

The Bolshevik leadership responded with predictable fury to Brutskus's prescient economic analysis and to Sorokin's wide-ranging sociological critique. From its perspective, a scientifically posed debunking of socialism was even more pernicious than Berdiaev's neo-idealist "mysticism" or Izgoev's Vekhist morality. An ideology claiming a monopoly on scientific truth could not allow *any* competing viewpoints, much less one that predicted its failure as a system for organizing society. The responses were swift and vehement. In his "On the Meaning of Militant Materialism," Lenin declared that Sorokin's views in "On the Influence of War" were those of a serf owner (*krepostnik*), reactionary, and "diplomatic lackey of clericalism [*popovshchiny*]." Such types, he hinted ominously, would be much better off living in one of the bourgeois "democracies" with which they were so enamored.[101] Bubnov added that Sorokin "regards the masses as a starving, unruly 'throng,' and treats Communist ideology as a vagabond ideology." He bitterly objected to the fact that "Mr. Sorokin teaches this most excellent 'sociology' in the worker-peasant state, at the expense of this state, to hundreds of youths, among which are both workers and peasants!"[102]

Other Bolshevik critics debunked the triumphal pessimism of these "anti-Soviet" economists. The traces of capitalist restoration that Sorokin, Brutskus, and others claimed to find in NEP had nothing to do with the failure of Communism, retorted the Petrograd Gosizdat journal *Kniga i revoliutsiia*. V. I. Nevskii, a Petrograd Narkompros leader, saw in Brutskus's portrayal of the genetic flaws in socialist economic practice yet another attempt of the defeated representatives of the bourgeoisie to find a ray of hope in the supposedly inevitable "transformation" of the Communist system. A comprehensive critique of Brutskus by the young economist V. E. Motylev noted that it was precisely the growing strength of Marxist economic theory that called forth such vicious attacks.[103] He asserted that there was not much science in Brutskus's piece, but that it demanded a response. In affirming that Marxism offered no economic blueprint, Brutskus was confusing scientific socialism with its utopian counterpart. Motylev insisted that socialism would be able to develop a rational system for determining value far superior to the arbitrary (*stikhiinyi*) processes of capitalism, and that this would indeed be based on the Marxist labor theory of value. He scathingly rejected Brutskus's insistence that the competition supposedly created under capitalist conditions was the only guarantor of true individual creativity. From the Bolshevik point of view, as P. Mesiatsev noted, Brutskus's work had nothing to do with economic science and everything to do with politics and propaganda.[104]

"On Anti-Soviet Groups among the Intelligentsia"

In addition to pointed replies to individual books and articles, the Bolshevik leadership began to develop a more holistic response to the resurgence of bourgeois ideology. Lenin ordered a counterattack, including the use of repressive measures and a resolution not to turn away from terror when necessary. The March 1922 Eleventh Party Congress reaffirmed a commitment to intensifying agitation and propaganda, especially in response to "bourgeois" efforts to influence the masses.[105] Lenin's rhetoric grew ever more vituperative, and he and Dzerzhinskii began to plan the expulsion of the most pestiferous intellectuals. The coincidence of Lenin's first directives on the expulsions with Semashko's warnings regarding the recent physicians' congress helped to cement further the leadership's conviction that the bourgeois publications were inextricably linked to the other manifestations of intellectual hostility in the public sphere: the struggle over university reform and the "corporatist," antistate stance of independent-minded *spets* societies. The Politburo, on

Lenin's urging, commissioned a GPU report on all these phenomena. The resulting memo, "On Anti-Soviet Groupings among the Intelligentsia," proved the catalyst for a multifaceted campaign against intellectuals with the deportations at its core.

Iakov Agranov, who drafted the memo, did not mince words; because of NEP, a clear and present danger had arisen. "The anti-Soviet intelligentsia is making broad use of the possibilities now open for organizing and gathering its forces created by the conciliatory course of the Soviet regime and the weakened activity of the repressive organs." Using scholarly societies and private publishers as their organizational base, they had new hope for their restorationist goals. Their "main arenas of struggle" were the VUZy, societies, the press, institutional congresses, theaters, cooperatives, trusts, and religious institutions. Agranov detailed the grim state of each, beginning with the struggle for autonomy in higher education, which was especially troubling because of the efforts of "counterrevolutionary elements" to inculcate an "anti-Communist and anti-Soviet spirit" in the studentry. He then briefly described the situation with scientific and cultural societies, with private publishers, *spets* congresses, cooperatives, and religious groups. It was imperative, he concluded, to recognize that these groups could in time become "a dangerous force" and must therefore be met with decisive measures.[106]

On 8 June 1922 Unshlikht reported to the Politburo, which approved a series of measures that came to serve as the regime's integrated response to the "renaissance of bourgeois ideology" in the public sphere.[107] The Politburo, GPU, and NKVD would oversee the purging of hostile professors and students from the nation's VUZy, the monitoring of professional and intellectual societies and their congresses, and the planning of the expulsions. In the area of the press and publishing, a special commission consisting of Kamenev, Unshlikht, and Commissar of Justice D. I. Kurskii, which was also placed in charge of coordinating the deportations, would work closely with the Gosizdat Politotdel in deciding further which journals and publishers "not consistent with the aims of Soviet politics" to eliminate.[108]

In addition, the Central Committee launched an integrated propaganda campaign led by Zinoviev and the Agitprop head, Andrei Bubnov, Lunacharskii's eventual replacement at Narkompros. Along with direct critiques in official journals, more broadly disseminated and comprehensive pronouncements were issued. The appearance of articles such as "The Illusion of Counterrevolutionary 'Democracy'" and Trotsky's "Dictatorship, Where Is Your Whip?" in May and June suggested the consideration of harsher punitive measures.[109] Planning was under way for the Twelfth Party Conference, with the campaign against "hostile intellectual groupings" to be the prime focus. Bubnov, who was the chief editor of Zinoviev's upcoming keynote speech, cautioned that the danger had become acute.[110] "We must oppose the front of reborn bourgeois ideology with a powerful, organized onslaught of the revolutionary ideology of Communism," he declared. The presence of the familiar old "rubbish" in the bookstores attested to just how energetic the enemy had become and how urgent was the task of preventing the spread of this infection. Although *Pod znamenem marksizma, Krasnaia nov'*, and the other Bolshevik thick journals had made great strides, marked improvement was critical, as was the coordination of these organs in a "united proletarian front."

The gathering storm achieved full public expression with Zinoviev's speech at the Twelfth Party Conference. In explicitly linking the anti-intellectual campaigns to the SR trial and the purging of Mensheviks from public institutions, Zinoviev differentiated little between declared foes and the nonparty intelligentsia. The "anti-Soviet camp," he explained, was in the process of a great reorganization, so the understanding of the enemy would have to change as well. For example, the actual number of Mensheviks or SRs at the recent doctors' congress and other *spets* conferences was less important than the appearance and success of "objectively" Menshevik and SR positions. In the face of the enemy's revival, it was critical that the party not allow any political relaxation to accompany the economic concessions. The Mensheviks and SRs must be completely liquidated; no less attention should be paid to those who had no formal party affiliation but, as Zinoviev insisted, shared their worldview. These individuals, he explained, were making insidious use of "Soviet legality" to continue their struggle against the dictatorship of the proletariat.[111]

The charges followed Agranov's outline: these groups put their "guild" interests above the common good; they controlled agricultural cooperatives; and they insisted on the false slogan of VUZ autonomy. They also assumed, Zinoviev remarked, that NEP meant "freedom of the press for the bourgeoisie. This, of course, is not so, comrades. We must keep in mind that a transition period is a transition period." The new journals (Zinoviev specifically censured *Ekonomist* and *Utrenniki*) had shown that they would support Sorokin's "Anglo-Saxon position" and dismiss the reality of Soviet rule. Zinoviev closely linked the intelligentsia with their supposed coconspirators in the emigration. At the same time, he admitted that the regime could not "struggle against bourgeois literature only by means of repression," and that not all professors, litterateurs, and doctors were anti-Soviet. It was critical to know the enemy thoroughly, to differentiate carefully among them, and to understand that non-Communist hands would be required in the building of socialism. But repression remained (in combination with other measures) a critical and irreplaceable weapon in their arsenal even in 1922, just as it had been in 1918.[112]

In the discussions following Zinoviev's diatribe, only N. Osinskii, recently a leader of the Democratic Centralists, questioned its core principles. Osinskii's was the sole suggestion from within the party leadership that the incessant search for enemies might cause more harm than the enemies themselves. "It seems to me," he remarked, "that what will really be most dangerous for us is if we become too afraid of our opponents and sound the alarm in response to the most minor instances of their appearance."[113] This may have been the appropriate response during Civil War, he added, but now the tasks were different, and it was more important to invest in constructive social activity. "I believe that we need to be much less afraid of our opponents; they are less terrifying than it seems." But Zinoviev and others flatly rejected Osinskii's response, and the conference agreed on a resolution that closely mirrored Zinoviev's remarks.[114]

The publication of Zinoviev's speech in the Communist dailies hailed the arrival of the storm that intellectuals had sensed brewing, and most of the arrests took place only a week after the conference. The expulsions, however, were not the end of this campaign. After the conference, Bubnov huddled with Agitprop operatives and Bolshevik journalists to fortify the party press. Tasks in the anti-intellectual campaign were more explicitly assigned: *Krasnaia nov'* was to be the primary organ for the "battle with the revival of bourgeois ideology," whereas *Pod znamenem marksizma* and *Pechat' i revoliutsiia* would stick to more specific issues. Over the next several months, during and after the expulsions, party publicists warned that vigilance must not be relaxed. Bubnov cautioned the newly formed press workers' section of Rabpros that the inimical journals represented a "united front of the reborn bourgeois ideology" that they must energetically oppose. *Pravda* complained that despite the great fanfare, little real progress had been made; the party press was still uncoordinated and unready for battle. In particular, provincial newspapers had not received the support, financial and ideological, necessary to wage this critical battle correctly.[115]

Among party notables, only Lunacharskii questioned the need for a further intensification of the struggle. At a November congress of Glavpolitprosvet (the Chief Committee for Political Enlightenment under Narkompros), he acknowledged that the tendencies against which Zinoviev had railed had indeed been a threat, but that the "well-known measures" taken in response had been sufficient. "All of this has been wiped off the face of the earth, as if it had never been."[116] But the commissar once again found himself isolated. Bubnov, while acknowledging that the party had delivered a major blow to its enemies, cautioned that this had been but the "first wave of the bourgeois mindset, born in the conditions and on the basis of NEP," and it would not be the last. "The wave has fallen, but it might rise anew." Although "the scholarly counterrevolution" had been "cut down," it had not disappeared entirely, and it was imperative that agitation and political education continue to be directed at strengthening the Communist position.[117]

Agitprop leaders stressed that although they had stymied the "renaissance of bourgeois ideology," they must remain vigilant, for it could arise anew at any moment. Still, Bubnov emulated Lenin's rejection of infantile leftism on the cultural front. Lenin angrily upbraided Nikolai Bukharin for publishing the Proletkult leader Pletnev's "On the Ideological Front" in *Pravda* in September 1922, and he insisted, over Bukharin's objections, that a response critiquing such absolutist views be printed.[118] The mandate to differentiate among intellectuals underlined even Bubnov's most militant pronouncements. At a November Agitprop conference in Petrograd, while warning against the potential revival of bourgeois ideology in the former capital and reiterating the urgency of efforts to "conquer" higher education, those assembled emphasized the necessity of the "attraction and utilization of nonparty '*spetsy*' on the cultural front."[119]

Bubnov and his colleagues continued to discuss this "wave" of struggle well into 1923, and the Orgburo ordered the publication of *On the Ideological Front of the Struggle with the Counterrevolution.*[120] Although retrospective and triumphalist, these essays asserted that this first wave of bourgeois restorationism was destined to reappear in another form. This first wave, Bubnov noted, had featured a confluence of economic liberalism; "academic counterrevolution," hidden behind the slogan of autonomy and "pure scholarship"; an "intensification, even an onslaught, of every type of idealism and clericalism [*popovshchina*] in scholarship"; and a growth in boulevard (popular lowbrow) and pornographic literature. A network of bourgeois-intellectual institutions, publishers, and the like had united these trends, in particular journals such as *Ekonomist, Utrenniki,* and *Mysl'*. The repressive measures had been effective, so far as they went, and although the proletariat would not conquer through repression alone, it would also not shy away from it when needed. The primary lesson of this wave, Bubnov concluded, was that the party propaganda machine must be fortified and never let its guard down.[121] The experience, added N. Alekseev, in combating the simultaneous appearance of intellectual counterrevolution in higher education, professional congresses, publications, and cooperatives had "demonstrated the possibility of our regulating not only the tempo but also the very character of public activities [*vystuplenii*]."[122]

Glavlit and the Coordination of Censorship

With the urging of the party leadership, the Gosizdat Politotdel and GPU censors grew increasingly interventionist in spring 1922. As noted above, several of the primary literary journals were abolished, and the censors became more likely to make changes in pieces submitted to them or to ban particular articles entirely.[123] Those like Dalmat Lutokhin who were most intimately involved in the process became very much aware of the increased scrutiny, while the barrage of articles in the Bolshevik press specifically lashing out at *Ekonomist, Utrenniki,* and other publications alerted those less directly connected. Lenin and his colleagues read Whiteguard journals and almanacs ever more voraciously, and the procedure for disseminating these publications among Politburo members was a frequent topic at their meetings. That the most important Bolshevik leaders, extremely busy with dozens of tasks, were assigned to read "enemy" publications attests to just how seriously these matters were taken.[124]

In enumerating for his colleagues in the Politburo and GPU which intellectuals to deport, Lenin looked closely at these journals. "*Ekonomist,*" he wrote to Dzerzhinskii, "is a manifest center of Whiteguards. In no. 3 . . . there is a list of contributors printed on the cover. They are, I think, *almost all* the most rightful candidates for deportation abroad." Even after his first stroke, he continued to insist that "*all* the contributors to *Ekonomist* are the most relentless enemies. Get all of them out of Russia." The same, he added, should be done with the writers for *Letopis' doma literatorov, Mysl',* and other journals.[125] Lenin underlined a number of names in his copy of *Utrenniki,* including Berdiaev, Bukshpan, Kizevetter, Kuskova, and Peshekhonov, and carefully marked up offensive articles, in particular Sorokin's speech at the Petrograd University jubilee and Izgoev's "Judgment on Terror."[126] He hesitated only concerning I. Lezhnev's Smenovekhovite journal *Novaia Rossiia,* which the Petrograd authorities had shut down. Unlike Zinoviev, Lenin still believed that these interstitial groups could be useful and that it was a bit early to close it. "*Not all* of this journal's contributors are candidates for deportation abroad," he instructed, and the Politburo allowed it to resume publication.[127]

In the meantime, with Glavlit still in formation, the Politotdel and GPU remained vigilant, although no less inconsistent. Particular attention was focused on Lutokhin's new almanac, *Utrenniki,* which had an even more publicistic bent than its predecessor, *Vestnik literatury.*[128] Sorokin's article "I Believe, O Lord" was prohibited for its overt pessimism, and Lutokhin's proposal that the Petrograd Politotdel chief, V. A. Bystrianskii, write a suitably optimistic official response was rejected. The censors also blocked two satirical pieces by M. Ia. Kozyrev. Other changes were more picayune: in a response by Izgoev to Voronskii's critique of his "Power and the Individual," the verb "reports" (*dokladyvaet*) was replaced with "informs" (*soobshchaet*). On several occasions, Lutokhin did not receive a copy of the mandated cuts, and one article by Professor F. F. Zelinskii made it all the way to the printer before the censor noticed the error.[129]

Eventually the Politburo and Politotdel had had enough and shut down a number of journals and almanacs in connection with the expulsions, including *Mysl', Ekonomist, Utrenniki, Literaturnye zapiski,* the successor to *Letopis' doma literatorov,* and the Pirogov Society's *Obshchestvennyi vrach.* The reason was their "tendentious and anti-Soviet inclination" or, in the case of *Mysl',* its "anti-Soviet and mystico-idealistic inclination." The indefatigable Lutokhin went to Bystrianskii the day before he was arrested to propose two new publications, *Ekonomisticheskii magazin* (The Economists' Shop) and an almanac called *Mlechnyi put'* (Milky Way), symbolizing that a broad swath of the population shared the views to be expressed therein. Bystrianskii, undoubtedly aware of the impending arrests, demurred.[130]

Soon after the deportations, several private and cooperative publishers, including Berdiaev, Stepun, and Frank's Bereg, were shut down. The closure of Mel'gunov's Zadruga came as a shock to its editorial board (despite the recent expulsion of most of its members), which protested after apartment searches conducted on the night of 26–27 October and of the Zadruga bookstore the next day. They begged Glavlit to reconsider, arguing that Zadruga was a writers' artel with purely "cultural-educational goals," and that it "never served the interest of any political party and includes people of various political convictions from the laboring Russian intelligentsia." The stated reasons for its closure—the posthumous publication abroad of Korolenko's critical letter to Lunacharskii under the unauthorized mark of Zadruga and the presence of several objectionable books in its store, including Miliukov's *History of the Russian Revolution*—were thought to be weak pretexts. Glavlit, not surprisingly, was unsympathetic to the appeal and refused to reconsider.[131]

Lenin's instructions to monitor carefully these journals and publishers in deciding whom to expel were followed closely. Among the deportees were many prominent editors and publishers, including Lutokhin, Khariton, Volkovyskii, Mel'gunov, Iretskii, V. M. Kudriavtsev, V. S. Ozeretskovskii, and Abram Kagan. Those who were deported because of their writings or simply because they were listed among the contributors included not only Brutskus, Sorokin, and Izgoev, but also the publicist Petrishchev, the bewildered technician and economist Efim Zubashev, and the cooperator L. M. Pumpianskii.[132] Especially indicative was the inclusion on the lists of "Chaadaev, P.," described simply as the "author of a vile article in the journal *Utrenniki.*"[133] Apparently the name of one of Russia's most famous nineteenth-century thinkers did not evoke any recognition among those investigating. Lutokhin recounted that during the August arrests, "a youth from [the GPU] came to me at one point and asked the address of a contributor to my publication named *Gadaev.* I said that I didn't know such a person, that there had been an article by P. Chaadaev, and that had been a pseudonym (of Sorokin) that had evoked much ridicule, since no one signs with the name of Goethe, Kant, Tolstoy, etc. He asked whether I could absolutely confirm *this* and left."[134]

The goal of unifying censorship resulted in the 6 June 1922 decree establishing the Main Administration on Matters of Literature and Publishing, or Glavlit. It and its local organs were to be given full control over all operations, including mandatory preliminary censorship for all printed material except for that officially connected to the regime. It was to forbid, among other things, publication of any "agitation against the Soviet regime," anything influencing "public opinion by way of false information," and pornographic materials. Although it was formally under the jurisdiction of Narkompros, it was to have very close ties with the military censors and the GPU. In fact, the GPU was to serve as Glavlit's executive arm, seizing works it banned, monitoring the sale of books and journals, keeping a close eye on what entered through customs, and battling underground publications. It was made very clear to those in charge of the printing presses that they would be held responsible for anything issued under their auspices that had not been given proper clearance.[135]

It was initially intended that Meshcheriakov, the Politotdel head, would run Glavlit, but in fact his deputy, Lebedev-Polianskii, was placed in charge. In October the Secretariat confirmed measures to coordinate censorship activities, including efforts to involve more high party officials.[136] Glavlit then instructed its local organs concerning their critical role and specific tasks. "The printed word, both in our hands and in the hands of our opponents, is taking on ever greater significance, and it is a powerful means of affecting the mood of various parts of the Republic's population. The particular conditions of the proletarian dictatorship in Russia, the presence of a significant emigration, and the strengthening of our internal opponents' material resources owing to NEP, have created an atmosphere conducive to their denunciations of us in the press. Censorship is a weapon for us to counteract the growing influence of bourgeois ideology." It was Glavlit's task to lead this charge, first through closing publishing houses, prohibiting specific publications, reducing press runs and circulation, and imposing fines and jail time; and second by means of more subtle "ideological pressure" applied to editors, by bringing in more suitable people, and by removing unacceptable individuals from leadership positions.[137]

All printed matter was to be submitted to Glavlit for approval except that emanating from explicitly exempted official organs, and new publishing entities had to receive Glavlit's blessing. Anything "hostile to the Communist Party and Soviet Russia" was to be categorically forbidden, especially when "hostile to our ideology in fundamental matters (public life [*obshchestvennost'*], religion, economics, the national question, the artistic sphere, etc)." The GPU would serve as the technical and executive arm of Glavlit in watching over the dissemination of publications, printing presses, the book trade, and the import and export of all printed products.[138] A reregistration of all private, cooperative, and institutional publishers was ordered to "clarify the physiognomy of every publisher from all sides." In particular, it was critical to identify the real financiers of private publishers, in order to reveal "formally scientific or artistic and completely, on appearances, apolitical" presses that were in fact covers for SR or Menshevik groups. Semiofficial and *profsoiuz* publishers must be purged of "politically suspicious" non-Communist individuals.[139]

The establishment of the surveillance apparatus proceeded rapidly.[140] Glavlit and its GPU executors made sure that copies of all publications were sent for registration to the Book Chamber (*Knizhnaia palata;* the Russian book registry), and the Orgburo delegated surveillance over the private book market to a bureau headed by Bubnov.[141] This commission issued a brief survey of private publishers in the two capitals, but it was decided that a more extensive and regular source of information was necessary, and Lebedev-Polianskii was assigned to edit a secret Glavlit bulletin.[142] These bulletins, the first of which appeared in January 1923, were distributed to a highly select group of party leaders. They described in qualitative and statistical detail all unofficial publishers and a great many individual publications, domestic and foreign.[143] Political and philosophical publications, which were easier for the average censor to dissect, were more likely than fiction to run into problems. Still, writers such as Zamiatin and Pil'niak already received careful scrutiny, and Glavlit exhorted its local organs to pay closer attention to how "misrepresentations" of the Revolution were hidden beneath artistic exteriors.[144] Despite the initial spate of journal and publisher closings, most publications were allowed, although cuts and alterations were common for private publishers. The import of foreign publications into Soviet Russia was forbidden as often as not.[145]

The immediate result of the formation of Glavlit, then, mirrored that of other institutions established during the campaign to root out anti-Soviet intellectuals. A few publishers deemed especially pernicious were closed, several prominent journals were banned, leading editors and contributors were deported, and a coordinated, centralized surveillance regime was instituted. The subsequent task was not the absolute prohibition of all independent publishing but its close circumscription through observation, frequent intervention, and the memory of this first warning.[146] The party, at Trotsky's urging, even encouraged its censors to play a "pedagogical" role, to "work with authors" and explain their mistakes.[147] Reregistration of publishers and submission to the local bureaucracy also played an important role in checking the flow of printed material.[148]

The importance of dismantling the system of journals and publishers that had arisen after the Civil War should not be underestimated. It signaled the end of real public criticism and sharply limited the space for cultural, scholarly, and especially publicistic journalism. The editors of *Literaturnye zapiski* lamented shortly before its prohibition that "in publishing matters, the hopes placed on NEP have proven unwarranted."[149] At an official congress of journalists in February 1923, the House of Litterateurs and other proponents of an independent press were portrayed as already defeated foes.[150] Criticism of the regime, even and especially when it did not explicitly claim to be such, was impermissible. Many of those who had clamored for freedom of the press a year or two before were no longer in the country, and, as Bubnov and his colleagues noted with no small satisfaction, the "renaissance of bourgeois ideology" could be considered utterly vanquished. Private publishing, although still extant, did not actively threaten ideological hegemony.[151] The prophets of doom were silenced or removed, as was any public expression of doubt over whether Soviet Russia was indeed becoming a socialist utopia.

6

The Deportations, Part I: Precedents and Planning

Our political attack will now develop, and we will fully liquidate these anti-Soviet groups, taking from them that which is valuable in their human material, that which is capable of supporting Soviet power, and smashing the rest.

—Grigorii Zinoviev, in a speech to the Petrograd soviet, 29 August 1922

Bolshevik leaders viewed the "renaissance of bourgeois ideology" as part of a coherent conspiracy. Although they took solace in the fragmentation that they observed among their foes, they also discerned an overarching unity in the enemy's use of "Soviet legality" for its own separatist purposes. Zinoviev warned the Twelfth Party Conference that "new formations have arisen in the anti-Soviet camp; there have occurred on new grounds a revival and a consolidation of anti-Soviet forces against us."[1] The Soviet regime and its security apparatus aimed to eliminate this threat while retaining those members of the intelligentsia who could be reformed and made useful. The construction of the hegemonic Soviet public sphere necessitated distinguishing between those who could be redeemed for service to the socialist state and those who refused to accept the terms of the new order. Those intellectuals who obeyed certain conventions, of which a public declaration of loyalty was the most effective, could avoid punishment, at least for the time being.

As we have seen, the regime objected not only to openly political opposition, but also to certain forms of autonomous social activity, "corporate" separatism, and the expression of heterodox opinions. The expulsion of intellectuals in 1922–23 was the climactic response to what was seen as an integrated conflict, the various aspects of which have been described in earlier chapters. First, the Bolsheviks vigilantly guarded against the rebirth of actual political conspiracy in the form of groups like the Tactical Center and Petrograd Battle Organization. Second, they worried that public organizations such as the famine relief committee or independent-minded professional and cultural societies could provide alternative social forums. Third, they were greatly alarmed by the professorial defense of university autonomy in open defiance of Soviet reforms. Fourth, they hoped to cleanse the public arena of ideologically unacceptable voices by centralizing censorship and initiating a broad propaganda campaign.

The Bolshevik leadership once again called upon the security apparatus to handle the situation. Although the Cheka was formally abolished in February 1922, limitations on the extralegal powers of the newly rechristened GPU not only did not last very long but served to incorporate these powers into the Soviet legal structure.[2] The GPU's reduced size and nominal subordination to legality did little to prevent the expansion of its surveillance operations and the removal of "socially harmful" elements. The GPU was able to exploit the party's broad understanding of what constituted an enemy, and the elasticity of terms such as *counterrevolutionary* and *anti-Soviet* formed the basis for criminal legislation.[3] Basing punitive action on these mutable terms allowed the security apparatus to make accusations predicated on highly subjective categorizations. The practice of hurling fiercely pejorative labels at alleged foes would soon become one of the most pervasive and infamous elements of Soviet discourse.

Thus, despite the superficial nod in the direction of "socialist legality," the GPU's authority remained undiminished, for the Bolsheviks retained the overarching belief that implacable enemies surrounded them on all sides. The GPU's rapid and incessant accrual of jurisdiction was an enormously important process that reified in peacetime circumstances most of the extraordinary powers given to the Cheka during the Civil War. Over the course of 1922 the GPU would oversee the expulsions, the development of a system of internal exile, the coordination of the censorship apparatus, and the registration of nongovernmental organizations and their congresses. In the process, it did much to consolidate its power, authority, and scope.[4]

Although the GPU implemented the arrests and expulsions, the decision to do so and even the names of particular individuals came first and foremost from

Lenin.[5] Even after his stroke in May 1922, he directed affairs through his colleagues as much as possible. In his absence over the summer, the operation was confirmed at every level by the Politburo. Lev Kamenev, despite having been an active proponent of "Soviet legality," participated as a primary actor in a process that would restore to the GPU all of the Cheka's former powers. The deportations were an affirmation by the party leadership that wartime methods of dealing with the population remained appropriate. After this event, deportation resumed its place as an important Russian institution. Along with other measures, such as the establishment of Glavlit as a central censorship body, the placing of controls over independent social organizations in the hands of the NKVD, and further cleansing of the universities, the deportations of intellectuals represented a major way station on the path toward the type of total control over society that the Bolsheviks never stopped intending to obtain.

Bolshevik leaders asserted to a world that often portrayed them as brutal, lawless usurpers that they had shown considerable restraint in deporting rather than executing their enemies.[6] While desperately trying to resuscitate a destroyed economy and feed a starving population, the new regime was also trying to gain international recognition and attract foreign investment. The need to take outside opinion into account was particularly palpable when dealing with internationally renowned intellectuals, as the bitter outcry following the SR trial demonstrated all too clearly.

Exile through 1921 and the Deportations of Mensheviks

The Bolsheviks started to banish political foes from urban centers not long after coming to power. Because of the negative connotations it had acquired under the old regime, they avoided using the terms *ssylka* or *vysylka,* denoting exile, and spoke instead of *udalenie,* meaning removal or sending away.[7] Although at first sentences were limited to one year, the terms soon grew longer and the areas more remote. The use of exile grew rapidly during 1921–22, and the regime resumed the use of the old terms. As was true in the tsarist era, there were several variants. *Vysylka* signified prohibition from living in a particular city or cities; *ssylka* meant that the individual was deported to a particular provincial location and prohibited from moving.[8] In addition, exile could be either on the basis of a court decision or due to extrajudicial or "administrative" decision.

Chekisty were told in early 1921 that existing conditions required an intensification of vigilance. "Having lost the battle on the external front," one directive declared, "the counterrevolution is focusing its efforts on overthrowing Soviet power from within. It will use any means for the attainment of this goal, using all of its rich experience, all of its techniques of betrayal."[9] The sense of urgency accorded to the battle on the internal front became particularly acute after Kronstadt, following which repression against political foes increased. Much of the impetus came from Iosif Unshlikht, whom Fëdor Dan called "the actual chairman of the Cheka" while Dzerzhinskii was preoccupied with his other posts.[10] Unshlikht outlined an ambitious plan for an "organized and systematic struggle with counterrevolutionary movements," including the Church, striking workers, rebelling peasants, and members or former members of other political parties. Of particular importance was the cleansing of Mensheviks and SRs from unions, agricultural cooperatives, government organs, and other positions of influence, to be followed by the final liquidation of the parties' central organs.[11]

In April 1921 dozens of socialist prisoners were beaten in Butyrka prison and then transferred to various locations. Most, however, were returned to Moscow after protests about terrible conditions in the provincial jails.[12] Mass arrests in July focused on the active Social Democratic youth organization; these students were deported to northern, non-university cities.[13] Six of the leaders of the public famine relief committee were deported to various provincial locations in fall 1921, and the pace of political arrests increased.[14] In November 1921 several dozen Mensheviks were sentenced to exile in Turkistan, which called forth vigorous objections. "A new weapon of terror has appeared," the Menshevik Moscow Committee declared. "The 'glorious' memory of tsarist administrative exile has been restored."[15] The deportations to Turkistan were halted, although some prisoners were still subject to deportation elsewhere.

Exile as yet had no administrative guidelines and no legal basis beyond the Cheka's extraordinary powers. In December 1921 the Politburo began to discuss the logistics of deportation.[16] It also directed Unshlikht to step up the purging of "dangerous" individuals from public life, in particular removing Mensheviks and SRs from *profsoiuzy*, cooperatives, economic organs, and other official institutions.[17] At year's end, Unshlikht moved forward with plans to deport a number of Mensheviks from Butyrka to various provincial locations. After some of the prisoners called a hunger strike on 4 January 1922, Ekaterina Peshkova, Gorky's first wife and head of the Political Red Cross, mediated a series of negotiations. The prisoners requested that they be offered the same choice they had under the tsarist regime—internal exile or deportation abroad. Despite some misgivings, the Politburo eventually agreed.[18]

The Mensheviks who chose internal exile were given seven days to settle their affairs and told to report to the Cheka's Secret Department with their documents. On reaching the place of exile, they registered with the local

Cheka organs, which kept watch over deportees. But for Fëdor Dan and others, Russia seemed already lost. Disheartened by the atmosphere in Moscow at the beginning of NEP, with the newly rich speculators, moral turpitude, and terrible poverty, Dan decided to go abroad.[19] On 26 January 1922 the eleven departing Mensheviks and their families were given thirteen dollars each to cover the cost of their German visas in Riga and escorted by the Cheka to the Latvian border. "At 8 o'clock the train started moving," Dan recounted, "taking us into foreign exile, which we endured so many times in tsarist times, but which was so unexpected now, in the fifth year of the Revolution. Our mood was miserable . . ."[20] As difficult as the decision to leave was for Dan and his colleagues, for some of the Mensheviks remaining in Moscow, their going was equivalent to leaving the field of battle. The Menshevik Central Committee was decimated by these departures, and a gulf opened up between those who remained in Russia and those abroad.[21]

The departure of the Mensheviks marked the regime's first use of expulsion as a means of getting rid of political opponents.[22] The episode foreshadowed the upcoming mass deportations, although it was unusual in that leaving the country was presented as a choice. Motivated by either vestigial sympathies for their former Social Democratic comrades or the desire to halt an embarrassing hunger strike as several international conferences were set to begin, the Bolsheviks gave in to their prisoners' demands.[23] This concession was immediately criticized within the leadership, and efforts to liquidate other political parties in Russia were redoubled. Lenin and Trotsky both instructed Unshlikht to hasten and intensify repression of the Mensheviks.[24]

Mensheviks were relentlessly purged from public life, especially from soviets, unions, and cooperatives, during 1922. Members of the Social Democratic youth organization were removed from important VUZy, including a significant number enrolled in the MGU Social Science Faculty. Trotsky and Lenin directed Unshlikht to arrest a significant portion of the youth group's Moscow-based leadership in February 1922, and in June and July a number of those arrested were deported to provincial towns.[25] Meanwhile, the still-legal parent party was also a frequent target. At the end of May, Zinoviev's Petrograd Party Committee resolved to cleanse the city and region of "counterrevolutionary" elements and deported a number of Mensheviks from the area. In June several members of the Menshevik Moscow Committee were arrested with the intention to deport them to Turkistan, but after another hunger strike they were released.[26] Measures were soon taken to ensure the destruction and illegalization of the Menshevik Party. In July the GPU disbanded its Central Committee, and active members were arrested or forced underground. The remaining Moscow Mensheviks realized the futility of attempting to act as a legal party and thenceforth resigned themselves to working as an underground organization.[27]

Linking Mensheviks to the general campaign against counterrevolutionary elements was an important act in both a literal and a rhetorical sense. While repression of Social Democrats continued unabated after the Civil War, the pejorative *Menshevism* came to be used as shorthand for all groups that hid their "counterrevolutionary" or "anti-Soviet" goals under the mask of socialism or neutrality. *Menshevism* quickly became one of the most prominent allegations hurled against purported enemies of the regime, the assumption being that the associations that the term had accrued would make apparent the true nature of the accused.[28] The removal of such individuals not only from important institutions, but also from the very locales where they might do the most harm, was seen as an important prophylactic measure necessary to maintain the health of the socialist state. To perform this prophylaxis, it was necessary to develop further those organs designed to excel in the locating and weeding out of dangerous elements.

Further Repression and the Formation of the GPU

When the Cheka was replaced by the GPU in February 1922, it was an apparent victory for the advocates of "revolutionary legality," including Lev Kamenev and Commissar of Justice Dmitrii Kurskii. Unlike the Cheka, the GPU would be subordinate to the existing state structure, specifically to the NKVD; it was also to share duties with the Commissariat of Justice. It quickly became apparent, however, that the GPU was hardly less potent than its predecessor. In fact, the formal subordination of the GPU to the NKVD—which meant little while Dzerzhinskii headed both institutions—had the effect of giving it a legitimacy it did not have previously.[29] Even among the proponents of socialist legality, the issue of the GPU's role in combating counterrevolution was not in question, as would become clear through Kamenev's and Kurskii's active participation in the deportations of intellectuals later in the year. As T. P. Samsonov, the director of the GPU's Secret Department, informed his colleagues, there had been significant organizational reforms, but this in no way lessened the importance of their task.[30]

The reforms did decrease the size of the GPU and increase the authority of other state institutions, most notably the Commissariat of Justice. Lenin's advocacy of "revolutionary legality," however, hardly meant an end to the struggle against "anti-Soviet forces," and he chided Kurskii for failing fully to grasp this fact. He argued that the Justice Commissariat should *also* be intimately involved in "intensifying repression against political enemies of Soviet power and agents of the bourgeoisie (*especially* the Mensheviks and SRs)," and that the spring 1922 criminal code should institute both capital punishment and exile for such opponents. "The courts should not eliminate the terror—to promise this would be deceitful and delusional—but provide foundation for and legalize it on principle, clearly, without falsity or embellishment."[31] Over the course of 1922, Narkomiust would orchestrate the public trials of SRs and church figures, whereas the GPU handled the preliminary investigation and arrests that preceded the expulsion of intellectuals. As quickly became clear, the GPU's sphere of jurisdiction was hardly any less than it had been. The Bolsheviks retained the overarching belief that they were surrounded by relentless foes whom they needed to battle by any means necessary.

The GPU occupied the nucleus of the surveillance apparatus. Its reports to party leaders aimed to maximize the sense of present danger and thus to highlight the continued importance of the security forces. The reports' descriptions of the population's political mood and attitude toward the regime tended toward hyperbole.[32] In early 1922 the GPU Secret Department directed the formation of Bureaus of Assistance (*buro sodeistviia*) in cooperatives, *profsoiuzy*, and economic organs.[33] The bureaus became a key part of its information-gathering system, with the task of "studying the personnel of all types at the given institution in terms of political reliability and party membership, and [determining] the distribution of both Communists and anti-Soviet elements by branch and department." They were to register all Mensheviks and SRs, to keep watch over "suspicious SR-izing and Menshevizing elements," and to present systematic data on these matters to the GPU Secret Department.[34] On 22 April 1922 the Secret Department directed its local organs to establish Bureaus of Assistance "in every state, public, cooperative, and private institution or enterprise, and also in VUZy where possible." The bureaus were "to undertake systematic collection of information on all types of phenomena of an anti-Soviet character, and also to discover counterrevolutionary elements in the given institution or enterprise, as well as outside it."[35]

The Bureaus of Assistance and similar bodies were designed to determine the strength and placement of perceived political foes. They were one of a variety of tools used during 1922–23 to aid in cleansing important public institutions of Mensheviks, SRs, and other "socially dangerous" persons. At the same time, the Bolshevik leadership decided that it was also necessary to expose the "true nature" of some of these enemies to the public, which it did through several propaganda trials, including a show trial of SR leaders and a series of campaigns against clergymen.

Weeding Out Ideological Enemies: The Church and SR Trials

As the crusade against religious idealism gained steam in early 1922, party leaders planned a more direct attack on the Orthodox Church itself. Lenin read antireligious literature voraciously, convinced of the need to intensify work in this area.[36] Although it deemed a frontal assault on religion inadvisable, the Politburo initiated a series of actions against both church leaders and recalcitrant parish priests, who were accused of corrupting the peasantry. The operation consisted of confiscating church valuables, purportedly to finance famine relief, and, when this met violent opposition, arresting eminent church figures such as Patriarch Tikhon and the Petrograd Metropolitan Veniamin. The ensuing trials were, along with the SR process, the first true Soviet show trials, designed to expose and isolate enemies of the people. It was contended that the accused had been continuously engaged in counterrevolutionary efforts, in coordination with émigré groups; that they had infected important segments of the population; but that space nevertheless remained for those willing openly to support the regime, in this case for the pro-Soviet renovationist church.[37]

In early 1922 Trotsky, the head of Bolshevik antireligious efforts, proposed the linkage of the seizure of church valuables with financing famine relief.[38] After a series of incidents in which believers resisted these appropriations, most notably a violent uprising in Shuia, northeast of Moscow, the Bolshevik leadership decided that it was time to take action.[39] In a 19 March memo to the Politburo, Lenin declared that it was clear that Tikhon and other "Blackhundred" church leaders were preparing a well-planned assault. He noted that the famine provided an excellent pretext to seize church valuables and made clear to his lieutenants that the financing of famine relief was not the primary reason. The strike was to be made quickly and efficiently. "We must initiate a decisive and merciless battle with the Blackhundred clergy immediately and suppress its opposition with such brutality that they will not forget it for many decades," he concluded. A representative was sent to Shuia so that the punitive organs might quickly initiate processes not only there, but also in Moscow and other important centers. Lenin ordered the GPU to put Tikhon under strict surveillance and for Dzerzhinskii or Unshlikht personally to report weekly on his activities to the Politburo. Meanwhile, the campaign to seize church valuables should be conducted mercilessly, and "the more reactionary clergymen that we are able to shoot on this pretext, the better."[40]

On Trotsky's initiative, the Politburo approved a plan to arrest the patriarch and members of the Synod in two weeks' time. An intense propaganda campaign stressed that the Bolshevik efforts were directed not against religion, but against the counterrevolutionary "princes of the Church."[41] It was explained that the church leaders were part of a larger anti-Soviet plot, and the Bolsheviks used the renovationists, whom Trotsky termed the leaders of the "*smena vekh* within the church," to show that cooperation between loyal clergy and the regime was possible.[42] Meanwhile, Unshlikht and Samsonov, the head of the GPU Secret Department, were vigorously gathering intelligence, and they soon asserted that "the GPU and its local organs already have sufficient grounds for the arrest of Tikhon and the most reactionary members of the Synod."[43] The ensuing punitive action against clergy leaders proved to be the first major instance in which the newly reformed security apparatus was allowed to reassert its former powers, and it was quickly made clear that the Politburo would continue to rely first and foremost on the GPU to execute its decisions in such matters.[44]

Just over a month later, the most important of a series of show trials of churchmen began in Moscow. The so-called Trial of the Fifty-Four featured a number of elements that would become standard in later Soviet trials.[45] First, the accusation was not merely of resisting the seizures of valuables, but of counterrevolution and a desire to overthrow the regime. Second, in a move consistent with their efforts to recruit temporary allies from their enemy's midst, the Bolsheviks called forth the renovationists to testify against the defendants. Third, the accused were explicitly tied to émigré church organizations.[46] Finally, in keeping with the ubiquitous lexicon of war and struggle, the press labeled Tikhon and his close colleagues the "general staff of the counterrevolution."[47] Eleven death sentences were handed down; this was later reduced to six, because of disagreement within the Politburo over the efficacy of execution and an appeal by one of the renovationist leaders.[48]

The Bolsheviks had succeeded in creating a Church schism and pointed to the renovationists as evidence that the arrests and executions were directed only against criminal clergy members, not the Church itself. The renovationists in turn acceded to a Bolshevik request to denounce the patriarch and Synod and call on believers to support the regime.[49] Metropolitan Veniamin responded by excommunicating the renovationist leader, Vvedenskii. In summer 1922 a second major Church trial, featuring Veniamin, began in Petrograd. The defendants were charged not only with having resisted the confiscation campaign, but also with using the so-called Society of Orthodox Parishes of Petrograd as a counterrevolutionary front in conjunction with the émigré church. Again, this fit the practice of contending that seemingly innocuous organizations were actually dedicated to overthrowing the regime. Ten defendants were sentenced to death, and, although six sentences were subsequently commuted, Metropolitan Veniamin and three others were executed on the night of 12–13 August 1922.[50]

The Petrograd Church trial reached its violent climax shortly after a more widely publicized process in Moscow: the show trial of the Socialist Revolutionaries. The SR trial was the public manifestation of the eradication of socialist opposition. In December 1921 Dzerzhinskii proposed arresting and trying leading SRs, and he, Kamenev, and Stalin formed a committee to plan the process. The propaganda battle was launched several months later with the publication of a pamphlet written in Berlin by the former SR Grigorii Semenov depicting the alleged terrorist activities of Socialist Revolutionaries during 1917–18.[51] Semenov and other penitent SRs were held up as positive examples and defended by Unshlikht himself against those Bolsheviks who did not accept them.[52] Extending the opportunity for forgiveness through repentance would become as important a weapon as punitive measures in eliminating the opposition, and it was a basic component of the party's strategy of divide and rule.

The trial was purposefully simultaneous with the ideological campaigns against the intelligentsia; the Bolsheviks hoped to show Russia and the world that their foes, including the moderate socialist opposition, were not merely "counterrevolutionary," but also criminal. The SRs' continued caché in the country, particularly among the more educated peasants in cooperatives, was seen as an even greater potential danger than the effects professors might have on students or Mensheviks on workers.[53] The anti-SR and Menshevik campaigns of 1922 both focused on removing them from cooperatives, unions, soviets, and other public institutions. A March 1922 GPU report to the Central Committee on moods among the workers and peasants and the activities of other parties warned that SRs still strove "to penetrate agricultural cooperative organs and thus to enter into intimate contact with the peasant masses."[54] The decision to put the SRs and churchmen on public trial while conducting extrajudicial repression against Mensheviks and other intellectuals might be explained by the fact that a much greater portion of the population stood to be infected by the insidious ideas of the SRs and church leaders. As Lenin had explained to Kurskii, the best method for combating this influence was to organize a very public exposition so as to reach as large an audience as possible with the "facts" of their crimes.[55] And as Lunacharskii noted at the trial, if given political liberties, the SRs would use them to "poison the backward or weary masses."[56]

Preparations for the SR trial took several months and exacerbated tensions between the Bolsheviks and foreign socialists, who quickly ascertained that the trial would be a produced event. The international socialist delegates taking part in the defense soon left in protest at the kangaroo-court nature of the proceedings. The public relations beating that the Bolsheviks subsequently received, particularly over their intention to use the death penalty, left a deep impression on them.[57] Especially grating were two letters written by Gorky in Germany, one to the Soviet government and the other a public missive to Anatole France. Gorky warned the Bolsheviks that if they went ahead with the "murder" of the SRs, this "crime" would not soon be forgiven. He beseeched Anatole France to support his protest, and France, whose response was also published, agreed completely. This exchange had several important consequences. First, any influence Gorky might have still had in Soviet Russia was completely undone. He was savaged in *Pravda* by Karl Radek and Demian Bednyi, and Lenin felt once again betrayed, although he forestalled inordinate denunciations of Gorky.[58] When mass arrests of intellectuals began in August, Gorky could not aspire to play his customary role as patron and protector. Second, the Bolsheviks became even more conscious of the need to present (occasionally) a gentler public face. The negative international reaction to the proposed use of the death penalty in the SR trial indisputably influenced how the Bolsheviks depicted their motivations for the expulsions, in particular their claims of "humaneness" and restraint.[59]

There were several other significant differences between the SR process and the expulsions. Most notably, Nakromiust and its most prominent prosecutor, Nikolai Krylenko, orchestrated the SR affair, since it had been organized as a trial rather than an administrative action. Though there were differences over who would control the process, sharp distinction between the legal and extralegal apparatus should not be overemphasized. The GPU operative Iakov Agranov, a key figure in the campaign against the intellectuals, was also in charge of the preliminary organization and investigation of the SR process. Despite real jurisdictional concerns, Narkomiust and the GPU operated in collaboration, even if sometimes the partnership was strained, during the struggle on the "third front" at the beginning of NEP. It was Agranov who selected and interrogated the most suitable defendants for the trial, and other SRs were kept in prison by the GPU or, like the Mensheviks, banished without trial to distant locations.[60]

Another major figure at the SR trial was Lunacharskii. He was Krylenko's right-hand man in drafting the indictment and viewed as the lead propagandist at the trial. The SRs, Lunacharskii declared, "are a petty bourgeois party," aiding the forces of reaction. The Bolsheviks were not fooled by the masks that hid the SRs' real agenda. He compared them to an insidious disease that threatened the weakened social organism: "The most piercing draught, the most abrupt transition from heat to cold, the deepest wounds would not be dangerous to a man if a whole world of microbes did not exist around him. . . . The SR Party consists of precisely such microbes. . . . The Soviet regime will never refuse to do battle with such elements, to employ the most severe punitive measures, and every Communist will valiantly take upon himself responsibility for such measures."[61] Thus, although he is frequently depicted as a soft-liner, Lunacharskii could be as adamant as any other Bolshevik when he believed that enemies needed to be exposed and punished.

In the end, the Bolsheviks, bowing to international pressure, commuted the death sentences against twelve of the defendants. As Marc Jansen has noted, this conditional death penalty allowed the regime to claim lenience while making clear that it would not be afraid to use capital punishment if necessary.[62] The trial was also not the end of the persecution of SRs. Immediately after its conclusion, Dzerzhinskii instructed Samsonov, "Now, after the sentence against the PSR central committee, we need to work out further action against that party."[63] There would be no more trials; as Jansen notes, "Legal prosecution of the Socialist Revolutionaries and of members of other 'anti-Soviet groupings' was the exception rather than the rule." Those arrested subsequently were, like the Mensheviks, sent into internal administrative exile and, more often, directly to concentration camps.[64] Even the usually alarmist GPU noted in its October 1922 report to the Central Committee that the SRs were no longer a threat.[65] At the same time, it orchestrated efforts to co-opt remaining SRs by convening a Smenovekhovite-style "All-Russian Congress of Ordinary Socialist Revolutionaries" in March 1923. This congress declared the PSR dead and called for "firm cooperation with the Communist Party as the only representative of 'genuine Socialist Revolutionary principles and traditions.' " Decimated by arrests and defections, the SR Party would last only a few more years.[66]

The creation of a forum through which former SRs could find amnesty and declare their loyalty to the regime was a widely used tactic to separate redeemable former enemies from those who had to be removed. A similar strategy had been utilized in forming a temporary alliance with the renovationist church. This variant of terror involved targeting a visible few and warning the rest that they would face similar punishment unless they mended their ways. The presence of an escape hatch shows that, at this point, the Bolsheviks preferred to allow most foes to leave behind their questionable past and join the creation of a socialist state.[67] Such a path was to be made available to intellectuals as well, even to some of those originally condemned to exile.

The show trials of SRs and churchmen aimed to expose political foes whose hostility to the regime could potentially corrupt a significant percentage of the population. In both cases, the security apparatus and justice organs were jointly employed: the former gathered information and executed the will of the Politburo, whereas the latter could conduct public trials with legalistic trappings. These efforts aimed to expose the supposed criminality and counterrevolutionary nature of particular church and opposition leaders while providing an out for those willing to declare their loyalty to the regime and denounce their former colleagues. Though succeeding in eliminating a handful of foes and assisting in the creation of small pro-Bolshevik defector organizations, these trials also encountered vocal opposition in and outside Russia, particularly concerning the use of the death penalty. This experience led the Bolsheviks to focus on more discreet methods of eliminating opponents, and show trials were not widely employed again until the end of the decade.

Initial Planning of the Expulsions of Intellectuals

Enemies were identified increasingly for intellectual as well as political reasons, although the Bolsheviks did not truly recognize a distinction between the two. The broadening of the "battle on the internal front" to include all perceived ideological foes became apparent by late April 1922, at which time the GPU's Bureaus of Assistance widened their scope from Mensheviks and SRs to all anti-Soviet or counterrevolutionary elements. The conviction that ideological disagreement concealed or led to political opposition is revealed in Lenin's complaint that the Oswald Spengler volume was "like 'a literary cover for a Whiteguard organization.' "[68] Lenin's article "On the Meaning of Militant Materialism" initiated a new phase of the propaganda war, highlighting the ties between intellectual and political enemies and exposing "nonpartyness" (*bespartiinost'*) as a facade and part of the dangerous new tactics of the opposition.[69] The tone of this campaign, of course, was not completely new: from the time of the October coup through the end of the Civil War, the Bolsheviks remained suspicious of the intelligentsia. Many of those targeted in 1922 had been arrested several times and implicated in the Tactical Center investigation or other purported plots. The difference in this particular operation was in its more holistic claims and tactics: rather than being presented as a move against a particular conspiracy, it was tied to the broader project of cleansing public life once and for all of unacceptable or "foreign" elements, in this case by deporting a number of important undesirables beyond the nation's borders.

In the weeks before the Eleventh Party Congress, Lenin continued to emphasize the need for repression. In a 6 March 1922 speech at a congress of metalworkers, he declared, "*If [terror] is demanded again, we will advance once again.* Not a single worker, not a single peasant doubts that it is necessary; other than intellectual hysterical women [*klikush*], no one doubts this."[70] The first explicit hint concerning the upcoming expulsions appeared in "On the Meaning of Militant Materialism." In an ominous conclusion, Lenin lamented: "The working class in Russia managed to win power, but it has not yet learned to use it, for otherwise it would have long ago most politely sent such instructors and members of scholarly societies to countries of bourgeois 'democracy.' That is the most natural place for such serf-owners [*krepostniki*]. It [the working class] will learn, were it to have the will to learn."[71] Several months passed before this threat was realized, during which time Lenin sent mixed signals. At the Party Congress, he noted the need to halt any political retreat associated with NEP and pronounced that "our revolutionary courts should employ execution for the public manifestation of Menshevism." Regarding other intellectuals, however, he showed his pragmatism, castigating Preobrazhenskii for being overzealous and too uncompromising toward the professoriat.[72]

The first official consideration of expelling intellectuals came in late April, when Unshlikht proposed to the Politburo that the exiled members of the famine relief committee choose between being sent to a provincial capital or deportation abroad.[73] The internal exile into which Ekaterina Kuskova and her husband, Sergei Prokopovich, had been forced weighed heavily upon both. In Vologda they tried desperately to continue playing the part of public intellectuals, but this was now quite difficult. They were sent at the end of January to Kashin, a small village in Tver province.[74] Kuskova attempted to continue writing but found that the isolation and inability to acquire materials in the provinces made this impossible. "Life here is unbelievably difficult without people we are close to," she wrote to Mel'gunov at the end of April, "and people close based on past relationships become somehow closer and dearer."[75]

The Prokopoviches, on Unshlikht's proposal, were then told that they could go to any Russian regional city (except for Vologda, Khar'kov, Odessa, Kiev, or Petrograd) or be deported abroad. On their choosing the latter, the GPU informed them that they had seven days to prepare, and that they were to go to Moscow "for further movement abroad." Kuskova wrote Dalmat Lutokhin that they would not have time to finish their articles for his journals; they had to sell most of their possessions to get money for travel. "And well, my head, to tell the truth, is spinning; I understand nothing. What kind of criminals we are, and why we can't live and work like everyone in our home in Moscow—I just don't know."[76] After a hectic week negotiating with the GPU to keep their manuscripts (Kuskova noted with pleasant surprise that "everything went well . . . it was all very cultured"), they left for Berlin, traveling through Latvia. Riga, Kuskova told her friend Praskovia Mel'gunova, was so beautiful, so elegant, that "one wants to cry when one remembers one's native land. It is sad, my dear."[77]

Kuskova and Prokopovich were among the last to be offered an ad hoc choice between internal exile and expulsion, and plans for a far more extensive and systematic campaign proceeded. In early May efforts were made to establish legal justification for both juridical and administrative exile, and GPU leaders pressed for the reinstatement of its extralegal rights. Unshlikht wrote to Stalin: "Considering the impossibility of resolving a whole series of matters within the court structure and the simultaneous necessity of freeing ourselves from impudent and harmful elements, the GPU proposes adding the following supplement to our statute: . . . The right to employ a) administrative exile to specific regions for a term of up to two years for anti-Soviet activities, participation in espionage, banditry, and counterrevolution, b) administrative exile beyond the boundaries of the RSFSR for a term of up to two years for ill-intentioned [*neblagonamerennykh*] Russian and foreign citizens."[78] This desire to have these GPU prerogatives officially ensconced was formally fulfilled only with the August VTsIK decree on administrative exile, but this was long after the operation to expel intellectuals under GPU guidance had already begun.

The GPU shared the task of combating political foes with other state organs. Although the GPU directed administrative exile and Narkomiust juridical exile, the rhetorical formulations used were the same. S. A. Krasil'nikov speaks of a situation of "dual power,"[79] but though there was certainly jurisdictional competition, there was little disagreement about either the goal or the means. Lenin proposed establishing juridical exile, which was more in line with "socialist legality," while simultaneously directing the GPU to take charge of his plan to expel intellectuals. The criminal code drafted by Kurskii in May included a set of counterrevolutionary activities to be punished by shooting. In response, Lenin listed several more potential offenses, noting that the use of execution should be broadened, but he added that in certain circumstances deportation abroad might be substituted. He proposed that such deportees be shot if they returned without permission, a formulation that would be used at the time of the expulsions. The duration of exile might be either for a specific length of time or indefinitely, an ambiguity that in Lenin's absence from the scene would lead to confusion as to whether expulsion was intended to be a permanent punishment.[80]

Although the final version of the criminal code did not emphasize deportation to the degree Lenin had suggested, it represented an important step in legalizing the conception of the enemy, of classifying what constituted an alien element.[81] It did this most notably in establishing a usefully elastic definition of *counterrevolutionary* in Article 57, the statute that would be used in the arrests of intellectuals. The ambiguity of laws such as Article 57 provided the party and GPU the latitude they needed while claiming to act within a system of legality.[82] Lenin hoped further to institutionalize the terror by shifting some of its implementation from the GPU to Narkomiust.

Lenin's notes to Kurskii illustrate both the depth of his suspicion of those he had decided to expel and the means of achieving this excision. First, he directed Kurskii to find a formulation explicitly connecting counterrevolutionary crimes "*with the international bourgeoisie* and its struggle with us (through buying the press and agents, preparations for war, etc.)." This echoed his oft-repeated conviction that the targets of this campaign were working—directly or indirectly—for foreign powers who would stop at nothing to overthrow the Soviet regime.[83] He wrote several drafts of a provision for the criminal code, noting that "propaganda, or agitation, or participation in an organization, or collaborating with an organization" that aided the international bourgeoisie must be met with the highest form of punishment—execution, or, given mitigating circumstances, exile abroad. Including such language in the code would help explain what was "motivating the *essence* and *justification* of the terror, its necessity, its range."[84]

Lenin did not explicitly state why he favored the occasional substitution of expulsion for execution, but it is clear it was for practical reasons: if the terror was to be increased significantly, then the Bolsheviks simply could not afford to appear too brutal in the eyes of either international opinion or those on whose productive labor they counted. The authors of the final version of the criminal code did not, however, place as much emphasis on the application of exile as Lenin had proposed,[85] and it was not often utilized by the Commissariat of Justice. The code's Article 57 would, however, become the central legal justification for the expulsions of intellectuals.

While the criminal code was finalized, Lenin moved to implement the expulsion of intellectuals. On 19 May he directed Dzerzhinskii to begin planning the process:

> Comrade Dzerzhinskii! On the question of the deportation abroad of writers and professors who are aiding the counterrevolution.
>
> We need to prepare this more carefully. Without preparation we will make fools of ourselves. I request that we discuss such measures of preparation.
>
> Gather a meeting of Messing, Mantsev, and one other person in Moscow.
>
> Require the members of the Politburo to set aside two to three hours a week for looking through a series of publications and books, *verifying* the

fulfillment [of this], *demanding written opinions* and obtaining dispatches to Moscow without delay of all non-Communist publications.

Obtain the opinions of a series of Communist-litterateurs (Steklov, Ol'minskii, Skvortsov, Bukharin, etc.).

Collect *systematic* information on the political record, work, and literary activity of professors and writers.

Assign all of this to an intelligent, educated, and thorough person in the *GPU.*

My opinions on two Petrograd publications:

Novaia Rossiia, No 2. Closed by our Petrograd comrades.

Isn't it early to close it? We need to send it out to all members of the *Politburo* and discuss it *more attentively.* Who is its editor *Lezhnev?* From [the newspaper] *Den'?* Would it be possible to gather some information about him? Of course, *not all* of the contributors to this journal are candidates for deportation abroad.

But the Petrograd journal *Ekonomist* published by the XIth Department of the Russian Technical Society is another matter altogether. This, in my opinion, is a manifest center of Whiteguards. In No 3 (*only* the third!!! this *nota bene!*) a list of contributors is printed on the cover. They are, I think, *almost all*—the most appropriate candidates for deportation abroad.

All of these are manifest counterrevolutionaries, accomplices of the Entente, the organization of its servants and spies and corrupters [*rastitelei*] of the studying youth. We need to establish the matter such that we search for and catch all of these "military spies" constantly and systematically and deport them abroad.

I ask you to show this secretly, without disseminating it, to *Politburo* members, *returning it to you and me,* and inform me of their opinions and your conclusion.[86]

The main features of the campaign are here already outlined: an exhaustive review of Whiteguard literature;[87] the development of information-gathering procedures and a system for classifying intellectuals; and the handling of all facets of the operation by the GPU. In addition, Lenin had outlined two key ideological charges against the accused counterrevolutionaries: that they served (consciously or unconsciously) as agents of foreign capitalism, and that the professoriat exercised a dangerous corrupting influence on the nation's future, its student youth.

Lenin's sense of urgency was amplified by a note from Commissar of Health Nikolai Semashko regarding the recent physicians' congresses. Semashko warned that "*important* and *dangerous* tendencies . . . are widespread among not only physicians, but also *spetsy* from other specialties (agronomists, engineers, technicians, and lawyers)." The doctors' "pronounced striving to stand outside the general workers' professional movement" was, Semashko felt, an attack by Kadets, Mensheviks, and SRs against Soviet medicine and demanded a harsh response.[88] Lenin alerted Stalin, Dzerzhinskii, and the Politburo, proposing that a plan of action be worked out within two weeks. On 24 May the Politburo concurred over the objection of Mikhail Tomskii, who, despite his upbraiding of the physicians, argued that "the question of the physicians' congress demands a different approach. We ourselves, and in particular comrade Semashko, are much to blame."[89]

Tomskii, however, was alone in his demurral, and the measures against doctors and other *spetsy* were thenceforth linked to the expulsions of writers and professors that Lenin had proposed to Dzerzhinskii. The Politburo adopted Lenin's directive to review Whiteguard literature; potentially pernicious books and journals were scoured for offensive content and their editors and contributors added to the list of deportees.[90] Lenin had his first stroke on 29 May, but even during his recuperation outside Moscow he continued to show vigorous interest in the process. The main features he had outlined were retained, and the lists by and large reflected his specific instructions.

The Case against the Intelligentsia

The first GPU policy document concerning the anti-intellectual campaigns was the report written by Iakov Agranov for the Politburo on 1 June 1922.[91] Agranov tied together the various areas of conflict to provide a holistic indictment of the intellectual public sphere. He asserted that the conflict over university autonomy was entirely political, aimed at limiting Communist authority in the nation's VUZy. Most ominously, the professors had an insidious corrupting effect on the studentry. The GPU had evidence, he claimed, that members of the Moscow and Petrograd professoriat were planning still more interruptions.[92] A similar explanation obtained for scientific and professional societies, which, Agranov contended, were also politically oriented. Even when, like the Pirogov Society's, their aims were "to some degree masked," in the end they aimed at overthrowing the regime. The *spets* congresses served as a means for SRs and Mensheviks to voice pernicious attacks on Soviet power, and cooperatives provided certain "elements" the opportunity to spread their ideas among "a wide spectrum of laboring elements." Journals and publishers provided an institutional foundation for former members of other political parties, and they disseminated counterrevolutionary literature. Finally, Agranov concluded, Blackhundreds had rallied around religion, particularly during the campaign to seize church valuables.[93]

Asserting that the enemy still posed a significant threat served the institutional interests of the GPU and boosted the case that its own task had in no way diminished.[94] Nevertheless, it would be a mistake to view the anti-intellectual campaigns of 1922 as arising from the GPU's institutional ideology and jurisdictional avarice. The conflicts outlined by Agranov raised the ire of Politburo members and frustrated state organs such as Narkomzdrav and Glavprofobr; the idea to link these matters and to initiate the expulsions was clearly Lenin's. The thirst for such a campaign was widespread within the party leadership. On 2 June Trotsky published an anonymous article in *Pravda* entitled "Dictatorship, Where Is Your Whip?" asserting that there was no difference between cultural and political foes and declaring that it had long since been time to take harsher measures.[95] With the exception of Tomskii, even those Bolsheviks who had either striven to limit the Cheka's power or stood to lose institutional authority did not oppose the establishment of GPU-directed administrative exile.[96]

The Politburo and GPU jointly orchestrated the expulsions of intellectuals. On 8 June the Politburo approved Unshlikht's proposal on what to do about "anti-Soviet groups among the intelligentsia," on how to eradicate the threats outlined in Agranov's note.[97] Unshlikht sketched a system of surveillance and control of the intelligentsia, and the Politburo added to this Lenin's plan for exiling selected prominent individuals. A commission was formed consisting of Unshlikht, Kurskii, and Kamenev for planning the deportation abroad of "the leadership [*verkhushki*] of the enemy intellectual groupings." In addition, it directed VTsIK to establish a special conference of representatives from the Commissariats of Justice and Internal Affairs to handle future deportations (either abroad or within Russia) when it was not necessary to "resort to more severe measures."[98]

As noted previously, the 8 June Politburo resolution also contained a number of other measures designed to place systematic restraints on the autonomous public sphere. In an effort to cleanse the VUZy before the next school year, there was to be a filtration of students, strict limits on accepting those of nonproletarian origin, and the erection of a system of verifying students' political reliability. Rules for the formation of professors' and students' organizations were also to be worked out. Second, the caste character of scholarly and professional organizations was to be sharply curtailed. Thenceforth, "not a single congress or all-Russian conference of *spetsy* (doctors, agronomists, engineers, lawyers, etc.) can convene without the corresponding permission of the NKVD"; all "scientific, religious, academic, etc." societies and unions were to be registered with the NKVD; and those that did not comply or were refused permission would be liquidated.

VTsSPS was directed to be extremely cautious in permitting *spets* unions and to require GPU permission for special sections within them. Third, the Politburo authorized the Unshlikht, Kurskii, Kamenev commission to shut down "publications and press organs not compatible with Soviet policies," and the censors to conduct a painstaking review of publications associated with "private societies and *spets* sections under the jurisdiction of *profsoiuzy* and certain People's Commissariats (Narkomzem, Narkompros, etc.)."[99]

The inclusion of these diverse measures demonstrates the holistic approach taken to the problem of eradicating problematic groups within the intelligentsia. Elements of civil society standing in even potential opposition to the regime were not to be tolerated. Independent-minded organizations or groups, no matter how fragile and ephemeral, were to be either eliminated or watched over and controlled. Those publishers and journals seen as giving voice to views openly critical of the regime were to be censored or liquidated. And those people perceived to be leaders of this separatist, corporate, or caste spirit deemed so injurious to state-sponsored harmony were to be taken out of the body politic by the relatively humane but dramatic act of expulsion. The repressive actions taken against a specific group of individuals, societies, and journals were accompanied by subtler, more pervasive restrictions—by the NKVD altering societies' charters, by censors making minor revisions, by specific individuals being prohibited from participating in certain organizations or teaching in certain departments. In addition, as the Bolsheviks repeatedly emphasized, the punitive measures were meant to be exemplary: to demonstrate to other intellectuals what the limits were, what types of things might be punished, and what type of punishment they might expect for transgressing these boundaries.

The Deportation of Medical Doctors

The May 1922 physicians' congress had helped catalyze the process, and as a result the punitive measures against doctors were both part of the general campaign and also a separate initiative.[100] Unshlikht introduced a second proposal to the Politburo on 8 June focusing on the errant physicians. Although most of the deportations were to be delayed until after the SR trial, the so-called interdepartmental ad hoc commission led by Unshlikht, Kurskii, and Kamenev initiated arrests of physicians immediately. Unshlikht reported to the Politburo on 22 June that the commission had compiled a list of doctors "subject to deportation . . . for utilizing their position for anti-Soviet agitation." The Politburo directed Unshlikht to divide these doctors into three categories: those to be arrested and deported immediately, those to be arrested and investigated for the dissemination of illegal literature, and those to be arrested and given a week to settle their affairs before deportation.[101]

At the end of June, the GPU arrested four members of the physicians' section Central Bureau (TsB) in Moscow: N. I. Gurevich, L. B. Granovskii, K. F. Stankevich, and G. A. Verkhovskii.[102] The TsB, led by Ia. Kats, petitioned on behalf of the four, contending that "the only type of public activity in which the arrested members of the TsB engaged was professional." They beseeched the VTsSPS Presidium to ascertain the reasons for the arrests and to accelerate the investigation.[103] The discrepancy between the TsB's protests and the GPU's terse explanation that those arrested had engaged in counterrevolutionary activity reflected the broader discord between intellectuals and the regime. The physicians claimed that the debates at the congress had been of a purely professional nature, whereas the Bolsheviks saw the call to develop alternatives to Soviet medicine as insurrectionary. The TsB complained that those arrested had been punished for professional opinions, but the GPU retorted that the arrests took place "for political, and not professional, activity."[104] Over the summer a number of physicians in other cities associated with the TsB or the congress were also arrested. M. M. Magula and G. I. Dembo, members of the TsB in Petrograd, were the first to be deported to provincial locations. Also arrested were TsB members V. M. Kogan in Kharkov and A. B. Iakhnina in Vitebsk, members of the presidium of the congress L. M. Gorovits-Vlasova and N. A. Vigdorchik in Petrograd, and delegates to the congress A. A. Lozinskii in Petrograd, Frumin in Kiev and D. I. Vostrov in Kaluga.[105]

The physicians' appeals fit a pattern that other institutions petitioning on behalf of intellectuals would use in the following months. The TsB adopted a dual strategy of addressing the GPU directly and of petitioning an intermediary organization, in this case the VTsSPS, which they thought would be sympathetic. Tomskii, despite his harsh warnings at the physicians' congress, resented the interference of the GPU in *spets* unions and similar organizations. But although the VTsSPS assured the TsB that Tomskii would look into the matter, nothing seems to have resulted from this. Tomskii was a dubious ally at best, and by the end of the year the leadership of the physicians' section had been replaced by one more loyal to the Party.

It is also true, however, that some of the most vocal and independent-minded physicians, in particular Kats himself, escaped arrest. Beyond the purposeful selection of several Mensheviks, it is not clear why some were deported and others spared. After the initial round of arrests and banishments in July, the Unshlikht, Kurskii, Kamenev commission sentenced a second group of physicians to exile as well. None was deported abroad; doctors were in too short supply at a time of widespread famine and disease, and even politically suspect ones were too valuable to expel. When the commission compiled the final list of intellectuals to deport at the end of July, it included eleven more physicians, but it resolved to exile all of them to "eastern regions [*guberniia*] of the Republic for use by their specialties for a term of two years."[106]

The Deportation of MVTU Students

Physicians were not the only group sent into internal exile while the expulsions were still in the planning stages. Whereas the doctors' arrests were explicitly connected to the anti-intellectual campaigns, others, like the Mensheviks and famine relief committee leaders, were deported on an ad hoc basis. In June 1922 the leaders of two important student associations at the Moscow Higher Technical School (MVTU), Russia's most important technical institute, were arrested and sent into internal exile.[107] The GPU labeled them "dangerous elements," and their relatives' and the MVTU administration's repeated appeals failed to achieve their release, at least through early 1923. The episode highlights the fact that the Bolsheviks found the control and direction of student organizations at least as important as authority over professors' groups, and that they refused to tolerate those who attempted to maintain the rebellious student tradition.

One of the central motives behind the Bolsheviks' campaign to reform the VUZy was to remold the studentry in their own image. They repeatedly purged the student body of nonproletarians and anyone deemed politically disloyal. The arrests at MVTU were part of a series of punitive actions against "dangerous" student leaders in summer 1922, preceding the deportation of their professors. The GPU uncovered student cells at both MGU and the second MGU, and at MVTU, the Institute of Transportation Engineers (IIPS), and the Petrovsko-Razumovskii Agricultural Academy, uniting "Kadet monarchists" and "right socialists" and conducting "intense anti-Soviet agitation in both academic and political matters." During June and July 1922, "the active part of this studentry was arrested and deported to northern and non-university cities of the RSFSR."[108]

At the end of June 1922, approximately a dozen MVTU students were arrested and sent to various provincial locations. Precise charges were not forthcoming, but they faced the same sort of general counterrevolutionary allegations that would be levied against their professors. In response to an inquiry by the MVTU rector M. G. Lukin, Glavprofobr chief Varvara Iakovleva looked into the matter. The news, she told Lukin, was not good. "The GPU promises to conduct the investigation of these students in a timely manner, but it does not consider it possible to free them before then, as the preliminary information is very serious."[109] She did not explain this information, but a week earlier, she herself had ordered the school's two official student groups, the Academic Section and the Cooperative Section, to be closed down for having taken on political functions.[110] At least six of the arrested students had recently been elected as representatives to these groups and at least one other had been among the active supporters of autonomy at the February student meetings.[111] The GPU had decided that mere removal from the student body was not, in this case, sufficient.

With all indications that they would be convicted, their wives and relatives turned to the MVTU board. Their appeals averred that those arrested had done nothing wrong and promised that they would abstain from all political activity. From a few meetings that they were granted with their arrested husbands or relatives, they had determined that the charges were unspecified and unfounded, although they understood that it was participation in the Academic and Cooperative sections that had motivated the arrests. "There is absolutely no substance to the accusations; moreover, they have already gotten several of the arrested students to sign their agreement to the fact that they will not participate in any kind of student social organizations."[112]

Repeated pleas from the MVTU board to Glavprofobr fell on deaf ears. At least ten of the arrested students remained in exile, and the board's appeals for their release were ineffective, even when it petitioned under the terms of the amnesty held in conjunction with the fifth anniversary of the October Revolution. As often happened, these petitions were passed on to the very highest organs of power, in this case VTsIK, the body in charge of coordinating the amnesties.[113]

Although the deportation of these students was an ad hoc action that took place before the planned expulsions, both were linked to the regime's desire to tightly control public discourse among the studentry. These arrests also foreshadowed the eventual explicit inclusion of students in the planned deportation campaigns and mass arrests among students in the fall. If a new, Soviet studentry was to be created, it was imperative to remove dangerous influences not just from among those who taught them, but from among those who studied alongside them as well.

The Interdepartmental Commission and the Development of the Campaign

These arrests were a start, but the comprehensive cleansing Lenin had in mind called for a more thoroughly planned process. As the doctors and students were exiled, the interdepartmental commission of Unshlikht, Kurskii, and

Kamenev compiled lists of intellectuals for deportation abroad. The makeup of the commission placed those who had been most wary of the Cheka's extralegal powers in a position to watch over this GPU action. By their very participation, however, Kamenev and Kurskii contributed to the expansion of the GPU's authority. The advisory bodies reporting to the commission were under Unshlikht's auspices; the other participants were GPU operatives such as Agranov and Genrikh Iagoda; and the timing of the arrests was fixed by the GPU Collegium.[114] Certain Bolsheviks would later question the list of intellectuals, but at the time they were compiled, neither Kamenev nor Kurskii seem to have objected.[115]

The assembling of names came from several interconnected sources and was directed by Lenin. In addition to those individuals he had originally mentioned to Dzerzhinskii, he singled out several more in a 16 July letter to Stalin from his convalescent home outside Moscow, in which he chided his colleagues for not bringing the process to completion more quickly. He identified potential deportees either by party affiliation or by connection to journals, private publishers, or literary or cultural organizations. He had continued his careful perusal of Whiteguard literature and directed the GPU to scan lists of journal contributors and arrest as many as possible:

> Decisively "root out" all the NSs [Popular Socialists]. *Peshekhonov,* Miakotin, Gornfel'd, Petrishchev, etc. In my opinion, deport them all. They are more harmful than any SR, because they are more cunning.
>
> Also A. N. Potresov, Izgoev, *and all* contributors to *Ekonomist* (Ozerov and *many, many* others). The Mensheviks Rozanov (a cunning enemy), Vigdorchik ([and] Migula [*sic*] or something along those lines);[116] Liubov' Nikolaevna Radchenko and her young daughter (who it is said are the most malicious enemies of Bolshevism). N. A. Rozhkov (need to deport him, we will not correct him); S. A. [*sic*] Frank (the author of the *Methodology*).[117] The Commission under the supervision of Mantsev, Messing, etc. should compile lists and we need to deport several *hundred* similar gentlemen without pity. We will cleanse Russia for a long time.
>
> Regarding Lezhnev (former [editor of] *Den'*), we should think about deporting him. He will always be most insidious, as far as I can judge by his articles that I have read.
>
> Ozerov, like *all* the contributors to *Ekonomist* are the most relentless enemies. Get all of them out of Russia.
>
> We need to do this immediately. Before the end of the SR trial, no later. Arrest several hundred and *without declaration* of motives—be gone, gentlemen! All the authors of the [*Letopis'*] *Dom literatorov,* of the Petersburg [journal] *Mysl';* ransack Kharkov, *we do not know it,* it is for us the "abroad." . . .

> Pay attention to the litterateurs in Petersburg (addresses are in *Novaia russkaia kniga* No. 4, 1922, p. 37) and to the list of private publishers (on p. 29).[118]

Thus, even after his stroke and removal from daily decision making, Lenin attempted to direct whom to expel and how quickly. The final lists of intellectuals approved closely echoed the individuals, journals, and organizations he had targeted. The extent to which the campaign depended on Lenin's initiative (even after his stroke) is extraordinary.[119] It was only after the arrests that appeals reduced the eventual number of deportees well below the several hundred that he had proposed. Even then, most of the appeals were done in accord with Lenin's oft-repeated directive that bourgeois *spetsy* be brought into the Soviet economic fold when possible.

On 20 July 1922 Unshlikht reported to the Politburo on the campaign's progress. The Politburo, following Lenin's remarks, declared that the lists of intellectuals needed to be both more extensive and more carefully explicated, and it directed the formation of specialized subcommissions to justify including specific individuals.[120] Such explanations were entirely for internal consumption and reflected the deeply ingrained desire to know and categorize the enemy, also manifest in the assigned reading of Whiteguard publications. As Unshlikht and his colleagues worked to elucidate the rationale for deporting particular intellectuals, party and GPU leaders began to consider how better to expand and systematize their database.

Shortly after the arrests of intellectuals, Dzerzhinskii wrote to Unshlikht that the GPU needed to rethink and improve how it gathered information on intellectuals.

> It is necessary to work out a plan, constantly correcting and supplementing it. We need to divide the entire intelligentsia by groups, for example:
>
> 1) belletrists,
> 2) publicists and politicals,
> 3) economists (here we need subgroups a) financial experts, b) fuel-related, c) transport-related, d) trade, e) cooperators),
> 4) technicals (here also subgroups a) engineers, b) agronomists, c) doctors, d) military officers),
> 5) professors and instructors, etc. etc.
>
> Information should be collected by all of our departments and be brought together in a department on the intelligentsia. For every intellectual there should be a file, each group and subgroup should be elucidated from all sides by competent comrades. . . . We need to remember that the task of

> our department should be not just deportation but assistance in the erection of a line in relation to the specialists, i.e., the introduction in their ranks of disintegration and the promotion [*vydvyzheniia*] of those who are prepared to support Soviet power without qualification.[121]

Dzerzhinskii was, in essence, proposing the creation of a taxonomic database of intellectuals, fitting each into a set of categories.[122] Within this database, there was to be an even more crucial binary distinction—whether the given individual was redeemable or irredeemable for Soviet power—and the promotion of those who were judged to be sufficiently supportive of the regime. Although he bemoaned the lack of cadres qualified to undertake this task, Dzerzhinskii nevertheless expressed the hope that the security apparatus would cultivate specialists who would possess expertise on all the various breeds of intellectuals.

Those directing the expulsions had in fact consulted ad hoc versions of several such bodies. On 22 July Unshlikht gathered a group of Bolshevik literary "experts," including Lebedev-Polianskii and I. I. Ionov, the head of the Petrograd Gosizdat, to discuss the characteristics of certain cultural figures. The experts were thus external to the actual security apparatus, and the categories with which they were dealing were extremely broad, centering on the term "litterateur," a catchall for writers, journalists, publicists, literary critics, historians, and philosophers. Moreover, the experts examined the entire Petrograd list, including people outside the competence of a strictly literary commission. A second, "economic" group consisted of the VSNKh chief Pëtr Bogdanov; S. P. Sereda, a high-level official in both VSNKh and Gosplan; L. M. Khinchuk, the former Menshevik chairman of Tsentrosoiuz; and V. M. Likhachev, chair of the Moscow city economic council. Third, Glavprofobr, in the person of Iakovleva, was asked its opinion of professors and of many other intellectuals (most with some connection to higher education) on the list.[123]

The 22 July literary subcommission, discussed many of those Lenin had mentioned, including the Popular Socialists A. V. Peshekhonov, V. A. Miakotin, and Aleksandr Iziumov, and those associated with Sergei Mel'gunov's publishing house, Zadruga, including A. A. Kizevetter, V. S. Ozeretskovskii, V. M. Kudriavtsev, the journalist V. A. Rozenberg, and the pedagogue V. I. Charnolusskii. The Petrograd lists singled out members of the House of Litterateurs, including Zamiatin, Petrishchev, Volkovyskii, and Boris Khariton; contributors to *Ekonomist* and other journals, including Lutokhin, Brutskus, and Efim Zubashev; and other professors and cooperators. The literary subcommission overwhelmingly supported the GPU lists with several notable exceptions: they advised that Zamiatin be deported internally, since "upon exile abroad he would become a dangerous leader," and Lebedev-Polianskii and Ionov also proposed exiling Aikhenval'd and Berdiaev internally for unspecified reasons.[124]

The second, economic, subcommission was consulted regarding a number of potential deportees with economic, technical, cooperative, or agricultural backgrounds, and it weighed in on other individuals as well. (Several other officials appear to have had their opinions solicited on an individual basis.) In a few instances, the consultants objected to expelling particular individuals, who as often as not were outside their purported area of expertise. Although it makes sense that Khinchuk was against deporting Viktor Krokhmal', a Menshevik Tsentrosoiuz colleague, and that Bogdanov opposed the deportation of several (but not all) of the engineers listed, it is curious that he opposed the deportation of the historian Miakotin "in view of his harmlessness," and that Commissar of Health Semashko, who had been instrumental in initiating the prosecution of physicians, came out against the deportation of Stepun (as did Bogdanov) but in favor of Frank's.[125]

In fact, these specialists were simply considered more knowledgeable about the intelligentsia in general, and their authority lent weight to the final lists. Their objections were minimal. Glavprofobr's Iakovleva, who had formerly been Unshlikht's colleague in the Cheka, was particularly supportive and did not oppose the inclusion of any of those on the final list.[126] It is no accident that Iakovleva and Lebedev-Polianskii assisted the process while their more conciliatory nominal boss, Lunacharskii, was out of the loop. The commissar of Enlightenment was occupied with the SR trial and then spent much of August abroad. He registered no opposition to the expulsions at the time; despite his moderate reputation and occasionally more lenient attitude toward intellectuals, he had made clear his fury with the professors and had helped quash their autonomous organizations. Still, Iakovleva was undoubtedly a more amenable adviser, and Lunacharskii had poor relations with Zinoviev, one of the leaders of the anti-intellectual campaigns.[127]

The annotations developed during these meetings joined generic political epitaphs with specific offenses. For example, the astronomer Vsevolod Stratonov, it was asserted, had edited a Blackhundred newspaper before the Revolution and was a decided anti-Semite, which made his evolution into a "ringleader" (*glavar'*) of the MGU professors' strikes a logical extension of his activities as a "malicious opponent of Soviet power." Moreover, it was claimed, he was not a particularly outstanding scholar. The engineering professor Ivan Kukolevskii "conducted anti-Soviet agitation, even during lectures," and had actively participated in the protests against the Glavprofobr-approved board at MVTU. They were both accused of being dangerous influences on the studentry: Stratonov by supporting the admission of bourgeois and Whiteguard students and Kukolevskii by spreading his pernicious views while teaching and at student assemblies. Nikolai Tiapkin, a professor at the Institute of Transportation Engineers, was a monarchist and had even dedicated a lecture to the memory of Nikolai II as founder of the institute; he had ties with unspecified White organizations and, in addition, had been a leader of the strikes at the institute.[128]

The most generally applicable of the political labels were "counterrevolutionary" and "anti-Soviet." The cooperator Ivan Matveev, "by political convictions a Kadet," had helped ensure that the selection of delegates at the All-Russian Congress of Agricultural Cooperatives had favored "the old cooperators of the kadetizing [*kadetstvuiushchego*] type, who had distinguished themselves by their anti-Soviet work." The institutional or publishing ties of, and recent works by, litterateurs were carefully registered, and their political tendencies were then exposed. Thus, it was noted that Sorokin had ties to *Ekonomicheskoe vozrozhdenie* and *Artel'noe delo;* that he was a former SR and "an unquestionably anti-Soviet figure"; and that his recent book, *Hunger as a Factor in Human Affairs,* was "hostile and contains a whole series of insinuations against Soviet power." Kizevetter was a board member of Zadruga, had been a member of the Kadet Central Committee, and was implicated in the Tactical Center affair; he could, then, "undoubtedly serve as a center of cohesion for anti-Soviet forces." The "best demonstration" that Efim Zubashev was a "dangerous person" was his articles in *Ekonomist,* and the ex-Bolshevik Zamiatin had proven himself a "hidden, inveterate Whiteguard" through his activities at the House of Litterateurs.[129]

Some were targeted simply for having contributed to a particular journal (following Lenin's orders to arrest every name on the masthead). As the case of "Chaadaev" shows,[130] a single act was enough to define an enemy. The behavior under scrutiny was said to be part of a larger pattern of anti-Soviet or counterrevolutionary activity, which was naturally consistent with an unalterably hostile political worldview, characterized as Kadet, Blackhundred, Whiteguard, and so on. These enemies, then, were defined not just for having committed specific acts or expressed particular views that were "harmful" or anti-Soviet, but as being irredeemable opponents. The only way to combat such inveterate foes was to remove them from the scene completely.

Enemy definition operated within the discourse of dialectical struggle; a Menshevik or a Kadet or a Whiteguard could be known by his activities, associations, and utterances and did not have to be a member of the Menshevik Party to "objectively" be a Menshevik. Others who were said to behave in a similar manner were then easily categorized.[131] The accusations against these intellectuals were more or less sincere rants against individuals who were held to be more insidious when they did not reveal their "true" nature (as Blackhundreds, Mensheviks, etc.) than when they did. Such internal enemies could not be tolerated, and an example had to be made of them.

Confirmation and Legislation

A sense of urgency developed as rumors of the impending deportations spread among intellectuals in Soviet Russia and in the émigré community.[132] On 27 July the Politburo directed the interdepartmental commission to settle the logistical matter of expenses and the acquisition of visas.[133] Several days later, the commission finalized the lists to expel "persons not reconciling with the regime in the course of the almost five-year existence of Soviet power and continuing counterrevolutionary activities at a moment of internal difficulties for the Soviet republic," a charge that would be the standard formulation throughout the process of arrest, interrogation, and expulsion. The accused were to be given three days to settle their affairs, and, if they refused to pay for their travel, the GPU was to be given funds to assist in their departure. The commission also confirmed the closure of *Utrenniki* and *Ekonomist* and banned several more journals, including *Ekonomicheskoe vozrozhdenie, Literaturnye zapiski, Vestnik sel'skogo khoziaistva,* and *Mysl'*.[134]

Unshlikht next moved to have the matter officially sanctioned by permanent party and state bodies. He sent Stalin the annotated lists on 2 August for Politburo approval, while simultaneously sending for VTsIK's ratification a draft decree on administrative exile, the adoption of which was a stipulation of the 8 June Politburo resolution.[135] The process was shelved for the duration of the Party Conference, at which Zinoviev's speech and the accompanying resolutions on anti-Soviet groups among the intelligentsia provided the intellectual public with its first real sense that the party was preparing some sort of action. It also led some Petrograd-based intellectuals to believe that Zinoviev was the driving force behind the entire process.[136] The Politburo approved the list of 217 anti-Soviet intellectuals from Moscow, Petrograd, and Ukraine on 10 August 1922; it directed the GPU to conduct apartment searches but arrest only those they thought might hide, allowing the rest to remain under house arrest.[137] The list was then approved by the GPU Collegium, which ordered searches and, contrary to the Politburo's directive, the arrest of *all* "indicated persons."[138]

Although the Politburo and GPU may have disagreed on certain details, both envisioned a speedy, predetermined process. Conviction came before arrest, and all evidence gathered through search and interrogation was meant merely to buttress the case and provide the appearance of due process. Why search and interrogation were considered necessary, since there was not even a mock trial, is not entirely clear. It was, however, quite consistent with the Bolsheviks' stress on following the form of the law, and, perhaps more important, on gathering for their own edification as much specific evidence proving their conclusions as they could. Though the party and GPU leaders had already proclaimed that these men were irreconcilable enemies, the trappings of an investigative process would make these assertions more substantial.

The third body formally approving the deportations was VTsIK. On Lenin's insistence, expulsion had been inserted into the criminal code as an alternative to capital punishment, but it was mentioned infrequently and without much explanation. The decree on administrative exile was designed to expand dramatically the place of exile in the punitive system. It also gave jurisdiction to the policing apparatus (the NKVD and GPU); Narkomiust had merely an advisory role. Hypothetically, then, a dual system was established in which exile could be decided either by executive order ("administratively") or by the formal judicial process in the courts. In practice, the institution of exile (which after 1923 was almost exclusively internal) was nearly always administrative and the province of the NKVD and OGPU.

There were several amendments made to the draft decree on administrative exile submitted by Unshlikht.[139] The final decree established a special commission, to be confirmed by VTsIK and under the auspices of the NKVD, for the employment of deportation either abroad or to distant regions within the RSFSR. Internal deportees would then be under the surveillance and control of the GPU. The maximum length of deportation was reduced from Unshlikht's proposed five to three years, and a clause allowing that deportation abroad might be indefinite was eliminated.[140] To maintain a semblance of legality, the subsequent development of the system of exile, as well as surveillance over and registration of societies and their congresses, was to remain in the hands of the NKVD apparatus. This, however, neither halted GPU involvement (and the deportations of intellectuals in particular was and remained a GPU affair), nor stopped the NKVD from also acquiring the characteristics of an unchecked secret police apparatus. In addition, while Dzerzhinskii headed both the NKVD and GPU, the jurisdictional divisions meant little. Only after the OGPU again became a self-standing entity in fall 1923 and Dzerzhinskii relinquished his position as commissar of Internal Affairs did an institutional rivalry erupt.[141]

Equally important was the GPU's and NKVD's ability to exploit the ambiguity inherent in the phrases "anti-Soviet" and "counterrevolutionary acts," the crimes for which deportation was originally designed as a punishment.[142] The accusations against intellectuals were framed so that opposition to particular policies or involvement with certain offensive publications was labeled "counterrevolutionary." This sort of rhetoric was an integral part of Bolshevik discourse, and the GPU simply followed the example of Lenin and other party leaders. Lenin himself had asserted that these intellectuals were counterrevolutionaries implicitly aiding the international bourgeoisie, and this struck a cord with the genuine anxiety and vigilance that predominated in the highest ranks. What some of Lenin's colleagues did not foresee was that this allocation to the policing apparatus of the right to interpret what constituted *counterrevolution* would provide a loophole around the limitations on its extraordinary powers, not only making a farce of the concept of socialist legality, but also providing it with a weapon that would eventually be used against many of them.

By August 1922 the Bolsheviks had initiated a series of operations to eliminate proven foes and send a strong warning. These punitive actions were aimed not only at open political opponents, but at anyone whose activities were antithetical to the establishment of a unitary public sphere. The corporate or caste spirit manifest in an insistence on cultural, intellectual, or professional autonomy was seen as not at all different from active Menshevik or SR opposition. The equivalency thus established, and the use of elastic and ever-expanding pejorative labels, allowed the security apparatus eventually to include more and more people within the various categories of enemy.

But at the time, the Bolsheviks' tentative grip on the reins of power dictated that they involve anyone of whose loyalty they could be convinced in the daunting task of rebuilding the nation's economy. As a result, the campaigns of 1922–23 were limited to a relatively small number of intellectuals, and efforts were made to differentiate those who could still assert their loyalty from those who were entirely irredeemable. This distinction, however, was not always clear to either side. As arrests began in mid-August, a cry of confusion arose from those who had foresworn political action and considered themselves loyal (or at least harmless). Although a number of them had had multiple experiences in Bolshevik prisons, this action caught many off guard.

7

The Deportations, Part II: Arrest, Negotiation, and Expulsion

I know some of these men personally and they assure me that they have kept out of politics and they have no idea why they are being sent out. One professor argued with the G.P.U. and asked to produce one single act against him. He was asked, "Are you for us or against us?" "I am not for you," he replied. "Then you had better leave the country." . . . I have been trying to account for it, but I am not sure I know what is in the head of the government aside from the desire to remove any influence which is in opposition to it. They are afraid of "ideology."

—From the diary and letters of Frank Golder, historian and ARA official, August 1922

In the early morning hours of 17 August 1922, security operatives fanned out across Moscow and Petrograd, jarring hundreds of intellectuals and their families awake. The *chekisty* rifled drawers looking for incriminating evidence, after which convoys whisked the dazed scholars away to the infamous Butyrka and Shpalernaia prisons. There an assortment of the most educated men in Russia shared jail cells and was marched through the interrogation chambers of the GPU. Over the next weeks and months, dozens of Russia's best-known professors, writers, and scientists were imprisoned, questioned, and ordered to leave the country. Bewildered, they hurried to gather themselves, their families, and their belongings in preparation for departure.

The arrested intellectuals reacted with a mixture of despair, defiance, and resignation. The yearlong propaganda campaign, and especially Zinoviev's virulent speech, had put them on alert. As the ARA official Frank Golder related a week before the arrests, "Since that speech was made and approved by the Party I have had occasion to talk to the professors and other intellectuals under fire and they said: 'We are not afraid. We are hardened to suffering. We can not be worse off than we are today. They can not kill us because they can not get along without us. Let them do their worst.'"[1] Despite this bravado, even those who had already spent time in Soviet jails were alarmed and mystified. While fearing the worst, most adamantly rejected the notion that their academic, cultural, and professional activities were politically disloyal or posed a threat to the regime.

Arrest and Imprisonment

After their apartments were searched, most of the intellectuals were imprisoned, some were instead placed under house arrest, and still others simply had certain documents confiscated and were told to prepare for departure. After the first round of searches in Moscow, according to the GPU, eleven people were under house arrest, fourteen were imprisoned, two had already been in prison, twenty-one were freed to prepare for departure abroad, eight had not been located, and eleven were in other cities.[2] It took some time for the GPU to locate everyone, since many were at their dachas or traveling for the summer. Iagoda reported to an impatient Lenin on 18 September, a month after the start of the arrests, making clear that a number of intellectuals had not yet been found.[3]

Word of the arrests spread quickly, although no one was sure of the exact implications. The philosopher Nikolai Losskii was in Tsarskoe Selo, and, on receiving instructions to appear at the Petrograd GPU, assumed he was to be allowed to travel on sabbatical. He went quite willingly and was promptly arrested. The agronomist Aleksandr Ugrimov was at a KUBU-run sanatorium when his Moscow apartment was searched, and, like Losskii, he voluntarily turned himself in. Venedikt Miakotin was ill in the country, and he himself phoned the authorities on his return to Moscow; the GPU operative N. I. Zaraiskii invited him for questioning, after which he was let go to prepare for departure. Fëdor Stepun, who was also in the countryside, found out through his sister that his apartment had been searched and received a GPU summons several days later. Stepun wondered anxiously, "Could one really believe the Cheka? Could one really know whether the rumors about expulsion were not perhaps started consciously, in order to extort an open confession?" But his fears were unfounded, and after his interrogation, he was released to prepare for departure.[4]

Nikolai Berdiaev, Mikhail Osorgin, and their families were in the small town of Barkhivi. Berdiaev recalled, "We forgot about the nightmare regime, one felt it less in the country. At one point I went for a day to Moscow. And precisely on that night, the only one all summer that I spent in our Moscow apartment, they came for a search and arrested me."[5] Word was soon sent to Barkhivi. "As we were accustomed to the nonsense of the time," Osorgin recalled, "Berdiaev's arrest did not surprise us. We heard also of others, just as alien to any active politics, just as far from being 'enemies of the Revolution,' and 'Whiteguards.'" Fearing arrest himself, and having only recently been allowed to return from internal exile, Osorgin hid in the countryside. On hearing the rumors of expulsion, he decided to risk it and called the GPU. Though friends and colleagues who said that they were fortunate to be going abroad congratulated them, Osorgin felt an understandable trepidation as he went to the Lubianka. There, he wryly recalled, the guards at first refused to let him in without a *propusk* (pass) before at last allowing him to be interrogated.[6]

Pitirim Sorokin was in Moscow when the GPU searched his home in Petrograd. He discovered that the friends he was visiting had been arrested and received a telegram from his wife with a cryptic warning: "Please detain my son. We have scarlet fever in our house." Sorokin remained in Moscow for a week, until he was certain that he did not face execution. "As soon as the fate of my arrested colleagues became known, I decided that my own banishment abroad was the best thing that could happen." The Moscow GPU at first refused to arrest him and told him to return to Petrograd. Sorokin, however, wanting to avoid imprisonment under the jurisdiction of the reviled Zinoviev, insisted that they arrest him in Moscow or not at all.[7]

The astronomer Vsevolod Stratonov, like Berdiaev, had just come home from his dacha. When the building *komandant,* a former student of his, arrived, Stratonov told his son to delay the *chekisty.* "I open[ed] the drawer of my writing desk. What was the most dangerous? Here—a few pages of my memoir notes. For keeping this diary, I could be shot." Hiding it in a secret drawer, he tried to stay calm while the operatives rifled through his things, but they did not find the diary. He gathered some food and sewed money into his clothes. By the time they sealed his office and the car came to take them away, it was 4:00 A.M. He shared the ride to prison with an unfamiliar man with a gray mustache who he later learned was A. D.

Arbuzov, a high-ranking tsarist official. "My perceptions were oddly deadened," Stratonov recalled, "the future was not yet alarming, the danger could not yet be sensed, . . . I turned to look around . . ."[8]

This sense of dislocation was common; it appears again in the recollections of one of Stratonov's colleagues, the zoologist and former MGU rector Mikhail Novikov. "At dawn, when the search was completed, my wife and I, exhausted by the difficult sleepless night, sat by the samovar in order to fortify ourselves with hot tea. The marvelous September weather continued—Indian summer, and the window of our spacious dining room was opened wide." V. P. Volgin, then the Communist rector of MGU, came later and expressed indignation at Novikov's house arrest. Several days later, Novikov was called into the GPU and informed that he was to be deported.[9]

Some were questioned immediately and allowed to go home; others were eventually called for interrogation from their cells. Those who remained in prison gradually realized the enormity of the situation. When Stratonov came upon Vsevolod Iasinskii, the deputy chair of KUBU, he realized that he would not receive help from the usual sources. "His face was pale and serious; no doubt I didn't look any better. And I had directed my son to turn especially to Iasinskii for assistance." These encounters led to an odd camaraderie among people who had little else in common. Sergei Trubetskoi met Semën Frank and several others: a cooperator, an artillery officer, a student, and so on, "a mix, which would seem unusual only to a person unfamiliar with the practices of the ChK-GPU."[10] The situation was much the same in Petrograd, where the intellectuals passed one another as they were being brought in, on their way to the interrogation chamber, and as they were taken together from the house of initial confinement to the main prison on Shpalernaia Street.[11]

The GPU also decided to deport several individuals who had already been imprisoned, including Sergei Mel'gunov, the head of Zadruga publishing.[12] Mel'gunov, who had been in prison since June, was released in extremely haggard condition to prepare for his departure. He was one of the few to be given the choice of expulsion or internal exile, as Kuskova and Prokopovich had. The Political Red Cross, fearing that Mel'gunov would face a worse fate if he remained, pressed for his expulsion. The GPU's Viacheslav Menzhinskii told Mel'gunov that the GPU preferred to send him to the far north, but it had relented and agreed to his deportation abroad.[13]

As the GPU and party leaders discussed adding more names to the lists, the Politburo approved an Unshlikht proposal to deport "enemy groups among the studentry." A troika of Kamenev, Unshlikht, and Preobrazhenskii was formed, and eighteen students were arrested on 31 August 1922.[14] They, too, were charged under Article 57 of the criminal code, some being sentenced to internal exile and others to expulsion abroad.[15] Gavril Goretskii, a student at the Petrovskii Agricultural Academy, was released after extensive petitioning on his behalf. Other than Vladimir Golovachev, a former member of the famine relief committee, few if any of these students actually left Russia. Nevertheless, these arrests, together with other punitive actions, indicated an intensification of the campaign to purify Russia's studentry of hostile and corrupting elements.

Publicity and Propaganda

Word spread quickly through educated circles and among foreigners in the two capitals.[16] The arrests and planned expulsions were soon covered in the foreign press,[17] and the Bolsheviks were forced to explain their motives, which at first they did with some uncertainty. Kamenev denied his role in the undertaking and claimed that the exiles would be allowed to return in a year; L. B. Krasin, according to Frank Golder, "is discouraged and says he does not know what it is all about"; Pëtr Smidovich, the recently appointed vice-chairman of VTsIK, which had not yet approved the lists, "said he knew nothing about it"; and Kurskii told the Associated Press correspondent that as many as fifteen hundred people would be expelled from Russia.[18]

In an interview with foreign correspondents on 25 August, Trotsky described the operation as a prophylactic device. "Russia should not have enemies in the rear. In view of the fact that the professors and their ilk have not been able to make peace with the Soviet [state] during the last five years, they must be regarded as enemies." Although the deportees were politically insignificant, they were "potential weapons in the hands of our possible enemies." In the case of a war, the regime would be forced to shoot these people, and, therefore it was acting with "farsighted humaneness," which he hoped the foreign correspondents would dutifully relate.[19] This emphasis on restraint was, of course, part of a larger campaign to soften the Bolsheviks' international image.

In a speech to the Petrograd soviet published in the local party organ, Zinoviev, too, spoke with an ear to external opinion: "We have selected the most humane measure, deportation abroad. Of course, this is the most humane measure. They portray us as beasts." He singled out his old nemesis, Gorky, who, having protested the SR trial, would likely complain that Soviet Russia was foolishly expelling its best men. Gorky, he noted bitingly, had a tendency to kowtow before intellectuals. The deportees were potential foes on the internal front serving the interests of émigré groups. The Bolsheviks very much valued intellectuals, but only those willing to work for the good of the state. "The meaning of this action undertaken against part of the intelligentsia might be concisely formulated as 'he who is not with us, and does not want to help the rebirth of Russia, is against us.'"[20] In these remarks we see both the vividness of the Soviet binary worldview and the claim to a stark equivalence between what was good for the Bolsheviks and what was good for Russia.

Though expulsion allowed the Bolsheviks to claim they had been merciful, it was also intended to demonstrate that they dealt firmly with their enemies. A 31 August *Pravda* article entitled "A First Warning" asserted that the regime had shown too much patience toward those who were working on behalf of the Whiteguard emigration. The deportations represented a first warning: the regime would use any means possible to uncover and eliminate hidden struggles against it. Even the notion that those who demonstrated their loyalty would avoid a similar fate was, like NEP, portrayed as a necessary but temporary concession; "this helps remind workers and peasants that they need to have their own worker-peasant intelligentsia as soon as possible."[21]

The rising intolerance of opposition led to numerous arrests not directly related to the expulsions, including continued harassment of Mensheviks. Stalin declared that "humanitarian" methods would not last indefinitely, and that the Bolsheviks would not hesitate to return to terror. "Let them recall that we fulfill our promises, and how we carry out our warnings—this should be familiar by recent experience. All those sympathizing with our political opponents should forewarn their friends who are going much too far, transgressing permitted boundaries and ever more openly acting out against the government."[22] If they did not heed this warning, he added, the Bolsheviks would be forced to use terror against both active opponents and those who sympathized with them.

Interrogations

The investigation was conducted with a typical attention to form. If in certain cases the verdict was later altered, this occurred because of discussions among party and state leaders and not because of anything said in the GPU's interrogation chambers. Unlike that in the recently completed SR show trial, the questioning was not meant to support a demonstrative, propagandistic prosecution, and no effort was made to force those questioned to admit their crimes. The interrogations were conducted out of a desire to corroborate conclusions that had already been reached. The GPU was expanding and justifying its analyses of the moods or attitudes of various segments of the population, and it was eager to gather information that might be used to highlight the dangers against which the proletarian state still had to protect itself.

The GPU asked each arrested intellectual an almost identical set of questions concerning the various arenas of "ideological struggle" motivating the expulsions.[23] They did not suspect the intellectuals of direct involvement in counterrevolutionary conspiracy; rather, their views and activities were taken as indication of their *potential* as enemies. First, a questionnaire ascertained personal data, including class origin, occupation, party affiliation, and political convictions.[24] During the interrogations themselves, the following questions were asked:

> State your views on the structure of the Soviet regime and the proletarian state system;
>
> State your views on the tasks of the intelligentsia and of the so-called "public" [*obshchestvennost'*];
>
> State your views on political parties in general and the Russian Communist Party in particular;
>
> State your attitude toward such methods of struggle with Soviet power as the professors' strikes;
>
> State your attitude toward *smenovekhovstvo,* Savinkov, and the SR trial;
>
> State your views on the Soviet regime's policies regarding higher education and your attitude toward its reforms;
>
> State your views on the prospects for the Russian emigration.

The GPU and party could thus gather information in sensitive areas from precisely those whom they deemed most threatening. In so doing they increased their understanding of the intelligentsia's mood and confirmed for themselves that those arrested were truly ideologically dangerous.

Their answers were alternately candid, defiant, or pleading. For some, the entire process was a farce, some hoped to mock the *chekisty,* whom they detested, others on the contrary tried to prove their innocence and loyalty, and others just wanted it to be over. Most rejected the charge that their cultural, academic, and professional activities could be considered politically disloyal. Osorgin went so far as to turn in an attestation denying any wrongdoing. "I not only do not confess guilt, but absolutely do not understand what provoked the given accusation. . . . I do not and could not engage in anti-Soviet activity, as I engage exclusively in artistic literature, alien to political colorings." Berdiaev and Kizevetter also submitted formal affidavits denying anti-Soviet activity.[25]

Several tried to differentiate their distaste for the Bolsheviks from disloyalty, a distinction the regime refused to accept. "By the cast of my thinking,"

Stratonov later summarized his replies, "I cannot sympathize with Communism. But in my work [*sluzhebnoi*] activities I have observed loyalty toward the Soviet regime." His GPU interrogator, however, wondered how he could consider organizing the professors' strikes as loyal behavior.[26] Others tried to insert even more nuance into their answers. Zamiatin, while decrying the use of repression, still believed that "Soviet power might in the future be one of the more successful state organizations, after the correction of 'small shortcomings of the mechanism' "; on the other hand, he felt that the task of the intelligentsia was "to be the brains of the nation, and, if it sees 'shortcomings of the mechanism'—to speak about them."[27]

Others did not hide their political and philosophical opposition. The Hegelian scholar Ivan Il'in declared that he considered the Soviet regime "a historically inevitable processing of a great social-spiritual ailment that has ripened in Russia over the course of the last several centuries." Berdiaev distanced himself from all class-based ideologies while simultaneously attacking basic egalitarianism. "My personal ideology I consider aristocratic, not in the estate sense, but in the sense of the rule of the best, the smartest, the most talented, the most educated, the most noble. I consider democracy a mistake, because it depends on the rule of the majority." He pointedly added, "I think there cannot be a proletarian state in Russia, because the majority of the Russian people are peasants." Sergei Trubetskoi wryly declared that he observed the development of the Soviet regime "with great interest," and later scoffed that his interrogator "didn't know how to ask a question clearly and understood the answers even less." Stepun, on the other hand, who feared getting into even greater trouble, avoided provocation. "I decided to respond completely openly, but softly, without fervor or any sort of harsh words, not as a political activist, which I had not considered myself since the downfall of February, but as a passive but honest and incorruptible contemplative observer of the occurring events." Like Stratonov, he attempted to make a distinction between his loyal political attitude toward the government and his philosophical conviction that Bolshevism was a "grave illness of the popular spirit."[28]

For various reasons, no one much liked *smenovekhovstvo*. "I consider the *smenovekhovtsy* unprincipled and hypocritical political opportunists," Il'in declared. Zamiatin saw them as "a bourgeois group, which sees in NEP a return . . . to bourgeois state organization. This is very far from socialism."[29] There were also few expressions of sympathy or affinity for the emigration.[30] In matters closer to home, opinions differed. No one had anything positive to say about the Bolsheviks' reforms of higher education, although not everyone was sure that the strikes had been useful. Berdiaev asserted, "If the professoriat struggles for the interest of science and knowledge, then this

I consider right-principled; if their struggle is based on a strictly economic point of view, I consider it mistaken." But, he added, "I do not sympathize with the policies of the Soviet regime regarding higher education, inasmuch as it destroys the freedom of science and teaching and constricts the freedom of traditional philosophy." Osorgin, on the other hand, said that he did not know enough about higher educational reform to comment.[31]

The subsequent charge was uniform and preordained. The GPU found, supposedly on the basis of the interrogation, that each of the accused "from the October Revolution to the present day has not only not reconciled with the worker-peasant regime that has existed for five years in Russia, but has also not for a moment ceased, and, at a time of external difficulties for the RSFSR, has intensified his anti-Soviet activity." Therefore, on the basis of Article 57 of the criminal code, he was sentenced to deportation abroad, made to sign a form agreeing to wrap up his affairs in seven days, and to acknowledge that, should he return to Russia without permission, he faced "the highest measure of punishment." The matter was then taken to the GPU Collegium for approval on a case-by-case basis.[32] The interrogations in fact had little to do with the actual sentencing. When Stratonov argued that not a single fact had been produced against him, the operative smiled and invited him to protest, and Osorgin signed his affidavit of expulsion before he had even been questioned.[33]

The deportees reacted differently. As Osorgin noted, "For many the departure was a genuine tragedy; no sort of Europe could lure them, all of their life and work was connected with Russia by a link which was unique and inseparable from the goal of existence."[34] Such was the reaction of the engineer A. V. Sakharov. "Where is there for me to go abroad?" he asked Stratonov. "I only just got myself set up, I earn good money . . . what is there for me to do abroad?"[35] Others, on the contrary, were greatly relieved at the opportunity to get out, and a few even used it as a means to transport distant relatives who had long wished to depart.[36]

Preparations, Departure, and Reaction

Most of the Moscow arrestees were released after a few days at the Lubianka to prepare for departure. In Petrograd, many remained in prison for several months, fueling further denunciations of Zinoviev's draconian regime. Nikolai Losskii recalled making great use of the decent prison library until he and the other elderly members of the Petrograd group were released.[37] Those let go set about selling their possessions; some had their way paid by the GPU, but the rest were expected to purchase their own tickets and support themselves. A complicated process of haggling over what they could take out of the country ensued. Those who left earlier were able to take much more than the usual hard currency limit of fifty dollars, and Soviet employees often did not know what documents and manuscripts they were allowed to take.[38]

Although the deportees came from different backgrounds and most had not known one another before the arrests, their common plight soon created a solid group identity that would last well into emigration. The groups in both capitals chose "elders" for the various negotiations with the regime and foreign embassies. In Moscow those selected were Iasinskii and the agronomist Ugrimov; in Petrograd, Losskii and the House of Litterateurs' leader Volkovyskii. I. F. Reshetov, head of the fourth division of the GPU's Secret Department, set departure for 28 August, but it was delayed several times. The first setback was the German government's refusal to issue visas "as if it were Siberia," a place to which the Soviet state could exile individuals at will. This was solved, ironically, by having the deportees themselves request the visas under threat of internal exile to northerly locations.[39]

During the time between arrest and departure, the Moscow group met regularly in KUBU's offices, where the elders discussed practical matters and how to deal with the GPU.[40] The anxiety caused by preparing for their forced departure and having to sell most of their worldly possessions was understandably very high. As the delay lengthened, the deportees started to give credence to rumors that they were to be sent instead to distant internal exile or perhaps even worse. When, at a meeting of the Moscow group on 2 September, the GPU operative Zaraiskii shouted, "Over here [*k stenochke*]!" most took this to mean "Against the wall [*k stenke*]!"—that is, that they were to be shot. In fact, Zaraiskii was separating out those who were to remain in Russia owing to a change in their sentences.[41] But the rumors that disagreements within the Bolshevik leadership were holding up the deportations continued to swirl.

The Bolshevik leaders were impatient, as Lenin's badgering of Unshlikht for updates makes clear. "Everything was very complicated," Osorgin noted, "and the Soviet machine at this time was not fit for such an enterprise." On 20 September Zaraiskii told the elders that departure must take place in two days, but visas had not yet been received. The numerous Soviet organs involved and the German mission's insistence that it deal with the Commissariat of Foreign Affairs and not the GPU continued to hold things up.[42] As Osorgin wryly recalled, "The all-powerful GPU turned out to be powerless to help our 'voluntary' departure beyond the boundaries of the motherland."[43] Once the visa issues were settled, tickets still had to be acquired. A few deportees, including Peshekhonov, Miakotin, and Sorokin, left by train on 23 September. They arrived in Riga three days later, after which most continued on to Berlin.[44] The rest of the Moscow contingent received their visas on 26 September. A meeting was held at KUBU on the eve of departure at which Iasinskii and Ugrimov gave out passports and announced the purchase of train tickets from Moscow to Petrograd and steamboat tickets from Petrograd to Stettin. One train left for Petrograd on the afternoon of the twenty-sixth and a second the next evening. The GPU wanted to include a convoy, but the elders insisted that all seats in their car were occupied. Nevertheless, most were of the view that an unfamiliar young couple with a baby (which they suspected was actually a doll) were in fact undercover agents. "The naive ones," Stratonov recalled, "they still thought that someone would want to remain."[45]

A small crowd saw the trainload of intellectuals off; those departing duly noted its size and composition. The deportees had been highly conscious of the response of their acquaintances and colleagues in the days between their arrest and departure. Some were encouraged by the support they found, but for the most part they were disappointed by what they felt was a silence born of fear. As one of the regime's primary motives was to cause terror in the remaining intelligentsia, this apparent quietism is an important indication of how successful the deportations were. The disappointment found in the deportees' memoirs must be taken for what it is, however, and not as a comprehensive or objective indicator of public reaction.

Nevertheless, there was no real public opposition to the expulsions; there was a reluctance to speak out loudly or show too much support. Trubetskoi's experience leaving the state agricultural syndicate where he worked was an exception: "Almost everyone . . .—bourgeois and Communist—very warmly parted with me and wished me well in my future life."[46] Osorgin was more typical in bitterly recalling the last meeting he attended at the Union of Writers. Although he and Berdiaev had been vice-chairs, no one spoke to thank them or bid farewell. "Five years of work together, in a group whose composition was almost unchanged, always amicable and always independent! A demonstration was not necessary, the Union needed to be protected, but even so, I could have used just the briefest emotional reaction [*rastrogannost'*], and so, I think, could have everyone."[47]

Unsurprisingly, those institutions still led by allies of the deportees tended to speak out more openly. The departing intellectuals also received support from some students, who, according to Novikov, were prominent among those seeing them off in Moscow.[48] Sorokin says that while en route from

Moscow to Riga, he and his companions on the first train read letters of farewell from students, professors, cooperatives, and others.[49] Frank's students presented him with a declaration that made clear his influence had been exactly of the sort that the Bolsheviks most feared: "It is sad for us to think that our studies under your direction have come to an end. We have worked with you for only a year, but, you have nevertheless managed in this short time to captivate us with your lectures, in which we saw . . . the living face of the divine total-unity. . . . We believe that the time will come, when once again we can work with you, dear Semyon Liudvigovich."[50] Students such as these were hardly being transformed into model Red scholars, and so it was precisely to counteract the influence of "corrupters of the youth" such as Frank that the deportations had been devised.

As the Moscow professors looked onto the train platform before being whisked to Petrograd, each saw the crowd somewhat differently. Stratonov was most acerbic: "We were seen off at the train station, but only by a few people. It would seem . . . that the seeing off of such an important party, based on its intellectual significance, which 'was suffering for ideas,' should have drawn to it many people, first of all the colleagues of the deported. . . . Alas, they were almost entirely absent, they were seized with an animal fear. Only the closest friends and relatives of the deported gathered."[51] Novikov, while noting the substantial group of students, also lamented the lack of public figures and colleagues. Others, however, recognized the danger of associating with the deportees in light of the obvious GPU presence. Vera Reshchikova, Ugrimov's daughter, recalled that "a fairly large group of people gathered to see us off, which was in those times a certain display of courage." Sorokin wrote, "In spite of prohibitions of the authorities, many friends and acquaintances came to see us off, with gifts of flowers, handclasps, and tears."[52] The Mel'gunovs, who left two weeks after the main group, held a farewell evening before the others departed that sixty people attended. "People were not as broken as they are now," Praskov'ia Mel'gunova recalled. "It was lively, everyone acted as if they believed in a better future." Sergei Mel'gunov was himself thrown a farewell dinner by Zadruga, the controversial cooperative publishing house he had headed, which would be shut down before the end of the year.[53] Such farewell evenings strongly suggest that many had not yet heeded the Bolshevik warning to disassociate themselves from "harmful elements."

The trains from Moscow arrived in Petrograd overnight and the deportees were forced to stay an additional day because of a delay with the German steamship. The local KUBU secretary arranged for hotel rooms, and they used the time to see acquaintances, including the Petrograd deportees, some of whom were still in prison.[54] An anxious atmosphere clouded these two days; fear that Zinoviev would halt their departure and perhaps do worse was on everyone's mind. Trubetskoi contrasted Moscow, which despite Bolshevik rule was full of life, with Petrograd, which he felt was empty and half dead.[55] Guided by their elders, the deportees finally lined up to board the *Oberbürgermeister Hakken* at 3 P.M. on 28 September. The families were called out and the GPU operatives took careful stock of the money and documents they were taking with them. The process took until 9 P.M. to complete, and they were unable to leave until the next morning. They left on 29 September at 8 A.M.; as Stratonov noted, they did not feel entirely free until the *chekisty* holding their passports were radioed and returned to shore on a small craft.[56]

Several members of the Petrograd group, including Losskii, watched their colleagues depart that morning, but it would be another month and a half before they themselves would leave. Most remained in prison, though a few were released because of their advanced ages. The conditions at Shpalernaia were harsh, and two other prisoners committed suicide during the time that the intellectuals were there. Because no explicit reasons were given for the delay, rumors swirled that Zinoviev had decided that exile abroad was too lenient. After they were released in mid- to late October, the Petrograd group hurried to turn to the German consulate for visas, understand the limits of what they might take, and deal with a labyrinth of Soviet institutions.[57]

As in Moscow, the departure of some of the city's most significant personages did not go unnoticed. On 9 November there was a farewell evening in honor of Losskii, his wife, and his mother-in-law, M. N. Stoiunina, the founder of a prominent girls' gymnasium.[58] Another evening several days later, attended by a number of Losskii's university colleagues, featured speeches paying homage not only to Stoiunina, but also to Losskii and their fellow deportee Sergei Polner. A third event, a farewell "tea" on Vasil'evskii Island, honored the three departing philosophers Losskii, Lapshin, and Karsavin. As Losskii's son Boris recalled, at one of these evenings a poetess read several verses she had written about Gumilev in the aftermath of his execution. "A similar performance could have hardly occurred without punishment three years later, when the GPU had perfected its investigative apparatus."[59] Izgoev wrote that a large group of students was among those who saw their boat off, even bringing flowers for the professors' wives and helping them carry their things. Clearly, as was true in Moscow, not all the remaining scholars, students, and other Petrograd intellectuals had been cowed into disassociating themselves from those whom the regime chose to cast out. Most of the Petrograd group, seventeen men and their families, boarded the steamship *Preussen* on 15 November and left for Stettin early the next morning.[60]

At the time, no one knew for certain that this banishment was for life. The official proclamation stated that the length of exile was three years, which led to a pervasive belief that they would be permitted to return. Various Bolshevik leaders lent credence to this idea during the period between arrest and departure, particularly Kamenev, who told several that they might be allowed to come back within a year; he even suggested to Novikov that if he did not like conditions abroad, he should write to Kamenev personally and he would help arrange his return.[61] It is difficult to know whether Kamenev truly believed this was the case or whether this was simply another instance of his presenting a more moderate face in public. According to Sorokin, Piatakov, with whom he had been friends as a student, told him that they might be invited back "after two or three years."[62] By 1 November, however, the Commissariat of Foreign Affairs had issued a secret circular noting that banishment should be considered "without time limit."[63]

Though some already suspected that this was the case, others refused to believe they would be gone very long, and so did many of their colleagues. Most of Stepun's friends assured him that he would return at the end of the three-year limit, and when he demurred that the Bolsheviks would hardly allow this, they laughed.[64] Reshchikova recalled her father, Ugrimov, saying as they departed, "Well, we will return in a year."[65] Sorokin wrote to the publisher Vitiazev on the day before he left, "I disagree only on whether we part for ever. I firmly believe that in two or three years we will meet again . . . , and that we will once again work together."[66] While aboard the *Preussen*, the publisher Abram Kagan wrote, "Departing into banishment, I dream about returning as soon as possible to my beloved motherland."[67]

Most, in fact, would never see Russia again. Though there was some indecision among the Bolsheviks over the length of the sentence, it was generally agreed that those deported were irredeemable. The agronomists Nikolai Liubimov and Ivan Matveev were permitted to return in 1923, but only a handful of others (as I will discuss in the epilogue) took the three-year limit seriously and tried to come back in the mid-1920s.[68] Although many never felt truly comfortable among the emigration, and some even held on to their Soviet passports, the fact that the regime neither weakened nor grew more moderate dashed any intentions most had of returning.

Additions and Stragglers

A handful of intellectuals were arrested in various Russian provincial cities.[69] Three Kazan professors, I. A. Stratonov, A. A. Ovchinnikov, and G. Ia. Troshin, were expelled, accused of resisting VUZ reforms and of having Blackhundred views.[70] In Ukraine, as we shall see, the entire campaign came under fierce scrutiny. Of the group of seventy-seven people arrested in five Ukrainian cities on the night of 18 August 1922, only three Odessan professors were deported abroad. The historian Antonii Florovskii, the physiologist B. P. Babkin, and G. A. Sekal', a teacher at the Odessa Economics Institute, arrived in Constantinople on 19 September 1922.[71]

We can gain some idea of how events proceeded in the provinces by looking at the fate of Sergei Bulgakov, who was in the Crimea when the initial round of arrests took place. The Crimean police followed direct orders from the GPU in Moscow. Bulgakov's house was searched on 20 September, but he was not arrested until 13 October, at which time he was taken to Simferopol. A week later, Menzhinskii sent an order from Moscow to sentence Bulgakov to expulsion under the same formulation used previously. Although Bulgakov filled out a questionnaire, he was not formally interrogated. He was released on 1 November but required to check in with the Yalta GPU every three days until his departure. Along with the standard charge, the local investigators accused Bulgakov of "political unreliability, concretely expressed in his active scholarly work against the workers' movement under the previous tsarist government."[72] In late December he boarded the Italian steamship *Jeanne* from Sevastopol to Constantinople. He wrote in his diary that although it was very difficult for him to leave his motherland, the experiences of the preceding several years suggested that it was perhaps God's will. "Russia," he wondered sadly, "how did you perish? How did you become a victim of the devils, your own children? What has happened to you? Never has an enigma been more enigmatic, more incomprehensible."[73]

Several Moscow and Petrograd intellectuals left after the main groups. Some haggling over his fate delayed Fëdor Stepun's departure.[74] The writer Viktor Iretskii left a month after the rest of the Petrograd group, during which time the possibility of overturning his sentence was being discussed.[75] Dalmat Lutokhin became deathly ill with rheumatism after being imprisoned and was released in early September, after which he was allowed to remain in Russia while he recuperated. During his illness, he was visited by many of the literary, scholarly, and publishing lights with whom he had worked as editor of several journals. Before he left on 11 February 1923, by train to Germany via Estonia, Zamiatin, Viacheslav Ivanov, and others came to see him off.[76]

On 27 December 1922 the NKVD special commission on administrative exile sentenced the Tolstoyan Valentin Bulgakov to three years of banishment, and Vladimir Chertkov, Tolstoy's most famous disciple, had to use all of his considerable influence to avoid the same fate.[77] Bulgakov's deportation was connected to the Bolsheviks' distrust of the burgeoning Tolstoyan movement, as well as their distaste for the ecumenical Free Association of Spiritual Tendencies. In addition, Bulgakov vocally opposed the collaborationist Living Church, which the Bolsheviks hoped to counterpose to the official Orthodox Church. His final public presentation was at a January 1923 debate with members of the Living Church, at which he denounced their hypocrisy.[78]

Bulgakov was given no more details about the reasons for his expulsion than the other deportees had been. "Undoubtedly, I, too, was included among those people who were shortsighted and stubborn—and not in the narrow, personal sense, but in terms of ideas." Bulgakov and his wife were stunned: the three years to which they thought they had been exiled seemed interminable. Bulgakov was granted a delay to get ready; the German government, now accustomed to giving visas to the deportees, did not give him any problems. Bulgakov stopped his friends from appealing on his behalf, truly believing that he would be allowed to return in three years.[79] On 5 March 1923 his friends held a farewell dinner at the Tolstoy Museum, at which many expressed great frustration and sorrow. I. I. Gorbunov-Posadov bitterly lamented: "Today we have met here to bid farewell to Valentin Fëdorovich. What is happening? Why? Why must he leave Russia? What sort of crime did he commit? What has he done that he must leave Russia at precisely the time when Russia needs such workers for its bright new life? . . . Apparently the vast majority of his guilt consists of the independent free speech with which he addresses people, and such a freedom of speech should be highly valued by a government that at all respects itself. . . . But no, the government says: leave, you, with your free independent voices. Russia must thus continue to be silent, to be voiceless; here it is permissible to speak only with the permission of the leaders, and we all must continue to be only mooing [*mychashchimi*] animals, as we had been previously." Bulgakov himself was less bitter, warmly thanking his friends and reiterating his Tolstoyan and pacifist principles. He declared, "Leaving Russia, I do not experience gloomy feelings or a gloomy mood."[80] On 30 March 1923 friends huddled at the Belorussia train station to bid farewell to him, his wife, and their daughter. Aleksandra Tolstaia shouted, "Come back soon!" as the train pulled away.[81]

The standing NKVD commission on administrative exile began to function in fall 1922, but it focused almost exclusively on internal exile. Why expulsion proved to be a short-lived instrument for eliminating enemies is unclear, but it likely had to do with a fear of strengthening opposition voices in the emigration, which, as we shall see shortly, had already changed the progress of the campaign in Ukraine.[82] Rumors soon circulated that the government regretted the expulsion of intellectuals from Russia.[83] Sorokin received a coded letter on arriving in Berlin that read, "Our grandmother [the GPU] is very sorry for having let you go without giving you her last and eternal blessing [execution]."[84] In any event, after this time the Soviet state rarely used expulsion and instead employed internal exile and more drastic measures to remove perceived foes.

Deportation in Ukraine

Events took a significantly different turn in Ukraine from those in the RSFSR. In June the Ukrainian Politburo discussed the "political actions of the professoriat" and resolved to root out opposition in institutions of higher education. The Ukrainian Narkompros was directed to compile a list of professors "who introduce the greatest disorder in academic life" for "transfer," including deportation "beyond the boundaries of the federation."[85] The Ukrainian GPU, with the active participation of the Ukrainian Narkompros, which was significantly more radical than its Russian counterpart,[86] soon put together a list of potential deportees no less comprehensive and even more vociferous in its denunciations than that compiled for Moscow and Petrograd.

The Ukrainian Bolsheviks, who had established control more recently, were even more likely to see evidence of conspiracy—and not all of these suspicions should be dismissed out of hand. Thus, a counterrevolutionary group was thought to exist around Ivan Krasutskii, the rector of Kharkov Technology Institute. "At the current time," the Ukrainian GPU lamented, "as rector he has managed to bring gradually under his control and submit to his influence those around him to such an extent that at all meetings of the professoriat his views on one question or another are accepted like a law." Krasutskii, it was reported, maintained connections not only with Kharkov professors (several of whom were named specifically) but across Ukraine.[87]

The Ukrainian report was insistent that those named were active foes and "harmful types." It painted a comprehensive portrait of intimately connected, cunning enemies who would stop at nothing to overthrow the regime. Ties to Denikin, Petliura, and other White and nationalist leaders were highlighted, as was their supposed anti-Semitism. Their deleterious influence on students was emphasized time and again. Thus, A. S. Muliukin, a professor at the Odessa Economics Institute, was said to "ironize and behave like a hooligan during lectures, which has a bad effect on the studentry." I. V. Kistiakovskii, one of the pro-rectors of the Kiev Medical Academy, "conducted active agitation among the studentry against Communist students." Professors who had opposed the radical VUZ reforms and participated in or called for strikes were also targeted.[88]

On 3 August 1922 the Ukrainian GPU marked seventy-seven professors, teachers, medical staff and other intellectuals from Kharkov, Odessa, Kiev, Podol'sk, and Ekaterinoslav for deportation, and this was confirmed by the Politburo commission a week later. As noted above, however, only three men would in the end be expelled from Soviet territory. In November the Ukrainian Politburo warned that in view of the strength of the Ukrainian émigré intelligentsia, the professors should not be deported abroad. Moscow at first denied this request, but Unshlikht did suggest that the GPU might consider permitting deportation to "distant points in the RSFSR" in place of expulsion. The Ukrainian Politburo then sent a second plea, noting that Ukrainian émigré professors were being met with open arms by the Czechoslovak government and were taking part in the new Ukrainian university there; the Ukrainian emigration should not be given further reinforcements.[89]

The matter was not decided for several months. While the Ukrainian Politburo listened to appeals and sought to alter some of the sentences, Unshlikht moved to have Moscow take control, unhappy that the emigration might take vacillation for weakness and displeased that matters were being decided on a local level. He thus opposed the creation of a separate standing commission on administrative exile under the Ukrainian NKVD. Eventually, after difficulties arose in arranging visas for the deportees, Unshlikht did support deportation to internal points in the RSFSR. The Politburo concurred, but it directed that the list should first be examined by the Unshlikht, Kamenev, Kurskii troika. It also ordered a further intensification by the GPU of surveillance of all members of "liberal professions." On 1 February 1923 the Unshlikht troika directed that the majority of arrested Ukrainian intellectuals be deported to Turkistan, Ufa, Orenburg, Viatka, and other distant locations. Several were sent to Moscow, where their expertise could be of use while they were removed from where they were most dangerous, and a few, in part on the basis of recommendations of the Ukrainian Politburo, remained in Ukraine.[90]

Thus, the advice of the Communist authorities in Kharkov having been followed, there was no flood of Ukrainian deportees into the emigration. At the same time, the GPU and Politburo in Moscow made clear that they were running the show. At a time when the Soviet Union was just being established, it was affirmed that exile was to be a unified institution and not the province of the separate republics. In the future, however, the central powers would recognize that it was easier to control their enemies by keeping them isolated but within their midst.

Appealing Expulsion

The intellectuals, their families, and friends were not the only ones dismayed by the arrests in Moscow and Petrograd in August 1922. Those institutions that depended on their irreplaceable expertise began to inquire into the possibility that some be allowed to remain, and organizations such as KUBU began to petition on their behalf. The appeals process thus occurred on several levels. In some instances, it was initiated by those arrested or their families, who appealed either to KUBU or to the institution of employment. In others, high state and party officials turned directly to the Politburo with a request that various important specialists be allowed to stay.

At the time, some of the traditional defenders of the intelligentsia were out of the picture, most notably Gorky and Lunacharskii. Gorky was abroad and not then in the Bolsheviks' good graces—he had been sharply attacked in the Bolshevik press by Radek[91]—and he could only watch from afar as Zinoviev led a campaign against those people and societies he had tried to protect. Although Gorky did not, as Zinoviev had predicted, issue an open condemnation of the deportations, his disappointment with Bolshevik policy toward the intelligentsia is clear. According to the poet Khodasevich, Gorky expressed frustration with Zinoviev and Kamenev for their participation in the anti-intellectual campaigns, and it was at Gorky's strong suggestion that Khodasevich wrote a critical article for the Berlin paper *Golos Rossii.*[92]

Gorky was more circumspect in his public pronouncements. Caught between his anger over the deportations and a lack of sympathy with some of the deportees—it is doubtful that he shed any tears for religious thinkers and celebrators of Dostoevsky—he sent a letter to the Smenovekhovite newspaper *Nakanune* that attempted to separate his support for the regime from his disapproval of the way it treated intellectuals. After his stance against the SR trial and the attacks on him in the Soviet press, he felt it more essential to emphasize the former point. "I find it necessary to declare that the Soviet regime is for me the sole force capable of overcoming the inertia of the Russian popular masses and awakening the energy of these masses toward the creation of new, more just, and wiser forms of life." Nevertheless, he affirmed, "by the entire structure of my psyche I cannot agree with the stance of the Soviet regime toward the intelligentsia. I consider this stance mistaken, . . . the ferocity unfounded and unjustified."[93] For this effort to find nuance, he was roundly criticized in both Soviet and émigré papers.[94]

Lunacharskii, too, remained largely uninvolved in the campaign. This can be attributed in part to the fact that his subordinates Iakovleva and Lebedev-Polianskii were more willing partners for the GPU, but it also resulted from Lunacharskii's own time-consuming and exhaustive participation in the SR prosecution. In fact, the commissar was not even in the country during the August arrests themselves. His anti-SR speeches, when taken together with his frustration with the professoriat, suggest that he was not opposed to weeding out bad elements, even if he tended to be more sympathetic to the intelligentsia than were his comrades. Although Lunacharskii was not on the best of terms with Zinoviev, his only public response to the virulent anti-intellectual speech at the Twelfth Party Conference was yet another plea to better fund Narkompros.[95] With the significant exception of his anti-SR speeches, he was not a vocal advocate of retribution against the intelligentsia. He did aid in the appeals of several of those arrested, including, surprisingly, the Petrograd philosopher Ivan Lapshin, but he does not appear to have been particularly proactive or to have made that much of a difference.[96] In a speech entitled "The Ideological Front against the Bourgeoisie," delivered on 9 October, he made clear that he wholeheartedly supported the attacks on bourgeois philosophy, religion, and social science, while cautioning that the country must value technology and the positive sciences.[97] In a letter to Kamenev shortly thereafter, while worrying that the campaign might be going overboard in Ukraine, Lunacharskii added that "here in Russia we deported only useless and presently harmful professors."[98]

Only several months into the process did the commissar of Enlightenment respond directly to the anti-intelligentsia campaigns, contending that the threat should not be exaggerated, and that the deportations had taken care of most of the danger: "I do not believe bourgeois ideology to be of any strength. All of what comrade Zinoviev pointed out at the Party [Conference] was sufficiently threatening—journals, brochures with wily attacks on the regime, advocating religion, idealist philosophy, etc.—but all of this has already been wiped off the face of the earth as if it had never existed. The well-known measures in regard to those individuals, useless to us in view of their counterrevolutionary propaganda, were sufficient so that all of this has disappeared. We have no hopes of turning all of these reactionary, bourgeois philistines, all of the professoriat, into Communists; to us it is important that they just do not carry on their propaganda."[99] Although his claim that further repressive measures were not *immediately* necessary jibed with the leadership's consensus, the general striving toward weeding out "bourgeois" ideology and combating the intelligentsia's influence certainly did not disappear.

Lunacharskii's influence, as we have suggested, was not then so great; those seeking amnesty more often turned to other sources of aid. Although there were still direct ties between nonparty and socialist intellectuals and certain high-level Bolsheviks, the appeals process usually went through several stages of intermediaries. By most accounts, Kamenev was the Politburo member most often approached by those petitioning on behalf of the arrested intellectuals.[100] As we have seen, however, despite his moderate reputation and promotion of "socialist legality," Kamenev had actively participated in the interdepartmental troika overseeing the expulsions. His participation in the appeals process should therefore be seen as that of responder and not initiator.

The officials most responsible for taking petitions from individuals and organizations to the high party leadership were often Bolsheviks with key positions in educational, agricultural, and other government institutions, including Iakovleva, P. A. Bogdanov, and I. A. Teodorovich. Most had assisted the interdepartmental troika as expert advisers and so had known of the deportations in advance. At this earlier stage there had been little talk of the need to retain irreplaceable professors and *spetsy.* Though there was some opposition to the deportation of particular individuals, there is no indication that anyone protested too loudly. That they were willing to be more vocal after the arrests is indicative of substantial institutional opposition to losing valuable experts. The signal that this was now politically viable came from an unusual source; the person most instrumental in the significant reductions made in those expelled was not a soft-line Bolshevik, but the man in charge of the secret police, Feliks Dzerzhinskii.

Although Lenin's initial directive on the deportations was sent to Dzerzhinskii, it was Unshlikht, as we have seen, who took control of the operations while his boss devoted himself to other matters, especially his duties as commissar of Transportation. Dzerzhinskii had already approved the list of deportees as a member of the GPU Collegium, but on 24 August the Politburo directed him to form a commission with the right to alter these decisions.[101] It was at this point that Dzerzhinskii suggested to Unshlikht and his other subordinates that the regime needed to look carefully at each individual intellectual, and that the GPU and NKVD should refine and augment the process of categorizing information.[102] Iron Feliks's role as a sometime benefactor of intellectuals is not as paradoxical as it first sounds, since this largely stemmed from his dual role in economic concerns such as Narkomput' and VSNKh. Most of those whose fate he was concerned with were *spetsy,* and indeed many *spetsy* came to see Dzerzhinskii as a protector, particularly against less pragmatic and more ideological Communists.[103]

At the same time, Dzerzhinskii remained the GPU's most influential proponent, and he continued to demand suppression of political parties and other "alien" formations.

In the days following the initial arrests, petitions and queries to the higher authorities trickled in; some were sent through intermediary organizations like TsKUBU, whereas others were addressed to Iakovleva, other leading Bolsheviks, or directly to the GPU. The fact that some of those sending queries held high positions of authority in the most directly affected institutions makes clear the extent to which the process remained limited to a select group of active planners. For university rectors and other institutional leaders, concern over the fate of their colleagues was mitigated by caution in how to proceed, as they sought to understand the situation and determine the degree of latitude they had in attempting to exercise influence.

Thus, in a 22 August memo, MGU's Communist rector, V. P. Volgin, addressed an inquiry to Glavprofobr's Council on VUZ Affairs, a body he had himself chaired until Iakovleva took over this position not long before the arrests.[104] Either unaware of her involvement or in an effort to keep an official tone, he informed her (although of course she knew) that a number of professors had been arrested by order of the GPU. "Bringing this to the attention of Glavprofobr, the University Board requests that you take measures to clarify the situation . . . , and, in the case that no serious charges are brought against the detained individuals, render all possible assistance to their being set free, as their absence from the university at the very start of the school year would reflect extremely unfavorably on the course of university teaching."[105] Iakovleva's reply a week later did little more than provide the formulaic charge against those arrested. Explaining that she had taken measures to clarify the circumstances (although as an advisor to Unshlikht's troika she was well aware of the campaign), she explained that they were charged with the fact that "for the five years of the existence of Soviet power, they did not reconcile with the Soviet regime and continued counterrevolutionary activity even at a moment of external danger."[106]

Other VUZy were less circumspect in appealing on their professors' behalf. They astutely stressed the critical issues around which the decision to expel had been reached: that the individuals in question were politically loyal, represented no danger to the Soviet regime, and were crucial and irreplaceable experts. An excellent example is the efforts of the Petrograd Technology Institute (PTI) on behalf of the agro-chemist Efim Zubashev. The rector N. Bartels and other board members explored multiple avenues. First, they wrote to the Petrograd branch of KUBU immediately upon Zubashev's arrest to request its mediation.[107] KUBU, or at least the Petrograd branch, forwarded such queries directly to the local GPU organs.[108] TsKUBU, along with Peshkova's Political Red Cross, had established itself as the premier intercessor on behalf of arrested intellectuals and was used frequently at this time.[109] Still, though TsKUBU survived the year's upheavals, it is unclear how much influence it had, with its main patron Gorky out of the picture and its de facto leader in Moscow, Vsevolod Iasinskii, among those sentenced to deportation.

Several days later, the PTI board tried to enlist the assistance of Leonid Krasin, the commissar for Foreign Trade, a well-known moderate who had remained close to non-Bolshevik intellectuals and even certain émigré circles.[110] "The Technology Institute earnestly asks your intercession for Professor Zubashev, who was arrested together with others on 17 August and according to rumors is to be deported somewhere. Zubashev has worked for years in Soviet institutions with irreproachable conscientiousness. . . . He is needed by the institute as an outstanding specialist and pedagogue. He is an old man, of seriously impaired health."[111] Several weeks later, a similar letter was sent to Iakovleva. Having ascertained from the newspaper accounts that Zubashev was to be deported abroad, the board and deans of PTI asked that he be freed and allowed to continue his teaching at the institute. "E. L. Zubashev is an irreplaceable worker, an outstanding specialist, . . . and a superlative professor-pedagogue. The expulsion of Professor Zubashev would deprive the Technology Institute of a great scientific force. And for E. L. Zubashev himself, it would undoubtedly shorten his days. He is 62 years old and his health is very shaky. . . . Knowing intimately and well all of Professor Zubashev's activities, we assert that never in any way or sense can they be called counterrevolutionary or directed against the Soviet regime."[112] The efforts on Zubashev's behalf were in vain, but many similar petitions were not. The points made in his support correctly highlighted those issues under consideration in the Bolsheviks' review of the expulsions: usefulness, loyalty, and advanced age or poor health.[113]

The Dzerzhinskii-run commission examining these appeals began to meet on 31 August. Reevaluation did not necessarily lead to exoneration; some were held for trial and others were deported to internal locations. Konstantin Savich, the Academy of Sciences administrator, was held along with several members of the regional craft cooperative for supposed anti-Soviet activity. Savich remained in prison for five months, until being told that he would be exiled to Tiumen province for three years, at which point he had a stroke and ended up in the prison hospital.[114] The defense lawyers in the SR trial, A. S. Tager and N. K. Murav'ev, were banished to Kazan, although they were allowed to return in July 1923. The prominent economist Nikolai

Kondrat'ev, on the other hand, who was charged with supporting the SRs, was released and even allowed to travel to Europe and America, after which he worked in Soviet institutions until his arrest in 1930.[115]

For the most part, the decisions made by the Dzerzhinskii commission led to the freeing—at least in the short term—of a number of those originally designated for deportation. It is noteworthy that Iakovleva and the VSNKh chief Pëtr Bogdanov, among others, now spoke up on behalf of individuals whose expulsions they had not opposed when advising the Unshlikht troika in July.[116] This indicates that they were serving as intermediaries, reacting to petitions, but also that they recognized that Dzerzhinskii's involvement had now made intercession politically viable.

The Dzerzhinskii commission listened to their assertions that certain essential specialists should not be deported. Thus, the deportations of the engineer Nikolai Parshin and Ivan Kukolevskii, the dean of the Moscow Higher Technical School Mechanical Faculty, were rescinded on the basis of Bogdanov's appeals. One of the primary mechanisms for prompting a reconsideration of exile was assurances from petitioners or a declaration by the deportee himself of his complete loyalty to the Soviet regime. As we have seen, this was not always sufficient; Osorgin and others had protested their loyalty in vain, and PTI's pleas on behalf of Zubashev went unheeded. These avowals were nevertheless the best first step for those wishing to stay. For example, Viktor Krokhmal', director of Tsentrosoiuz's office, was freed on the basis of an affirmation of his loyalty to Dzerzhinskii, along with Bogdanov's petitions on his behalf.[117]

Some appeals were quickly decided, but others dragged on for months, which caused a great deal of angst. The freeing of some intellectuals provoked opposition from Unshlikht, Zinoviev, and other advocates of deportation. Lenin, still in Gorki recuperating from his illness, did not take direct part in the process of reconsideration and had to limit himself to continually demanding updates on the status of the deportees. A response from Iagoda to Lenin in mid-September indicated that a significant number had already had their sentences altered.[118]

As it became clear that needed specialists could be retained, more economic and agricultural officials petitioned Dzerzhinskii's commission. Thus, Grigorii Kaminskii, a Bolshevik delegate in the agricultural cooperative union Sel'skosoiuz, and Boris Kushner, a Bolshevik with positions in various economic agencies, backed the release of the agronomists I. P. Matveev, N. I. Liubimov, and A. I. Sigirskii. They argued that removing prominent non-Communists from Sel'sksoiuz would be seen as a naked power grab, and that a more conciliatory approach was needed: "The *kooperatory* suppose that

. . . we will attain *three spaces* in the Sel'skosoiuz board. The coincidence of this number with the number of deported members of the board . . . will, naturally, give grounds for the belief that the deportation is nothing other than the freeing of the number of vacancies needed by the Communists and the simultaneous removal of dangerous currents."[119] The party leadership, however, very much intended to complete the bolshevization of cooperatives and to remove those who might infect educated peasants with "SR tendencies." On Molotov's suggestion, the Secretariat turned down the requested amnesty, and all three men were deported.[120] Even after their departure, however, appeals continued, and in fall 1923 the Politburo permitted Liubimov and Matveev to return to Russia, the only deportees to be allowed to return so soon.[121]

The appeals of prominent agronomists received a great deal of attention. The debate over these appeals foreshadowed a pattern of conflict between the practical leaders of the Commissariat of Agriculture (and other state institutions) and the conflict-oriented GPU during the course of the decade over the presence of nonparty *spetsy.*[122] The MGU professor Nikolai Oganovskii, for instance, received the backing of both the university and the former Menshevik chairman of Tsentrosoiuz L. M. Khinchuk. Unshlikht and Samsonov protested bitterly that this public person (*obshchestvennik*) would strengthen anti-Soviet activity in the Free Economic Society and the Moscow Agricultural Society, and that allowing him to remain would set a bad precedent. Several months later, it was decided to rescind his expulsion.[123]

Most of those who had their cases reviewed were *spetsy,* in particular agronomists and engineers. For the few humanists and litterateurs whose sentences were reconsidered, the decision was more complicated, and the process of petitions extended into the winter. One example of both the inconsistencies in the process and the patronage relationships that determined it involves one of the most well-known intellectuals marked for exile, Zamiatin, author of the famous anti-utopian novel *We.* Officially targeted for two short stories he had written, Zamiatin was also associated with both the House of Litterateurs and the House of Arts. After Zamiatin's arrest, his friend the writer Boris Pil'niak went to Aleksei Voronskii, the editor of the journal *Krasnaia nov',* who in turn went to Kamenev. Zamiatin was freed over the bitter objection of Zinoviev's Petrograd soviet, but his case continued to be debated over several months. After the Politburo discussed the issue a number of times, and even ordered one of his plays be read over, Zamiatin's sentence was revoked.[124]

Voronskii, like most of those who were now coming to the assistance of the deportees, was not entirely consistent. The man who saved Zamiatin from deportation had been among several who had attacked him in the press earlier in the year.[125] Voronskii had criticized the message inherent in the stories for which Zamiatin was now under scrutiny and had found the unabashed parody of a rationalist utopia in *We* extremely troublesome. But, as elsewhere, these ideological boundaries were neither consistently drawn nor etched in stone. Although he criticized *We* on a number of levels, Voronskii suggested that with certain (rather drastic) changes, it might even be published in Soviet Russia, something to which Lebedev-Polianskii certainly would never have agreed.[126]

As it turned out, Zamiatin did not want to be "saved" and was unaware of the appeals on his behalf. In a letter to Voronskii immediately after his release from prison, he thanked him for having interceded but went on to say that he was looking forward to his departure: "To do some work abroad, perhaps that will be to my advantage."[127] Having changed their minds, the Politburo now made it difficult to *leave*. As Pil'niak lamented in a letter to his friend, "Well, you understand what a stupid position I am in—a month ago we wanted it so that you did not go, now we need to rearrange our entire artillery for just the opposite [goal]."[128] Zamiatin spent a year trying to receive permission to depart, a process that included at least one face-to-face meeting with Kamenev, before reconciling himself to remaining in Soviet Russia.[129] He would again ask to be allowed to leave almost a decade later in a letter to Stalin during a particularly virulent campaign directed at him and Pil'niak. This time, with the help of the returned-to-glory Gorky, he was allowed to leave the country.

Unlike Zamiatin, the pedagogue and former Popular Socialist Vladimir Charnolusskii actively petitioned to have his expulsion rescinded. His appeal contained many of the central motifs found in such declarations of loyalty, but it was also more pointed than most. Charnolusskii was arrested on 23 October, after the main group had already left. The explanation he received for his pending deportation was more detailed than the simple accusation of anti-Soviet activity leveled at most of the deportees, and, in his appeal, originally sent to the dean of the MGU Social Science Faculty, Charnolusskii refuted these charges point by point, starting with the professors' strikes: "The given 'strike' occurred almost a year ago, had no political character, and ceased without any repression toward anyone. I did not take part in a single meeting preceding the 'strike.' Only having just been named a professor at the university, I was extremely poorly oriented in university affairs. I regarded the given 'strike' negatively, but when it took place and classes at the university temporarily came to a halt, I did not come to one of my lectures. Both at the time of the 'strike,' as well as currently, in terms of what I am charged with, not a single professor at the university was presented an accusation for participation in it and no one was arrested." Similarly, he noted that the cooperative publisher Zadruga, his participation in which constituted the second charge against him, had no connection to any kind of political activity. "It is obvious," he averred (wrongly, since such charges were, as we have seen, taken quite seriously) "that both . . . charges against me have a purely formal character and cannot make up the basis for the repressive measures taken against me." He was not entirely incorrect, however, in surmising that it was a "general relation" to him and his past activity that constituted the "true reason" for his expulsion. Finally, he added the key points that would form the basis of Iakovleva's eventual appeal on his behalf: his advanced age; his long-standing scholarly, educational, and revolutionary work; his "completely loyal relation to Soviet power"; and the fact that allowing him to continue his scientific work represented no danger to the Soviet regime and in fact would be extremely useful in helping raise the country's cultural level, one of the central goals of Bolshevik enlightenment.[130]

The MGU rector V. P. Volgin forwarded the appeal to Iakovleva, adding that Charnolusskii was "an irreplaceable educational worker,"[131] and Iakovleva then met with Iakov Agranov.[132] She received an explanation from Unshlikht and Samsonov reiterating the charges against Charnolusskii (including his membership in the NS central committee and his work with Zadruga).[133] Although Iakovleva had not previously objected to Charnolusskii's expulsion, she now met with Unshlikht and made every effort to overturn it. At a meeting in January 1923, the Politburo, following a presentation by Dzerzhinskii, came down on the side of allowing him to remain in Russia.[134]

Although the appeals frequently involved the high Bolshevik leadership, Lenin's name, despite his return in fall 1922, rarely appears in these discussions. Over the summer, while recuperating, he had made several exhortations to add *more* names to the lists being compiled. One of the few cases under reconsideration in which he became directly involved was that of the Menshevik historian Nikolai Rozhkov, whose sentencing was repeatedly debated at the highest levels of government over several months. Rozhkov had initiated a correspondence with Lenin during and after the Civil War in which he both criticized the regime and followed the Menshevik strategy of performing the role of loyal opposition. He expressed great hopes that the New Economic Policy would herald a new beginning.[135] Rozhkov was prominent in Marxist scholarly circles, which the Bolsheviks were desperately cultivating to counter the caste organizations of the old professoriat.[136] At the same time, both he and Lenin were well aware that their differences were substantial. Lenin eventually decided that Rozhkov's views were intolerable, directed that he be imprisoned with other Mensheviks in 1921, complained to Zinoviev about his release in January 1922, and, in his July 1922 letter to Stalin, specifically noted that Rozhkov was incorrigible and must be expelled.[137]

Varvara Iakovleva once again mediated on Rozhkov's behalf, and the case was put before the Politburo.[138] At issue was whether disavowal of past political ties was sufficient to prove loyalty. The acceptance of recalcitrant Mensheviks and SRs and even their entrance into the Bolshevik Party was not uncommon at the time and often used for propaganda purposes.[139] The question of how to measure a declaration of loyalty was central to reconsidering a sentence of deportation, and it was answered differently in different cases. For Rozhkov the process took an unusual number of twists and turns. On 19 October the Politburo (in Lenin's absence) decided to postpone his expulsion, "taking into account the firm declaration of Rozhkov that he has become convinced of the counterrevolutionary nature of the Mensheviks and his declaration of this publicly." But at another meeting a week later, after a report by Zinoviev, the Politburo reversed itself and decided to expel him after all.[140]

The matter remained unresolved for several months. On 7 December, waiting until Lenin had departed, the Politburo decided to cancel Rozhkov's expulsion and to publish his declaration on his complete break with the Menshevik platform.[141] The next day Lenin furiously wrote to Stalin, declaring this illegal and insisting that the matter be discussed in his presence.[142] Lenin wrote to Zinoviev that he did not trust Rozhkov's assertions of loyalty. "Comrade Zinoviev! I don't suspect you of having the *smallest drop* of partiality toward Rozhkov. *Not the smallest drop!* But I am quite concerned: he will lie as much as he likes, *even in the press*. He will lie, and we will be circumvented. This is what I am afraid of. They have a slogan: lie, leave the party, and stay in Russia. This is what we need to think about and discuss."[143] In a memo to Stalin the day before the matter was brought up again, Lenin laid out his views, highlighting the differences within the Politburo concerning Rozhkov: Lenin and Stalin were in disagreement; after Rozhkov had given a new formulation of his views, Trotsky, who had at first opposed the deportation, concluded that Rozhkov was insincere. "I fully agree with Zinoviev," Lenin continued, "that Rozhkov is a man of firm and stubborn convictions."[144]

The Bolshevik leadership faced a dilemma in judging the sincerity of such declarations of loyalty; at stake was nothing less than the granting of full membership in the Soviet public sphere. During the appeals process, intellectuals were encouraged to make public assertions of loyalty, to disavow "anti-Soviet beliefs," and to disassociate themselves from other political parties. This device, which had been frequently employed with recalcitrant SRs and Mensheviks, was meant to signal the possibility of repentance and to attract prodigal sons willing to work for the proletarian dictatorship.[145] But an equally prominent strain in Bolshevik discourse, expressed forcefully in Zinoviev's conference speech, contended that a Menshevik could be defined objectively and that actual party affiliation did not matter. In other words, the logic went, former foes could not simply declare that they had renounced their faith and be trusted thenceforth as reformed and loyal subjects.

In the end, Lenin allowed that for reasons of age Rozhkov might instead be sent somewhere out of the way, such as Pskov. The Politburo concurred, placing him under strict surveillance to observe his adherence to what he professed. The matter of publishing his declaration of loyalty was confirmed, but it was brought up again at the beginning of February, before it was finally resolved at the end of February to publish it along with criticism of Rozhkov.[146] Rozhkov spent several years in Pskov, where he was eventually allowed to teach, before being permitted to return.

The MGU economist Iakov Bukshpan, by contrast, had earned the Bolsheviks' wrath for contributing to the 1922 Spengler volume but had not been marked for deportation. When he traveled to Europe in summer 1923, however, the GPU declared that he should be considered expelled, and he was refused permission to return, much to his bewilderment. "Upon my departure no one told me anything about the fact that I was deported," he complained to Volgin. "My conduct abroad was completely loyal, and I don't feel that I did anything aimed against the Soviet regime either directly or indirectly. If there is a charge against me, I am prepared to answer it in court."[147] He also turned to Zakharii Grinberg, a Narkompros official in Berlin. Bukshpan's appeal made its way through the usual channels. Grinberg passed it along to Iakovleva, noting that P. A. Bogdanov and I. T. Smilga, the chair and deputy chair of VSNKh, both agreed. Iakovleva met with Iagoda on 2 October 1923, after which she directed Grinberg to have Bukshpan petition the GPU directly. In the end, Bukshpan was allowed to return and even teach at MGU, albeit on a provisional basis.[148]

Through the process of appeals, the Soviet economic and educational elite was able to come to defend those individuals whose rare skills and education made them difficult to replace. Where they could establish usefulness, the matter came down to a question of how loyalty to the Soviet state could be proven. As Rozhkov's case shows, the sincerity of this register was openly questioned by Lenin and other Bolshevik leaders, but in many cases it did succeed in halting expulsions. Nevertheless, most of those who had been marked by the Unshlikht, Kamenev, Kurskii troika did not return to the fold completely; many of them were eased from teaching positions to keep them from influencing the studentry, and few would survive the purges of the late 1920s.[149]

The NKVD Commission and Administrative Exile

The campaign against the intelligentsia was quickly proclaimed a great success, although it was simultaneously asserted that vigilance must be maintained. By the end of the year, the GPU reported in its secret bulletin that "the activity of counterrevolutionary forces continues to weaken with progressive quickness" and that "the activity of anti-Soviet parties in Soviet Russia remains almost completely unnoticeable."[150] At the same time, and somewhat paradoxically, Unshlikht warned the Politburo that their information suggested an upsurge in Menshevik activities, and that the GPU must therefore intensify its struggle with them.[151] The result was a quieting of the public nature of the battle, but a simultaneous institutionalization of the powers of the security apparatus to ferret out and eliminate "harmful" political, cultural, or intellectual tendencies. First and foremost, exile and forced labor were established as fundamental features of the Soviet system.

The NKVD special commission on administrative exile began to function in fall 1922. The operations were handled by both the NKVD and the GPU; the personnel overlapped considerably, and the special commission, which had no standing body, developed into a creature of both. At the same time, a Special Bureau was formed within the GPU Secret Department to manage the expulsion of intellectuals.[152] The NKVD commission's decisions in fall 1922 were formally confirmed by VTsIK rather than the Politburo. This quasi-legal oversight, however, only served to strengthen the extralegal functions that Unshlikht had striven to preserve for the GPU and its sister organs. Dzerzhinskii was given control over the NKVD commission, and in his absence this again fell to Unshlikht. A mid-October set of instructions on administrative exile not only maintained the GPU's role, but expanded its powers by adding forced labor to exile as a punitive instrument and including recidivist criminals among those under its scope. It explicitly added that Articles 60, 61, and 62 of the criminal code, concerning membership in other political parties, should be considered reason for exile. A further clarification stressed that being labeled counterrevolutionary did not necessitate belonging to a specific organization, thus furthering an extremely broad use of the statute on administrative exile and forced labor.[153] The 10 August 1922 decree on administrative exile and its subsequent clarifications, which had as their proximate motivation the deportation of intellectuals, would become one of the foundational blocks in the Soviet punitive system.

Two additional contemporaneous sets of expulsions deserve mention here. First, in fall 1922, dozens of Mensheviks were deported after the Bolshevik takeover of independent Georgia.[154] Second, a group of Moscow Mensheviks, including Boris Dvinov and Pëtr Garvi, were informed in fall 1922 that they, too, were to be expelled. They demanded to know for what crime they were being punished, but received no response. This group of five left in January 1923, except for Boris Bogdanov, who was thrown in prison and charged with fomenting anti-Soviet activity among his VSNKh coworkers. The NKVD commission on exile sentenced him to two years in the newly formed forced labor camps. A series of appeals failed owing to the resolute resistance of the GPU Secret Department, and he was sent to Solovki. His fate was similar to that of a number of Mensheviks and SRs who were exiled internally in late 1922 and 1923.[155] Led by Unshlikht, Dzerzhinskii, and the Politburo, the anti-Menshevik campaigns continued unabated into the following year.

Thenceforth, defiant intellectuals and politicals were not the only targets of exile.[156] Rather, the understanding of deviance developed during the Civil War was made even more elastic. Those exiled after this, in addition to Mensheviks and SRs, were primarily common criminals, but labeled in such a way to make their differences from the "politicals" seem superficial. The term "socially dangerous," shifted from those spreading dangerous ideologies to anyone deemed potentially harmful to the larger community. Among those deported were recidivist criminals and bandits who still terrorized the nation's infrastructure. These elements could contaminate their communities, just as the intellectuals were suspected of infecting students and other educated citizens, and so it was thought that removing them from their localities would have a similar prophylactic effect.[157]

The NKVD commission on administrative exile was one of several institutions arising at this moment to increase surveillance and control over the public sphere. The others included Glavlit, which worked closely with the GPU in obtaining information about and determining the status of journals and publishers; the Scientific-Political Section of the State Academic Council (GUS), which enlisted GPU assistance in keeping track of and removing politically unreliable professors; and the NKVD commissions on the registration of cultural, intellectual, and *spets* societies and organizations and on the authorization of their congresses. The surveillance apparatus was under constant expansion, including the increased use of Communist student cells. This ever-developing network pursued Dzerzhinskii's goal of developing a thickly detailed, taxonomically subdivided chart of every intellectual in the nation—and, eventually, of all other citizens.

Although the expulsion of intellectuals proved to be a relatively unusual event, the series of repressions of which it was a part showed no immediate signs of abating. Despite having driven Mensheviks out of almost all areas of public life, Unshlikht intensified the campaign against them in 1923. The weeding out of enemies in higher education continued, with further purges of students and faculty in 1923 and 1924. As times changed, so too did the name applied to the enemies, and it would not be long before bitter recriminations against the bourgeois intellectuals and Mensheviks gave way to campaigns against Trotskyites. At the same time, the pattern of flattening the differences between these various perceived inimical groups, all at various times classified as "counterrevolutionary," "anti-Soviet," "socially harmful," grew only more ingrained in Bolshevik discourse. The manufacture of seemingly incongruous discursive epithets would reach its logical conclusion in the Great Terror of the late 1930s.

A second legacy of these campaigns was the ever-growing authority of the security apparatus. The transformation of the Cheka into the GPU at last put it within the bounds of the Soviet legal apparatus; its size was diminished and its scope seemingly narrowed. Other institutions, such as Narkomiust, were expected to share its punitive functions. But because of the ambiguity inherent in the statutes describing whom the GPU might send into administrative exile, and because the Bolshevik leadership, and most prominently Lenin, shared the GPU's belief that a broad range of intellectual action could be considered counterrevolutionary, Unshlikht and Dzerzhinskii were quickly able to expand the jurisdiction of the GPU and its nominal parent organization, the NKVD. Its increased responsibilities extended also to its surveillance operations, as Bolshevik efforts to know and categorize the population over which they ruled became more comprehensive.

The limits placed on the scope of the operation were practical more than legal; they were based on exploiting a network of personal connections in a way that would become a key feature of the Soviet polity. Members of the Bolshevik leadership, including Dzerzhinskii, recognized that their ideological push to eliminate enemies, and to convince remaining intellectuals not to overstep similar bounds, should not be allowed to deprive the talent-poor regime of those individuals whose skills could provide a valuable service. The same elasticity that allowed the GPU to use the term "counterrevolutionary" so freely provided in its opposite form the possibility for some of the accused to claim loyalty to the Soviet state. Not all these apparent enemies were entirely irredeemable. Through declarations of fidelity, disavowals of opposition, and, where applicable, condemnation of their former parties, these individuals could serve (so the Bolsheviks hoped) as reminders that those willing to accept the regime's strict conditions could still find a place within the fold.

The deported intellectuals reacted with almost universal defiance to the charge that they were engaged in any sort of direct political activity. Allowing for the possibility of a certain degree of disingenuousness, it is clear that even those who most hated the Soviet state did not recognize the various activities that had so infuriated the Bolsheviks, from professors' strikes to writing critical articles to participating in independent-minded societies, as constituting counterrevolutionary behavior. Though some left Russia with a sense of relief, most experienced the forced separation from their homeland as a great tragedy.

It is difficult to generalize about the effect of this operation on the remaining intelligentsia. Some kept their distance, but others shared the frustration and confusion of their exiled friends and colleagues. But although not all of these men and women were cowed into silence, and not all universities came under complete Soviet control, and not all scholarly, professional, and cultural societies were bolshevized, and not all independent publications disappeared immediately, crucial steps had been taken in limiting the size and scope of the autonomous public sphere.

Epilogue: The Deportees in Emigration

> *I take up a glass, I stand up, and, seeing through the window the last strip of Russian shoreline disappearing into the blue expanse, I say suddenly and awkwardly: "We will drink . . . to the happiness of Russia, which . . . has thrown us out . . ."*
>
> —*Mikhail Osorgin, describing departure aboard the Oberbürgermeister Hakken*

The emigration's conservative majority met the deportees with suspicion, and there were even rumors on the far right that they were Soviet agents.[1] Their friends and colleagues, however, received them with enthusiasm; as bearers of fresh news, they were a unique and privileged group.[2] The émigré public, eager for reports from recent arrivals, listened attentively to their speeches and discussions. Their common fate gave the deportees a sense of collective identity, especially while most of them lived in Berlin, and they gathered as a group several times in the months following their arrival. The first such evening took place on 14 November 1922. Among the speakers were Frank, Stepun, and Vsevolod Iasinskii, and Ivan Il'in expressed the prevailing sense that there was a sharp distinction between those who had departed earlier and even the more conservative deportees. "Voluntarily we would never have abandoned our Native Land," Il'in intoned, "all the more so when she is in such black despair."[3] Upon the arrival of the Petrograd deportees, their Moscow colleagues warmly welcomed them and organized a general bureau led by Iasinskii. In January 1923 a dinner was held for all those expelled and their families. When Dalmat Lutokhin arrived in mid-February, he became the newest celebrity and spoke at another meeting of deportees, including Kuskova, Izgoev, Petrishchev, Peshekhonov, and Kuzmin-Karavaev.[4]

Having been stymied in their efforts to contribute to the Soviet public sphere, the deportees took eager part in the vibrant network of Russian émigré organizations that served as an alternative *obshchestvennost'*.[5] Where institutions did not already exist, they formed their own, which often closely mimicked the ones they had been forced to leave behind. The deportees dominated the Berlin Academic Group, which promoted the corporate interests of professors and collegial ties in the emigration.[6] With the assistance of the YMCA, Berdiaev, Stepun, and others formed the Russian Religious Philosophical Academy as a successor to the Free Spiritual Academy.[7] Those who had belonged to the House of Litterateurs and the Moscow Union of Writers founded the Writers' Club in Berlin and congregated around the Union of Russian Journalists and Litterateurs.[8]

The plethora of émigré newspapers and journals offered a decided advantage over the always-precarious independent periodicals of Soviet Russia. Kuskova, Osorgin, Petrishchev, and other left-leaning deportees gravitated to Kerensky's Berlin-based *Dni*, whereas Miliukov's liberal daily *Poslednie novosti* served as a forum for varied points of view. Izgoev, Kizevetter, Aikhenval'd, and others wrote for the right-Kadet Berlin daily *Rul'*. Thick journals such as *Sovremennye zapiski* and the Prague-based *Volia Rossii* published more extensive essays, and the many émigré publishers allowed the deportees to put out works they had been unable to issue in Soviet Russia. A. S. Kagan re-formed his publishing house Petropolis, prominent until its closure by the Nazis in 1938. Mel'gunov and his colleagues, including V. M. Kudriavtsev, V. S. Ozeretskovskii, Venedikt Miakotin, and Aleksandr Kizevetter formed a branch of Zadruga in Berlin and issued a journal entitled *Na chuzhoi storone,* which featured accounts of days gone by and the years of the Revolution.[9]

The deportees were also active in the informal manifestations of the émigré public sphere, in particular cultural *kruzhki*. In Berlin, cafés like the Leon and the Landgraf became lively centers of Russian public life; "it was not unusual in 1922 to find four or five separate literary gatherings or poetry readings going on simultaneously on a given evening."[10] Mel'gunov's colleagues from Zadruga, including Miakotin, the Peshekhonovs, and Osorgin, met on Mondays at Schellia. As the center of emigration shifted in 1923–24 from Berlin to Paris and Prague (where the Czech government warmly welcomed and supported Russian émigrés), many of the deportees who had originally settled in Germany followed. In the mid-1920s, cafés and restaurants on Montparnasse were filled with Russian intellectuals debating art and politics. Religious-philosophical *kruzhki* also arose, including the Brotherhood of St. Sophia, with which Frank and Losskii were affiliated. In the town of Zbraslav, outside Prague, a lively and extremely diverse circle of "*Piatnitsy*" (Friday gatherers), including Kizevetter, Losskii, Lutokhin, Valentin Bulgakov, Ivan Lapshin, Antonii Florovskii, and Stratonov, met on Friday afternoons in a local *biergarten.*[11]

The deportees were also active in erecting a network of émigré scholarly and educational establishments. First among these was the Russian Scientific Institute in Berlin, founded with the aid of the German government, whose initiators were almost entirely deportees, including Berdiaev, Aikhenval'd, Zubashev, Karsavin, Kizevetter, Odintsov, and Stratonov. It aimed to provide a Russian education for émigré youth, to assist scholars in their research and publications, and to arrange public lectures and discussions. The always-active Iasinskii chaired the organizational committee, and Il'in and Novikov spoke at its opening in February 1923. Despite its auspicious start, the Scientific Institute did not long remain the focal point of Russian academic life abroad. As the political situation and living conditions worsened in Germany, there was an exodus of scholars from Berlin to Prague, which became the center of émigré scholarly life until the late 1930s. The Czech government's generous Russian Action plan helped establish an impressive set of institutions there, including the Russian Juridical Faculty, Prokopovich's Economic Cabinet, and the Russian Popular University, where Novikov would take up the familiar role of rector.[12]

Many of the deportees felt uncomfortable, surrounded as they were by stalwarts of the old regime. In the early twenties, borders were not as fixed as they would later become, and a number of intellectuals living abroad, including Andrei Belyi, Viktor Shklovskii, and Ilya Ehrenburg returned to Soviet Russia. Aleksei Tolstoi publicly excoriated the emigration, asserting that it was time to "recognize the reality of the government that exists in Russia."[13] Other intellectuals and *spetsy,* buoyed by the belief that NEP signaled an opportunity to resume productive work, also began to consider the possibility of going back.[14] The Soviet regime was particularly interested in convincing Russian students to return to the motherland, and the GPU began to infiltrate nonparty student organizations in Prague and Berlin to encourage them to come back.[15]

Although the specific principles of *smenovekhovstvo* did not attract many of those expelled, the left-leaning among them began to talk of returning. Most recognized that they had been banished indefinitely, but others took seriously the official three-year term. A number of those expelled held on to their Soviet passports rather than trade them in for the Nansen passport that had been established for "stateless" people after the Great War.[16] Soon Soviet trade missions in Europe were querying the Central Committee concerning requests from deportees (in particular Iasinskii) that they might work within these institutions; these requests were denied forthwith.[17]

Prokopovich and Kuskova, the first deportees to arrive "on alien shores," created immediate controversy with their provocative assessments of the Revolution. The Soviet regime, Kuskova held, could not be divorced from the Revolution as a whole, and in some ways was its natural and inevitable consequence. "The Bolsheviks are our children," she declared. "In Bolshevism there is something purely Russian. The October Revolution is a national revolution." She expressed great dismay that the emigration was so cut off from the way people thought at home. Russia would arise again, and the emigration should not rejoice in the Bolsheviks' struggles, which were also Russia's struggles.[18] "I consider it necessary to establish a different, 'non-émigré' line," Kuskova wrote to Vasilii Maklakov, the Kadet and former Provisional Government ambassador to France. The single-mindedness of the emigration and its "primitive" Manichaean opposition she saw as a useless and dangerous pose. "Intervention from outside has outlived itself. . . . Only internal processes will resolve the fate of Bolshevism and Russia itself."[19]

Pitirim Sorokin was one of a number of deportees who sharply disagreed with Kuskova's optimism. The devastation, the cruelty of the bloody war and the Revolution, which had significantly impaired the moral and physical capabilities of the population, led him to doubt the likelihood of a quick recovery. Despite the minor improvements of NEP, it would take "years and years to heal even in part the deep wounds inflicted on the spirit of the people by the war and Revolution."[20] Kizevetter agreed, arguing that Bolshevism, far from being an "embodiment of the Russian national spirit," was instead a misfortune "issuing not from the innermost depths of the popular spirit but as a result of a fatal combination of ephemeral historical conditions." Kuskova's and others' belief that NEP was a first step toward normalcy was, he declared, a "spectacular fantasy," which evinced the same delusions as those that had led them to form the ill-fated famine relief committee. "It is *impossible* to do any sort of useful public activity there. Only more 'Prokukishes' are possible."[21]

Kuskova was not alone, however, in her discomfort with the emigration.[22] Osorgin, A. B. Petrishchev, and others rejected Sorokin's pessimism, insisted that they shared Russia's suffering, and proclaimed that the emigration was hopelessly out of touch with Russian realities.[23] Stepun chastised the emigration for its backward-looking intransigence and its failure to acknowledge the progress that had been made since the Revolution. The "*emigrantshchina*" did not recognize that the real Russia was *in* Russia.[24] The emigration, Osorgin added, wrongly confused the Revolution—and even Russia itself—with the Bolsheviks. "Every humiliation of Russia is our humiliation," he maintained. "Each success is our success. . . . And the Revolution (all of it, as a whole, in all of its stages) we consider not an illness from which the country is now recovering, but a difficult operation helping it to overcome a long-standing and terrible chronic illness." Its survival of "a monstrous catastrophe," was even "to its advantage," he declared. "Russia lives, and—no matter what kind of regime there might be—is being reborn."[25]

Although such remarks were met with heavy scorn by conservative émigrés, this irritation paled in comparison with the scandal following the publication of Peshekhonov's brochure, *Why Didn't I Emigrate?*[26] which alleged that the emigration was doomed to become ever more estranged from the motherland. Emigrés, he asserted, must recognize the Soviet regime and return to Russia, which was desperately in need of talented and educated people. He suggested that much good had come of the Revolution and Bolshevik rule—especially the restoration of a capable state—although he still condemned the means. For those inside Russia, he held, acceptance of the Soviet state was a simple recognition of an undeniable fact. And he defended his and others' efforts to cooperate with the Bolsheviks: "By staying in Soviet service, I hoped to serve Russia."[27]

The reaction to this pamphlet ranged from outrage to disbelief. Not only the conservative émigrés, but longtime comrades from the Popular Socialist Party, such as Miakotin and Mel'gunov, disavowed it. Miakotin maintained that the very fact of Peshekhonov's (and his own) expulsion "proved that it was impossible to work constructively under the Bolsheviks." As to protecting the gains of the Revolution, nothing could be worse than the current regime. Miakotin also defended the emigration's usefulness in propagating Russian culture and preserving its intellectual forces. Mel'gunov questioned the sharp distinction between the emigration and intellectuals remaining in Russia, noting that many differences existed within these groups as well. In addition, he cautioned against any attempt to dictate what it really meant to be "close to the people."[28]

Osorgin and Kuskova, on the other hand, shared Peshekhonov's conviction that nothing productive would emanate from the emigration. In summer and fall 1925, taking the nominal three-year term of exile literally, several deportees explored the idea of going home.[29] Although most of those expelled rejected *vozvrashchenstvo* ("returnism") and neither wished to return nor took seriously the supposed expiration of their term,[30] Peshekhonov was not alone. Kuskova declared that the time had come to "fill in the trenches of the Civil War" and claimed that *vozvrashchenstvo* had already become a "current" among the émigrés. Osorgin added that émigrés should aim not at defending "pickled 'precepts' [*marinovannye zaveti*]," but at attaining "union with the Russian people, accepting its new faith and its new methods of struggle."[31] These views were anathema to many leading émigrés. When Osorgin proclaimed that he accepted the Revolution as a whole, in all its phases, Kerensky angrily retorted that Osorgin was no longer welcome to write for *Dni*.[32]

Despite their vocal criticism of the emigration, neither Kuskova nor Osorgin made any apparent effort to return. Peshekhonov, on the other hand, publicly announced that he was ready to return as soon as possible.[33] He began to make inquiries as early as spring 1924. The Politburo quickly rejected his request, despite the unlikely support of the GPU's Menzhinskii. Peshekhonov continued to pursue the matter, and in May 1925 he made a formal request that he be allowed to return now that his three-year term had expired. Despite the intervention of the moderate Bolshevik leader Leonid Krasin, the assistance of Vera Figner, and Peshekhonov's persistence, he was told that although he might work for Soviet institutions in Europe, he could not enter Russia itself.[34] In summer 1927, to the great consternation of his former Popular Socialist colleagues and under heavy criticism, he went to Riga to accept a position with the Soviet trade mission.[35]

Dalmat Lutokhin, the former editor of *Ekonomist* and *Utrenniki,* had not been as vocal as Peshekhonov, but privately he felt the same misgivings toward the emigration.[36] His personal views drew him closer to Osorgin, Kuskova, and Peshekhonov and caused a rift with his former colleague Sorokin.[37] He maintained that despite the absence of rights, public work was still possible in Soviet Russia. And in spite of the "starving or half-starving" state of those who did not work directly for the regime, he discerned the (not yet complete) consolidation of a united front, a movement of the people. The emigration, he had discovered, was extremely ill informed and entertained fantastic delusions of divisions among the Bolsheviks and peasant rebellions. The émigré press "creates the dangerous illusion of the possibility of an imminent return to Russia, to the *old* Russia." But the old Russia had disappeared for good.[38] Soon Lutokhin's numerous talks on Russian literature made him a controversial figure known for his "pro-Soviet" views.

Lutokhin admired Peshekhonov for his courage in the face of public ridicule, and he began to look into the possibility of returning himself.[39] Pil'niak made inquiries on his behalf, and his father, A. P. Lutokhin, appealed to VTsIK, averring that his son was in an "extremely difficult moral and material position, being by conviction an ally of the Soviet Union—he has completely broken off with the Russian emigration, he is an alien in their midst." Most important, perhaps, during his time abroad, Lutokhin had become close to Gorky, who after seven years was also preparing to return to Russia, where he would receive a hero's welcome. Undoubtedly, Gorky's intervention was of great assistance to Lutokhin, who, unlike Peshekhonov, was after some hesitation granted permission to return in fall 1927.[40]

Though only a handful of deportees shared Peshekhonov's and Lutokhin's preference for Soviet Russia over the emigration, few went so far in the other direction as Ivan Il'in, one of the few unequivocal defenders of the White movement.[41] Il'in developed a close relationship with Pëtr Struve, became an active contributor to Struve's newspaper, *Vozrozhdenie* (Rebirth), and shared the conviction that not only should the emigration not reconcile itself to the Soviet state, but it should renew attempts to overthrow it by means of armed intervention.[42] The publication of Il'in's *On the Resistance of Evil by Force* in 1925 became as controversial an event as had Peshekhonov's diametrically opposed remarks.[43] Il'in argued that Tolstoy's doctrine of nonresistance naively placed the virtuous man in the position of passively accepting and therefore condoning evil, thus weakening his principles and character. In certain situations, if an enemy was truly evil and the warrior truly righteous, force was not only justified but morally imperative.[44] Il'in's book amounted to a theological-philosophical justification of armed struggle against the Bolsheviks.

A split among the *Vekhisty* and their associates was evident soon after their arrival in Berlin; at a gathering at Berdiaev's flat, Frank and Izgoev joined their host in rejecting Struve and Il'in's conservative nationalism.[45] Two years later, after the publication of Il'in's screed, Berdiaev wrote, "I have rarely had to read such a nightmarish and torturous book as I. Il'in's *On the Resistance of Evil by Force*. The book is capable of inducing a revulsion to 'good,' it creates an atmosphere of spiritual suffocation, it plunges into the torture chamber of moral inquisition."[46] In fact, even most of the religiously oriented deportees distanced themselves from direct struggle with Bolshevism. Berdiaev immediately felt uneasy among the emigration—he felt that the Whites were generally no less hostile to freedom than were the Bolsheviks—and he rejected the idea of military intervention. Like the *vozvrashchentsy*, he called for a "regeneration from within" Russia, although the means he proposed were quite different.[47] Even Struve's close friend Frank broke with him over the advisability of armed conflict and echoed Berdiaev's call for a spiritual regeneration in the spirit of *Vekhi.* Political change was irrelevant if it did not address the inner disease, and "fact acceptance" of the Revolution was a necessary step in the path toward moral recovery.[48]

Most deportees took just such an unlikely, nuanced position between the advocates of total war and quiet reconciliation. Fëdor Stepun suggested that both Il'in and Peshekhonov were sincere patriots in their own way, but, expressing what were undoubtedly the sentiments of many deportees, he could not go as far as either. He insisted that a united front with Il'in, intransigently rejecting the Revolution and confusing the emigration with "authentic Russia," was impossible for democratic-minded émigrés; the *vozvrashchentsy,* on the other hand, in their utter antipathy for the emigration, confused the true Russia with the Soviet Union and Bolshevik rule. Thus, both sides subscribed to the dominant and dangerous notion that the only choices for Russia were monarchy and Bolshevism. Russia abroad needed neither a counterproductive armed struggle in alliance with reactionaries nor dull and hopeless acceptance of Bolshevik rule. "The task of the emigration, of course, is not in the restoration of the past, but in the conservation for the future of the eternal character of Russia."[49]

The eventual fate of the deportees was as diverse as their political views and professional backgrounds. Most lived the ordinary lives of émigré intellectuals, teaching, writing, and polemicizing before dying natural deaths in France, Germany, and Czechoslovakia during the interwar period. Others met different tragic ends: Aikhenval'd was run over by a tram in 1928; Stratonov, lonely and depressed, committed suicide in 1938. Lev Karsavin, having moved to Kaunas to teach, died in a Stalinist camp in 1952 after the Soviet absorption of Lithuania. Sorokin, convinced that Russia would not soon recover, was one of the few to cross the Atlantic, teaching first at the University of Minnesota and then for many years at Harvard. After the Second World War, several of those who had survived, including Mikhail Novikov, moved to the United States. Antonii Florovskii remained in Communist Czechoslovakia and continued a productive academic career that brought him into contact with a new generation of Soviet historians.[50] The Tolstoyan Valentin Bulgakov and the agronomist Aleksandr Ugrimov joined those émigrés who returned after the Second World War on Stalin's invitation, having at last been convinced that the only life possible for a Russian intellectual was in the Soviet Union.[51]

Conclusion: The Intelligentsia in Soviet Russia

There may be individual intellectuals, but there is no intelligentsia as a class. There used to be an intelligentsia, . . . but, as a group, the intellectuals have been destroyed as a useless body; they have been destroyed by the logical processes of history itself. . . . What are we? An amputated limb, a useless fragment, a piece of emptiness, internal émigrés—oh, hell! isn't that what we are?

—The teacher N. P. Ozhegov, July 1925,
in the novel The Diary of Kostia Riabtsev

By mid-1923 a softening in Bolshevik rhetoric signaled that the skirmish in the struggle on the ideological front had been deemed a success. Even the zealous Zinoviev offered an olive branch at a national meeting of Rabpros's scientific workers' section, into which all professors had been involuntarily impressed after the dissolution of their autonomous organizations. While recalling the "sabotage" in which many intellectuals had engaged after the Revolution, Zinoviev suggested that a corner had been turned in the relationship between people of science and the dictatorship of the proletariat. The Soviet state had had to restrain the perfectly understandable anti-intelligentsia sentiments prevalent among workers, peasants, and soldiers. Now, he maintained, open hostility was giving way to greater accommodation.

"Circumstances are developing under which the intelligentsia, as a group, as a certain stratum, is changing its orientation."

Still, he cautioned, this was not yet a full transformation: even those intellectuals who had come to terms with the Revolution had in fact accepted only NEP. As long as the renowned Pavlov made naive political remarks in his classroom, and especially as long as a significant portion of the Russian intelligentsia remained in the counterrevolutionary emigration, it was not yet time to declare a complete reconciliation. Still, even abroad there were positive signs, and he noted with satisfaction Peshekhonov's acknowledgment of the achievements of the Soviet state. Within Russia, those intellectuals who had witnessed how the regime defended the country's core interests could not help having evolved in their regard for it. The working class, which was not vengeful, would then forgive the intelligentsia its misdeeds and work toward developing a new relationship.[1]

Zinoviev's conciliatory words took place in a setting carefully orchestrated to demonstrate the absence of rancor between intellectuals and the proletariat. Trotsky concurred that the former clannishness of the intelligentsia was fading, and that it was time to draw it into closer collaboration in constructing the socialist economy. He optimistically predicted that the ensuing rapprochement would be the basis for a "new public sphere [*obshchestvennost'*]."[2] Having removed a significant number of the most visible (and most recalcitrant) old intellectuals, the Bolshevik leadership now focused on developing an understanding with the remaining mass of "scientific workers," whose expertise it needed to build a new society. *Spetsy* with practical technical and scientific skills were of greater value than, and should be treated differently from, the cultural or humanistic intelligentsia. As Bubnov remarked, "If Prof. Kizevetter causes harm with his reactionary lectures, then we send him packing out of the country. But if the famous physiologist Pavlov scolds us Communists in the introductions to his lectures, we cannot chase him out, for he also does tremendous work that is extremely useful for us. We must arrange things so that Pavlov does needed and useful things for the Soviet state, and we must somehow remove his negative characteristics."[3] With the closure of journals and the circumscription of autonomy for scholarly and professional societies, criticism of the regime was noticeably more muted than it had been a year earlier. Even the GPU was pleased with its efforts to reduce Menshevik and SR activities, particularly among the studentry. The change in atmosphere was especially obvious in the universities; by mid-1923 the movement for university autonomy had been soundly routed and a working system of appointments established.

The conciliatory rhetoric continued into 1925 in a series of debates on the roles of art and literature in a socialist society. The advocates of relative permissiveness included such diverse party leaders as Lunacharskii, Trotsky, and Bukharin, who were able to keep at bay the demands for uniformity emanating from proletarian maximalists.[4] The lack of an unequivocal cultural dictum should not, however, be confused with advocacy of pluralism. Bukharin himself cautioned at these same debates that politics and culture were inextricably linked.[5] Although societies and *kruzhki* could continue to gather, belletrists to write and be published, and scholars to pursue their research relatively unhindered, all were kept under tight surveillance. Most important, such activities could be kept from entering the broader public sphere. Police informants were ready to take away the ability of associations to organize or disperse "seditious" gatherings; Glavlit could eliminate offensive passages and sharply curtail the circulation of a particular publication; and a scholar preaching idealist philosophy or defending the bourgeoisie could be removed from his teaching duties. In addition, although expulsion from the Soviet Union was employed infrequently after 1923, the use of internal exile and forced labor against perceived enemies intensified.

The inconsistency in dealing with intellectuals during the 1920s had more to do with the regime's youth and relative frailty than with its moderation. Even during the rhetorical relaxation following the expulsions, Bubnov warned that the recent skirmish had represented only the first wave, and it was just a matter of time before the next round of conflict. Throughout the 1920s, those who continued to view the intelligentsia with suspicion and even outright hostility—and they were vocal—waited for the moment when the second wave would arise.[6] Efforts to purge the public sphere continued: the NKVD consistently advocated the elimination of autonomous organizations; Glavlit frequently took censorship further than Lunacharskii thought prudent; and the OGPU was not afraid to take action against "politicals" and "counterrevolutionaries" long after the elimination of their organizational structures. At the same time, the party accelerated the construction of Soviet *obshchestvennost'*, an increasingly developed but ultimately univocal network of institutions in which intellectuals were expected to participate, in harmony and unity with the rest of society, putting separate interests aside.

Tolerance of reconciled former foes was a provisional tactic, as demonstrated by the demise of *smenovekhovstvo*. Criticism within the Bolshevik Party of the tenuous alliance with the Smenovekhovites had been considerable, and support for the newspaper *Nakanune* ended in mid-1924. Two years later, *Novaia Rossiia*, which Lenin himself had saved from closure in 1922, was shut down as well. Its editor, I. G. Lezhnev, was accused of advocating a separatist ideology for *spetsy*, of attempting "to turn [his] press organ into an organizational center for all dissatisfied employed intellectuals," and he was expelled from the Soviet Union in 1926 in a unique and demonstrative echo of the events of 1922–23.[7]

Compared to what followed, the 1922–23 expulsion of intellectuals was indeed, as Trotsky claimed, a humane operation. By the time that Stalin expelled Trotsky himself from the Soviet Union in 1929, the incessant hunt for internal enemies zeroed in on both the remaining bourgeois intellectuals and on the upper party leadership. During the 1920s Bolsheviks always sharply distinguished between themselves and the "old" intelligentsia, but they were in many ways its apotheosis, and it was only logical that their deep distrust of undisciplined and discordant intellectuals, of their potential deviance, would eventually reach inward. The rhetoric deployed during the great purges was strikingly similar to the discourse of exclusion used during the earlier anti-intellectual campaigns. The enemy, who was depicted as ever more devious and ever more pernicious as he was discovered ever closer to the center of the new social hierarchy, was vilified for introducing division into a people who would be unified.[8] This impurity could not be allowed to remain in a position to infect immature but critical elements of the population.

Shortly after his expulsion, Pitirim Sorokin argued that a sea change in the composition and character of the intelligentsia had already occurred. The "penitent intellectual" with an innate sense of debt toward the masses had disappeared. The representatives of the thinking classes were now more inwardly focused, businesslike, and practical, and thus more willing quietly to serve the new order as *spetsy* without an agenda.[9] Mikhail Osorgin disagreed with Sorokin, asserting that the traditional intellectual values of social conscience and public activity had persevered. Everyday intellectuals—teachers and factory doctors, minor agronomists and librarians, leaders of workers' circles and directors of reading halls, had the opportunity to serve the people in a small-scale but direct and hands-on manner that demonstrated the survival of intellectual public-spiritedness.[10]

The Communist Party reserved for itself the privilege of speaking for the people, and it proposed a new role for the intelligentsia, more limited in its mission but broader in its composition. Intellectuals were from that point on to advance the greater interest of the people—and they would be rewarded for this—but only as the nation's servant, as directed by the avant-garde of the proletariat.[11] Intellectuals would no longer be permitted to pose as the conscience of the nation; instead, *intelligentsia* would merely be the collective noun used in referring to all those performing mental labor in the service of their country. To what degree and how quickly the Bolsheviks succeeded in transfiguring the scope and character of intellectual participation in the public sphere would be played out not only during NEP but over the next seventy years of Soviet rule. As Doug Weiner has demonstrated, even the enforced uniformity that was the primary characteristic of the Soviet public sphere had within it at least one "little corner of freedom."[12]

Nevertheless, the struggle on the ideological front in the early 1920s had had its effect on limiting these pockets of autonomy and shaping an outwardly harmonious and unitary *obshchestvennost'*. The old intelligentsia had had its ranks dramatically thinned, and a new generation of mental laborers infused with a different understanding of their role in society was emerging to take its place. The institutions of state control and practices of power that would thenceforth characterize the Soviet system had been established, and an emphatic first warning had been delivered concerning the limits of autonomous activity in the public sphere.

Appendix
Intellectuals Expelled from Soviet Russia, 1922–1923

This list includes those intellectuals expelled from the country as part of the concerted GPU-directed operation during 1922–23. It does not include Mensheviks, anarchists, or students expelled in related but separate actions, and it does not include intellectuals sent to internal deportation within Russia.

Abrikosov, V. V.	Catholic priest. Leader of Catholic-Orthodox unity circle in Moscow.
Aikhenval'd, Iu. I.	Literary critic. Member of board of All-Russian Union of Writers in Moscow. Participated on the All-Russian Famine Relief Committee.
Arbuzov, A. D.	Part of Abrikosov group in Moscow. Senator under old regime.
Babkin, B. P.	Professor of physiology, Odessa. Worked for the American Relief Administration.
Baikov, A. L.	Professor of international law at Moscow State University and in the Crimea. Connected to Abrikosov group.
Bakkal, I. Iu.	Active in Tsentrosoiuz (consumer cooperative board). Member of Legalist wing of Left-Socialist Revolutionary Party.
Bardygin, V. M.	Professor at the Archeological Institute, Moscow.

Berdiaev, N. A.	Religious philosopher, contributor to *Vekhi* and *Iz glubiny*, temporarily professor at Moscow University, involved with Bereg press, founder of Free Spiritual Academy, deputy chair of All-Russian Union of Writers.
Bogolepov, A. A.	Professor of administrative law at Petrograd State University, former vice-rector. Active in professors' groups.
Brutskus, B. D.	Economist and agronomist, professor in Petrograd, cooperator, wrote for and was on editorial board of Ekonomist.
Bulatov, A. A.	Head of craft-industrial cooperative organization in Novgorod. Member of Kadet Party. Served in *zemstvo* under old regime and as a Provisional Government representative in Novgorod.
Bulgakov, S. N.	Religious philosopher, later a priest. Lived in Crimea after the Revolution. Contributor to *Vekhi* and *Iz glubiny*.
Bulgakov, V. F.	Tolstoy's last secretary, one of leaders of Tolstoyan movement. Founder and head of Tolstoy Museum in Moscow. Pacifist. Returned to Soviet Union in 1948.
Florovskii, A. V.	Historian at Odessa Archeological Institute, member of Odessa Society of History and Antiquity.
Frank, S. L.	Religious philosopher, dean of Historical-Philological Faculty at Saratov University until 1921, and then briefly professor at Moscow University. Participated in Free Spiritual Academy and involved with Bereg press. Contributor to *Vekhi* and *Iz glubiny*.
Golovachev, V. D.	Head of Moscow student organization in 1921. Head of student section of All-Russian Famine Relief Committee.
Iasinskii, V. I.	Professor at Moscow Higher Technical School, engineer. Head of Moscow commission for improving the life of scholars (KUBU), and chairman (1921) of Moscow Union of Scientific Actors.
Il'in, I. A.	Philosopher, expert on Hegel, professor at Moscow University. Head of Moscow Psychological Society. Later a monarchist.
Iretskii, V. Ia.	Writer and journalist. Board member and librarian at the House of Litterateurs. Secretary of Petrograd branch of Union of Writers. Contributor to *Letopis' doma literatorov* and *Literaturnye zapiski*.
Iushtim, I. I.	Member of the commission on improving the condition of engineers. Secretary of Presidium of Petrograd branch of All-Russian Union of Engineers.

Izgoev, A. S.	Philosopher and publicist. Member of Kadet Party. Wrote for journals *Utrenniki* and *Parfenon*. Member of House of Litterateurs in Petrograd. Contributed to *Vekhi* and *Iz glubiny*.
Iziumov, A. F.	Archivist in Moscow regional administration. Historian. Cooperator. Member of Popular Socialist (NS) Party.
Kagan, A. S.	Professor at Agronomical Institute. Publisher, on editorial board of *Ekonomist*. Deputy chair, Petrograd Union of Cooperative Publishers.
Karsavin, L. P.	Professor at Petrograd University, at one point member of its administrative board. Historian, medievalist, philosopher, theologian.
Khariton, B. O.	One of leaders of House of Litterateurs and Petrograd branch of Union of Writers, editor of *Literaturnye zapiski*.
Kizevetter, A. A.	Historian, professor at Moscow University. Associated with Zadruga press. Member of Kadet Party.
Kozlov, N. P.	Civil engineer. Member of commission on improving condition of engineers, Petrograd.
Kudriavtsev, V. M.	Cooperator, deputy director of Zadruga press. Member of Popular Socialist Party.
Kuskova, E. D.	Publicist. A founder and leading member of All-Russian Committee to Aid the Starving. Married to S. N. Prokopovich.
Kuzmin-Karavaev, D. V.	Jurist. Catholic, monarchist. Connected to Abrikosov group. Worked for state forestry committee (Glavleskom).
Lapshin, I. I.	Professor at Petrograd University. Philosopher, art theoretician. Member of Academy of Sciences.
Liubimov, N. I.	Agronomist, board member of Sel'skosoiuz (agricultural cooperative board). Allowed to return in 1923.
Losskii, N. O.	Philosopher, professor at Petrograd University. One of leaders of Philosophical Society at Petrograd University. Coeditor of *Mysl'* (Thought). Member of Kadet Party through 1917.
Lutokhin, D. A.	Engineer, economist, litterateur. Editor of *Utrenniki* and *Ekonomist*. Worked for Soviet paper trust in Petrograd. Allowed to return in 1927.
Maloletenkov, N. V.	One of founders of All-Russian Society of Agronomists. Prominent in cooperative organizations.
Martsinkovskii, V. F.	Prominent in evangelical Russian Christian Student Movement.

Matusevich, I. A.	Journalist. Officer in All-Russian Union of Writers.
Matveev, I. P.	Member of board of Sel'skosoiuz (agricultural cooperative board) and of Moscow Agricultural Society. Member of All-Russian Committee to Aid the Starving. Allowed to return in 1923.
Mel'gunov, S. P.	Historian. Implicated in Tactical Center trial. Director of Zadruga press, editor of *Golos Minuvshego*. Member of Popular Socialist Party.
Miakotin, V. A.	Historian, publicist. Associated with Zadruga press. Member of Popular Socialist Party.
Novikov, M. M.	Zoologist, professor, rector of Moscow University in 1920. Former member of Kadet Party. Leader of Provisional Government committee on reforming higher education.
Odintsov, B. N.	Professor of agronomy and pro-rector at Petrograd University. Active in Petrograd United Council of Professors.
Osokin, V. M.	One of leaders of Petrograd (northern) regional craft-industrial cooperative union.
Osorgin, M. A.	Publicist, writer. Chairman of All-Russian Union of Journalists, deputy chairman of All-Russian Union of Writers. One of proprietors of Moscow Writers' Book Store. Participated on All-Russian Committee to Aid the Starving and edited its journal, *Pomoshch'* (Aid).
Ovchinnikov, A. A.	Professor. Rector at Kazan University, former rector at Petrograd University, statistician
Ozeretskovskii, V. S.	Member of board of Zadruga press. Member of Popular Socialist Party.
Peshekhonov, A. V.	Agronomist, cooperator, statistician, historian. Provisional Government Minister of Food Supply. Member of Popular Socialist Party. Worked in Soviet statistical administration. Participated on All-Russian Committee to Aid the Starving. Attempted to return to Soviet Union in mid-1920s.
Petrishchev, A. B.	Publicist, active member of House of Litterateurs in Petrograd.
Poletika, V. P.	Professor at Petrograd Geographical Institute, meteorologist. Secretary of United Council of Professors in Petrograd.
Polner, S. I.	Professor at Petrograd University, mathematician.
Prokopovich, S. N.	Economist, formerly professor and dean of Juridical Faculty at Moscow University. Minister of Trade and Industry and Minister of Food Supply in Provisional Government.

	Cooperator and one of leaders of All-Russian Committee to Aid the Starving. Married to E. D. Kuskova.
Pumpianskii, L. M.	Cooperator, contributor to *Ekonomist.*
Romodanovskii, N. P.	Member of council of All-Russian Society of Agronomists in Moscow. Former member of Kadet Party.
Rozenberg, V. A.	Journalist, former editor of prerevolutionary newspaper *Russkie vedomosti.* Associated with Zadruga press.
Sekal', G. A.	Instructor at Odessa Institute of Agriculture.
Selivanov, D. F.	Professor at Petrograd University, mathematician.
Shishkin, M. D.	Agronomist, cooperator. Member of Menshevik Party. Participated on All-Russian Committee to Aid the Starving.
Sigirskii, A. I.	Cooperator, agronomist. Board member of All-Russian Society of Agronomists and of Sel'skosoiuz (agricultural cooperative board). Member of Popular Socialist Party.
Sorokin, P. A.	Professor at Petrograd University, sociologist. Former member of SR Party and Kerensky's secretary in 1917. Active contributor to *Ekonomist* and other journals.
Stepun, F. A.	Writer and religious philosopher, formerly associated with right SRs. Associated with Bereg press and Free Spiritual Academy in Moscow. Edited literary almanac *Shipovnik.*
Stratonov, I. A.	Professor at Kazan University, historian.
Stratonov, V. V.	Astronomer, professor and dean of Math and Physics Faculty at Moscow University. Active supporter of university autonomy and member of professors' organizations. One of founders of Main Astrophysics Observatory in 1921.
Troshin, G. Ia.	Psychiatrist, professor, dean of Medical Faculty at Kazan University.
Trubetskoi, S. E.	Publicist, associated with Bereg press. Implicated in Tactical Center trial. Worked for state agricultural syndicate. Monarchist.
Tsvetkov, N. A.	Professor at Archeological Institute in Moscow.
Ugrimov, A. I.	Agronomist, chairman of Moscow Agricultural Society and of Free Economic Society. Participated on All-Russian Committee to Aid the Starving. Returned to Soviet Union in 1947.
Visloukh, S. M.	Botanist, member of Petrograd professors' organizations. Professor at Petrograd Institute of Agronomics. Head of Hydrobiology Station.
Volkovyskii, N. M.	Journalist. One of leaders of House of Litterateurs in Petrograd. Deputy chair of Petrograd branch Union of Writers.

Zubashev, E. L.	Professor at Petrograd Technology Institute. Founder and former director of Tomsk Technology Institute. Wrote for and was on editorial board of *Ekonomist*.
Zvorykin, V. V.	Engineer, professor at Moscow Higher Technical School.

Glossary

Bolshevik (Communist) Party (RKP)

Politburo (Policy Bureau)—Highest decision-making organ; in the early 1920s there were between seven and nine members.

Orgburo (Organizational Bureau)—Organ directly below Politburo. In the early 1920s the jurisdictional divisions between it and the Politburo were not well established.

Secretariat—In 1922 basically indistinguishable from the Orgburo.

Central Committee—Broader decision-making body that confirmed decisions of the Politburo.

Agitprop—Central Committee's bureau on agitation and propaganda.

Ukrainian Communist Party—KPU. Theoretically still independent of the RKP.

Ukrainian Politburo—The KPU's highest organ.

Soviet State Institutions

Sovnarkom—Council of People's Commissars. The state's highest administrative organ, it theoretically coordinated the work of the Commissariats.

VTsIK—All-Russian Central Executive Committee. The standing executive arm of the Congress of People's Deputies, its Presidium was the state's highest executive organ. In 1922 the jurisdictional divisions between Sovnarkom and VTsIK were not yet well established.

Narkompros—Commissariat of Enlightenment.

Glavprofobr—Chief Committee on Professional Education. Narkompros organ in charge of all higher education as of 1921.

Glavlit—Central censorship organ, formed in June 1922, nominally under the aegis of Narkompros.

Gosizdat—State publishing house, under Narkompros.

Gosizdat Politotdel—Gosizdat's political department. In charge of most censorship until the formation of Glavlit. Headed by N. L. Meshcheriakov and P. I. Lebedev-Polianskii.

Glavpolitprosvet—Main Political Enlightenment Committee. State committee in charge of propaganda; worked in the shadow of Agitprop.

NKVD (Narkomvnudel)—Commissariat of Internal Affairs. Feliks Dzerzhinskii was its commissar during 1922.

VChK (Vecheka or Cheka)—All-Russian Extraordinary Committee for the Combating of Counterrevolutionary Activities. Independent of NKVD. Disbanded in February 1922 and reconstituted as the GPU.

GPU (Gosudarstvennoe Politicheskoe Upravlenie)—State Political Administration. Formed in February 1922. Theoretically subordinate to the NKVD until its reformation as the OGPU in late 1923. Dzerzhinskii was its head, though Unshlikht ran daily affairs.

Narkomindel—Commissariat of Foreign Affairs.

Narkomiust—Commissariat of Justice.

Narkomput'—Commissariat of Transport.

Narkomvneshtorg—Commissariat of Foreign Trade.

Narkomzdrav—Commissariat of Health.

Narkomzem—Commissariat of Agriculture.

VSNKh—Supreme Council of the People's Economy. Highest state economic organ, it had the status of a commissariat.

Gosplan—State Planning Committee. Body created to oversee production plans for all economic agencies.

Unions and Cooperatives

VTsSPS—All-Union Central Council of Professional [Trade] Unions. Central Bolshevik-controlled body in charge of the official unions.

Sel'skosoiuz—Central union of agricultural cooperatives.

Tsentrosoiuz—Central union of consumer cooperatives.

Vsemediksantrud—Union of medical and sanitary workers (including doctors).

Vserabotpros or Rabpros—Union of educational workers (eventually including professors).

TsKUBU (or KUBU)—Central Committee to Improve the Life of Scholars

Higher Educational Institutions

VUZ (Vysshee uchebnoe zavedenie; plural VUZy)—Higher educational institution. VUZy included universities, institutes, and higher technical schools.

FON (Fakul'tet obshchestvennykh nauk)—Social Science Faculty. Formed in early 1920s to replace old historico-philological and law faculties.

MGU—Moscow State University.
MVTU—Moscow Higher Technical School.
PGU—Petrograd State University.
PTI—Petrograd Technology Institute.

Other Political Parties

Kadets (Constitutional Democrats)—Liberal democratic party that included among its membership many professors and other intellectuals.
Mensheviks—Moderate Marxist socialists, formerly the Menshevik faction of the RSDRP.
NSs (Popular Socialists or Narodno-sotsialisty)—Smaller populist socialist party that split from the SRs well before the revolution.
SRs (Socialists-Revolutionaries)—Non-Marxist or populist socialists, split into radical (left SR) and moderate factions. Won a majority in the Constituent Assembly, which was disbanded by the Bolsheviks before it could meet in January 1918.

Notes

Introduction

Epigraph: Plato, *Selections*, ed. Raphael Demos (New York: Charles Scribner's Sons, 1955), 19, 28.

1. "Zapisi pod chertoi," *Novyi zhurnal*, no. 40 (1955): 269–74. The original notebook, "On board the 'Preussen,' 18–19 November 1922," is in the N. N. Evreinov Collection, Anna Aleksandrovna Evreinova Folder, Bakhmeteff Archive, Columbia University, New York.

2. In Russia the deportations have been at the center of a reconsideration by scholars, journalists, and others of the fate of the intelligentsia at the start of the Soviet era, as well as part of a revival of interest in the first wave of emigration. There have been a number of articles, document publications, and even a documentary and an exhibition at the Russian state archive. The most comprehensive contribution has been the collection of documents and commentary in V. G. Makarov and V. S. Khristoforov, eds., *Vysylka vmesto rasstrela. Deportatsiia intelligentsii v dokumentakh VChK-GPU. 1921–1923* (Moscow: Russkii put,' 2005). See also S. S. Khoruzhii, "Filosofskii parokhod: Kak eto bylo," *Literaturnaia gazeta*, 9 May and 6 June 1990; T. A. Krasovitskaia, "Chto imeem, ne khranim. Neizvestnye fakty o prichinakh i obstoiatel'stvakh vysylki iz Sovetskoi Rossii v 1922 g. elity gumanitarnoi intelligentsii," *Moskovskie novosti*, 20 May 1990; A. M. Gak, A. S. Masalskaia, and I. N. Selezneva, "Deportatsiia inakomysliashchikh v 1922 g. (Pozitsiia V. I. Lenina)," *Kentavr*, 1993, no. 5: 75–89; L. A. Kogan, "'Vyslat' za granitsu bezzhalostno' (Novoe ob izgnanii dukhovnoi elity)," *Voprosy filosofii*, 1993, no. 9: 61–84; S. A. Krasil'nikov, "Vysylka i ssylka intelligentsii kak element Sovetskoi karatel'noi politiki

20-kh—nachala 30-kh gg.," in *Diskriminatsiia intelligentsii v poslerevoliutsionnoi Sibiri (1920–1930-e gg.)*, ed. Krasil'nikov and L. I. Pystina (Novosibirsk: Sibirskoe otdelenie Institut istorii RAN, 1994), 24–60; V. L. Soskin, "'Filosofskii parokhod'—Tragediia rossiiskoi intelligentsii," in *Perekhod k NEPu i Kul'tura (1921–1923 gg.)* (Novosibirsk: Novosibirskii gosudarstvennyi universitet, 1997), 62–84; I. N. Selezneva, comp., "Intellektualam v Sovetskoi Rossii mesta net," *Vestnik Rossiiskoi akademii nauk* 71, no. 8 (2001): 738–47; M. E. Glavatskii, *'Filosofskii parokhod': god 1922-i. Istoriograficheskie etiudi* (Ekaterinburg: Izdatel'stvo Ural'skogo universiteta, 2002); V. G. Makarov, comp., "Arkhivnye tainy: intelligentsiia i vlast'," *Voprosy filosofii*, 2002, no. 10: 108–55; V. S. Khristoforov, comp., "'Filosofskii parokhod.' Vysylka uchenykh i deiatelei kul'tury iz Rossii v 1922 g.," *Novaia i noveishaia istoriia*, 2002, no. 5: 126–70; and A. N. Artizov, comp., "'Ochistim Rossiiu nadolgo.' K istorii vysylki intelligentsii v 1922g.," *Otechestvennye arkhivy*, 2003, no. 1: 64–96. The first monographic treatment in English on the expulsions of intellectuals appeared as this book was being prepared for publication: Lesley Chamberlain, *The Philosophy Steamer: Lenin and the Exile of the Intelligentsia* (London: Atlantic Books, 2006). Chamberlain vividly traces the events and the reactions of the individuals involved, in particular the philosophers, and a substantial portion of the work is devoted to their fate after their emigration. Her book does not, however, use original archival research, nor is it entirely integrated with the scholarly literature, either on the deportations or more broadly on the early Soviet period. The only substantial article to have appeared in a Western publication until recently was Michel Heller, "Premier avertissement: Un coup de fouet (l'histoire de l'expulsion des personnalités culturelles hors de l'Union soviétique en 1922)," *Cahiers du monde russe et soviétique* 20, no. 2 (1979): 131–72. This article was also published in Russian as Mikhail Geller, "'Pervoe predosterezhenie'—udar khlystom. (K istorii vysylki iz Sovetskogo Soiuza deiatelei kul'tury v 1922 g.)." in the émigré journal *Vestnik russkogo khristianskogo dvizheniia* 1978, no. 4: 187–232, and translated into English as "First Warning" in *Survey* 24, no. 3 (Summer 1979): 159–89.

3. See in particular the collection of articles in A. S. Bubnov et al., *Na ideologicheskom fronte bor'by s kontre-revoliutsiei* (Moscow: Krasnaia Nov', 1923). The various arenas that constituted the "ideological front" were also summarized in several GPU (the State Political Administration) operational reports, including "Overview on the activities of the anti-Soviet intelligentsia for 1921–22," dated 23 November 1922, in Makarov and Khristoforov, *Vysylka vmesto rasstrela*, 139–64.

4. In a highly influential article, Sheila Fitzpatrick has asserted that a so-called soft line in culture, led by Commissar of Enlightenment Anatolii Lunacharskii, not only existed but was de facto state policy. Support for literary fellow travelers, a laissez-faire attitude toward higher education, and experimentation and achievement in the fine arts characterized cultural policy in the 1920s ("The 'Soft' Line on Culture and Its Enemies: Soviet Cultural Policy, 1922–1927," *Slavic Review* 33 [June 1974]: 267–87). Peter Kenez has similarly argued that during this time Soviet leaders accepted that culture was apolitical, and that "it was only the Stalinist generation of leaders that defined politics so broadly as to kill independent thought." At the same time, he allows that "what made the Soviet Union different from pluralist societies was that the boundaries [of discourse] could be consciously changed and manipulated by a political elite and that the public sphere even in the 1920s was remarkably narrow" (*The Birth of the Propaganda*

State: Soviet Methods of Mass Mobilization, 1917–1929 [New York: Cambridge University Press, 1985], 12, 233). Other scholars have increasingly challenged the soft-line thesis. Katerina Clark has argued that it was in fact during the 1920s that "Russian intellectual life was sovietized. . . . NEP should not be defined, as it so often is, as a period of relative intellectual freedom before the 'great breakthrough' (*velikii perelom*) of the Cultural Revolution" ("The 'Quiet Revolution' in Soviet Intellectual Life," in *Russia in the Era of NEP: Explorations in Soviet Society and Culture*, ed. Sheila Fitzpatrick et al. [Bloomington: Indiana University Press, 1991], 210–11). See also Christopher Read, *Culture and Power in Revolutionary Russia: The Intelligentsia and the Transition from Tsarism to Communism* (London: Macmillan, 1990).

5. The same bargain held for the creative intelligentsia; as Barbara Walker notes, in return for perks and privileges, "writers owed the state loyalty, obedience, and support" (*Maximilian Voloshin and the Russian Literary Circle: Culture and Survival in Revolutionary Times* [Bloomington: Indiana University Press, 2005], 5).

6. On voluntary organizations in the early Soviet period see I. N. Il'ina, *Obshchestvennye organizatsii Rossii v 1920-e gody* (Moscow: Institut rossiiskii istorii RAN, 2000); Michael David-Fox's review of that work in *Kritika* 3, no. 1 (Winter 2002): 173–81; and Dzh. Bredli [Joseph Bradley], "Dobrovol'nye obshchestva v Sovetskoi Rossii, 1917–1932 gg.," *Vestnik Moskovskogo universiteta*, ser. 8: *Istoriia*, 1994, no. 4: 34–44.

7. David-Fox, review of Il'ina, *Obshchestvennye organizatsii Rossii*, 173.

8. Pitirim Sorokin, "Ob 'anglo-saksonskoi' pozitsii," *Utrenniki* (Petrograd), no. 1 (1922): 15–18, and Sorokin, "'Smena vekh' kak sotsial'nyi simptom," *Vestnik literatury*, 1921, no. 12 (December): 1–3.

9. Israel Getzler has argued that Lenin "understood revolution solely in the narrow terms of civil war where there are no compromises, no neutrals, where his favourite question was 'Who devours whom?'" ("Lenin's Conception of Revolution as Civil War," *Slavic and East European Review* 74, no. 3 [July 1996]: 47).

10. See Bradley, "Dobrovol'nye obshchestva," and Lewis Siegelbaum, *Soviet State and Society between Revolutions, 1918–1929* (Cambridge: Cambridge University Press, 1992), 4, 84, 136. Richard Sakwa rebuts the idea that civil society survived in "The Soviet State, Civil Society, and Moscow Politics: Stability and Order in Early NEP, 1921–1924," in *Soviet History, 1917–1953: Essays in Honour of R. W. Davies*, ed. Julian Cooper, Maureen Perrie, and E. A. Rees (New York: St. Martin's Press, 1995), 42–43.

11. Among the seminal histories of the Russian intelligentsia are Isaiah Berlin, "A Marvellous Decade, 1838–1848: The Birth of the Russian Intelligentsia," *Encounter* 4, no. 6 (June 1955): 27–39; Martin Malia, "What Is the Intelligentsia?" and Richard Pipes, "The Historical Evolution of the Russian Intelligentsia," both in *The Russian Intelligentsia*, ed. Pipes (New York: Columbia University Press, 1961); Martin Malia, *Alexander Herzen and the Birth of Russian Socialism, 1812–1855* (Cambridge: Harvard University Press, 1961); Michael Confino, "On Intellectuals and Intellectual Traditions in Eighteenth- and Nineteenth-Century Russia," *Daedalus* 101, no. 2 (Spring 1972): 117–49; and Andrzej Walicki, *A History of Russian Thought from the Enlightenment to Marxism*, trans. Hilda Andrews-Rusiecka (Stanford: Stanford University Press, 1979). Two recent reexaminations are Jane Burbank, "Were the Russian *Intelligenty* Organic Intellectuals?" in *Intellectuals and Public Life: Between Radicalism and Reform*, ed. Leon Fink, Stephen T. Leonard, and Donald M. Reid (Ithaca: Cornell University Press,

1996), 97–120, and Igal Halfin, *From Darkness to Light: Class, Consciousness, and Salvation in Revolutionary Russia* (Pittsburgh: University of Pittsburgh Press, 2000), 149–204.

12. Malia, "What Is the Intelligentsia?" 1–3.

13. The most comprehensive reassertion of the traditional role of the intellectual was R. V. Ivanov-Razumnik, *Istoriia Russkoi obshchestvennoi mysli: Individualizm i meshchanstvo v russkoi literature i zhizni XIXv.*, 2 vols. (St. Petersburg: Tipografiia M. M. Stasiulevicha, 1907). Aleksandr Izgoev proposed a redefinition of intellectual mission that squared more with the liberal ethos of developing an autonomous citizenry (A. S. Izgoev, "Intelligentsiia, kak sotsial'naia gruppa," *Obrazovanie* 13, no. 1, pt. 2 [January 1904]: 72–94).

14. Christopher Read, *Religion, Revolution, and the Russian Intelligentsia, 1900–1912: The "Vekhi" Debate and Its Intellectual Background* (London: Macmillan, 1979), 9, 115–19; Jane Burbank, *Intelligentsia and Revolution: Russian Views of Bolshevism, 1917–1922* (New York: Oxford University Press, 1986), 8–11; Katerina Clark, "The Image of the *Intelligent* in Soviet Prose Fiction, 1917–1932" (Ph.D. diss., Yale University, 1971), 13–14.

15. Marshall S. Shatz and Judith E. Zimmerman, eds. and trans., *Vekhi = Landmarks: A Collection of Articles about the Russian Intelligentsia* (Armonk, N.Y.: M. E. Sharpe, 1994).

16. Read, *Religion*, 141–61.

17. Samuel D. Kassow, James L. West, and Edith W. Clowes, "Introduction: The Problem of the Middle in Late Imperial Russian Society," in *Between Tsar and People: Educated Society and the Quest for Public Identity in Late Imperial Russia*, ed. Edith W. Clowes, Samuel D. Kassow, and James L. West (Princeton: Princeton University Press, 1991), 3–9; Abbott Gleason, "The Terms of Russian Social History," in Clowes et al., *Between Tsar and People*, 15, 18–23; Joseph Bradley, "Subjects into Citizens: Societies, Civil Society, and Autocracy in Tsarist Russia," *American Historical Review* 107, no. 4 (2002): 1094–1123; Bradley, "Voluntary Associations, Civic Culture, and *Obshchestvennost'* in Moscow," in Clowes et al., *Between Tsar and People*, 131–48; David Wartenweiler, *Civil Society and Academic Debate in Russia, 1905–1914* (Oxford: Clarendon Press, 1999); Manfred Hagen, *Die Entfaltung Politischer Öffentlichkeit in Russland, 1906–1914* (Wiesbaden: Steiner, 1982); and Hagen, " 'Obshchestvennost'': Formative Changes in Russian Society before 1917," *Sbornik: Papers of the Study Group on the Russian Revolution*, no. 10 (1984): 23–36.

18. Catriona Kelly and Vadim Volkov, "*Obshchestvennost', Sobornost'*: Collective Identities," in *Constructing Russian Culture in the Age of Revolution: 1881–1940*, ed. Catriona Kelly and David Shepherd (Oxford: Oxford University Press, 1998), 26–27.

19. Bradley, "Voluntary Associations"; Wartenweiler, *Civil Society*, 1–42, 82–126. As Samuel Kassow argues, "The rise of voluntary societies, the steady if slow development of respect for property rights, the rapid expansion of higher and secondary education, artistic patronage, the growth of professions, the rite of a multilayered press, the emergence of the Duma as a forum for political articulation, the unrelenting assault on the *soslovie* system, philanthropy, new opportunities afforded by municipal government—all pointed toward the creation of what Habermas would call a 'public sphere' " ("Russia's Unrealized Civil Society," in Clowes et al., *Between Tsar and People*, 367).

20. Paradoxically, "Russia's professionals sought to reduce state interference in their activities while still requiring state power to achieve their professional programs" (Harley Balzer, "The Problem of Professions in Imperial Russia," in Clowes et al., *Between Tsar and People,*" 184).

21. Boris Kolonitskii, "Antibourgeois Propaganda and Anti-'*Burzhui*' Consciousness in 1917," *Russian Review* 53, no. 2 (April 1994): 183–96; Charles Rougle, "The Intelligentsia Debate in Russia, 1917–1918," in *Art, Society, Revolution: Russia, 1917–1921,* ed. Nils Åke Nilsson (Stockholm: Amqvist and Wiksell, 1979), 54–105.

22. Pitirim Sorokin, "Ob 'anglo-saksonskoi' pozitsii," and Sorokin, "'Smena vekh' kak sotsial'nyi simptom."

23. William F. Woehrlin, ed. and trans., *Out of the Depths (De Profundis): A Collection of Articles on the Russian Revolution* (Irvine, Calif.: Charles Schlacks Jr., 1986).

24. A. S. Izgoev, "Vlast' i lichnost'," *Vestnik literatury,* 1922, no. 1 (January): 3; Izgoev, "O zadachakh intelligentsii," *Parfenon* (Petrograd), no. 1 (1922): 32–39. Sorokin responded that he had no intention of suggesting, as Izgoev implied, that the erection of a public sphere was possible without the necessary political liberties and rule of law.

25. Burbank, "Russian *Intelligenty,*" 114. See also Burbank, *Intelligentsia and Revolution,* 238; Halfin, *Darkness to Light,* 196.

26. Jochen Hellbeck details the effect of this pressure to integrate with the "laboring collective" on the teacher and agronomist Zinaida Denisevskaya in *Revolution on My Mind: Writing a Diary under Stalin* (Cambridge: Harvard University Press, 2006), 115–64. As David L. Hoffmann notes, the creation of a New Soviet Person "prepared to sacrifice his or her individual interests for the good of the collective, in sharp contrast to the ideal of liberal individualism," was an essential part of the broader project of cultivating "cultured" Soviet citizens (*Stalinist Values: The Cultural Norms of Soviet Modernity, 1917–1941* [Ithaca: Cornell University Press, 2003], 10).

27. *Izvestiia,* 30 August 1922; *Petrogradskaia pravda,* 30 August 1922.

28. "Pervoe predosterezhenie," *Pravda,* 31 August 1922.

29. As quoted in "Stalin preduprezhdaet o novoi polose krasnogo terrora," *Segodnia* (Riga), 16 September 1922.

30. Makarov and Khristoforov, in their introduction to *Vysylka vmesto rasstrela,* note that several different figures were put out at the time and conclude that of 228 individuals originally considered for expulsion, 67 were actually deported abroad during 1922–23 and another 49 faced internal exile (*Vysylka vmesto rasstrela,* 40–42).

31. It is asserted in quite a few places that 160 intellectuals were deported. This number, of uncertain origin, is undoubtedly incorrect, unless it is meant to include family members.

32. Expulsion as such has received remarkably little theoretical attention. A notable exception is Benjamin Z. Kedar, "Expulsion as an Issue of World History," *Journal of World History* 7, no. 2 (Fall 1996): 165–80. Focusing on the banishments of Jews in the Middle Ages, Kedar traces "the convergence of an intense, feverish preoccupation with the defense of purity and the rise of a new ethic of governance enunciated by rulers wielding an ever more efficient state machinery," which "rendered orderly governmental expulsion a viable mode of coping with perceived internal foes whose physical annihilation was usually precluded by cultural constraints" (177). These characterizations of the employment of expulsion can be applied to the current study with only minimal revision.

33. Claude Lefort, *The Political Forms of Modern Society,* ed. John B. Thompson (Cambridge: MIT Press, 1986), 297. Many of the ideas in this section have been developed in

Amir Weiner, *Making Sense of War: The Second World War and the Fate of the Bolshevik Revolution* (Princeton: Princeton University Press, 2001), introduction. Tim McDaniel has advanced an analysis similar to Lefort's, but it is tied to the ever-elusive "Russian Idea" rather than an inherent "logic of totalitarianism." For McDaniel the political principle of the Russian Idea holds that "truth is unitary and compulsory. . . . The community must also be unitary. Opposition and diversity is falsehood and therefore deserves no hearing." This faith found ample echoes in the Bolshevik interpretation of Marxism, for which any departure from enforced harmony was equivalent to direct opposition. "In such a vision of the world, there can be no differentiation of spheres in society and no neutral behavior." (Tim McDaniel, *The Agony of the Russian Idea* [Princeton: Princeton University Press, 1996], esp. 35–39, 86–117.)

34. Lefort, *Political Forms*, 287, 298, 288–90.

35. Peter Holquist, "State Violence as Technique: The Logic of Violence in Soviet Totalitarianism," in *Landscaping the Human Garden: Twentieth-Century Population Management in a Comparative Framework*, ed. Amir Weiner (Stanford: Stanford University Press, 2003), 19–45. (See also Holquist, "To Count, to Extract, to Exterminate: The 'Rise of the Social' and Population Politics in Late Imperial and Soviet Russia," in *A State of Nations: Empire and Nation-Making in the Age of Lenin and Stalin*, ed. Ronald Grigor Suny and Terry Martin [New York: Oxford University Press, 2001], 111–44.) Peter Kenez has made a similar point, noting that "Soviet institutions, and to a considerable extent the mentality of those who created those institutions, were formed during the difficult days of the Civil War" (*Birth of the Propaganda State*, 4).

36. As Golfo Alexopoulos has noted, "Politics designed to excise dangerous alien elements from the civic body require extensive state and public participation for the surveillance, identification, and classification of individuals" (*Stalin's Outcasts: Aliens, Citizens, and the Soviet State, 1926–1936* [Ithaca: Cornell University Press, 2003], 4). For a thorough and well-considered study of the growth of the surveillance apparatus and state control, see V. S. Izmozik, *Glaza i ushi rezhima: Gosudarstvennyi politicheskii kontrol' za naseleniem sovetskoi Rossii v 1918–1928 godakh* (St. Petersburg: Izdatel'stvo Sankt-Peterburgskogo Universiteta Ekonomiki i Finansov, 1995).

37. Peter Holquist, " 'Information Is the Alpha and Omega of Our Work': Bolshevik Surveillance in Its Pan-European Context," *Journal of Modern History* 69 (September 1997): 415–50.

38. Nicolas Berdyaev, *The Origin of Russian Communism*, trans. R. M. French (Ann Arbor: University of Michigan Press, 1960), 183–84, italics in original.

39. As Clark notes, the rejection of the possibility of political neutrality was commonly expressed in the slogan " '*ili* . . . *ili* . . . ,' i.e., 'Either you are with us, or you are against us,' " which the Bolsheviks frequently hurled at the intelligentsia at the time (Clark, "Image of the *Intelligent*," 30).

40. Jürgen Habermas, *The Structural Transformation of the Public Sphere: An Inquiry into a Category of Bourgeois Society*, trans. Thomas Burger (Cambridge: MIT Press, 1989), xvii.

41. Philip C. C. Huang, " 'Public Sphere'/'Civil Society' in China? The Third Realm between State and Society," *Modern China* 19, no. 2 (April 1993): 216–40, esp. 216–17. The debate on the appropriateness of using the term *public sphere* has been particularly animated among historians of China. In addition to Huang, see the other articles in the special issue of *Modern China* (19, no. 2 [1993]) on the public sphere and civil society,

including Frederick Wakeman Jr., "The Civil Society and Public Sphere Debate: Western Reflections on Chinese Political Culture," 108–38; Mary B. Rankin, "Some Observations on a Chinese Public Sphere," 158–82; and Richard Madsen, "The Public Sphere, Civil Society, and Moral Community," 183–98. See also, inter alia, Rudolf G. Wagner, "The Role of the Foreign Community in the Chinese Public Sphere," *China Quarterly*, no. 142 (June 1995): 423–43; Frederick Wakeman Jr., "Boundaries of the Public Sphere in Ming and Qing China," *Daedalus* 127, no. 3 (Summer 1998): 167–89; and Guobin Yang, "Civil Society in China: A Dynamic Field of Study," *China Review International* 9, no. 1 (Spring 2002): 1–16. As Yang notes, China scholars who still employ the term "public sphere" use it in the broader sense, "loosened and freed from its Habermasian origins" ("Civil Society," 6).

42. Jürgen Habermas, "The Public Sphere: An Encyclopedia Article (1964)," *New German Critique*, no. 3 (Autumn 1974): 49.

43. Habermas, *Structural Transformation*, xvii.

44. Kenez, *Birth of the Propaganda State*, e.g., 8–9.

Chapter 1. The Russian Intelligentsia and the Bolsheviks at the End of the Civil War

Epigraph: Lenin to Gorky, 15 September 1919, in *Revelations from the Russian Archives*, ed. Diane P. Koenker and Ronald D. Bachman (Washington, D.C.: Library of Congress, 1997), 229.

1. Halfin, *Darkness to Light*, 193–98; Rougle, "The Intelligentsia Debate," 81–82; James C. McClelland, "The Professoriate in the Russian Civil War," in *Party, State, and Society in the Russian Civil War: Explorations in Social History*, ed. Diane P. Koenker, William G. Rosenberg, and Ronald Grigor Suny (Bloomington: Indiana University Press, 1989), 243–44; Kendall E. Bailes, "Natural Scientists and the Soviet System," ibid., 268; Sheila Fitzpatrick, *The Commissariat of Enlightenment: Soviet Organization of Education and the Arts under Lunacharsky, October 1917–1921* (Cambridge: Cambridge University Press, 1970), 34–35; Read, *Culture and Power*, 46–48; and Vera Tolz, *Russian Academicians and the Revolution: Combining Professionalism and Politics* (London: Macmillan, 1997), 27–28.

2. Molotov and Dzerzhinskii, top secret Cheka circular, [not before 17 February 1921], Rossiiskii gosudarstvennyi arkhiv sotsial'no-politicheskoi istorii (henceforth RGASPI) f.17, op.84, d.228, l.52.

3. Several hundred prominent scholars died between 1917 and 1922. "Personalia. Skonchavshiesia v techenie poslednykh trekh let," *Nauka i ee rabotniki*, 1921, no. 3: 34–38, and 1922, no. 2: 37–40. The suffering is poignantly described in many of the memoirs from the period. See, e.g., Pitirim Sorokin, *Leaves from a Russian Diary* (New York: E. P. Dutton, 1924), 217–34; and Viktor Shklovsky, *A Sentimental Journey: Memoirs, 1917–1922*, trans. and ed. Richard Sheldon (Ithaca: Cornell University Press, 1984), 175–76, 196, 231–32, 242–43.

4. I. A. Reviakina and I. N. Selezneva, eds. and comps., "Pis'ma M. Gor'kogo k V. I. Leninu," in *Gor'kii i ego epokha: Materialy i issledovania*, vol. 3, *Neizvestnyi Gor'kii (k 125-letiiu so dnia rozhdeniia)* (Moscow: Nasledie, 1994), 7–69; Reviakina and Selezneva, eds. and comps., "'Zachem fabrikovat' muchenikov?' (Pis'ma M. Gor'kogo k V. I. Leninu i v Sovet Narodnykh Komissarov)," in *M. Gor'kii. Materialy i issledovaniia*, vol.

5, *M. Gor'kii. Neizdannaia perepiska s Bogdanovym, Leninym, Stalinym, Zinov'evym, Kamenevym, Korolenko* (Moscow: Nasledie, 1998), 95–135; L. Spiridonova, ed. and comp., "'Ia vas serdechno liubil . . . ,' (M. Gor'kii i L. Kamenev)," ibid., 228–74; N. N. Primochkina, E. N. Nikitin, and S. D. Ostrovskaia, eds. and comps., "Gor'kii v bor'be za sokhranenie kul'tury (iz epistoliarnogo naslediia 1919–1920 gg.)," *Izvestiia AN. Seriia literatury i iazika* 57, no. 3 (1998): 57–66; Paul R. Josephson, "Maksim Gor'kii, Science and the Russian Revolution," *Soviet and Post-Soviet Review* 22, no. 1 (1995): 15–39.

5. Lenin to Gorky, 15 September 1919, in Koenker and Bachman, *Revelations from the Russian Archives*, 229–30.

6. There is no English term that entirely captures the combination of duty, participation in social life, and celebrity signified in the term "*obshchestvennyi deiatel'.*" I have chosen to use "public figure" chiefly because it is less awkward than "social actor" or "public activist."

7. Burbank, *Intelligentsia and Revolution*, 7–11.

8. V. V. Shelokhaev et al., eds., *Vserossiiskii natsional'nyi tsentr* (Moscow: Rosspen, 2001); S. E. Trubetskoi, *Minuvshee* (Moscow: Dem, 1991), 190; Christopher Lazarski, "The Politics of Fragmentation: The Anti-Bolshevik Opposition—Moscow, Kiev, Odessa, 1917–19" (Ph.D. diss., Georgetown University, 1993), 128–44; A. S. Velidov, ed., *Krasnaia kniga VChK*, 2nd ed. (Moscow: Izdatel'stvo politicheskoi literatury, 1989), 2: 38–52, 131–71; Lennard D. Gerson, *The Secret Police in Lenin's Russia* (Philadelphia: Temple University Press, 1976), 157.

9. V. Miakotin, "Iz nedalekogo proshlogo (otryvki vospominaniia)," *Na chuzhoi storone* 2 (1923): 187.

10. Miakotin, "Iz nedalekogo," *Na chuzhoi storone* 2 (1923): 178–99; 5 (1924): 251–68; 6 (1924): 73–99; 9 (1925): 279–302; 11 (1925): 205–36; 13 (1925): 193–227; Jason Antevil, "The Politics of Russian Populism, 1894–1929: V. A. Miakotin, A. V. Peshekhonov, and the Popular Socialist Party" (Ph.D. diss., Stanford University, 1998), 548–57, 566–76, 584–86; Lazarski, "Politics of Fragmentation," 157–64; Velidov, *Krasnaia kniga*, 2: 32–38, 79–131.

11. Sergei Mel'gunov denied there was any such organization, but S. E. Trubetskoi proudly confirmed that he, Mel'gunov, and S. M. Leont'ev formed its "military commission." Leont'ev declared in a deposition that the center had neither monetary means nor contact with émigré groups. The "military commission" never dealt with any real operational questions and predated the existence of the Tactical Center (Miakotin, "Iz nedalekogo," *Na chuzhoi storone* 6 [1924]: 81, 87–93, and 13 [1925]: 214–15, 223–24; S. P. Mel'gunov, *Vospominaniia i dnevniki*, 2 vols. [Paris: Editeurs Reuins, 1964], 2: 16–18; Mel'gunov, "'Sud istorii nad intelligentsiei.' [K delu 'Takticheskogo Tsentra'],'" *Na chuzhoi storone* 3 [1923]: 137–63; Trubetskoi, *Minuvshee*, 190–91, 212–13; "'Takticheskii tsentr' i sostoiavshaia pri nem voennaia komissiia," in Velidov, *Krasnaia kniga*, 2: 52–59; P. E. Mel'gunova, "Prodolzhenie," in Mel'gunov, *Vospominaniia*, 2: 60–73; "Takticheskii tsentr (Istoricheskaia spravka S. M. Leont'eva)," in Velidov, *Krasnaia kniga*, 2: 208–14; and Antevil, "Politics of Russian Populism," 575–76, 581–82, 589–92).

12. Mel'gunov, "Sud istorii," 139.

13. N. V. Krylenko, *Za piat' let, 1918–1922 g.g. Obvinitel'nye rechi* (Moscow: Gosizdat, 1923), 54. Reports on the trial are in *Izvestiia*, 17, 19, 21, and 22 August 1920.

14. Mel'gunova, "Prodolzhenie," 62–63, 70–72; Trubetskoi, *Minuvshee*, 215–26; Mel'gunov, "Sud istorii," 142–46, 156–58; Krylenko, *Piat' let*, 55–56; D. L. Golinkov, *Krushenie antisovetskogo podpol'ia v SSSR*, 3rd ed. (Moscow: Politizdat, 1980), 2: 11–17. None ended up actually serving the full ten-year sentence.

15. The most comprehensive account of the Kronstadt rebellion in English remains Paul Avrich, *Kronstadt 1921* (Princeton: Princeton University Press, 1970). See also Israel Getzler, *Kronstadt 1917–1921: The Fate of a Soviet Democracy* (Cambridge: Cambridge University Press, 1983); and V. P. Kozlov et al., eds., *Kronshtadtskaia tragediia 1921 goda. Dokumenty v dvukh knigakh* (Moscow: Rosspen, 1999).

16. Lenin was quite explicit in linking "the lesson of Kronstadt" with "greater struggle against the Mensheviks and Socialist Revolutionaries" (Avrich, *Kronstadt*, 225–26). See also Mary McAuley, *Bread and Justice: State and Society in Petrograd, 1917–1922* (New York: Oxford University Press, 1991), 408–9.

17. Krylenko, *Piat' let*, 369–404; "Revtribunal. Prigovor po delu Glavtopa," *Izvestiia*, 18 May 1921, 2; Ronald George Charbonneau, "Non-Communist Hands: Bourgeois Specialists in Soviet Russia, 1917–1927" (Ph.D. diss., Concordia University, 1981), 315–18; Aleksandr I. Solzhenitsyn, *The Gulag Archipelago, 1918–1956: An Experiment in Literary Investigation*, trans. Thomas P. Whitney (New York: Harper and Row, 1973), 1: 334–35.

18. "Vyderzhki iz doklada Vserossiiskoi Chrezvychainoi Komissii o raskrytykh i likvidirovannykh na territorii R.S.F.S.R. zagovorakh protiv Sovetskoi vlasti v period maia-iiunia 1921 g.," *Izvestiia*, 24 July 1921, 2; "Uroki zagovora," *Petrogradskaia pravda*, 27 July 1921, 1; "O raskrytom v Petrograde zagovore protiv Sovetskoi vlasti (Ot Vserossiiskoi Chrezvychainoi Komissii)," *Petrogradskaia pravda*, 1 September 1921, 2; "Bankroty kontr-revoliutsii," *Pravda* 31 August 1921, 1; Iu. Shchetinov, "Vvedenie," in Kozlov et al., *Kronshtadtskaia tragediia*, 1: 7–10; F. Perchenok and D. Zubarev, "Na polputi ot polupravd. O tagantsevskom dele i ne tol'ko o nem," in *In Memoriam: Istoricheskii sbornik pamiati F. F. Perchenka* (Moscow: Feniks and Athenium, 1995), 362–70; George Leggett, *The Cheka: Lenin's Political Police. The All-Russian Extraordinary Commission for Combating Counter-Revolution and Sabotage (December 1917 to February 1922)* (Oxford: Clarendon Press, 1981), 288–89; Golinkov, *Krushenie*, 2:110–16; Charbonneau, "Non-Communist Hands," 323–24; Avrich, *Kronstadt*, 127–28.

19. Gorky to Lenin, 29 or 30 July 1921, and annotations, in Reviakina and Selezneva, "Pis'ma M. Gor'kogo k V. I. Leninu," 38–39, 62–64; I. N. Selezneva and Ia. G. Iashin, "Mishen'—Rossiiskaia nauka" and "Chetyre pis'ma V. I. Leninu," *Vestnik Rossiiskoi akademii nauk* 64, no. 9 (1994): 821–27; Dzerzhinskii to Lenin, 19 June 1921, Unshlikht to Lenin, 29 July 1921, and Lenin to L. A. Fotieva, 10 August 1921, in *V. I. Lenin i VChK. Sbornik dokumentov (1917–1922 gg.)*, 2nd ed. (Moscow: Politizdat, 1987), 434–35, 452, 457; Sorokin, *Leaves*, 277–78.

20. "O raskrytom," *Petrogradskaia pravda*, 1 September 1921, 2.

21. Shchetinov, "Vvedenie"; Perchenok and Zubarev, "Na polputi"; M. N. Petrov, *VChK-OGPU: pervoe desiatletie (na materialakh Severo-Zapada Rossii)* (Novgorod: Novgorodskii gosudarstvennyi universitet, 1995), 93–95; and V. Iu. Cherniaev, "Finliandskii sled v 'dele Tagantseva,'" *Rossiia i Finliandiia v XX veke* (Saint Petersburg: Evropeiskii dom, 1997), 180–200. Agranov duped Tagantsev into confessing by promising that none of his comrades would be executed. (Tagantsev's confessions of 29–30 July 1921 are published as "Pokazaniia V. N. Tagantseva o prichinakh soglasiia na

predlozhenie prezidiuma VChK dat' podrobnye svedeniia o deiatel'nosti PBO," in Kozlov et al., *Kronshtadtskaia tragediia,* 2: 177–81, 184–88.)

22. According to Sorokin, he was known in popular parlance as "Grisha the Third" (Sorokin, *Leaves,* 238, 281). The first two "Grishas" were Gregory Otrepiev (the False Dmitrii) and Rasputin.

23. Ibid., 280.

24. A. P. Karpinskii to V. I. Lenin, 21 September 1921, in "Chetyre pis'ma," 826–27.

25. Lenin to N. P. Gorbunov, 3 September 1921, in V. I. Lenin, *Polnoe sobranie sochinenii,* 5th ed., 55 vols. (Moscow: Izdatel'stvo politicheskoi literatury, 1958–65) (henceforth *PSS*), 53: 169.

26. "Pokazaniia V. N. Tagantseva," 188.

27. E. Kuskova, "Mesiats 'soglashatel'stva,'" part 1, *Volia Rossii,* 1928, no. 3 (March): 53–55.

28. Ibid., 58–59; N.S., "Pis'mo iz Moskvy," *Segodnia,* 31 August 1921, 2.

29. Kuskova, "Mesiats," part 1, 59, italics in original; "Istoriia obrazovaniia Vserossiiskogo Komiteta Pomoshchi Golodaiushchim," *Pomoshch',* no. 1 (16 August 1921), 2; "Postanovleniia Vserossiiskogo S"ezda po sel. khoz. opytnomu delu 15–25 iiunia 1921 g. (prodolzhenie)," *Vestnik sel'skogo khoziaistva,* 1921, no. 7 (10 December): 12; M. V. Sabashnikov to Z. P. Izmailova, 16 July 1921, in "'V uspekh ne veriu, no dolg velit.' K istorii Vserossiiskogo Komiteta Pomoshchi Golodaiushchim: Pis'ma M. V. Sabashnikova," *Istochnik,* 1999, no. 1: 60; Charles M. Edmondson, "The Politics of Hunger: The Soviet Response to Famine, 1921," *Soviet Studies* 29 (October 1977): 513; Geller, "Pervoe predosterezhenie," 197.

30. Kuskova would later contend that "in 1921, when a shocking famine raged, Gorky displayed a shocking indifference," and that when the public figures finally convinced him to approach the Kremlin, he did so "listlessly, without any enthusiasm" (E. D. Kuskova, "Tragediia Maksima Gor'kogo," *Novyi zhurnal,* no. 38 [1954]: 235–36).

31. Lenin to I. A. Teodorovich, 28 June 1921, *PSS,* 53: 4; and excerpts from Politburo protocols, 29 June 1921, in Irina Kondakova, ed., "'Stol' uspeshnoe vtiranie ochkov vsemu svetu.' Neizvestnye dokumenty o Vserossiiskom komitete pomoshchi golodaiushchim," *Istochnik,* 1995, no. 3: 53. On Sadyrin's role see V. F. Bulgakov, "Kak prozhita zhizn'," part 11, "Poslednie gody zhizni v Moskve," Rossiiskii gosudarstvennyi arkhiv literatury i iskusstva (henceforth RGALI) f.2226, op.1, d.60, l.41.

32. "Istoriia obrazovaniia," 2; Kuskova, "Mesiats," part 1, 59–62; Benjamin Weissman, *Herbert Hoover and Famine Relief to Soviet Russia* (Stanford: Hoover Institution Press, 1974), 12–13; Edmondson, "Politics," 513. Bertram Wolfe vividly retells the committee's brief history, based on Kuskova's account, in *The Bridge and the Abyss: The Troubled Friendship of Maxim Gorky and V. I. Lenin* (Stanford: Hoover Institution Press, 1967), 108–17.

33. Protocols of preliminary meetings of the All-Russian Committee to Aid the Starving, 9 and 12 July 1921; protocols of special meeting of the All-Russian Committee to Aid the Starving, 19 July 1921, Gosudarstvennyi arkhiv Rossiiskoi federatsii (henceforth GARF) f.1064, op.1, d.15, l.3, 32–33, 79.

34. The appeals appeared in a number of places, including the *New York Times,* 31 July 1921, 2. (Tikhon's appeal was printed in part in the 19 July *Times.*) See also Weissman, *Hoover,* 46; and Edmondson, "Politics," 515.

35. Lenin to Semashko, 12 July 1921, *PSS*, 53: 24, italics in original (cited in Weissman, *Hoover*, 14).

36. Although some historians refer to both organizations as Pomgol, I will follow contemporary usage and avoid confusion by referring to the public committee as VKPG and only the official VTsIK commission as Pomgol.

37. Excerpts from Politburo protocols of 12 and 15 July 1921, in Kondakova, " 'Stol' uspeshnoe,' " 53–54; excerpts from Politburo protocols of 15 July 1921, GARF f.1235, op.38, d.50, l.9–9ob.

38. Iu. N. Maksimov, "Komitet pomoshchi golodaiushchim," intro. R. Guleev [B. A. Ravdin], *Pamiat': Istoricheskii sbornik*, no. 4 (Paris: YMCA Press, 1981), 387–89; Boris Zaitsev, *Moskva* (Paris: Russkie zapiski, 1939), 241; and V. F. Bulgakov, "Kak prozhita," RGALI f.2226, op.1, d.60, l.40.

39. See, e.g., I. Vetrinskii, "'V golodnyi god,' (V. G. Korolenko i ego kniga o golode 1891–1892 gg.)," *Pomoshch'*, no. 3 (29 August 1921): 1.

40. "Istoriia obrazovaniia," 2; Kuskova, "Mesiats," part 2, *Volia Rossii*, 1928, no. 4 (April): 43–46; "Zasedanie Vseros. Komit. pomoshchi golodaiushchim," *Izvestiia*, 22 July 1921, 2; "Zasedanie Vseros. komiteta pomoshchi golodaiushchim," *Pravda*, 21 July 1921, 2; "Vo Vserossiiskom Komitete Pomoshchi Golodaiushchim," *Izvestiia*, 21 July 1921, 2; Bulgakov, "Kak prozhita," RGALI f.2226, op.1, d.60, l.42–43.

41. Kuskova, "Mesiats," part 2, 46.

42. VTsIK protocols, 18 and 21 July 1921, and Decree on All-Russian Committee to Aid the Starving, GARF f.1235, op.38, d.50, l.3, and d.51, l.4, 26–29. The official Pomgol protocols are in GARF f.1064, op.1, d.3 and d.4. The VTsIK decree and a list of the committee's members are in *Izvestiia*, 23 July 1921, 1; "Istoriia Obrazovaniia," 2; and *Na bor'bu s golodom (sbornik statei i materialov)* (Moscow: Gosizdat, 1921), 127–31.

43. Kuskova, "Mesiats," part 3, *Volia Rossii*, 1928, no. 5 (May): 63. Zaitsev concurred that Kamenev was "the best bridge to us," but that Rykov was always drunk and slurred his speech (Zaitsev, *Moskva*, 242).

44. [Osorgin], "Ot redaktsii," *Pomoshch'*, no. 1 (16 August 1921): 1; Ek. Kuskova, "Pod Krasnyi Krest," ibid., 1; Vera Figner, "Prezhde i teper', " ibid., 1; A. Lunacharskii, "Bor'ba za rebenka," ibid., 1.

45. V. G. Korolenko to A. M. Gorky, 10 August 1921, in "V. G. Korolenko i golod v poslerevoliutsionnoi Rossii," *Pamiat'*, no. 4 (1981): 399; Sabashnikov to Z. P. Izmailova, 5 July 1921, in "V uspekh ne veriu," 60.

46. Kuskova, "Mesiats," part 1, 63. Zaitsev recalled seeing a crowd reading a wall newspaper listing the participants and hearing one cynic remark, "A personnel list of idiots" (*Moskva*, 240). Mel'gunov and Prokopovich would later bitterly debate how much the "public" had supported the committee (S. Mel'gunov, "Odin dokument [po povodu obshchestvennogo komit. pomoshchi golodaiushchim]," *Poslednie novosti*, 3 May 1923, 2; S. Prokopovich, "Kak eto bylo. Pis'mo v redaktsiiu," *Poslednie novosti*, 17 May 1923, 2–3; Mel'gunov, "Vynuzhdennyi otvet," *Poslednie novosti*, 31 May 1923, 2).

47. I. Got'e, diary entry for 22 July 1921, in *Time of Troubles: The Diary of Iurii Vladimirovich Got'e: Moscow, July 8, 1917, to July 23, 1922*, trans., ed., and intro. Terence Emmons (Princeton: Princeton University Press, 1988), 418.

48. Kuskova, "Mesiats," part 1, 54–57.

49. Mikh. Osorgin, "N. N. Kutler," *Poslednie novosti,* 20 May 1924, 2.

50. Figner, "Prezhde i teper'," 1.

51. Sabashnikov to Z. P. Izmailova, 5 and 17 July 17 1921, in "V uspekh ne veriu," 60–61. Sabashnikov later added that only the committee could procure aid from foreign sources (Sabashnikov to Izmailova, 24 July 1921, ibid., 61).

52. "O Vserossiiskom komitete pomoshchi golodaiushchim. (Iz besedy s t. Kamenevym)," *Izvestiia,* 4 August, 1921, 2. For a similar account see Karl Radek, "My, golod i oni," *Pravda,* 2 August 1921, 1. Both Kamenev and Radek insisted that the committee had agreed to work "under the leadership of Soviet power," which upset the public figures, who felt that Kamenev had betrayed his guarantee of noninterference (Kuskova, "Mesiats," part 3, 64–65).

53. RCP Secretary V. Molotov and Deputy Chair of VTsIK Commission L. Kamenev to Gubispolkom secretaries and chairpersons, "top secret" circular, 11 August 1921, RGASPI f.17, op.84, d.178, l.36; later printed in *Spravochnik partiinogo rabotnika,* vol. 2 (1922), 159–61.

54. Bertrand M. Patenaude, *Big Show in Bololand: The American Relief Expedition to Soviet Russia in the Famine of 1921* (Stanford: Stanford University Press, 2002), 18.

55. "Istoriia obrazovaniia," 2–3; "Zasedanie Vserossiiskogo Komiteta pomoshchi golodaiushchim," *Izvestiia,* 24 July 1921, 1; "Na bor'bu s golodom. Zasedanie Vser. Komiteta pomoshchi golodaiushchim," *Izvestiia,* 3 August 1921, 1; and Kuskova, "Mesiats," part 2, 47–48, and part 3, 59.

56. The first admission that something worse than a bad harvest was occurring appeared in *Pravda* at the end of June. Even after this, information was, as always, carefully controlled. (See Preliminary Committee protocols, 9 July 1921, GARF f.1064, op.1, d.15, l.3.)

57. "V Komissiiakh. Literaturnaia. Khudozhestvennaia. Teatral'naia," *Pomoshch',* no. 1 (16 August 1921): 3; "Otklik soiuza pisatelei," *Pomoshch',* no. 1 (16 August 1921): 3; Kuskova, "Mesiats," part 2, 46–47.

58. "Zasedanie gruppy kooperatorov," *Pomoshch',* no. 1 (16 August 1921): 3; Kuskova, "Mesiats," part 2, 47.

59. A. I. Ugrimov, "Golod i agronomicheskaia pomoshch', " *Pomoshch',* no. 1 (16 August 1921): 1. Aleksandr Chaianov, in examining the steps necessary for improving the following year's harvest, more carefully avoided elliptical suggestions of blame ("Chto znachit' golod dlia zemledeliia," *Pomoshch',* no. 1 [16 August 1921]: 3).

60. D. Korobov, "Bor'ba s golodom i s-kh. kooperatsiia," *Pomoshch',* no. 2 (22 August 1921): 1; "Vozzvanie Rossiiskikh kooperativnykh organizatsii," *Golos Rossii,* 2 August 1921, reprinted in *Pomoshch',* no. 2 (22 August 1921): 1; "Protokoly zasedanii Vserossiiskogo s"ezda sel'skokhoziaistvennoi kooperatsii, 20–24 avgusta 1921 g.," in *Kooperativno-kolkhoznoe stroitel'stvo v SSSR, 1917–1922. Dokumenty i materialy,* ed. V. P. Danilov et al. (Moscow: Nauka, 1990), 270–316; "S"ezd Sel'sko-khoziaistvennoi kooperatsii," *Pomoshch',* no. 3 (29 August 1921): 3. References to the confiscated third and final issue of *Pomoshch'* are to its recent reprint (London: Overseas Publications Interchange, 1991). The controversial Sel'skosoiuz congress will be discussed in chapter 4.

61. These literary organizations will be discussed in detail in chapter 5.

62. "V Petrogradskom komitete pomoshchi golodaiushchim," and "Petrogradskoe otdelenie vserossiiskogo komiteta," *Petrogradskaia pravda,* 28 July 1921, 2; "V Petrogradskom otdele vserossiiskogo komiteta pomoshchi golodaiushchim," *Petrogradskaia*

pravda, 4 August 1921, 2; "V Petrogradskom otdele vseross. komiteta pomoshchi golodaiushchim," *Krasnaia gazeta*, 6 August 1921, 3; "Petrograd na pomoshch' golodaiushchim. Otdelenii Vserossiiskogo komiteta," *Petrogradskaia pravda*, 10 August 1921, 2; "Bor'ba s golodom. V Petrograde," *Izvestiia*, 10 August, 1921, 1; "V Petrogradskom otdelenii Vserossiiskogo komiteta," *Petrogradskaia pravda*, 12 August 1921, 2. "Bor'ba s golodom. V Petrograde," *Izvestiia*, 16 August 1921, 1; "Polozhenie o Petrogradskom Oblastnom Komitete Pomoshchi Golodaiushchim," *Pomoshch'*, no. 2 (22 August 1921): 4.

63. Gorky to Lenin, 29 or 30 July 1921, in Reviakina and Selezneva, "Pis'ma M. Gor'kogo k V. I. Leninu," 39, 66n13; Petrogubispolkom Large Presidium protocols, 20 August 1921, GARF f.393, op.28, d.207, l.117; and L. Spiridonova, " 'Ia vas serdechno liubil . . . ' (M. Gor'kii i L. Kamenev)," 231.

64. "V Petrogradskom otdelenii vserossiiskogo komiteta," *Petrogradskaia pravda*, 19 August 1921, 2.

65. Redaktsiia, "Mestnye komitety" and "Polozhenie o mestnykh sovetakh i otdelakh Vs.K.P.G.," *Pomoshch'*, no. 2 (22 August 1921): 4; "Vladimirskii Gub. K.P.G.," "Cherepovetskii komitet," "Simbirskii komitet," and "Podol'skii Uezdnyi Komitet," ibid.; "Mestnye komitety," *Pomoshch'*, no. 3 (29 August 1921): 3.

66. "V Tsentral'noi Komissii pomoshchi golodaiushchim pri V.Ts.I.K." *Izvestiia*, 16 August 1921, 1; circular to Gubispolkoms, RGASPI f.17, op.84, d.178, l.36.

67. "Studencheskaia sektsiia," *Pomoshch'*, no. 1 (16 August 1921): 3; "Studencheskaia sektsiia," *Pomoshch'*, no. 2 (22 August 1921): 3; Iu. N. Maksimov, "Komitet," 382–93; Kuskova, "Mesiats," part 2, 46.

68. "Ko vsemu russkomu studenchestvu" and "K molodezhi," *Pomoshch'*, no. 1 (16 August 1921): 4. These appeals were reprinted in the confiscated *Pomoshch'*, no. 3 (29 August 1921): 4.

69. Excerpts from Moscow Bureau protocols, sent to VUZ Party Bureaus, 11 August 1921, and protocols of the conference of secretaries of VUZ Communist cells, 11 August 1921, RGASPI f.17, op.60, d.76, l.50, 5.

70. "Pomoshch' golodaiushchim. Golos Moskovskogo studenchestva," *Izvestiia*, 17 August 1921, 1.

71. Kuskova, "Mesiats," part 2, 49–53; "Organizatsiia Tserkovnogo Komiteta" and "Vozzvanie Patriarkha Moskovskogo i Vseia Rossii Tikhona o pomoshchi golodaiushchim," *Pomoshch'*, no. 2 (22 August 1921): 3, 4.

72. Kuskova, "Mesiats," part 3, 66–67; Sabashnikov to Z. P. Izmailova, 16 August 1921, in "V uspekh ne veriu," 62; Bulgakov, "Kak prozhita," RGALI f.2226, op.1, d.60, l.46; Zaitsev, *Moskva*, 241. The Cheka would later take to task its editor, Osorgin, chiefly on account of this external resemblance.

73. [Osorgin], "Vivos voco!" Ek. Kuskova, "Pod Krasnyi Krest," and A. Lunacharskii, "Bor'ba za rebenka," *Pomoshch'*, no. 1 (16 August 1921): 1. (Osorgin's authorship is verified in N. Barmache, D. M. Fiene, and T. Ossorguine, eds., *Bibliographie des oeuvres de Michel Ossorguine* [Paris: Institut d'Etudes slaves, 1973], 65.)

74. Publishing and the reinstitution of censorship will be discussed in greater detail in chapter 5.

75. [Osorgin], "Moskva, 22 avgusta," *Pomoshch'*, no. 2 (22 August 1921): 2.

76. In. Stukov to the Orgburo, [August 1921, before 22 August], RGASPI f.17, op.84, d.250, l.50; "V kraiu golodnom," *Pomoshch'*, no. 2 (22 August 1921): 2.

77. Orgburo protocols, 22 August 1921, RGASPI f.17, op.112, d.200, l.5.

78. M. A. Osorgin, "L. D. Trotskomu—naputstvennoe," *Dni,* 22 January 1928, 1.

79. According to Osorgin, the page proofs were in his briefcase at the time of his arrest. As noted in n. 60, this issue has recently been reprinted along with the other two.

80. Hodgson was indeed a British intelligence agent (Stephen White, *The Origins of Détente: The Genoa Conference and Soviet-Western Relations, 1921–1922* [Cambridge: Cambridge University Press, 1985], 99–100, 199, 204).

81. Kuskova, "Mesiats," part 2, 53–54. Another replied that foreign contacts were the committee's second "crime"—the first had been already committed through its *smychka* with the Church.

82. "Protokol zasedaniia Parizhskoi Demokraticheskoi gruppy Partii Narodnoi Svobody, 18 avgusta 1921 g.," in *Protokoly zagranichnykh grupp konstitutsionno-demokraticheskoi partii,* vol. 5, *Iiun'-dekabr' 1921 g.* (Moscow: Rosspen, 1997), 202–5; "Na puti k novoi vlasti? Bol'sheviki ukhodiat'?" *Poslednie novosti,* 3 August 1921, 1; "Bor'ba ili sotrudnichestvo," *Poslednie novosti,* 4 August 1921, 1. There were even reports that Soviet authorities in the famine regions had entirely abandoned their duties to the local VKPG plenipotentiaries. "Vlast' na mestakh," *Poslednie novosti,* 21 August 1921, 1; and "Vlast' na mestakh i golod," *Poslednie novosti,* 22 August 1921, 1.

83. "Pervye shagi Moskovskogo komiteta," *Poslednie novosti,* 16 August 1921, 1. The more conservative Kadet faction in Paris fiercely debated whether to help in the aid efforts (*Protokoly zagranichnykh grupp,* 136–39, 150–54).

84. Vl. Burtsev, "Pri bol'shevikakh nevozmozhna bor'ba s golodom!" *Obshchee delo,* 29 July 1921, 1; Burtsev, "Kapituliatsiia bol'shevikov," *Obshchee delo,* 4 August 1921, 1; Burtsev, "Krakh vsego dela bol'shevikov. Bor'ba a ne soglashenie!" *Obshchee delo,* 5 August 1921, 1.

85. "Postanovlenie prezidiuma Vserossiiskogo Komiteta pomoshchi golodaiushchim," *Izvestiia,* 14 August 1921, 1; and Kuskova, "Mesiats," part 3, 65–66.

86. Information on the formation and activities of the foreign branch committees appeared regularly in *Poslednie novosti* and other émigré newspapers, as well as in *Pomoshch'.*

87. Berzin (in London, in the name of Krasin) to Chicherin, telegram, "top secret," 4 August 1921; V. L. Kopp (in Berlin, in the name of Chicherin) to Kamenev, coded telegram, 29 July 1921; Kopp (in Berlin, in the name of Chicherin) to Kamenev, telegram, "top secret," 31 July 1921; Kamenev to Kopp (at Berlin mission), coded cipher, 3 August 1921; all in GARF f.1235, op.140, d.43, l.7, 19–21 (formerly f.1235 s. ch., op.2, d.10).

88. "Memorandum Regarding Conversation between C. A. Herter and Mr. Paul Riabouchinsky, Jr.," 8 August 1921, Hoover Institution Archives, American Relief Administration, Russian Unit (henceforth Hoover Archives, ARA R.U.), box 22, folder 9 (cited in Weissman, *Hoover,* 49–50).

89. Brodovskii (in Paris) to Chicherin, coded telegram, 10 August 1921, GARF f.1235, op.140, d.43, l.28–29. One American observer wrote to Secretary of State Charles Evans Hughes that the VKPG might serve not only as "an agency through which we can hope to extend assistance and relief to the people of Russia without strengthening the Bolshevist regime, but, what is more important perhaps, a group actively functioning in Russia, which, if it is properly and adequately supported by the generous cooperation of

this and other nations, can develop into the representative government of Russia" (John Spargo to Secretary of State, 25 July 1921, cited in Weissman, *Hoover,* 15).

90. Patenaude, *Big Show in Boboland.*

91. "Non-political Character of the Russian Mission and General Directions for Preliminary Organizations. Mr. Hoover to Walter Lyman Brown," 9 August 1921, Hoover Archives, ARA R.U., box 22, folder 9 (cited in Weissman, *Hoover,* 51). See also Patenaude, *Big Show in Boboland,* and Edmondson, "Politics," 518.

92. M. M. Litvinov to G. V. Chicherin, telegrams, 12 and 13 August 1921, in " 'Ara k nam idet bez zadnikh myslei, no vozni s nei budet mnogo.' Deiatel'nost' Amerikanskoi administratsii pomoshchi v Rossii. 1921–1923 gg.," *Istoricheskii arkhiv,* 1993, no. 6: 78, 79; and Edgar Rickard, "General Memorandum to the American Relief Administration," 25 August 1921, Hoover Archives, ARA R.U., folder 22, box 9.

93. As we shall see in later chapters, attempting to maintain autonomy while depending on official support was a common dilemma for intellectual groups.

94. Kuskova, "Mesiats," part 2, 56–57; "Istoriia obrazovaniia," *Pomoshch',* no. 1 (16 August 1921): 3; "V komitete. Pozhertvovaniia," *Pomoshch',* no. 3 (29 August 1921): 3.

95. "Delegatsiia zagranitsu," *Pomoshch',* no. 1 (16 August 1921): 3; F. Golovin, "Zadachi delegatsii," *Pomoshch',* no. 2 (22 August 1921): 1; "Obrashchenie obshchestvennogo Vserossiiskogo Komiteta Pomoshchi Golodaiushchim za granitsu," *Pomoshch',* no. 2 (22 August 1921): 1.

96. Kuskova, "Mesiats," part 3, 60–61; "Rabota komiteta. Polozhenie o zagranichnoi delegatsii Vserossiiskogo Komiteta Pomoshchi Golodaiushchim," *Pomoshch',* no. 2 (22 August 1921): 3; "Bor'ba s golodom. Zasedanie Vser. Komiteta pomoshchi golodaiushchim," *Izvestiia,* 3 August 1921, 1.

97. Pavel Biriukov to Pëtr Vasilevich Verigin and Ivan Evseevich Konkin, 11 August 1921, GARF f.353, op.4, d.418, l.6–8; "Beseda s P. I. Biriukovym," *Poslednie novosti,* 16 August 1921, 2; "Kongress Krasnogo Kresta," *Poslednie novosti,* 18 August 1921, 1; "Otklik zagranitsy. Mezhdunarodnaia konferentsiia" and "Zarubezhnaia Rossiia," *Pomoshch',* no. 3 (29 August 1921): 4.

98. Kuskova, "Mesiats," part 3, 61–62; "Rabota komiteta. Ot"ezd delegatsii," *Pomoshch',* no. 2 (22 August 1921): 2.

99. This delegation was to include Gorky, Rykov, and others (protocols of VTsIK Pomgol Presidium, 2 August 1921, GARF f.1064, op.1, d.4, l.180).

100. Gorky to Lenin, 29 or 30 July 1921, in Reviakina and Selezneva, "Pis'ma M. Gor'kogo k V. I. Leninu," 38–39; and Gorky to M. A. Peshkov, summer 1921, excerpted in A. M. Gor'kii, *Arkhiv A. M. Gor'kogo,* vol. 9, *Pis'ma k E. P. Peshkovoi, 1906–1932* (Moscow: Khudozhestvennaia literatura, 1966), 390.

101. G. V. Chicherin to V. I. Lenin, 18 August 1921, RGASPI f.17, op.84, d.250, l.30–31.

102. L. B. Krasin to V. I. Lenin, 19 August 1921, in Kondakova, " 'Stol' uspeshnoe,' " 57.

103. Politburo protocols, 18 August 1921, RGASPI f.17, op.3, d.193, l.1. VTsIK issued a secret addendum stipulating that if the committee members refused to work in the localities, they be ordered to go to specifically appointed regions (VTsIK Presidium protocols, 18 August 1921 [copy sent to NKVD], GARF f.393, op.26, d.4, l.90).

104. Kuskova, "Mesiats," part 3, 70.

105. Resolution of the All-Russian Committee to Aid the Starving, 23 August 1921, sent to Lenin 26 August 1921, in Kondakova, "'Stol' uspeshnoe,'" 57–58.

106. Politburo protocols, 25 August 1921, RGASPI f.17, op.3, d.194, l.1; A. Lunacharskii, A. Emshanov, and I. Teodorovich to Politburo, 27 August 1921, in Kondakova, "'Stol' uspeshnoe,'" 58–59.

107. Kuskova, "Mesiats," part 3, 71; Bulgakov, "Kak prozhita," RGALI f.2226, op.1, d.60, l.47–48.

108. Gorky to Peshkova, 24 August 1921, in Gor'kii, *Pis'ma k Peshkovoi,* 211–12. The Petrograd authorities were prepared to permit the local branch to function if they could control its membership. As late as 27 August, when the Moscow committee was dispersed, they confirmed a presidium consisting of Soviet officials and a few trusted intellectuals (Petrogubispolkom Presidium protocols, 27 August 1921 [copy sent to NKVD], GARF f.393, op.28, d.207, l.131).

109. Gorky to Kamenev as chair of VKPG, 24 August 1921, in S. V. Zaika, L. A. Spiridonova, and I. I. Vainberga, eds. and comps., "Pistael' i vozhd' (Iz istorii vzaimootnoshenii M. Gor'kogo i I. Stalina)," in *M. Gor'kii. Neizdannia perepiska,* 241; and Gorky to Korolenko, 31 August 1921, in O. V. Shugan, "'Skol'ko tragicheskikh pisem chitaiu ia . . . ' (Iz perepiski M. Gor'kogo i V. G. Korolenko)," ibid., 170–71.

110. Vladislav Khodasevich, "Gor'kii," *Sovremennye zapiski,* no. 70 (1940): 141.

111. V. G. Korolenko and [his daughter] S. Korolenko to A. M. Gorky, 14 September 1921, in "V. G. Korolenko i golod," 400–401; and Kuskova to Korolenko, 22 August 1921, cited in O. V. Shugan, "Skol'ko tragicheskikh pisem," 191n2.

112. "V Petrogradskom otdelenii vserossiiskogo komiteta," *Petrogradskaia pravda,* 19 August 1921, 2.

113. Lenin to Stalin and all members of the Politburo, 26 August 1921, *PSS,* 53: 140–42, italics in original. I. S. Unshlikht, "Vospominaniia o Vladimire Il'iche," *Voprosy istorii KPSS,* 1965, no. 4: 99.

114. Politburo protocols, 27 August 1921, RGASPI f.17, op.3, d.195, l.1; "Postanovlenie prezidiuma V.Ts.I.K., 27 avgusta 1921 g.," *Petrogradskaia pravda,* 31 August 1921, 1.

115. Kuskova, "Mesiats," part 3, 72.

116. Others were arrested at a cooperators' meeting on the premises of the Moscow Agricultural Society (Kuskova, "Mesiats," part 3, 72–73; Sabashnikov to Z. P. Izmailova, 15 January 1922, in "V uspekh ne veriu," 62–63; M. A. Osorgin, *Vremena: avtobiograficheskoe povestvovanie, romany,* ed. N. M. Pirumova [Moscow: Sovremennik, 1989], 133; Zaitsev, *Moskva,* 245–46; M. Mironov, "Podrobnosti i prichina," *Poslednie novosti,* 1 September 1921, 1; "Poslednee zasedanie komiteta pomoshchi golodaiushchim," *Poslednie novosti,* 29 October 1921, 2; "Spisok arestovannykh chlenov vserossiiskogo komiteta pomoshchi golodaiushchim, sluzhashchikh komiteta i sviazannykh s nim lits," in *Diplomaticheskii ezhegodnik* [1992]: 398–99; and "Spisok arestovannykh chlenov Pomgola, soderzhashchikhsia v VChK ot 29 avgusta 1921 g.," in Makarov and Khristoforov, *Vysylka vmesto rasstrela,* 54–56).

117. Osorgin, "Chtoby luchshe oshchushchat' svobodu (Iz 'vospominanii')," *Na chuzhoi storone,* no. 8 (1924): 109–12; Osorgin, "Kutler," 2; Osorgin, "O Borise Zaitseve," *Poslednie novosti,* 9 December 1926, 3.

118. "Zasedanie plenuma Moskovskogo Soveta R.K. i K.D. 30 avgusta 1921 goda," *Stenograficheskie otchety Moskovskogo Soveta Rabochikh i Krasnoarmeiskikh Deputatov,* 1921, no. 6: 5.

119. "Soobshchenie V.Ch.K. ob arestakh vo Vserossiiskom Komitete pomoshchi golodaiushchim," *Izvestiia*, 8 September 1921, 2; "Pravitel'stvennoe soobshchenie," *Kommunisticheskii trud*, 30 August 1921; "S golodom ne igraiut," *Pravda*, 30 August 1921; Iak. Okunev, "Komitet pomoshchi . . . kontr-revoliutsii," *Kommunisticheskii trud*, 30 August 1921; "Etogo my ne pozvolim," *Pravda*, 8 September 1921, 1; Iak. Okunev, "'Interesnaia rabota,'" *Kommunisticheskii trud*, 9 September 1921, 1; Valentin Bulgakov to Cheka Presidium, 9 and 13 September 1921; and V. F. Bulgakov to Sovnarkom Chair V. I. Lenin, 14 September 1921, GARF f.353, op.4, d.418, l.9–14, and RGALI f.2226, op.1, d.403, l.1–5. Oddly, a summary of Bulgakov's response was printed in *Kommunisticheskii trud*, a rare occurrence ("Raz"iasnenie V. F. Bulgakova (Iz pis'ma v redaktsiiu)," *Kommunisticheskii trud*, 18 September 1921, 4; Geller, "Pervoe predosterezhenie," 208).

120. Lenin did, however, ask whether several agricultural experts who worked for Narkomzem might be released (*Lenin i VChK*, 468, 470, 473, 483; Unshlikht, "Vospominaniia," 99–101).

121. *Protokoly zagranichnykh grupp*, 317; N. D. Avksent'ev, chair of Russian Committee for Famine Relief in France, to English Prime Minister Lloyd George, Hoover, Nansen, and Gustave Ador, 22 September 1921; High Commissioner Nansen to N. D. Avksent'ev, 29 September 1921; and Chicherin to Nansen, International Committee of the Red Cross, Geneva, all in *Poslednie novosti*, 2 October 1921, 1.

122. Hoover to Walter Brown, received 24 September 1921, and American Embassy in London to American Commission in Riga, 24 September 1921, both in Hoover Archives, ARA R.U., box 499, folder 3.

123. W. M. Haskell to Kamenev, 29 September 1921, Hoover Archives, ARA R.U., box 19, folder 6. My thanks to Bert Patenaude for first bringing this document to my attention.

124. Haskell to Brown, 3 October 1921 (citing Kamenev's denial), Hoover Archives, ARA R.U., box 499, folder 3.

125. Elmer J. Burland, ARA in Moscow, to London offices, 11 September 1921, Hoover Archives, ARA R.U., box 22, folder 9.

126. V. F. Bulgakov to M. I. Kalinin, [before 11 April 1922], RGALI f.2226, op.1, d.294, l.1–20b.; E. Iaroslavskii to Bulgakov, 11 April 1922, quoted in Bulgakov, "Kak prozhita," RGALI f.2226, op.1, d.60, l.51.

127. Lenin to Molotov, 23 August 1921, Library of Congress, Volkogonov Papers, box 23, folder 4; Politburo protocols, 25 August 1921, RGASPI f.17, op.3, d.194, l.1–2.

128. VTsIK Pomgol Presidium protocols, 31 August 1921, GARF f.1064, op.1, d.6, l.33.

129. Politburo protocols, 20 October 1921, RGASPI f.17, op.3, d.219, l.5; VChK Deputy Chair Unshlikht, for the VChK Secret Department, to Mikhailov, CC RCP, RGASPI f.17, op.84, d.227, l.63.

130. The decision to expel members of the famine relief committee was made at a Politburo meeting several weeks before Lenin wrote to Dzerzhinskii ordering the mass deportations, as will be discussed in chapter 7 (Politburo protocols, 27 April 1922, RGASPI f.17, op.3, d.290, l.4).

131. A. I. Rykov, Deputy Chair of Sovnarkom and STO (the Council of Labor and Defense), to CC RCP Secretariat, 14 July 1922 (sent by Molotov to GPU for its response,

17 July 1922), and I. Reshetov, Head of the GPU Secret Department's Fourth Division, "Conclusion," 20 July 1922, GARF f.5446s. op.55, d.88, l.7, 3.

132. As I will describe in chapter 7, a number of *spetsy* whom the GPU wished to deport were pardoned through the intercession of Soviet leaders who argued that their value to the regime outweighed their political liabilities.

133. Gorky's departure came at Lenin's insistence, purportedly for health reasons. Some scholars have suggested that his leaving was itself a quasi exile and a (provisional) victory for his nemesis, Zinoviev, who proceeded to dismantle or bolshevize the organizations that Gorky had patronized. Orlando Figes contends that Gorky was "the first in a long line of dissident writers forced into exile by the Soviet regime" ("Maxim Gorky and the Russian Revolution," *History Today* 46, no. 6 [June 1996]: 19–20). See also Geller, "Pervoe predosterezhenie," 224–27.

134. "Doklad t. Zinov'eva" and "Rezoliutsiia Vserossiiskoi konferentsii R.K.P. po dokladu t. Zinov'eva," in G. E. Zinov'ev, *Ob antisovetskikh partiiakh i techeniiakh: Rech´ na Vserossiiskoi konferentsii RKP(b) s prilozheniem rezoliutsii* (Moscow: Gosizdat, 1922), 32–33, 49–50.

Chapter 2. Bolsheviks and Professors: The Struggle over University Autonomy

Epigraph: V. I. Lenin, *PSS*, 45: 52.

1. Sorokin, *Leaves*, 212. Also see Michael David-Fox, "The Emergence of a 1920s Academic Order in Soviet Russia," *East/West Education* 18 no. 2 (1997): 112.

2. The term *VUZy* encompasses both universities and specialized institutes.

3. Sheila Fitzpatrick has contended that changes in the structure of higher education during NEP were minimal: the professoriat remained a privileged class and the universities a bastion of heterodox thought until the onset of the cultural revolution in 1928. But, although many older professors stayed on until the end of the decade, the process of bolshevizing Soviet higher educational institutions began significantly earlier. Not only did the regime, as James McClelland has demonstrated, replace professorial control with centrally appointed administrations by 1923, but it also managed to make significant changes in the humanities and social sciences. As Michael David-Fox has argued, the years 1920–22 featured a confrontation that was followed by a period of stabilization and more gradual transformation (Sheila Fitzpatrick, "Professors and Soviet Power," in *The Cultural Front: Power and Culture in Revolutionary Russia* [Ithaca: Cornell University Press, 1992], 37–64; James McClelland, "Bolshevik Approaches to Higher Education, 1917–1921," *Slavic Review* 30, no. 4 [December 1971]: 818–31; McClelland, "Bolsheviks, Professors, and Reform of Higher Education in Soviet Russia, 1917–1921" [Ph.D. diss., Princeton University, 1970]; and David-Fox, "Emergence," 106–42).

4. McClelland, "The Professoriate in the Russian Civil War," and McClelland, "Bolsheviks, Professors, and Reform." See also firsthand accounts by two of the exiled professors: V. V. Stratonov, "Poteria Moskovskim Universitetom svobody," and M. M. Novikov, "Moskovskii Universitet v pervyi period bol'shevistskogo rezhima," in *Moskovskii Universitet, 1755–1930*, ed. V. B. Eliashevich, A. A. Kizevetter, and M. M. Novikov (Paris: Sovremennye zapiski, 1930).

5. This was at a speech to local education officials in November 1920, in *V. I. Lenin o nauke i vysshem obrazovanii* (Moscow: Izdatel'stvo politicheskoi literatury, 1967), 150–51.

6. As Anne Gorsuch has noted, "Youth was the guarantor of future social and political hegemony, insofar as they were able, or willing, to replicate the ideology and culture of the Bolshevik party" (Anne E. Gorsuch, *Youth in Revolutionary Russia: Enthusiasts, Bohemians, Delinquents* [Bloomington: Indiana University Press, 2000], 1).

7. See Samuel D. Kassow, *Students, Professors, and the State in Tsarist Russia* (Berkeley: University of California Press, 1989), and James C. McClelland, *Autocrats and Academics. Education, Culture, and Society in Tsarist Russia* (Chicago: University of Chicago Press, 1979).

8. The term "ideology of *nauka*" is introduced by Kassow in *Students, Professors, and the State*, 4–5.

9. This was the so-called Declaration of 342 (ibid., 219–22).

10. I have used *professoriat* and *studentry* to retain the sense of corporate identity implicit in *professura* and *studenchestvo*. Despite signs that these group identities were already breaking down by the start of World War I, the terms remained in widespread discursive use through the 1920s. (See Kassow, *Students, Professors, and the State;* Susan Morrissey, *Heralds of Revolution: Russian Students and the Mythologies of Radicalism* [New York: Oxford University Press, 1998]; and Peter Konecny, *Builders and Deserters: Students, State, and Community in Leningrad, 1917–1941* [Montreal: McGill-Queen's University Press, 1999].)

11. Pitirim Sorokin, *Leaves*, 25; Mikhail Novikov, *Ot Moskvy do N'iu-Iorka: Moia zhizn' v nauke i politike* (New York: Izdatel'stvo imeni chekhova, 1952), 220; M. G. Vandalkovskaia, "Aleksandr Aleksandrovich Kizevetter," *Russian Studies in History* 36, no. 4 (Spring 1998): 58.

12. Novikov, *Ot Moskvy*, 269–76; Paul J. Novgorotsev, "Universities and Higher Technical Schools," in *Russian Schools and Universities in the World War*, ed. Paul N. Ignatiev, Dimitry M. Odinetz, and Paul J. Novgorotsev (New Haven: Yale University Press, 1929), 232–33; notes of the Commission for Reform of Higher Schools, GARF, f.6767, op.1, d.73, l.2–8.

13. Konecny, *Builders*, 40–42; Morrissey, *Heralds*, 225; Novgorotsev, "Universities," 222–23.

14. McClelland, "The Professoriate in the Russian Civil War," 243–44.

15. Peter Konecny, "Conflict and Community at Leningrad University, 1917–1941" (Ph.D. diss., University of Toronto, 1994), 57–58. See also E. M. Brusnikin, "Iz istorii bor'by Kommunisticheskoi partii za vuzovskuiu intelligentsiiu v 1917–1922 gg.," *Voprosy istorii KPSS*, 1972, no. 8: 84.

16. As detailed in McClelland, "Bolsheviks, Professors, and Reform," chaps. 1–4.

17. McClelland, "Bolshevik Approaches," 822–23; N. L. Safraz'ian, *Bor'ba KPSS za stroitel'stvo sovetskoi vysshei shkoly, 1921–1927* (Moscow: Izdatel'stvo Moskovskogo Universiteta, 1977), 11–12; T. M. Smirnova, "Istoriia razrabotki i provedeniia v zhizn' pervogo sovetskogo ustava vysshei shkoly," in *Gosudarstvennoe rukovodstvo vysshei shkoloi v dorevoliutsionnoi Rossii i v SSSR. Sbornik statei* (Moscow: MGIAI, 1979), 12.

18. The number of VUZy in the country tripled between 1914 and 1921 (McClelland, "Bolsheviks, Professors, and Reform," 146–59), although many did not last into NEP.

19. McClelland, "The Professoriate in the Russian Civil War," 248–58; Smirnova, "Istoriia razrabotki," 7–10; Sh. Kh. Chanbarisov, *Formirovanie sovetskoi universitetskoi sistemy (1917–1938 gg.)* (Ufa: Bashkirskoe knizhnoe izdatel'stvo, 1973), 105–21. Lunacharskii angrily warned that the professoriat was mistaken if it thought autonomy could protect it from the forward march of the Revolution (N. A. Konstantinov et al., eds., *A. V. Lunacharskii o narodnom obrazovanii* [Moscow: Izdatel'stvo Akademii pedagogicheskikh nauk RSFSR, 1958], 43).

20. Smirnova, "Istoriia razrabotki," 10–17; McClelland "Bolsheviks, Professors, and Reform," 159–66.

21. McClelland, "The Professoriate in the Russian Civil War," 259. According to one local Bolshevik, the Kazan professoriat was "ecstatic" when Czech forces occupied that city in 1918 (Mikhail Korbut, *Kazanskii Gosudarstvennyi Universitet imeni V. I. Ul'ianova-Lenina za 125 let. 1804/05–1929/30* [Kazan: Izdanie Kazanskogo Universiteta, 1930], 2: 303).

22. See Sorokin, *Leaves,* 217–34, and N. O. Losskii, *Vospominaniia: zhizn' i filosofskii put'* (St. Petersburg: Izdatel'stvo S-Peterburgskogo universiteta, 1994), 225–31.

23. *Shest' mesiatsev raboty Tsentral'noi Komissii po uluchsheniiu byta uchenykh pri Sovete Narodnykh Komissarov (TseKUBU). Kratkii otchet* (Moscow: TsKUBU, 1922); Fitzpatrick, *Commissariat,* 82–83.

24. McClelland, "Bolsheviks, Professors, and Reform," 223–30.

25. On Glavprofobr's early history see Otto Shmidt, "Pervyi god raboty glavprofobra" (29 January 1921), in Shmidt's collection at Arkhiv Rossiiskoi Akademii Nauk (henceforth ARAN), f.496, op.2, d.114, l.1–9.

26. McClelland, "Bolsheviks, Professors, and Reform," 251, 232. Shmidt quickly set about reforming the nation's technical institutes to make them directly useful to the Soviet state (O. Iu. Shmidt, "The Meaning and Role of Professional Education in the Transition to Socialism. [Theses of Glavprofobr]," ARAN f.496, op.2, d.122, l.1ob., and *Reforma Vysshei Tekhnicheskoi Shkoly. Chast 2-ia: Vserossiiskaia Konferentsiia Vysshikh Tekhnicheskikh Uchebnykh Zavedenii 18 iiunia 1920 goda,* vol. 4 of *Materialy po professional'no-tekhnicheskomu obrazovaniiu* [Moscow, 1920], ARAN f.496, op.2, d.108, l.27–48).

27. McClelland, "Bolsheviks, Professors, and Reform," 258–60, 271–75. As Kendall Bailes notes, scientists "generally stressed the need for state direction and regulation of the economy" (Bailes, "Natural Scientists," 269; Bailes, *Technology and Society under Lenin and Stalin: Origins of the Soviet Technical Intelligentsia* [Princeton: Princeton University Press, 1978], 21).

28. The participation of non-Communist professors in Soviet organs will be discussed more in chapter 3.

29. McClelland, "Bolsheviks, Professors, and Reform," 283–99.

30. Ia. Riappo, "O reforme Vysshei Shkoly na Ukraine" and "O blizhaishikh zadachakh Sovetskogo studenchestva," in *Reforma vysshei shkoly na Ukraine v gody revoliutsii (1920–1924): Sbornik statei i dokladov* (Khar'kov: Gosudarstvennoe Izdatel'stvo Ukrainy, 1925), 91, 67.

31. E. Preobrazhenskii, "To, o chem nado skazat,'" *Pravda,* 16 July 1921, and Preobrazhenskii, "O professional'no-tekhnicheskom obrazovanii," *Pravda,* 10 September 1921, 2.

32. A. Lunacharskii, "Ekonomiia i kul'tura," *Narodnoe prosveshchenie* (weekly), no. 84 (10 August 1921): 2; and Lunacharskii, "O vysshei shkole," *Narodnoe prosveshchenie* (weekly), no. 83 (20 July 1921): 2. See also Fitzpatrick, *Commissariat,* 215–20.

33. Fitzpatrick, *Commissariat,* 79; Fitzpatrick, "Professors and Soviet Power," 44–45. Lenin and Pokrovskii complained that prominent Bolsheviks neglected their teaching duties, but Pokrovskii himself had to apologize for being too busy (M. Pokrovskii to Dean of the MGU Social Science Faculty, 31 October 1921, GARF f.298, op.2, d.29, l.461).

34. When Bukharin was appointed to teach at MGU, Prokopovich retorted, "I know of no such economist. Please list his scholarly works" (Fitzpatrick, *Commissariat,* 78–79). Provincial VUZy often ignored GUS in making faculty appointments; see, e.g., Iaroslavl University rector to GUS, January 1921, GARF f.298, op.2, d.29, l.47.

35. "Postanovlenie Soveta Narodnykh Komissarov o plane organizatsii fakul'tetov obshchestvennykh nauk rossiiskikh universitetov, 4/III-1921 g.," in *Narodnoe prosveshchenie* (weekly), no. 80 (20 March 1921): 16. See also Chanbarisov, *Formirovanie,* 168–72; Safraz'ian, *Bor'ba,* 16.

36. Shimkevich, rector of PGU, to Lenin, telegram, 10 May 1921, with copies to Lunacharskii and Preobrazhenskii, GARF f.2306, op.1, d.598, l.387.

37. Resolution on the Scientific-Political Section of the State Academic Council (GUS), 16 July 1921, GARF f.2306, op.1, d.600, l.43–43ob.; and "Ekzamenatsionnyi minimum dlia perekhoda s kursa na kurs F.O.N. 1-go M.G.U.," *Vestnik FON'a* (MGU), 1922, no. 1 (November): 42–44.

38. "Postanovlenie Soveta Narodnykh Komissarov ob ustanovlenii obshchego nauchnogo minimuma, obiazatel'nogo dlia prepodavaniia vo vsekh vysshikh shkolakh R.S.F.S.R., 4 Marta 1921," in *Narodnoe Prosveshchenie* (weekly), no. 80 (20 March 1921): 16; and MGU Presidium, signed by D. N. Bogolepov, to FON Presidium, memo, 27 April 1921, RGASPI f.17, op.60, d.78, l.7–7ob.

39. Still, the production of Marxist social science scholars lagged, and in mid-1925 Pokrovskii lamented that it would take another six years to fill all positions with Communists. The Socialist (later Communist) Academy never had the influence its proponents hoped for, and debate over how the social sciences should be taught continued into the 1930s. (See Michael David-Fox, *Revolution of the Mind: Higher Learning among the Bolsheviks, 1918–1929* [Ithaca: Cornell University Press, 1997], esp. 50–51, 133–40, and 192–95. Pokrovskii is cited ibid., 80.)

40. MGU rector (D. N. Bogolepov) to Narkompros Presidium, 31 March 1921, and Pokrovskii, Academic Center Chair, to MGU Presidium, 6 April 1921, GARF f.298, op.2, d.29, l.175, 184; GUS to MGU Presidium, memo, 7 May 1921, GARF f.298, op.2, d.15, l.55–55ob.; List of MGU Social Science Faculty Professors and Instructors, 18 June 1921, and Glavprofobr to MGU, memo on professors confirmed by GUS, 10 October 1921, Tsentral'nyi Munitsipal'nyi Arkhiv gorod Moskvy (henceforth TsMAM) f.1609, op.5, d.73, l.51–55, 15–15ob.

41. Losskii, *Vospominaniia,* 232–33.

42. M. P. Polivanov, "Memoirs on Yaroslavl University, 1918–1924," draft (1952–53), Polivanov collection, Bakhmeteff Archive, Columbia University, 5; V. A. Bazhanov, *Prervannyi polet: Istoriia "universitetskoi" filosofii i logiki v Rossii* (Moscow: Izdatel'stvo Moskovskogo universiteta, 1995), 70–76; Philip Boobbyer, *S. L. Frank: The Life and Work of a Russian Philosopher, 1877–1950* (Athens: Ohio University Press, 1995), 112.

43. Sorokin, *Leaves,* 247; also Polivanov, "Yaroslavl University," 13, and David-Fox, "Emergence," 125.

44. Losskii, *Vospominaniia,* 232.

45. Gustav Shpet as director of the institute to MGU Presidium, 28 September 1921, TsMAM f.1609, op.5, d.77, l.23–23ob. Frank and Il'in were both to teach four hours a week. See also L. A. Kogan, "Neprochitannaia stranitsa (G. G. Shpet—direktor Instituta nauchnoi filosofii: 1921–1923)," *Voprosy filosofii,* 1995, no. 10: 95–117; Nicolas Berdyaev, *Dream and Reality: An Essay in Autobiography,* trans. Katherine Lampert (London: Geoffrey Bles, 1950), 234–36; Fëdor Stepun, *Byvshee i nebyvsheesia* (New York: Chekhov Publishing House, 1956), 2: 272–79; Boobbyer, *S. L. Frank,* 112–13. The Free Academy of Spiritual Culture will be discussed in more detail in chapter 4.

46. Regulations, programs, and curricula for VUZ Social Science Faculties (FONy) for 1921–22, GARF f.298, op.1, d.23, and Head of GUS Secretariat P. Dekhterev to Glavprofobr Division on VUZy, 9 July 1921, GARF f.298, op.2, d.29, l.392. From the 1921 MGU plans, only the Communist Professor Magerovskii's "The State Structure of the R.S.F.S.R." followed a strictly Bolshevik line (GARF f.298, op.1, d.23, l.30–31, 29–29ob.).

47. The repeated tinkering with social science and humanities curricula during the 1920s was due in large part to disagreement within the regime over whether to teach these subjects in a practical or theoretical manner (Chanbarisov, *Formirovanie,* 172–73, 243–44; Konecny, *Builders,* 143–46; Fitzpatrick, "Professors and Soviet Power," 45–46).

48. Academic Center protocols (Pokrovskii, chair), 21 July 1921, GARF f.2306, op.1, d.600, l.42–43ob.; K. G. Sharikov, "Universitet na pod"eme," in *Na shturm nauke: Vospominaniia byvshikh studentov fakul'teta obshchestvennykh nauk Leningradskogo universiteta,* ed. V. V. Mavrodin (Leningrad: Izdatel'stvo Leningradskogo Universiteta, 1971), 34; L. V. Ivanova, *Formirovanie Sovetskoi nauchnoi intelligentsii (1917–1927 gg.)* (Moscow: Nauka, 1980), 37–41.

49. GARF f.298, op.2, d.64 (excerpts from protocols on the confirmation of professors and instructors, biographies of candidates for positions, information on their scientific activities); David-Fox, *Revolution of the Mind,* 51; Konecny, *Builders,* 65–66. The evidence refutes the idea that there was little conflict over appointments (as suggested in Fitzpatrick, "Professors and Soviet Power," 40). For example, professors bitterly objected to GUS's appointments to the MGU anthropology department (GARF f.2306, op.1, d.1322, l.103ob.–104). On objections to Communist appointees at PGU, see Sorokin, *Leaves,* 247–48.

50. See Peter Konecny, "Revolution and Rebellion: Students in Soviet Institutions of Higher Education, 1921–1928," *Canadian Journal of History* 27, no. 3 (December 1992): 452.

51. For two different views, see David Lane, "The Impact of Revolution: The Case of Selection of Students for Higher Education in Soviet Russia, 1917–1928," *Sociology* 7 (May 1973): 241–52; and James C. McClelland, "Proletarianizing the Student Body: The Soviet Experience during the New Economic Policy," *Past and Present* 80 (August 1978): 122–46.

52. Peter Konecny, "Chaos on Campus: The 1924 Student *Proverka* in Leningrad," *Europe-Asia Studies* 46, no. 4 (1994): 619.

53. Sorokin notes that they called the unprepared "Zero students" (*Leaves,* 226–27).

54. The results at the MGU FON were particularly dramatic: of 1,808 students accepted for the 1922–23 year, almost 60 percent were Communists or Komsomol members (I. Udal'tsov, "K poslednemu priemu," *Vestnik FON'a. Ezhemesiachnyi organ Ispolbiuro fakul'teta obshchestvennykh nauk 1-go M.G.U.,* 1922, no. 1 [November]: 5). On the increases in Communists at PGU, see Sharikov, "Universitet," 23, 32, 39–40.

55. See, e.g., G. V. Burtsev, "Politekhnicheskii institut v pervye gody sovetskoi vlasti (1918–1922 gg.)," *Trudy Leningradskogo Politekhnicheskogo Instituta*, no. 190 (1957): 102–3.

56. Sergei Zhaba, *Petrogradskoe studenchestvo v bor'be za svobodnuiu vysshuiu shkolu* (Paris: J. Povolozky, 1922), 37, 40, 41; Sharikov, "Universitet," 34, 39–40; Konecny, *Builders*, 50–52.

57. See several memoir-essays in Mavrodin, *Na shturm nauke*; Zhaba, *Petrogradskoe studenchestvo*, 26–27; Sorokin, *Leaves*, 226; and Konecny, *Builders*, 45–46. The Bolshevik professor M. Smit-Falkner gave a poignant report in 1921, in which she called the misery of student life "the most shocking evil, under which only a few fortunate souls can put themselves on the road to knowledge and its practical utilization in life. This situation should be changed no matter what" (RGASPI f.17, op.60, d.78, l.20b.).

58. "Academic sections" were to deal with instructional matters and "cooperative sections" with material concerns (V. Volgin, Glavprofobr deputy chair, to all VUZ boards, 8 December 1921, Tsentral'nyi gosudarstvennyi arkhiv Sankt-Peterburga [henceforth TsGA SPb] f.7240, op.14, d.145, l.27).

59. Zhaba, *Petrogradskoe studenchestvo*, 49; announcement of MVTU board, 30 June 1922 (on the abolition of student sections), TsMAM f.1992, op.1, d.152, l.77; excerpt from Secretariat protocols, 22 February 1923, RGASPI f.17, op.60, d.202, l.36.

60. According to a February 1923 PGU party bureau report, 30 percent of the students were Communist; 20–25 percent were "White Guards"; 15–20 percent wavered between these groups; and 35–40percent were apathetic (Konecny, "Chaos on Campus," 620).

61. Konecny, "Revolution and Rebellion," 463–66, 472–73.

62. As I will discuss in chapter 6.

63. I will use the terms *regulations* and *charter* for *polozhenie* and *ustav*.

64. "Polozhenie o vremennom Prezidiume Moskovskogo Gosudarstvennogo Universiteta (Utverzhdeno Kollegiei Nauchnogo Sektora Narkomprosa 29 sentiabria 1920 goda)," *Narodnoe prosveshchenie* (weekly), nos. 69–70 (6 July [*sic*] 1920): 14; McClelland, "Bolsheviks, Professors, and Reform," 339–40; Smirnova, "Istoriia razrabotki," 18–20.

65. M. Novikov, "Sud'ba rossiiskikh universitetov," *Russkaia shkola za rubezhom*, nos. 5–6 (1924): 8–9; "Polozhenie o vremennom Prezidiume," 14.

66. As cited in Smirnova, "Istoriia razrabotki," 18.

67. According to M. M. Novikov, Pokrovskii furiously screamed that he would not tolerate Kadet speeches; Novikov believed this confrontation precipitated a bitter grudge that led to his own deportation two years later (Novikov, "Moskovskii universitet," 191). For a slightly different account of the confrontation, see V. V. Stratonov, "Po volnam zhizni." Vospominaniia. III chast', 1914–1922, GARF f.5881, op.2, d.669, l.222 (p. 429).

68. Safraz'ian, *Bor'ba*, 16–17.

69. D. Bogolepov, "Vysshaia shkola i kommunizm," *Pravda*, 27 February 1921, 1.

70. MGU Rector Bogolepov and Secretary Preobrazhenskii to the MGU Physics-Math Faculty, 6 April 1921, and Dean of the MGU Physics-Math Faculty V. Stratonov and Secretary Lange to the Glavprofobr department on VUZy, [between 6 and 15 April 1921], GARF f.298, op.2, d.29, l.225–25ob., 226–26ob.

71. M. Pokrovskii as Chair of the Narkompros Academic Center to the Dean of the MGU Physics-Math Faculty, 21 April 1921, and M. Pokrovskii as Chair of the

Narkompros Academic Center to the MGU Presidium, "secret," 21 April 1921, GARF f.298, op.2, d.29, l.242, 243; Safraz'ian, *Bor'ba,* 17.

72. McClelland, "Bolsheviks, Professors, and Reform," 299–310.

73. "Partiinoe soveshchanie po voprosam narodnogo obrazovaniia. Tezisi vvodnogo doklada t. Lunacharskogo," *Rabotnik prosveshcheniia,* nos. 2–3 (1921): 28–29.

74. A copy of this draft is in GARF f.2306, op.1, d.596, l.17–17ob. Bogolepov actually thought the charter did not go far enough ("Vysshaia shkola i kommunizm"), a charge that Pokrovskii angrily refuted ("Vysshaia shkola i studenchestvo," *Pravda,* 2 March 1921, 1).

75. Lunacharskii to Lenin, 13 April 1921, in *Literaturnoe nasledstvo,* vol. 80, *V. I. Lenin i A. V. Lunacharskii. Perepiska, doklady, dokumenty* (Moscow: Nauka, 1971), 272–73.

76. Smirnova, "Istoriia razrabotki," 19–20; Protocols of the Moscow City Komsomol Conference, 12 March 1921, RGASPI f.17, op.60, d.76, l.1aob.

77. Lunacharskii to Lenin, 13 April 1921, in *Lenin i Lunacharskii,* 273; Brusnikin, "Iz istorii bor'by," 88.

78. Politburo protocols, 14 and 19 April 1921, RGASPI f.17, op.3, d.150, l.1, and d.152, l.1.

79. "Ot narodnogo komissariata po prosveshcheniiu," *Pravda,* 19 April 1921, 2.

80. Lenin to Preobrazhenskii, 19 April 1921, *PSS,* 52: 155.

81. Lunacharskii to Lenin, 13 April 1921, and Lunacharskii to Lenin, 11 September 1921, in *Lenin i Lunacharskii,* 274–75, 318–21. See also Fitzpatrick, *Commissariat,* 201–4.

82. Politburo protocols, 14 April 1921, RGASPI f.17, op.3, d.150, l.1; Safraz'ian, *Bor'ba,* 20–21.

83. A detailed look at the fate of scholarly associations is in Ivanova, *Formirovanie,* 211–19.

84. Chairman Iasinskii of Moscow Union of Scientific Actors to Mossovet Justice Department, 18 February 1921; charter of Moscow Union of Scientific Actors sent to Mossovet Administrative Department, [February 1921]; and excerpt from Mossovet resolution of 11 February 1921, sent to Moscow Department of Education (MONO) and the Moscow Union of Scientific Actors, 19 February 1921, GARF f.5446, op.72., d.336, l.6–8ob., l.20–20ob.; Stratonov, "Poteria," 211–13, 218n.

85. Firsov, as chairman of MONO, memo on the reasons for its rejection of a union of VUZ instructors, [February 1921], GARF f.5446, op.72, d.336, l.21.

86. Excerpts from Academic Center Collegium protocols, 24 February [1921], GARF f.5446, op.72, d.336, l.25; protocols of Politburo Commission for Investigating the Society of Scientific Actors, 1 April 1921; and Report of Commission on the Union of Scientific Actors, [April 1921], GARF f.5462, op.3, d.125, l.2, 4–40b.

87. "O zakrytii soiuza nauchnykh deiatelei," "Ko vsem nauchnym rabotnikam, k professoram i prepodavateliam vysshei shkoly," and "Nauchnye rabotniki i Vserabotpros," *Rabotnik prosveshcheniia,* 1921, nos. 4–5: 37, 13, 12.

88. "Groznaia opasnost' russkoi nauke," "Po povodu 'groznoi opasnosti russkoi nauke'," *Rabotnik prosveshcheniia,* 1921, no. 6, 36–37, 37–38. The Academic Center quickly quashed attempts to resuscitate the union under a different name (Chief Decree on Organizing Sections of Scientific Workers in the Union of Educational and Artistic Workers [Rabpros], protocols of meeting on confirming the charter of the Moscow Association of Scientific Actors, 14 July 1921, and excerpts from Academic Center Protocols, 15 July 1921, GARF f.5446, op.72, d.336, l.11–13, 141–43).

89. Reports from the directorate of the Voronezh Rabpros branch to the Rabpros CC, 19 November 1921, and from the Tomsk branch of Rabpros to the Rabpros CC, 12 May 1921, GARF f.5462, op.3, d.125, l.15–15ob., 22. See also A. P. Kupaigorodskaia, "Kratkaia istoriia ob"edinennogo soveta nauchnykh uchrezhdenii i vysshikh uchebnykh zavedenii Petrograda (1917–1922)," in *Rossiia v XIX–XX vv. Sbornik statei k 70-letiiu so dnia rozhdeniia Rafaila Sholomovicha Ganelina*, ed. A. A. Fursenko (St. Petersburg: Dmitrii Bulanin, 1998), 328.

90. Deputy Commissar of Enlightenment M. Pokrovskii to Lenin, 28 June 1921, with postscript by Lunacharskii, in *Lenin i Lunacharskii*, 291. Although some believed that the United Council was more "neutral" than the Moscow Union of Scientific Actors, Petrograd authorities vociferously denounced it and pushed for its closure (Kupaigorodskaia, "Kratkaia istoriia," 327–29).

91. Of the 296 delegates with voting rights, 165 were Bolsheviks, and there were only 43 rectors and 46 other professors, compared to 136 students and 71 representatives of Narkompros and other Soviet organs ("Vserossiiskaia konferentsiia v.u.z.," *Narodnoe prosveshchenie* [weekly], no. 82 [20 May (*sic*) 1921], 7–8).

92. Ibid.

93. It proposed amendments to, inter alia, retain broad assemblies instead of centralized boards, keep large faculty councils in place of the proposed dean's offices, and eliminate the newly created "subject commissions." They were all defeated by large margins (GARF f.2306, op.1, d.597, l.7–9).

94. Stratonov, "Poteria," 215–16.

95. "Polozhenie o vysshikh uchebnykh zavedeniiakh," in *Professional'no-tekhnicheskoe obrazovanie v Rossii za 1917–1921 gg. Iubileinyi sbornik*, ed. O. G. Anikst (Moscow: Gosizdat, 1922), 66–71. For analysis of the charter, see McClelland, "Bolsheviks, Professors, and Reform," 364–74; Smirnova, "Istoriia razrabotki," 24–26; and Chanbarisov, *Formirovanie*, 257–60.

96. Four "curiae" were to present a list of candidates to Narkompros (in practice to Glavprofobr's Council on VUZ Affairs): professors; instructors and "scientific workers"; students; and members of "interested" institutions, including unions, local Soviet executive committees, and local education departments. Glavprofobr would then appoint a board of three to five members from these candidates, including a rector and a pro-rector in charge of "scientific-instructional" matters.

97. "Polozhenie o vysshikh uchebnykh zavedeniiakh," 66–68, 71–72. The "subject commissions," which straddled the boundary between divisions (*otdeleniia*) and departments (*kafedry*), were intended to challenge professorial supremacy by including younger teachers and students. (See McClelland "Bolsheviks, Professors, and Reform," 369–71; Chanbarisov, *Formirovanie*, 259.)

98. Council on VUZ Affairs protocols (V. P. Volgin, chair), 12 October 1921, and Volgin to all Boards of Higher Educational Institutions, 26 October 1921, RGASPI f.17, op.60, d.75, l.2, 7. The establishment of an employees' curia was apparently an innovation of these instructions.

99. Communist student cell report to Preobrazhenskii, head of Glavprofobr, 2 December 1921, RGASPI f.17, op.60, d.75, l.52.

100. Protocols of Moscow citywide Communist VUZ cell conference, 14 October 1921; protocols of VUZ bureau cells, 8 December 1921; protocols of Moscow student bureau, 16 and 19 December 1921, RGASPI f.17, op.60, d.76, l.12–12ob., 16ob., 45–45ob., 47–47ob.

101. Glavprofobr Council on VUZ Affairs protocols, 21 December 1921, GARF f.1565, op.3, d.96, l.3; Glavprofobr Presidium protocols, 30 December 1921, GARF f.2306, op.1, d.596, l.120–120ob. (For the battle over new boards at other Moscow VUZy, see Moscow Institute of Transportation Engineers Communist Cell to the All-Moscow Student Bureau, memo, 17 December 1921, RGASPI f.17, op.60, d.76, l.68–68ob.; and Declaration to the CC of the RCP by the Karl Marx Institute student cell, 23 January 1922, RGASPI f.17, op.84, d.422, l.2–3ob.)

102. A special commission to implement the charter in Petrograd was formed in November 1921 (Head of Petrograd Regional Department of Education and Narkompros Plenipotentiary Kuzmin to Petroprofobr and all Petrograd VUZ boards, copies to Glavprofobr and Deputy Commissar of Enlightenment E. Litkens, TsGA SPb f.7240, op.14, d.145, l.14; see also A. P. Kupaigorodskaia, *Vysshaia shkola Leningrada v pervye gody sovetskoi vlasti [1917–1925]* [Leningrad: Nauka, 1984], 99).

103. Conclusion of the Council of the Technological Institute on the new VUZ regulations, 21 November 1921, sent to comrade Sotnikov, chair of Petroprofobr, 20 January 1922, GARF f.1565, op.18, d.21, l.127.

104. PGU Administrative Dept. (signed by V. Shimkevich, rector) to Rabpros, 19 November 1921; PGU Administrative Dept. to Rabpros, 3 December 1921; PGU Administrative Dept. to Vsemediksantrud, December 1921; PGU Administrative Dept. to Petrograd Gubispolkom, December 1921; PGU Administrative Dept. to Petrograd Gubnarobraz, December 1921, TsGA SPb f.7240, op.14, d.145, l.4–8ob.

105. V. Shimkevich, rector, report of Petrograd University board, December 1921 [after 21 December], TsGA SPb f.7240, op.14, d.145, l.22ob.–24. Most students did not even know when and where the meeting was being held.

106. Meeting of Glavprofobr Collegium Presidium (V. P. Volgin, chair), 26 December 1921, RGASPI f.17, op.60, d.75, l.15–15ob., and Glavprofobr Collegium Extraordinary Meeting (E. A. Preobrazhenskii, chair), 28 December 1921, GARF f.2306, op.1, d.596, l.118; Kupaigorodskaia, *Vysshaia shkola Leningrada*, 102. The Petrograd Polytechnic Institute remained closed from January to April 1922 (G. V. Burtsev, "Politekhnicheskii institut," 106).

107. Resolution of the General Meeting of the Council of Scientific Institutions and VUZy, 26 January 1922, TsGA SPb f.7240, op.14, d.16, l.217–18, and GARF f.1565, op.18, d.21, l.134, 135–35ob.

108. PGU memo, 27 February 1922, TsGA SPb f.7240, op.14, d.16, l.212–14ob.; and PGU Council Resolution, memo on PGU and VUZy in general, 20 February 1922, sent to Lunacharskii on 20 March, GARF f.2306, op.1, d.598, l.231–35ob.

109. Petrograd State University Council protocols (Rector V. Shimkevich, chair), 20 February 1922, TsGA SPb f.7240, op.14, d.16, l.206–6ob.; Glavprofobr Council on VUZ Affairs protocols (V. P. Volgin, chair), 22 February 1922, GARF f.1565, op.3, d.96, l.36.

110. Petrograd State University Council protocols (Rector V. Shimkevich, chair), 16 March 1922, TsGA SPb f.7240, op.14, d.16, l.210ob.–211.

111. Petrograd State University Council protocols (Rector V. Shimkevich, chair), 20 March 1922, with reports of B. N. Odintsov and [student] E. M. Aizenshtadt, TsGA SPb f.7240, op.14, d.16, l.225–27ob.; Petrograd University board protocols, 23 March and 6 April 1922, TsGA SPb f.7240, op.14, d.150, l.65ob.–66, 74ob.–75; Petroprofobr to the rector of Petrograd University, 1 July 1922; and excerpt from protocols

of the Petrograd regional bureau of the RCP, 9 November 1922, TsGA SPb. f.2556, op.1, d.319, l.3, 8. Derzhavin was in fact appointed by Zinoviev and the Petrograd authorities and then confirmed by Glavprofobr (excerpt from Petrogubispolkom small presidium protocols, 3 May 1922, TsGA SPb f.2556, p.1, d.319, l.1; and Glavprofobr Council on VUZ Affairs protocols [V. P. Volgin, chair], 17 May 1922, GARF f.1565, op.3, d.96, l.81; and Kupaigorodskaia, *Vysshaia shkola Leningrada,* 109).

112. Resolution of extraordinary meeting of Physics-Mathematics Faculty, 27 January 1922, on calling an all-university assembly of professors and instructors for discussing the university's material conditions, TsMAM f.1609, op.1, d.610, l.1–2; and Stratonov, "Poteria," 219–20.

113. Notes from MGU board and presidium meeting, 28 January 1922, TsMAM f.1609, op.1, d.531, l.1–3ob.

114. Stratonov, "Poteria," 221–22. The strike was not supported unanimously; the historian Iurii Got'e thought it pointless and was surprised at its success (*Time of Troubles,* 444–45).

115. Resolution of the United Council of Professors of [Moscow] University, 1 February 1922, sent to the Council of People's Commissars (Sovnarkom), GARF f.130, op.6, d.871, l.2–5.

116. Politburo protocols, 2 February 1922, RGASPI f.17, op.3, d.259, l.3; stenogram of MGU delegation's audience with Tsiurupa, 4 February 1922, GARF f.2306, op.1, d.598, l.253–65; Tsiurupa to Stratonov, 4 February 1922, GARF f.130, op.6, d.863, l.104; Stratonov, "Poteria," 223–26; and S. A. Krasil'nikov, "Politbiuro, GPU i intelligentsiia v 1922–1923 gg.," in *Intelligentsiia, obshchestvo, vlast': Opyt vzaimootnoshenii (1917–1930-kh g.g.),* ed. S. A. Krasil'nikov and T. N. Ostashko (Novosibirsk: Sibirskoe otdelenie institut istorii RAN, 1995), 44–45.

117. V. S. Gulevich, V. A. Kostitsyn, A. P. Pavlov, D. D. Pletnev, G. V. Sergievskii, and V. V. Stratonov (Moscow University instructors) to the Council of People's Commissars, [6 or 7 February 1922], GARF f.2306, op.1, d.1322, l.15–16ob.; also GARF f.2306, op.1, d.598, l.356–56ob.

118. Resolution of a general meeting of the Moscow Higher Technical School (MVTU) instructors' collegium (Prof. P. Khudiakov, chair), 4 January 1922 (accepted unanimously by 145 professors and instructors present), GARF f.1565, op.18, d.5, l.60.

119. Minutes of second meeting of the new MVTU Board, 6 January 1922, TsMAM f.1992, op.1, d.159, l.2; excerpts from protocols of general meetings of the MVTU instructors' collegium, 16 and 23 January 1922, TsMAM f.1992, op.1, d.159, l.5–5ob., and GARF f.1565, op.18, d.5, l.48–48ob., 59–59ob.; declaration of the newly appointed MVTU Board, 23 January 1922, TsMAM f.1992, op.1, d.159, l.10; F. K. Gerke to Head of Glavprofobr, 24 January 1922, GARF f.1565, op.18, d.5, l.57–57ob.; Prof. Lukin to Chair of Glavprofobr, 25 January 1922, GARF f.1565, op.18, d.5, l.47; resignations of K. A. Krug, dean of Electronics Faculty, A. M. Bochvar, dean of Chemistry Faculty, P. A. Velikhov, dean of Engineering-Construction Faculty, and I. I. Kukolevskii, dean of Mechanical Faculty, and resignations of faculty secretaries; minutes of a meeting of the new MVTU board with the old board, 25 January 1922, GARF f.1565, op.18, d.5, l.49–56ob., and TsMAM f.1992, op.1, d.159, l.11; Head of Glavprofobr Preobrazhenskii to the new MVTU board, with copy to former Rector Kalinnikov, 30 January 1922, TsMAM f.1992, op.1, d.159, l.13; announcement of Rector Iv. Kalinnikov, 31 January 1922, TsMAM f.1992, op.1, d.152, l.17; Kalinnikov

and Tishchenko, declaration, 1 February 1922, TsMAM f.1992, op.1, d.152, l.14; announcement [of Kalinnikov], 1 February 1922, TsMAM f.1992, op.1, d.152, l.24; announcement of F. Gerke, 10 February, 1922, TsMAM f.1992, op.1, d.152, l.33; protocols of MVTU board, 8 February 1922, TsMAM f.1992, op.1, d.163, l.16–16ob.

120. Excerpts from protocols of the general meeting of MVTU instructors' collegium, 13 February 1922, GARF f.1565, op.18, d.5, l.39; stenograms of meeting of representatives of Higher Technical Educational Institutions with Tsiurupa and Stalin, 14 February 1922, GARF f.1565, op.18, d.5, l.21–38. Stalin asked the delegates what they thought of Preobrazhenskii's deputy Varvara Iakovleva, to which one professor replied, "I don't know, but the mood is against her. It is said that she served in the Cheka." Stalin answered vaguely, "It seems that at some point she served," to which the professor wryly responded, "And see, that creates a special aura."

121. G. V. Akimov, secretary of RKP collective, and Kuznetsov, RKP member, to the MVTU board, forwarded to Glavprofobr by board member V. Tsudek, memo, 15 February 1922; and resolution of MVTU general student meeting, 18 February 1922, GARF f.1565, op.18, d.5, l.18, 16; protocols of MVTU all-student assembly, 18 February 1922, TsMAM f.1992, op.1, d.163, l.53–54ob.; VChK information branch to Iakovleva, secret *svodki* (reports), 20, 21, and 25 February 1922, GARF f.1565, op.18, d.5, l.9, 8, 7.

122. Tsiurupa, deputy chair of SNK, to representatives of MVTU professoriat, Profs. Ramzim and Krug, with copies to Lunacharskii, Iakovleva, and MVTU board, telegram, 17 February 1922, TsMAM f.1992, op.1, d.159, l.30; excerpts from protocols of general meeting of the MVTU instructors' collegium, 20 February 1922 , GARF f.1565, op.18, d.5, l.14; Glavprofobr to the MVTU board (signed by V. Volgin, chair of Council on VUZ Affairs), 7 March 1922, TsMAM f.1992, op.1, d.163, l.37.

123. *Odinnadtsatyi s"ezd Rossiiskoi Kommunisticheskoi Partii (Bol'shevikov). Stenograficheskii Otchet. 27 marta–2 aprelia 1922 g.* (Moscow: Izdatel'skoe otdelenie Ts.K.R.K.P., 1922); see especially Preobrazhenskii's criticism of the concessions (75–76) and Lenin's response (126–27).

124. Commissar of Enlightenment A. Lunacharskii, "To the professors and students of Moscow VUZy," February 1922 [before 7 February], TsMAM f.1992, op.1, d.163, l.18–19. The Narkompros officials at these meetings included Lunacharskii, Pokrovskii, Litkens, Iakovleva, Volgin, and (at the first one only) Preobrazhenskii.

125. Summaries of the four meetings of Narkompros with the professoriat's representatives, February–March 1922, and Changes in the Regulations on VUZy Suggested by the Elected Representatives of Professors and Instructors, GARF f.2306, op.1, d.1322, l.18–48, 81–96ob., and 119–20. See also Stratonov, "Poteria," 226–30.

126. Interdepartmental Commission on VUZy, transcripts of 21 and 25 February 1922; Lunacharskii's report to this commission; and selected commissariats' lists of important VUZy, GARF f.2306, op.1, d.1322, l.49–69, 73.

127. See Krasil'nikov, "Politbiuro, GPU i intelligentsiia," 46.

128. It used as "proof" a *Poslednie novosti* article in which Miliukov urged Russian professors to move from passive to active resistance (Ia. Ia., "Kadety za rabotoi" and "Miliukov tol'ko predpolagaet," *Pravda,* 17 and 21 February 1922).

129. Lenin to Kamenev and Stalin, 21 February 1922, *PSS,* 54: 177.

130. Mikh. Korbut, "Direktiv Miliukova i kazanskaia professura," *Pravda,* 3 March 1922, 4. On the Kazan professors' protests and their aftermath, see Korbut, "Vysshaia shkola i komstudenchestvo," *Kommunisticheskii put'* (Kazan) no. 8 (15) (July 1922):

15–18; Student medik, "Poslednie 'mogikane,'" *Kommunisticheskii put'* (Kazan) no. 8 (15) (July 1922): 18–21; Korbut, *Kazanskii Gosudarstvennyi Universitet,* 314–17; and S. Iu. Malysheva, "Kazanskie professora—passazhiry 'filosofskogo' parokhoda," in *Rossiiskoe zarubezh'e: Istoriia i sovremennost',* ed. A. V. Kvakin et al. (Moscow: Rossiiskii institut kul'turologii, 1998), 53–60.

131. V. Lenin, "O znachenii voinstvuiushchego materializma," *Pod znamenem marksizma,* 1922, no. 3: 12.

132. MVTU instructors' collegium to Chairman of Council of People's Commissars (Sovnarkom), 17 March 1922, TsMAM f.1992, op.1, d.159, l.49–50.

133. Report on the position of higher education and on measures necessary for its revival, presented by the delegates of the MVTU instructors' collegium at the meeting called by the Commissar of Enlightenment, [March 1922], GARF f.2306, op.1, d.1322, l.103–70b., and Vl. Gulevich, V. Kostitsyn, V. Stratonov, A. Chichibabin (representatives of the instructors of Moscow VUZy) to Sovnarkom, [April 1922], GARF f.1565, op.18, d.3, l.26–270b.

134. Startlingly, Lunacharskii and Pokrovskii's amendments to the charter were rebuffed at these meetings. The Politburo approved them nonetheless, while ordering Narkompros to present monthly reports on the rectors' political tendencies (Krasil'nikov, "Politbiuro, GPU i intelligentsiia," 46–47). Communist students were greatly disappointed with the revised charter, which they called a "serious political concession" (Resolutions of the All-Russian Conference of VUZ Communist Cells, 26–30 April 1922, sent to Molotov, RGASPI f.17, op.84, d.422, l.4–50b.).

135. Stratonov, "Poteria," 232–34; and Sovnarkom Resolution of 10 May 1922, GARF f.130, op.6, d.1a, l.151–52.

136. Amendments to VUZ charter, [May 1922], GARF f.2306, op.1, d.1077, l.17–18. These changes remained in the final version ratified in July (*Polozhenie o vysshikh uchebnykh zavedeniiakh* [Moscow: Glavprofobr, 1922]). The professors' proposals are in GARF f.2306, op.1, d.598, l.163–64. Instructions on implementing the revised charter are in Glavprofobr Collegium Circular to VUZ boards, 24 July 1922, TsMAM f.1992, op.1, d.159, l.131–310b.

137. Narkompros Collegium Presidium protocols (Lunacharskii, chair), 16 May 1922, GARF f.2306, op.1, d.1227, l.1; and Glavprofobr Head V. Iakovleva to all VUZ Boards, 18 May 1922, TsMAM f.1992, op.1, d.159, l.87–88. Even the MGU Physics-Math Faculty realized that defiance was no longer prudent (MGU Physics-Math Faculty protocols, 31 May 1922, TsMAM f.1609, op.1, d.587, l.6–8). At its first and only formal meeting, on 19 May 1922, the United Convention of Moscow VUZy reiterated that the government was to blame for the difficult material conditions facing VUZy (GARF f.2306, op.1, d.1077, l.36).

138. As Volgin proclaimed, the goal was to establish "the importance of joint work of the professoriate and Glavprofobr" (protocols of rectors' conference on VUZ questions, under the auspices of Glavprofobr, meetings 1–6 [9 May–10 October 1922], TsMAM f.1609, op.1, d.529, l.1–150b.).

139. Iakov Agranov, report on anti-Soviet groups among the intelligentsia, sent to GPU chair Dzerzhinskii, "top secret," 1 June 1922, f.17, op.86, d.17, l.55–56. This report will be discussed in greater detail in chapter 6.

140. Politburo protocols, 8 June 1922, RGASPI f.17, op.3, d.296, l.2–3.

141. Protocols of the general meeting of professors on the selection of instructors onto the MGU board and council, 21 October–28 December 1922, TsMAM f.1609,

op.1, d.530, l.1–28ob. A small group protested in vain against this new, loyalist domination of the professors' council (ibid., esp. l.2–3).

142. Communications from higher educational institutions on reconstructive work in connection with the implementation of the new VUZ charter, May–December 1923, GARF f.1565, op.18, d.11.

143. V. N. Iakovleva, "Organizatsiia vysshei shkoly," in *Vysshaia shkola v R.S.F.S.R. i novoe studenchestvo,* ed. F. M. Seniushkin et al. (Moscow: Izdanie komissii pomoshchi proletarskomu studenchestvu VTsSPS tsentral'nykh komitetov profsoiuzov i mezhdunarodnogo komiteta rabochei pomoshchi, 1923), 22.

144. As described by Konecny, "Chaos on Campus," and Halfin, *Darkness to Light,* 264–82, 287–319.

145. As implied in Fitzpatrick, "Professors and Soviet Power," 41, 60. That a significant number of those professors purged during the cultural revolution were able to return to their positions during the 1930s suggests further problems with considering the period 1928–32 as the one and only "great break" in higher education.

Chapter 3. Exposing the Caste Spirit in Professional and Scientific Organizations

Epigraph: Pitirim Sorokin, "Ob 'anglo-saksonskoi,'" 16, italics in original.

1. Peter Holquist, *Making War, Forging Revolution: Russia's Continuum of Crisis, 1914–1921* (Cambridge: Harvard University Press, 2002), 4, 21.

2. Il'ina, *Obshchestvennye organizatsii Rossii,* discusses the work of these commissions in some detail.

3. Jay B. Sorensen, *The Life and Death of Soviet Trade Unionism* (New York: Atherton Press, 1969), 43–60; Diane P. Koenker, "Labor Relations in Socialist Russia: Class Values and Production Values in the Printers' Union, 1917–1921," in *Making Workers Soviet: Power, Class, and Identity,* ed. Lewis H. Siegelbaum and Ronald Grigor Suny (Ithaca: Cornell University Press, 1994), 181–82, 190–93; John B. Hatch, "Labor Conflict in Moscow, 1921–1925," in Fitzpatrick et al., *Russia in the Era of NEP,* 58–71.

4. Edward Hallett Carr, *The Bolshevik Revolution, 1917–1923* (London: Macmillan, 1952), 2: 317–31; Robert Daniels, *The Conscience of the Revolution: Communist Opposition in Soviet Russia* (Cambridge: Harvard University Press, 1960), 119–36; Leonard Schapiro, *The Origin of the Communist Autocracy: Political Opposition to the Soviet State, First Phase, 1917–1922,* 2nd ed. (Cambridge: Harvard University Press, 1977), 273–95; Sorensen, *Life and Death,* 88–128.

5. Jonathan Aves, *Workers against Lenin: Labour Protest and the Bolshevik Dictatorship* (London: Tauris Academic Studies, 1996), 175–78; Aves, "The Demise of Non-Bolshevik Trade Unionism in Moscow: 1920–21," *Revolutionary Russia* 2, no. 1 (June 1989): 101–33; and Vera Broido, *Lenin and the Mensheviks: The Persecution of Socialists under Bolshevism* (Aldershot, U.K.: Gower, 1987), 67–72.

6. Balzer, "Problem of Professions," 189; Nancy Mandelker Frieden, *Russian Physicians in an Era of Reform and Revolution, 1856–1905* (Princeton: Princeton University Press, 1979), 106–9; Peter Francis Krug, "Russian Public Physicians and Revolution: The Pirogov Society, 1917–1920" (Ph.D. diss., University of Wisconsin, 1979), 1–65; John F. Hutchinson, *Politics and Public Health in Revolutionary Russia, 1900–1918*

(Baltimore: Johns Hopkins University Press, 1990); and Hutchinson, "'Who Killed Cock Robin?' An Inquiry into the Death of Zemstvo Medicine," in *Health and Society in Revolutionary Russia,* ed. Susan Gross Solomon and John F. Hutchinson (Bloomington: Indiana University Press, 1990), 3–26. Both the broader unity behind *zemstvo* ideals and confidence in the Pirogov Society, which had never spoken for all Russian doctors, began to fray after the failure of the 1905 Revolution.

7. Peter Krug and other scholars have argued that the most vocal opposition soon died down and that many prominent physicians quickly found places within Soviet public health institutions (Krug, "Russian Public Physicians,' 101–33, 128–267, 281–92; Hutchinson, "Who Killed Cock Robin," 19–20; Christopher Williams, "War, Revolution and Medicine: The Case of the Petrograd Doctors, 1917–20," *Revolutionary Russia* 4, no. 2 [December 1991]: 259–87).

8. Krug concludes that "it is difficult to imagine that at the peak of the NEP period the regime would have moved with sufficient force to close the Pirogov society for this reason alone." In fact, however, this is precisely what happened (Krug, "Russian Public Physicians," 268–92 [quote on 272]; see also Hutchinson, "Who Killed Cock Robin," and Williams, "War, Revolution and Medicine").

9. On the creation of Vsemediksantrud, see Williams, "War, Revolution and Medicine," 268.

10. A. Aluf, *Za piat' let. Ocherk razvitiia i deiatel'nosti soiuza Vsemediksantrud s 1919 po 1924 god* (Moscow: Ts.K. Vsemediksantrud, 1924), 7–9. See also Krug, "Russian Public Physicians," 229–41.

11. Aluf, *Za piat' let,* 7–9; *Izvestiia narodnogo komissariata zdravookhraneniia,* nos. 3–4 (1920). See also Mark G. Field, *Doctor and Patient in Soviet Russia* (Cambridge: Harvard University Press, 1957), 53; E. I. Rodionova, *Ocherki istorii professional'nogo dvizheniia meditsinskikh rabotnikov* (Moscow: Medgiz, 1962), 94, 97; and Krug, "Russian Public Physicians," 249–59.

12. Ia. Iu. Kats and N. A. Vigdorchik, "Zdravookhraneniia i novaia ekonomicheskaia politika," *Vrachebnyi zhurnal,* 1922, nos. 2–3 (March–April): 46–55.

13. The plenum concluded that if their section could not be offered real autonomy, then it was time for doctors to leave the union. "Iz obshchego sobraniia Petrogradskikh vrachei, sozvannykh biuro sektsii vrachei soiuza Vsemediksantruda. Zasedanie 21 fevralia 1922 g.," *Vrachebnyi zhurnal,* 1922, nos. 2–3 (March–April): 66–67.

14. "3-ia gubernskaia konferentsiia chlenov Petrogradskoi sektsii vrachei soiuza Vsemediksantrud 31 marta [1922 g.]," *Vrachebnyi zhurnal,* 1922, nos. 2–3 (March–April): 67–68.

15. D. N. Zhbankov, "Pirogovskaia khronika: Soveshchanie vrachei 9 maia 1922 goda," *Obshchestvennyi vrach,* 1922, no. 2: 119–21. Tarasevich, among others, had been a member of the public famine relief committee in 1921.

16. Protocols of the All-Russian Physicians' Congress (All-Russian Congress of the Vsemediksantrud Physicians' Section), 10–14 May 1922, GARF f.5465, op.4, d.286a, l.2–3.

17. Ibid., l.3–4.

18. Ibid., l.4–40b.

19. The congress's resolutions were published together with the harshly critical replies from the Vsemediksantrud Central Committee: *II Vserossiiskii s"ezd sektsii vrachei Soiuza Vsemediksantrud (10–14 maia 1922 g.) (Rezoliutsii s"ezda i postanovleniia Tsentr.*

Komiteta 'Vsemediksantrud') (Moscow: Tsentral'nyi Komitet "Vsemediksantrud," 1922), 21–23. Also see GARF f.5465, op.4, d.286a, l.16.

20. *Vserossiiskii s"ezd sektsii vrachei*, 19; also GARF f.5465, op.4, d.286a, l.17.

21. "Physicians' professional associations and the tasks of the physicians' section," resolution based on the report of Dr. Bashenin at the All-Russian Physicians' Congress, 10 May 1922, GARF f.5465, op.4., d.286a, l.8–9ob.

22. Semashko to Politburo members, "extremely secret," 21 May 1922, RGASPI f.2, op.1, d.23224, l.1–1ob. The underlining is Lenin's on his copy of the letter; capitals in original.

23. "Predosterezhenie," *Biulleten' Narodnogo komissariata zdravookhraneniia*, no. 9 (15 May 1922): 2.

24. A. Aluf, "II Vserossiiskii s"ezd vrachei," *Meditsinskii rabotnik* 1922, no. 5 (1 July): 3–4. The journal published a second account by Kats, with a caveat that the editors disagreed with him but wished to expose the section's views (Ia. Kats, "II Vserossiiskii s"ezd vrachebnykh sektsii," *Meditsinskii rabotnik* 1922, no. 5 [1 July]: 5–6).

25. For more details on these arrests, see chapter 6. Kats himself escaped arrest, perhaps because of his tendency to mix his criticism with conciliatory remarks.

26. Central Bureau (TsB) of the Vsemediksantrud Physicians' Section protocols, 27 July 1922, signed by chairman Kats, GARF f.5465, op.4, d.287, l.38–38ob.

27. Expanded Meeting of the TsB, protocols, 10–12 September 1922, GARF f.5465, op.4, d.287, l.50–57ob.

28. Expanded Meeting of the TsB, protocols, 10–12 December 1922, report by Ia. Kats, GARF f.5465, op.4, d.287, l.71–73; Resolutions of the Expanded Plenum of the TsB, GARF f.5465, op.4, d.290, l.15–15ob., 19–19ob. On the fourth Vsemediksantrud congress (29 November—5 December 1922), at which 128 of the 170 delegates were Communists, see Aluf, *Za Piat let'*, 56–57.

29. Central Bureau (TsB) of the Vsemediksantrud Physicians' Section protocols, 27 December 1922, GARF f.5465, op.4, d.287, l.81–81ob.

30. Protocols of NKVD commission on confirmation of charters for not-for-profit societies, 16 November 1922 (V. Menzhinskii chair), GARF f.393, op.43a, d.1817a, l.5; Commissar of Health N. Semashko to NKVD Administrative Branch, 28 September 1922, GARF f.393, op.43a, d.1822, l.312; NKVD Administrative Branch chair Zaitsev to GPU Secret Branch, 10 October 1922, with note from S. Ravich of 5 October 1922, GARF f.393, op.43a, d.1822, l.312–13, 315.

31. Vsemediksantrud CC to NKVD Administrative Branch, 25 October 1922, GARF f.5465, op.4, d.295, l.1–1ob. (also GARF f.393, op.43a, d.1822, l.316–16ob.); GPU Secret Branch (signed by Unshlikht) to NKVD Administrative-Organizational Directorate, 10 November 1922, GARF f.393, op.43a, d.1822, l.318.

32. NKVD Commission on the confirmation of charters for nonprofit societies (Unshlikht, chair), 8 February 1923, GARF f.393, op.43a, d.1817a, l.26. The supposition that Tomskii appealed on behalf of the Pirogov is suggested by a note attached to the draft of the protocol directing the general *otdel* to "negotiate" with him (ibid., l.27).

33. "Pirogovskoe Obshchestvo: deiatel'nost' D.N. Zhbankova v etom obshchestve. 1889–1892 i 1904–1925," supplement to D. N. Zhbankov, "Protokol zhizni cheloveka 'Malykh del.' Vospominaniia" (manuscript, 1928), RGALI f.199, op.1, d.24, l.147–48.

34. Board of the Pirogov Society (signed by Chairman F. Rein and Secretary D. Zhbankov) to NKVD Administrative Branch, 2 January 1925, GARF f.393, op.43a, d.1822, l.288–88ob.; OGPU Secret Branch to NKVD Administrative Branch, "top

secret," 3 December 1924, GARF f.393, op.43a, d.1822, l.287; Zhbankov, "Pirogovskoe Obshchestvo," RGALI f.199, op.1, d.24, l.175, 203; Zaitsev, deputy director of NKVD Central Administrative Directorate, to Moscow Regional Administrative Branch, "urgent, secret," 19 December 1924, and responses of 17 February and 14 April 1925 from Krushinin, head of Mossovet Administrative Branch, Secret Branch, GARF f.393, op.43a, d.1822, l.286, 284, and 282.

35. The venerable Pirogovite L. A. Tarasevich even relayed the mistaken belief that Semashko had tried to *save*, not eliminate, the Pirogov Society (V. I. Vernadskii, *Dnevniki: mart 1921–avgust 1925*, ed. V. P. Volkov [Moscow: Nauka, 1998], 91).

36. Bailes, *Technology and Society*, 44–66; and Nicholas Lampert, *The Technical Intelligentsia and the Soviet State* (London: Macmillan, 1979), 25–28.

37. S. P. Strekopytov, *Vysshii sovet narodnogo khoziaistva i sovetskaia nauka, 1917–1932 gg.* (Moscow: MGIAI, 1990), 9–27; Ronald G. Charbonneau, "Non-Communist Hands, 109–12; V. N. Ipatieff, *The Life of a Chemist: Memoirs of Vladimir N. Ipatieff*, ed. Xenia Joukoff Eudin, Helen Dwight Fisher, and Harold H. Fisher, trans. Vladimir Haensel and Mrs. Ralph H. Lusher (Stanford: Stanford University Press, 1946), 288, 295, 310–11, 350–65; Bailes, *Technology and Society*, 56–57; and M. S. Bastrakova, *Stanovlenie Sovetskoi sistemy organizatsii nauki (1917–1922)* (Moscow: Nauka, 1973), 170–77.

38. On the scientific commission, see Novikov, *Ot Moskvy*, 303–25; Novikov, "Otchet o deiatel'nosti nauchnoi komissii za 1919–1921 gg.," GARF f.6767, op.1, d.73, l.9–34; Strekopytov, *Vysshii sovet narodnogo khoziaistva*, 22–25.

39. Novikov, *Ot Moskvy*, 303. According to Novikov, its various specialized sections had between them more than four hundred meetings in 1919, even more in 1920, and over six hundred in 1921 (ibid., 314–15).

40. Ibid., 307–8; Strekopytov, *Vysshii sovet narodnogo khoziaistva*, 22–25.

41. Novikov, *Ot Moskvy*, 321–25; Strekopytov, *Vysshii sovet narodnogo khoziaistva*, 28–33.

42. Bailes, *Technology and Society*, 41–43; Strekopytov, *Vysshii sovet narodnogo khoziaistva*, 26–27.

43. Charbonneau, "Non-Communist Hands," 232–36, 291–97.

44. Ibid., 297; Ipatieff, *Life*, 361–63.

45. Russian Academy of Sciences (signed by permanent secretary Sergei Ol'denburg) to the Commissar of Enlightenment, 12 February 1922, and decree on organizing a Scientific Committee, GARF f.130, op.6, d.863, l.3–6ob.; Decree of the Council of People's Commissars, 20 June 1922, GARF f.130, op.6, d.1a, l.239; Bastrakova, *Stanovlenie*, 259–64.

46. Rykov to Radek, 2 September 1922, and V. Nesterov (Rykov's secretary), [late summer 1922], information regarding the "special committee under the Council of People's Commissars," GARF f.5446s, op.55, d.79, l.34–36, 29–33.

47. The editor of VAI's journal, I. A. Kalinnikov, was the rector whose dismissal had led to the 1921 strike; he was also involved in the February 1922 protests (Bailes, *Technology and Society*, 103–4).

48. Tomskii, the head of VTsSPS, explicitly rejected the formation of a discrete engineers' union (*Stenograficheskii otchet rabot I-go Vserossiiskogo s"ezda inzhenerov, chlenov profsoiuzov. 16–22 dekabria 1922 goda* [Moscow, 1923], 34).

49. Ibid., 8–11, 161–64.

50. Ibid., 160 (cited in S. A. Fediukin, *Bor'ba s burzhuaznoi ideologiei v usloviiakh perekhoda k NEPu* [Moscow: Nauka, 1977], 279.)

51. Cited in Bailes, *Technology and Society,* 103.

52. VSNKh Presidium to NKVD, 2 November 1922, GARF f.393, op.43a, d.20, l.40.

53. NKVD Admorgupravlenie (signed by Deputy Commissar of Internal Affairs Beloborodov, Director of Admorgupravlenie Ravich, and Director of the Administrative Branch Zaitsev) to the Presidium of the All-Russian Association of Engineers, 9 June 1923, GARF f.393, op.43a, d.20, l.65–65ob.

54. S. Khrennikov, VAI chairman, to NKVD Central Administrative Directorate, 5 March 1923 (dated thus, but it could not have been before 21 November 1923), GARF f.393, op.43a, d.20, l.55. (Further correspondence can be found ibid., l.66–72, 75.)

55. S. Khrennikov, VAI chairman, to NKVD Admorgupravlenie, 16 August 1923, GARF f.393, op.43a, d.20, l.79.

56. The correspondence concerning permission for the VAI congress and the sending of *propuski* (passes) to the GPU is in GARF f.393, op.43a, d.11, l.432–58.

57. *Ekonomist*'s criticism of the regime and its subsequent closure are discussed in chapter 5. Several of those associated with RTO's Eleventh Department also belonged to the venerable Free Economic Society, which had briefly resumed its activities in 1922. A. I. Ugrimov, for instance, was sentenced to deportation owing in part to his involvement with it (RGASPI f.2, op.2, d.1245, l.3). The only Soviet history of the Free Economic Society notes that its "counterrevolutionary" opposition to the Revolution was the reason for its closure (V. V. Oreshkin, *Vol'noe ekonomicheskoe obshchestvo, 1765–1917* [Moscow: Izdatel'stvo Akademii Nauk, 1963], 57).

58. Protocols of NKVD commission on the confirmation of charters for societies not pursuing the goal of obtaining profits (G. Iagoda chair), 15 October 1923 and 14 April 1924, GARF f.393, op.43a, d.1817a, l.51, 60.

59. I. A. Garaevskaia, *Pëtr Pal'chinskii. Biografiia inzhenera na fone voin i revoliutsii* (Moscow: Rossiia molodaia, 1996), 134–37.

60. Declaration of P. A. Pal'chinskii to the Presidium of the Leningrad Branch of VAI, [December 1924], GARF f.3348, op.1, d.41, l.2–2ob.

61. Cited in Loren R. Graham, *The Ghost of the Executed Engineer: Technology and the Fall of the Soviet Union* (Cambridge: Harvard University Press, 1993), 31–32. See also Garaevskaia, *Pal'chinskii,* 138.

62. Protocols of NKVD commission on the confirmation of charters for societies not pursuing the goal of obtaining profits (Beloborodov, chair), 20 June and 12 July 1924, GARF f.393, op.43a, d.1817a, l.62–62ob., 64.

63. NKVD Central Administrative Directorate (signed by Commissar of Internal Affairs Beloborodov and Deputy Chief of Administrative Directorate Zaitsev) to VTsSPS, 2 July 1924, GARF f.393, op.43a. d.20, l.59.

64. VTsSPS to NKVD, 5 January 1925, GARF f.393, op.43a, d.20, l.63; Charbonneau, "Non-Communist Hands," 446–47.

65. The closure of VAI is detailed in GARF f.393, op.43a, d.20, l.191–95; the OGPU's relentless and eventually successful efforts to shut down the RTO from 1925 to 1929 are described in GARF f.393, op.43a, d.1060.

66. S. V. Veselov, "The Cooperative Movement and Soviet Rule: The Period of 'War Communism,'" *Russian Studies in History* 33, no. 1 (Summer 1994): 52–71.

67. [Osinskii], "S-khoziaistvennaia politika v sviazi s obshchei ekonomicheskoi politikoi Sovetskoi vlasti" (report to Agronomist Congress), *Vestnik sel'skogo khoziaistva,* 1922, nos. 6–7 (15 March): 30–33; and "Agronomicheskii s"ezd. Zadachi Narkomzema. Doklad tov. Osinskogo," *Bednota,* 5 March 1922, 2.

68. "III-i Vserossiiskii Agronomicheskii S"ezd," *Vestnik sel'skogo khoziaistva,* 1922, nos. 6–7 (15 March): 4.

69. "Griadushchee sel'skogo khoziaistva. Disput v Dome Soiuzov," *Bednota,* 12 March 1922, 2.

70. V. V. Simonov and N. K. Figurovskaia, "Posleslovie. Osoboe mnenie," in N. D. Kondrat'ev, *Osoboe mnenie. Izbrannye proizvedeniia v 2-kh knigakh,* vol. 1, ed. V. V. Simonov (Moscow: Nauka, 1993), 525–31.

71. Brutskus's speech is in "Ekonomicheskie predposilki vozrozhdeniia sel'skogo khoziaistva," *Vestnik sel'skogo khoziaistva,* 1922, nos. 6–7 (15 March): 22–26. (Osinskii's speech, as noted above, is ibid., 30–33.)

72. "Vserossiiskoe soveshchanie predstavitelei sel'sko-khoziaistvennykh obshchestv, sozyvaemoe sovetom MOSKh 25–29 ianvaria 1922 g. v g. Moskve," *Vestnik sel'skogo khoziaistva,* 1922, no. 2 (15 January): 6–8. Perhaps the most thorough indictment of Soviet agricultural policy was B. D. Brutskus, "Problemy narodnogo khoziaistva pri sotsialisticheskom stroe," *Ekonomist,* no. 1 (1922): 48–65; no. 2 (1922): 163–83; no. 3 (1922): 54–72.

73. "Agronomicheskii s"ezd. Zadachi Narkomzema. Doklad tov. Osinskogo," *Bednota,* 5 March 1922, 2.

74. Sergei B—oi [N. Alekseev], "Formy razvitiia burzhuaznoi ideologii v usloviiakh NEPa," in *Na ideologicheskom fronte bor'by s kontr-revoliutsiei,* ed. A. Bubnov (Moscow: "Krasnaia Nov'," 1923), 72.

75. James Heinzen, "'Alien' Personnel in the Soviet State: The People's Commissariat of Agriculture under Proletarian Dictatorship, 1918–1929," *Slavic Review* 56, no. 1 (Spring 1997): 73–100.

76. V. I. Lenin to N. Osinskii, 16 May 1922, and commentary in *PSS,* 54: 262, 646–47. Pressure to get rid of non-Communist specialists came in particular, but not only, from Rabkrin, the Workers' and Peasants' Inspectorate (Heinzen, "'Alien' Personnel," 81–82, 87–92, 98–100).

77. V. V. Kabanov, *Kooperatsiia, revoliutsiia, sotsializm* (Moscow: Nauka, 1996), 114–39; Veselov, "Cooperative Movement"; E. N. Kozlova, "Sovet Vserossiiskikh kooperativnykh s"ezdov," *Kooperatsiia. Stranitsy istorii* 1 (1991): 117–19; Iu. A. Reent, *Kooperatsiia i NEP* (Riazan: Riazanskii institut prava i ekonomiki, 1997), 8–11.

78. Reent, *Kooperatsiia,* 11; A. V. Voronin, *Sovetskaia vlast' i kooperatsiia.* (*Kooperativnaia politika sovetskoi vlasti: tsentr i mestnye vlasti Evropeiskogo Severa v 1917–nachale 30-kh gg.*) (Petrozavodsk: Izdatel'stvo Petrozavodskogo universiteta, 1997), 80.

79. See chapter 1.

80. "Protokoly zasedanii Vserossiiskogo s"ezda sel'skokhoziaistvennoi kooperatsii, 20–24 avgusta 1921 g.," and "Soobshchenie Sel'skosoiuza o s"ezde upolnomochennykh sel'skokhoziaistvennykh kooperativnykh soiuzov, 20 sentiabria 1921 g.," in Danilov,

Kooperativno-kolkhoznoe stroitel'stvo, 270–316, 319–20; Voronin, *Vlast' i kooperatsiia,* 78–80; L. E. Fain, *Otechestvennaia kooperatsiia: Istoricheskii opyt* (Ivanovo: Ivanovskii gosudarstvennyi universitet, 1994), 200–201; Kabanov, *Kooperatsiia,* 139.

81. Unshlikht to Lenin, 4 June 1921, section VIII: "o merakh v otnoshenii kooperativnykh organov," in "Stsenarii 'dolikvidatsii.' Planovost' v rabote VChK-GPU," *Nezavisimaia gazeta,* 8 May 1992, 5.

82. Eduard Filat'ev, "Aresty 1922 goda. Kak chekisty 'chistili' sel'khozkooperatsiiu," *Nezavisimaia gazeta,* 8 May 1992, 5.

83. Ia. S. Agranov, Report to Politburo, RGASPI f.17, op.86, d.17, l.55–59.

84. *Vserossiiskaia konferentsiia R.K.P. (bol'shevikov) 4–7 avgusta 1922 g. Biulleten',* no. 2 (6 August 1922): 31–69. The quotes from Kuibyshev are on 34 and 64, Osinskii's comments on 46.

85. A more detailed account of the arrests, deportations, and appeals process is in chapter 7.

86. A Sel'skosoiuz appeal on behalf of arrested colleagues is in Filat'ev, "Aresty"; on Kondrat'ev's quick release, see Simonov and Figurovskaia, "Posleslovie," 450.

87. Reent, *Kooperatsiia,* 11–15.

88. Correspondence between the NKVD and the GPU, Narkomzem, Narkomvneshtorg, and MOSKh, November 1922–February 1925, GARF f.393, op.43a, d.1827, l.2–89.

89. Narkomzem to NKVD, 26 September 1922; S. Ravich, head of NKVD Admorgupravlenie, et al., to All-Russian Society of Agronomists, [October 1922]; Iagoda, deputy chair of GPU, et al., to NKVD Admorgupravlenie, 3 October 1922; GPU Secret Branch (signed by GPU deputy chair Unshlikht et al.) to Ravich, NKVD Admorgupravlenie, 20 November 1922, GARF f.393, op.43a, d.1827, l.117–18, 121, 123.

90. Deputy Commissar of Internal Affairs Beloborodov et al. to VTsIK, "secret," 29 March 1923, GARF f.393, op.43a, d.1827, l.129–29ob.

91. Correspondence among VOA, Moscow authorities, NKVD, and GPU on delay of VOA congress, GARF f.393, op.43a, d.75, l.144–45, and d.58, l.188–92; and VOA to NKVD, 6 March 1924; NKVD to GPU Secret Branch, 21 March 1924; and NKVD to Moscow Regional Branch, 4 April 1924, GARF f.393, op.43a, d.1827, l.151–53ob.

Chapter 4. Cultural, Literary, Philosophical, and Spiritual Societies

Epigraph: Fëdor Stepun, *The Russian Soul and Revolution,* trans. Erminie Huntress (New York: Charles Scribner's Sons, 1935), 150–51.

1. On the more informal literary circles, or *kruzhki,* see, inter alia, Walker, *Voloshin.*

2. Shklovsky, *Sentimental Journey,* 189–90. Katerina Clark has suggested that Gorky played "such an extensive role as intelligentsia patron that he could be called with some justification a Soviet Lorenzo the Magnificent" (Katernia Clark, *Petersburg, Crucible of Cultural Revolution* [Cambridge: Harvard University Press, 1995], 102).

3. "Dom literatorov," *Vestnik literatury,* 1919, nos. 1–2 (February): 9; "Godovshchina Doma literatorov," *Vestnik literatury,* 1919, no. 12 (December): 16; and N. Volkovyskii, "'Dom literatorov.' (K godovshchine ego osnovaniia)," *Vestnik literatury* 1920, no. 1 (January): 14–15. On the House of Litterateurs see, inter alia, T. A. Kukushkina, "'Vseob"emliushchii i shiroko gostepriimnyi . . . ' Dom literatorov

(1918–1922)," in *Ezhegodnik rukopisnogo otdela Pushkinsogo doma na 1998–1999 god* (Saint Petersburg: RAN IRLI [Pushkinskii dom], 2003), 77–95; Barry Scherr, "Notes on Literary Life in Petrograd, 1918–1922: A Tale of Three Houses," *Slavic Review* 36, no. 2 (June 1977): 256–67; and I. F. Martynov and T. P. Klein, "K istorii literaturnykh ob"edinenii pervykh let sovetskoi vlasti (Petrogradskii Dom literatorov, 1918–1922)," *Russkaia literatura* 14, no. 1 (1971): 125–34.

4. "Khronika. Dom literatorov," *Dom iskusstv*, 1921, no. 1: 71.

5. Kukushkina, " 'Vseob"emliushchii,' " 80; Martynov and Klein, "Dom literatorov," 126. For a detailed description of the cafeteria, see "Dom Literatorov v Petrograde 1919–1921 godov (Vospominaniia A. V. Amfiteatrova)," in *Vstrechi s proshlym* (Moscow: Russkaia kniga, 1996), 8: 149–51.

6. "Vospominaniia Amfiteatrova," 150, 156–58; Kukushkina, " 'Vseob"emliushchii,' " 85; Martynov and Klein, "Dom literatorov," 127; appeal from House of Litterateurs to Petrograd Academic Center, TsGA SPb f.2555, op.1, d.396, l.1, 3, 7–8. Bonch-Bruevich argued that the House of Litterateurs kept the Soviet state from having to provide directly for hundreds of sick and elderly intellectuals.

7. This short-lived organization had over 160 members. Sologub was soon deposed as chair, which exacerbated tensions that hastened its quick demise, as did a scandal involving another member, Iu. L. Slezkin. For a contemporary account, see F. K. Sologub, "O Soiuze deiatelei khudozhestvennoi literatury," *Vestnik literatury*, 1919, no. 4 (April): 10–11; "Krizis v Soiuze deiatelei khudozhestvennoi literatury," *Vestnik literatury*, 1919, no. 5 (May): 10; "Na sud obshchestvennosti" and "K delam Soiuza deiatelei khudozhestvennoi literatury," *Vestnik literatury*, 1919, no. 11 (November): 3–5, 14–15; and the documents in V. P. Muromskii, "Soiuz deiatelei khudozhestvennoi literatury (1918–1919 gody)," *Russkaia literatura*, 1995, no. 2: 183–233.

8. On the House of Arts see Scherr, "Notes on Literary Life"; Martha Hickey, "Maksim Gor'kii in the House of Arts (Gor'kii and the Petrograd Literary Intelligentsia)," *Soviet and Post-Soviet Review* 22, no. 1 (1995): 40–64; A. D. Zaidman, "Literaturnye studii 'Vsemirnoi literatury' i 'Doma iskusstv' (1919–1921 gody)," *Russkaia literatura* 16, no. 1 (1973): 141–47; S. S. Shul'ts, *Dom iskusstv* (Saint Petersburg: Almaz, 1997); and S. Timina, *Kul'turnyi Peterburg: DISK. 1920-e gody* (Saint Petersburg: Logos, 2001).

9. On the formation and inaugural meeting of the House of Arts, see "Dom iskusstva v Petrograde," *Vestnik literatury*, 1919, no. 11 (November): 13; "V Dome iskusstv," *Vestnik literatury*, 1919, no. 12 (December): 16; and E. Ts. Chukovskaia, ed., *Chukokkala: Rukopisnyi al'manakh Korneia Chukovskogo* (Moscow: Prem'era, 1999), 151–53. For a vivid description of the meals served there, see Avgusta Damanskaia, "'Dom iskusstv' v Petrograde," *Slovo*, 1992, nos. 11–12: 54–55.

10. Martynov and Klein, "Dom literatorov," 125–28; Scherr, "Notes on Literary Life," 256–63; and McAuley, *Bread and Justice*, 331.

11. N. Iakhontov, "Iz istorii i deiatel'nosti Doma Uchenykh," *Nauka i ee rabotniki*, 1921, no. 2: 3–10; Scherr, "Notes on Literary Life," 266–67.

12. Shklovsky, *Sentimental Journey*, 196.

13. Scherr, "Notes on Literary Life," 261; Kukushkina, " 'Vseob"emliushchii,' " 80.

14. See, e.g.,Vladislav Khodasevich, " 'Dom iskusstv,' " in Khodasevich, *Izbrannaia proza*, ed. N. Berberova (New York: Russica Publishers, 1982), 324–25.

15. On the effort to save Blok, see Gorky to Lunacharskii, 29 May 1921, and Lunacharskii to Lenin and the CC, 11 July 1921, in *Lenin i Lunacharskii,* 292–93, and Lenin to V. R. Menzhinskii, 11 July 1921, in *Leninskii sbornik* 39 (1980): 305–6. The Politburo at last decided to allow Blok to go abroad at the end of July, but by then he was too ill and passed away several weeks later (*Lenin i Lunacharskii,* 294).

16. Robert A. Maguire, *Red Virgin Soil: Soviet Literature in the 1920's* (Princeton: Princeton University Press, 1968), 4. A number of memoirs emphasize that Blok's death was widely viewed as the end of an era. See, inter alia, Boris Zaitsev, *Dalekoe* (Washington: Inter-Language Literary Associates, 1965), 16–18. Fëdor Stepun recalled that "the days of his sickness and suffering . . . followed by his death and burial were elevated by the catacomb spirit in Bolshevik Russia to truly national days of solemnity and mourning" (*Russian Soul,* 151).

17. Clark, *Petersburg,* 150. Mary McAuley makes a similar point in *Bread and Justice,* 335–36.

18. In addition to "Spravka o Deiatel'nosti Doma Literatorov v 1920–1921 g.g.," August 1921, and "Spravka," [1921], TsGA SPb f.2555, op.1, d.396, l.5–5ob., 6–6ob., the activities of the House are thoroughly documented in *Vestnik literatury, Letopis' doma literatorov, Literaturnye zapiski,* and other journals. (See also Martynov and Klein, "Dom literatorov," 129–30.) In 1920–21 there were over two hundred reports, lectures, and debates, along with several literary competitions. Announcements and schedules for the various lectures, readings, concerts, and plays are also in Rukopisnyi otdel Institut russkoi literatury (Pushkinskii Dom) (henceforth RO IRLI), f.98, op.1, d.67, 73. On the library, see "Vospominaniia Amfiteatrova," 152–53.

19. Correspondence between the House and officials, including the House's accounts of and requests for permission for activities and the Petrograd authorities' request for tickets, is in RO IRLI f.98, op.1, d.23.

20. As Katerina Clark notes, whereas the Dostoevsky jubilees were met with expressive interpretation, the Pushkin celebrations were part and parcel of the institutionalization of Pushkin and as such were part of a broader movement toward cultural preservationism (*Petersburg,* 155–59). The different jubilees are described in depth in the contemporary journals cited in note 18 above; see also "Vospominaniia Amfiteatrova," 155–56.

21. This position is most openly stated in an editorial, most likely written by Khariton, entitled "Svoboda i nezavisimost'," in *Letopis' doma literatorov,* no. 4 (20 December 1921): 1, and "Peterburg, 1-oe fevralia," *Letopis' doma literatorov,* no. 7 (1 February 1922): 1. The word *publicistic* connotes writing that is essayistic, intended for a public audience, with an element of what we would call op-ed, except that it isn't necessarily as directly stated an opinion piece.

22. These events are detailed in *Letopis' doma literatorov* and *Literaturnye zapiski.* Also see "Vospominaniia Amfiteatrova," 154–55.

23. Clark, *Petersburg,* 155.

24. The Changing Signposts movement (*smenovekhovstvo*) will be discussed further in chapter 5.

25. The debates took place from November 1921 to January 1922. "Dva sobesedovaniia v Dome literatorov o sbornike 'Smena vekh,'" *Letopis' doma literatorov,* no. 3 (1 December 1921): 11; "'Vekhi' i 'Smena vekh,'" *Letopis' doma literatorov,* nos. 5–6 (15 January 1922): 10–11.

26. "Literaturnaia studiia Doma iskusstv," *Dom iskusstv,* 1921, no. 1: 70–71; Damanskaia, "Dom iskusstv," 55; Khodasevich, " 'Dom iskusstv,' " 326–37; Shklovsky, *Sentimental Journey,* 231–38; and Scherr, "Notes on Literary Life," 261–62. The lectures, concerts, and readings are detailed in "V Peterburge. Dom iskusstv," *Pechat' i revoliutsiia,* 1921, no. 1 (May–July): 180–81; "Chteniia, doklady, lektsii. V Dome Iskusstv," *Letopis' doma literatorov,* no. 1 (1 November 1921): 7; "Literaturnaia khronika," *Letopis' doma literatorov,* no. 2 (15 November 1921): 8; and "V dome iskusstv," *Letopis' doma literatorov,* nos. 5–6 (15 January 1922): 6. For an evocative description of the Serapion Brothers at the House of Arts, see Shklovsky, *Sentimental Journey,* 266–69.

27. A. Lunacharskii, review of *Dom iskusstv,* in *Pechat' i revoliutsiia,* 1921, no. 2 (August–October): 224–25.

28. A. S. Izgoev et al., *O smene vekh* (Petrograd: "Logos" pri dome literatorov, 1922); *Pushkin—Dostoevskii* (Petrograd: Dom literatorov, 1921). One planned collection of articles, to have been entitled "A Reflection of the Epoch," would have examined "how the events we have lived through—the war and Revolution—have been reflected in literature, art, spoken and literary language, in the psychology of adults and children, in law, in religious moods, etc." ("Literaturnaia khronika," *Letopis' doma literatorov,* no. 1 [1 November 1921]: 8; and "V Peterburge," *Pechat' i revoliutsiia,* 1921, no. 3 [November–December]: 301). We can guess that such an exploration, which found its way into the work of Pitirim Sorokin, would not have been overly sympathetic to the regime.

29. "Vserossiiskii soiuz pisatelei," *Novaia russkaia kniga,* 1922, no. 4 (April): 26; S. I. Subbotin, "O sostave Moskovskogo professional'nogo soiuza pisatelei (1919) i Vserossiiskogo professional'nogo soiuza pisatelei (1920)," *Novoe literaturnoe obozrenie,* 1995, no. 11: 185–94. The All-Russian Union was officially born on 1 January 1921.

30. See, inter alia, "V Peterburge. Soiuz Pisatelei," *Pechat' i revoliutsiia,* 1921, no. 1 (May–July): 181.

31. "Vserossiiskii soiuz pisatelei," 26.

32. See, inter alia, "Vserossiiskii soiuz pisatelei," *Rossiia,* 1922, no. 1 (August): 20.

33. "Vserossiiskii soiuz pisatelei," *Novaia russkaia kniga,* 26; "Vserossiiskii soiuz pisatelei," *Rossiia,* 20; P. I. N—v, "Pis'mo iz Moskvy," *Utrenniki* (Petrograd), no. 1 (1922): 129–30. These groups, whose constituents overlapped, included the *kruzhok* Nikitinskie subbotniki (Saturdays at Nikitin's) and the connected groups Literaturnoe zveno (Literary Link) and Literaturnyi osobniak (Literary Mansion). Topics at their lectures and meetings were similar to those of the larger organizations (*Svitok* [Moscow], no. 2 [1922]: 127–28; D. M. Fel'dman, *Salon-predpriatie: Pisatel'skoe ob"edinenie i kooperativnoe izdatel'stvo "Nikitinskie subbotniki" v kontekste literaturnogo protsessa 1920–1930-kh godov* [Moscow: Rossiiskii gosudarstvennyi gumanitarnyi universitet, 1998]).

34. "Vserossiiskii soiuz pisatelei," *Novaia russkaia kniga,* 26.

35. Mikh. Osorgin, "Knizhnaia lavka pisatelei," *Novaia russkaia kniga,* 1923, nos. 3–4 (March–April): 38–40 (quote from 39); see also Osorgin, "Knizhnaia lavka pisatelei," *Nashe nasledie,* 1989, no. 6: 124–31.

36. Zaitsev, *Moskva,* 236–38; Zaitsev, *Dalekoe,* 14, 64–65, 109–10; Osorgin, "Knizhnaia lavka," *Novaia russkaia kniga,* 38–40; and Osorgin, "Knizhnaia lavka," *Nashe nasledie,* 124–31. Some of the small-circulation publications for sale are in RGALI f.1182. The appearance of other stores and the lively book trading business in 1922 Moscow are detailed in Iu. F. Gekker, "Po knizhnym lavkam Moskvy. (Pis'mo amerikanskogo zhurnalista iz Moskvy)," *Novaia russkaia kniga,* 1922, no. 2 (February): 27–28.

37. Berdyaev, *Dream,* 231–32. An apologetic Kamenev not only released Osorgin from one "accidental" arrest (on Berdiaev's intervention) but offered to give him a ride home (Osorgin, *Vremena,* 123).

38. N. Kotliarevskii (chair of House of Litterateurs), A. L. Volynskii (chair of Petrograd branch of All-Russian Union of Writers), A. Blok (chair of Petrograd branch of All-Russian Union of Poets), A. Fed'ko (chair of literary fund), and A. E. Kaufman (chair of Society for Mutual Aid for Litterateurs and Scientists), to Kalinin, Lenin, Dzerzhinskii, Lunacharskii, Kurskii, and Kamenev, telegram, 20 February 1921, in "Otrezan, zabyt, zdes' i pogibnesh' . . . ," *Literaturnaia gazeta,* 12 July 1995, 6 (copy in RO IRLI f.98, op.1, d.26, l.1).

39. A. S. Izgoev, "Piat' let v Sovetskoi Rossii," *Arkhiv russkoi revoliutsii* (Berlin) 10 (1923): 7–9.

40. Zaitsev, *Dalekoe,* 109.

41. Zaitsev, *Moskva,* 130. Zaitsev added, "No wonder they in the end of ends expelled [Aikhenval'd]."

42. Berdiaev, Aikhenval'd, and Iosif Matusevich were the future deportees who signed the letter (A. Blium, "Protesty Vserossiiskogo soiuza pisatelei protiv tsenzurnogo terrora," *Voprosy literatury,* 1994, no. 4: 275–89. The letters and replies, which I discuss in detail in chapter 5, are in GARF f.2306, op.1, d.1164, and reprinted in part in Blium).

43. Some of the weapons they created, Glavlit on the one hand and new Bolshevik ideological journals on the other, will be discussed in chapter 5.

44. Protocols of the Combined Meetings of the Collegium of Agitprop, 21 and 28 February 1922, RGASPI f.17, op.60, d.141, l.16–19ob.; K. M. Polivanov, "K istorii 'arteli' pisatelei 'Krug,'" *De Visu,* 1993, no. 10 (11): 5. Voronskii persistently advanced the need to separate the "young" from the "old" writers in several articles and in an April 1922 letter to Lenin (A. Voronskii, "Literaturnye otkliki," *Krasnaia nov',* 1922, no. 2 [6] [March–April]: 258–75).

45. Orgburo protocols, 27 February 1922, RGASPI f.17, op.112, d.293, l.2, 5–7.

46. See Lynn Mally, *Culture of the Future: The Proletkult Movement in Revolutionary Russia* (Berkeley: University of California Press, 1990); and Maguire, *Red Virgin Soil,* 157–59.

47. Politburo protocols, 6 July 1922, with addendum (Trotsky proposal on young writers and artists), RGASPI f.17, op.3, d.302, l.2, 7–8.

48. Protocols of the commission for organizing writers and poets into an independent society, 11, 17, and 19 July 1922, with attachments (Voronskii's lists of suggested members for society, divided into three groups, with additions by Lebedev-Polianskii), RGASPI f.17, op.60, d.175, l.1–7ob.; Politburo protocols, 20 July 1922, RGASPI f.17, op.3, d.304, l.4.

49. The Politburo debates over Pil'niak's prose will be discussed in chapter 5.

50. The subsidies are discussed in the commission protocols cited in note 48 above and confirmed (to the tune of 150 billion 1921 rubles) in Politburo protocols, 17 August 1922, RGASPI f.17, op.3, d.308, l.5.

51. Cited in Polivanov, "K istorii 'arteli' pisatelei," 5.

52. Maguire, *Red Virgin Soil,* 392–93, 408–9.

53. "Vospominaniia Amfiteatrova," 158–59.

54. The closure of these and other journals will be discussed in chapter 5.

55. Pavel Smyshliaevskii, "Mertvyi dom," *Petrogradskaia pravda,* 17 May 1922, 3.

56. One observer warned that the need for an organization providing such services and aid for writers was as palpable as it had ever been (Ia. Livshits, "Peterburgskie Pis'ma [Knizhnyi krizis'—Vozrozhdenie zhurnalistiki—Dom Literatorov]," *Novaia russkaia kniga,* no. 6 [June 1922]: 25; "Iz zhizni literaturnykh organizatsii," *Novaia russkaia kniga,* no. 8 [August 1922]: 27–28).

57. The financial crisis became the central theme of the House of Litterateurs' committee meetings by late 1921. See the "V Dome literatorov" rubric in the *Letopis' doma literatorov,* no. 2 (15 November 1921): 6; nos. 5–6 (15 January 1922): 6; no. 7 (1 February 1922): 8; also the agenda for the "obshchee sobranie deistvitel'nykh chlenov Doma literatorov," in nos. 8–9 (25 February 1922): 1. On the introduction of membership fees, see "V Dome literatorov," *Literaturnye zapiski,* no. 3 (1 August 1922): 23.

58. Shklovskii, a prominent member of the House of Arts, had fled Russia in the spring to avoid being arrested in connection with the upcoming SR trial. Unhappy in the emigration, he returned the following year with Gorky's assistance (Shklovsky, *Sentimental Journey,* 270–71, and "V. B. Shklovskii. Pis'ma M. Gor'komu [1917–1923 gg.]," *De Visu,* 1993, no. 1 [2]: 30–40). Khodasevich also emigrated at this time; he claimed that he later heard rumors that he would have been among those expelled (Inna Andreeva, ed., "Perepiska V. F. Khodasevicha i M. O. Gershenzona," *De Visu,* 1993, no. 5 [6]: 30).

59. Stenographic record of the Petrograd soviet, report on the Counterrevolutionary Intelligentsia, 29 August 1922, TsGA SPb f.1000, op.6, d.276, l.31.

60. "Vse—na pisatelei," *Golos Rossii,* 16 September 1922; reprinted in V. F. Khodasevich, *Sobranie sochinenii,* vol. 2, ed. John Malmstad and Robert Hughes (Ann Arbor: Ardis, 1983), 337.

61. Khodasevich makes a similar comment on Zinoviev closing the House of Arts in "'Dom iskusstv,'" 337.

62. Martynov and Klein, "Dom literatorov," 133–34.

63. McAuley, *Bread and Justice,* 334–35.

64. From Petrograd Directorate of Scholarly and Scholarly-Artistic Organizations, of the Narkompros Academic Center, to Petrogubispolkom Directorate, 10 October 1922, TsGA SPb f.1001, op.6, d.32, l.9.

65. Deputy head of Petrograd Ispolkom Administrative Branch Il'in and head of commission on registering societies and unions Larionov to Petrograd Directorate of Scholarly Organizations, Academic Center, "secret," 31 October 1922, TsGA SPb f.1001, op.6, d.32, l.13; Kukushkina, "'Vseob"emliushchii,'" 88.

66. Plenipotentiaries of the former Committee of the House of Litterateurs to the Petrograd branch of the Academic Center, 24 November 1922, TsGA SPb f.2555, op.1, d.396, l.10–10ob.; deputy head of the Administrative Branch of Petrograd Ispolkom Il'in and head of the commission on registering societies and unions Larionov to Administrative Branch of the Central District, 31 October 1922; and "AKT," 8 November 1922, signed by coworkers of the Administrative Branch of the Central District and V. Rozenblium, TsGA SPb f.1001, op.6, d.32, l.14–15.

67. A. Volynskii, chair of the Petrograd branch of the All-Russian Union of Writers, to the Academic Center, [after 20 December 1922], TsGA SPb f.2555, op.1, d.561, l.8; excerpts from Petrogubispolkom Presidium protocols, 2 December 1922 (forwarded to Petrograd Academic Center 29 December 1922), TsGA SPb f.2555, op.1, d.396, l.14. Also see Martynov and Klein, "Dom literatorov," 133. Months later, Volynskii was still

lobbying the authorities to turn the building on Bassenaia street over to the Union of Writers (A. Volynskii, chair of Petrograd branch of the All-Russian Union of Writers, to Petrograd Academic Center, 7 March 1923, TsGA SPb f.2555, op.1, d.561, l.9).

68. NKVD Commission on Confirmation of Societies protocols, 16 November 1922, GARF f.393, op.43a, d.1817a, l.4–40b.; correspondence between GPU and NKVD Administrative Branch, September–October 1922, and NKVD Administrative Branch to All-Russian Union of Artistic Workers (Vserabis) Central Committee, "secret," 10 January 1923, GARF f.393, op.43a, d.1724, l.64–66; excerpts from Mossovet resolution, 31 January 1923, sent to NKVD Administrative Directorate 2 February 1923, and NKVD Administrative Branch to Mossovet, "urgent" and "secret," 15 February 1923, GARF f.393, op.43a, d.1729, l.194–95ob.; NKVD Commission on Confirmation of Societies protocols, 8 February 1923, GARF f.393, op.43a, d.1817a, l.26–26ob.

69. Maguire, *Red Virgin Soil,* 32, 392–93, 408–9.

70. *Ves' Leningrad na 1926 god* (Leningrad: Leningrad Gubispolkom, 1927), 182. Sologub died in late 1927.

71. Maguire, *Red Virgin Soil,* 159–75; "Fundamental Position. Report of comrade Voronskii on the question of our Party's artistic policy," presented to the Communist Party CC convention on the question of party policy in literature, RGASPI f.17, op.60, d.271, l.208–12.

72. Maguire, *Red Virgin Soil,* 408–12; "Iz dokumentov 'Partiinogo dela' A. K. Voronskogo, (1927–35)," *Voprosy literatury,* 1995, no. 3: 269–92.

73. Andrei Belyi, "Vol'naia filosofskaia assotsiatsiia," *Novaia russkaia kniga,* 1922, no. 1 (January): 32; V. S. Fëdorov, "'Akademiia iskanii': Petrogradskaia Vol'fila (1919–1924 gg.)," *Iz istorii literaturnykh ob"edinenii Petrograda–Leningrada 1910–1930-x godov, issledovaniia i materialy,* vol. 1, ed. V. P. Muromskii (St. Petersburg: Nauka, 2002), 204–7. Vol'fila, while representing a variety of views, spoke for "a spiritual revolution that will lead to the emancipation of man on all paths of spiritual creation" ("Vol'fila," *Zhizn',* 1922, no. 1: 174). Belyi and Ivanov-Razumnik did not, however, necessarily link this spiritual transformation to the Bolshevik Revolution.

74. Belyi, "Vol'naia," 32–33; "Vol'fila," *Zhizn',* 174–75; "Vol'fila—Bloku," *Letopis' doma literatorov,* nos. 5–6 (15 January 1922): 7; "V Vol'file," *Literaturnye zapiski,* no. 3 (1 August 1922): 23; "Beseda o proletarskoi kul'ture v Vol'file," *De Visu,* 1993, no. 7 (8): 5–27; Fëdorov, "'Akademiia iskanii,'" 207–28; B. G. Belous, *Petrogradskaia Vol'naia Filosofskaia Assotsiatsiia (1919–1924)—antitotalitarnyi eksperiment v kommunisticheskoi strane* (Moscow: Magistr, 1997), 6–9, 22–24; Renata von Maydell, "Anthroposophy in Russia," in *The Occult in Russian and Soviet Culture,* ed. Bernice Glatzer Rosenthal (Ithaca: Cornell University Press, 1997), 162–63; and Maria Carlson, *"No Religion Higher Than Truth": A History of the Theosophical Movement in Russia, 1875–1922* (Princeton: Princeton University Press, 1993), 175–76.

75. Losskii, *Vospominaniia,* 229–30.

76. Berdiaev, Gershenzon, and Vysheslavtsev were active members of the Moscow Vol'fila. When Belyi left the country for a time, he founded a Berlin branch of Vol'fila, which no doubt contributed to Bolshevik fears about ties between émigré and still-native Russian intellectuals (Belous, *Petrogradskaia,* 25–28).

77. See, inter alia, Stepun, *Byvshee,* 2: 272–73, and A. V. Vadimov, *Zhizn' Berdiaeva: Rossiia* (Oakland, Calif.: Berkeley Slavic Specialties, 1993), 186–90.

78. "Vol'naia Akademiia Dukhovnoi Kul'tury v Moskve," in *Sofiia. Problemy dukhovnoi kul'tury i religioznoi filosofii*, ed. N. A. Berdiaev (Berlin: Obelisk, 1923), 135–36; Charter of the Free Academy of Spiritual Culture, registered 26 September 1919 by the Moscow soviet, GARF f.393, op.43a, d.1822, l.470–71ob.; Berdiaev, *Dream*, 234–35; Boobbyer, *S. L. Frank*, 112–13; and B. A. Chagin and V. I. Klushin, *Bor'ba za istoricheskii materializm v SSSR v 20-e gody* (Leningrad: Nauka, 1975), 42–43.

79. Berdiaev, *Dream*, 234.

80. The Mossovet sanction is noted on its charter (GARF f.393, op.43a, d.1822, l.471ob.).

81. "Vol'naia Akademiia," 135–36, and Stepun, *Byvshee*, 2: 275–79. The Spengler volume and the reaction to it will be discussed further in chapter 5.

82. Berdiaev, *Dream*, 235–36; Vadimov, *Zhizn' Berdiaeva*, 207–10, 223–24, 228;

83. "Vol'naia Akademiia," 136.

84. Randall Poole, *Neo-Idealist Philosophy in the Russian Liberation Movement: The Moscow Psychological Society and Its Symposium "Problems of Idealism,"* Kennan Institute for Advanced Russian Studies Occasional Paper no. 262 (Washington, D.C.: Woodrow Wilson Center, 1996).

85. "Khronika. Deiatel'nost' Psikhologicheskogo Obshchestva pri Moskovskom universitete za poslednie 4 goda (1918–1922)," *Mysl'*, 1922, no. 3 (May–June): 186–87.

86. Ibid.; Chagin and Klushin, *Bor'ba*, 44.

87. Kogan, "Neprochitannaia stranitsa," 95–117; see also List of Active Members of the [MGU] Scientific Research Institute, and Gustav Shpet as Director of the Institute of Scientific Philosophy to the MGU Presidium, 28 September 1921, TsMAM f.1609, op.5, d.77, l.18–19ob., 23–23ob.

88. The Philosophy Society's charter and other registration materials, filed with Petrograd Glavnauka in spring 1922, are in TsGA SPb f.2555, op.1, d.530, l.2–13.

89. "Filosofskoe obshchestvo pri Petrogradskom Universitete," *Mysl'*, 1922, no. 1 (January–February): 187–88; "Peterburgskoe Filosofskoe Obshchestvo," *Mysl'*, 1922, no. 2 (March–April): 157; "Trudy Peterburgskogo Filosofskogo O-va.," and "Filosofskii kruzhok pri Petrogradskom universitete," *Mysl'*, 1922, no. 3 (May–June): 189–90; and V. I. Klushin, *Pervye uchenye-marksisty Petrograda* (Leningrad: Lenizdat, 1971), 45–50, 68–69.

90. Klushin, *Pervye*, 45, 56–62, 65–67.

91. Petrograd Department of Education Politprosvet to Department of Education Presidium, 27 February 1922; correspondence between NKVD and Petrograd Administrative Department, February–April 1922; and excerpt from Petrogubispolkom interdepartmental commission on registration of noncommercial societies protocols, 4 March 1922, GARF f.393, op.43a, d.27, 33–38. The Anthroposophical Society held to Rudolf Steiner's more rationalized version of the murky blend of Western and Eastern mysticism that was the province of the Theosophical Society (Carlson, *No Religion* [for their post-1917 activities, see 173–80], and von Maydell, "Anthroposophy," 153–67).

92. V. F. Martsinkovskii, *Zapiski Veruiushchego: Iz istorii religioznogo dvizheniia v Sovetskoi Rossii (1917–1923)* (Prague: by the author, 1929), 263.

93. Charter of Russian Christian Student Union submitted to NKVD, 23 August 1922, GARF f.393, op.43a, d.1818, l.59–60ob.

94. Paul Mailleux, *Exarch Leonid Feodorov: Bridgebuilder between Rome and Moscow* (New York: P. J. Kennedy and Sons, 1964), 127–30; I. I. Osipova, "V iazvakh

svoikh sokroi menia . . ." in *Goneniia na Katolicheskuiu Tserkov' v SSSR. Po materialam sledstvennykh i lagernykh del* (Moscow: Serebrianye niti, 1996), 9–10; M. V. Shkarovskii et al., *Rimsko-katolicheskaia tserkov' na severo-zapade Rossii v 1917–1945 gg.* (St. Petersburg: Nestor, 1998), 47–48; James J. Zatko, *Descent into Darkness: The Destruction of the Roman Catholic Church in Russia, 1917–1923* (Notre Dame: University of Notre Dame Press, 1965), 179–90.

95. On the other hand, Abrikosov told his adherents to avoid the *kruzhok* at Berdiaev's apartment, which he considered too free-thinking (Donald Lowrie, *Rebellious Prophet: A Life of Nicolai Berdyaev* [New York: Harper, 1960], 138, 179; Vadimov, *Zhizn' Berdiaeva*, 182–83).

96. These GPU reports are in "List of Anti-Soviet Intellectuals," [July 1922], TsA FSB f.1, op.6, d.160E, l.64–65.

97. See William Edgerton, introduction to *Memoirs of Peasant Tolstoyans in Soviet Russia*, ed. Edgerton (Bloomington: Indiana University Press, 1993), xii–xiii.

98. V. F. Bulgakov to E. M. Iaroslavskii, July 1921 [before 27 July], RGALI f.2226, op.1, d.398, l.1–8.

99. Ibid., l.6. On the United Council of Religious Communes and Groups, Its Charter and List of Founding Members, GARF f.393, op.43a, d.1818, l.52–54, 50.

100. Iaroslavskii to V. F. Bulgakov, 27 July 1921, included in Bulgakov's unpublished memoirs, "Kak prozhita zhizn'," part 11, "Poslednie gody zhizni v Moskvy," RGALI f.2226, op.1, d.60, l.57–62.

101. Iaroslavskii's attitude was in contrast to that of V. D. Bonch-Bruevich, who was far more sympathetic to sectarians and looked, at least initially, for ways that they could work with the regime (Alexei Zverev and Bruno Coppieters, "V. D. Bonch-Bruevich and the Doukhobors: On the Conscientious Objection Policies of the Bolsheviks," *Canadian Ethnic Studies* 27, no. 3 [1995]: 72–90; and Kathy Rousselet, "Utopies socio-religieuses et révolution politique dans les années 1920," *Revue des Etudes Slaves* 69, nos. 1–2 [1997]: 257–71).

102. Charter and List of Founding Members of the Free Association of Spiritual Tendencies, and protocols of the Founding Meeting of the Free Association of Spiritual Tendencies, 3 May 1922, GARF f.393, op.43a, d.1822, l.72–73, 76, 78–78ob.; Bulgakov, "Kak prozhita," RGALI f.2226, op.1, d.60, l.99–108; Carlson, *No Religion*, 176.

103. The Free Academy was particularly hard hit—in addition to these philosophers, Aikhenval'd was expelled, the legal scholar M. S. Fel'dshtein was arrested, and a year later the economist Iakov Bukshpan was refused reentry to Russia from a trip abroad. Vysheslavtsev, often listed among the deportees, in fact left at the same time of his own accord.

104. Protocols of the NKVD commission on confirmation of charters, 7 December 1922, GARF f.393, op.43a, d.1817a, l.16–16ob.; Narkompros administrative directorate, signed by Deputy Commissar Maksimov et al., to the NKVD, 11 November 1922, and registration materials submitted by the Free Academy of Spiritual Culture, GARF f.393, op.43a, d.1822, l.462–71ob.

105. Fëdorov, "Akademiia iskanii," 241; Belous, *Vol'fila*, 29–30. By the time of its final meeting in 1924, Vol'fila had already been officially liquidated (von Maydell, "Anthroposophy," 163n).

106. NKVD Commission on Confirmation of Charters protocols, 16 November and 7 December 1922, GARF f.393, op.43a, d.1817a, l.4–5, l.16–16ob. The Vegetarian Society

was at the center of Tolstoyan life in Moscow; its regulars also included a number of anthroposophists (A. B. Roginskii, "Primechaniia," in *Vospominaniia Krest'ian-Tolstovtsev 1910–1930-e gody* [Moscow: Kniga, 1989], 460–62; von Maydell, "Anthroposophy," 161).

107. NKVD Commission on Confirmation of Charters protocols, 16 November 1922; Deputy Commissar of Enlightenment V. Maksimov et al. to NKVD, "urgent," 4 October 1922; conclusion of NKVD consultative bureau on the charter of the Russian Christian Student Union, [before 31 October 1922], GARF f.393, op.43a, d.1817a, l.5, 11–11ob., 38–38ob.; d.1818, l.20, 57. Although similar groups such as the Martinists and Russian Spiritualist Society were also banned, unofficial new-age circles were able to continue into the 1920s, particularly outside Moscow and Petrograd (Carlson, *No Religion,* 176–79).

108. Bulgakov, "Kak prozhita," RGALI f.2226, op.1, d.60, l.113–38; Martsinkovskii, *Zapiski,* 275–91 (quote from 278). Chertkov's appeal of his deportation will be discussed in chapter 7.

109. The NKVD and Narkomiust established the commission on the registration of religious societies in spring 1923. "Postanovlenie narodnykh komissariatov Iustitsii i Vnutrennykh Del. Instruktsiia o poriadke registratsii religioznykh obshchestv i vydachi reshenii na sozyv s"ezdov takovykh" and "Prilozhenie k st. 384. Ustav," *Sobranie uzakonenii i rasporiazhenii rabochego krest'ianskogo pravitel'stva. Sbornik dekretov* (henceforth *SUR*), 1923, art. 384, pp. 692–95. Correspondence between local administrative departments and the NKVD on the question of registration of religious groups is in GARF f.393, op.43a, d.71, 72, 73.

110. J. A. Helby, *Protestants in Russia,* trans. John Pott (Belfast: Christian Journals, 1976), 89–95; and Martsinkovskii, *Zapiski,* 291–95.

111. Mossovet resolution, 31 January 1923, GARF f.393, op.43a, d.1729, l.195–95ob.; protocols of NKVD commission on societies (Unshlikht, chair), 8 February 1923, GARF f.393, op.43a, d.1817a, l.26; correspondence between NKVD and Mossovet, February–June 1923, GARF f.393, op.43a, d.1729, l.189–94.

112. Both the newsletter and the society were shut down at the end of the decade (Roginskii, "Primechaniia," 460–62; Mikhail Gorbunov-Posadov, "Foreword," in Edgerton, *Peasant Tolstoyans,* 1–2).

113. Shkarovskii, *Rimsko-katolicheskaia,* 52–58; Mailleux, *Exarch,* 163–77; Zatko, *Descent,* 180–84; Osipova, "V iazvakh," 11–17.

114. Lenin to N. P. Gorbunov, 5 March 1922, *PSS,* 54: 198.

115. Protocols of NKVD commission on societies, 19 April 1923, 7 June 1923, 12 July 1923, and 7 December 1926, GARF f.393, op.43a, d.1817a, l.36, 41–41ob., 46, 83–83ob., and various NKVD materials on the Moscow Archaeological Society, f.393, op.43a, d.1822, l.321–51.

116. Klushin, *Pervye,* 95–130.

117. "Dekret VTsIK. O poriadke sozyva s"ezdov i vserossiiskikh soveshchanii razlichnykh soiuzov i ob"edinenii i o registratsii etikh organizatsii," 12 June 1922; "Dekret VTsIK i SNK. O poriadke utverzhdeniia i registratsiia obshchestv i soiuzov, ne presleduiushchikh tselei izvlecheniia pribyli i poriadke nadzora za nimi," 3 August 1922; "Dekret VTsIK. Instruktsiia po registratsii obshchestv, soiuzov i ob"edinenii," 10 August 1922; "Dekret VTsIK. Instruktsiia po vydache razresheniia na sozyv s"ezdov i sobranii razlichnykh organizatsii, soiuzov i ob"edinenii," 10 August 1922, all in *SUR,*

1922, no. 40, p. 650, and no. 49, pp. 787–90; and NKVD secret circular to regional organs, 1922 [no exact date], GARF f.393, op.43a, d.6, l.2.

118. The regular provision of tickets for the congresses is discussed in the correspondence among the NKVD commissions, the GPU, and the societies, in GARF f.393, op.43a, d.11, 58.

119. "Kostromskoe Filosofskoe Obshchestvo," *Mysl'*, 1922, no. 2 (March–April): 158; "Filosofskoe Ob-vo pri Donskom Universitete," *Mysl'*, 1922, no. 3 (May–June): 187–88; Klushin, *Pervye*, 49–50.

120. In summer 1921 the Nevel and Vitebsk regional executive committees requested that the House of Litterateurs organize lectures in these locations (RO IRLI f.98, op.1, d.23, l.39–40).

121. NKVD Administrative Department to Saratov Regional Admin. Dept., [1923], GARF f.393, op.43a, d.1729, l.387. (An almost identical directive was sent a year later; ibid., l.368.) Very similar explanatory letters were sent out to other regional bureaus.

122. Correspondence of NKVD with Don region public prosecutor, Voronezh Admin. Dept., Orlov Admin. Dept., Iaroslavl Admin. Dept., Ivanovo-Voznensk Admin. Dept., and with the VAI Presidium, February–August 1923, GARF f.393, op.43a, d.71, l.16–17, 506–8; d.72, l.95–101; d.73, l.201–4; and d.1729, l.114.

123. This fact has been established by the work of a number of scholars, beginning with the seminal work of Merle Fainsod in *Smolensk under Soviet Rule* (Cambridge: Harvard University Press, 1958).

124. On the survival of Maximilian Voloshin's *kruzhok* into the early 1930s, see Walker, *Voloshin*, esp. 167–93.

Chapter 5. Publishing, Censorship, and Ideological Struggles

Epigraph: A. Lunacharskii, "Svoboda knigi i revoliutsiia," *Pechat' i revoliutsiia*, no. 1 (May–June 1921): 4–7.

1. Lenin to Miasnikov, 5 August 1921, *PSS*, 44: 79, italics in original; Roger Pethybridge, "Concern for Bolshevik Ideological Predominance at the Start of NEP," *Russian Review* 41, no. 4 (October 1982): 445–53.

2. Edward Brown, *Russian Literature since the Revolution*, rev. ed. (Cambridge: Harvard University Press, 1982), esp. 70–104; Maguire, *Red Virgin Soil;* Fitzpatrick, " 'Soft' Line," 278–85. Even so, vocal criticism of anti-Soviet fiction was already quite plentiful. (See, e.g., A. Voronskii, "Iz sovremennykh literaturnykh nastroenii," *Pravda*, 28 June 1922, 2; N. Meshcheriakov, "Literatura i iskusstvo. Svezhii rostok," *Pravda*, 6 May 1922, 3; P. S. Kogan, "Literaturnye zametki. I. Pisatel' Zamiatin," *Pravda*, 22 March 1922, 4; and, most extensively, in Trotsky's series "Vne-oktiabrskaia literatura," *Pravda*, September–October 1922. See also Marc Slonim, *Soviet Russian Literature: Writers and Problems* [New York: Oxford University Press, 1964], 40–58; Victor Erlich, *Modernism and Revolution: Russian Literature in Transition* [Cambridge: Harvard University Press, 1994], 12–13.)

3. On publishing during the Civil War period and NEP see, inter alia, Kenez, *Birth of the Propaganda State*, 96–104, 239–50. While stressing the "freedoms" still present in publishing, Kenez admits that 1922 was a watershed year, after which it became more difficult to publish ideologically suspect work (ibid., 246).

4. D. Lutokhin, "Vnutrennyi russkii knizhnyi rynok," *Novaia russkaia kniga*, 1923, no. 2: 38–39; A. V. Blium, *Za kulisami "ministerstva pravdy." Tainaia istoriia Sovetskoi tsenzury, 1917–1929* (St. Petersburg: Akademicheskii proekt, 1994), 74–75, 134–41; V. V. Gulev, "Organizatsiia izdatel'skogo dela i bor'ba protiv burzhuaznoi ideologii v pervye gody Sovetskoi vlasti (1918–1921 gg.)," *Istoricheskie zapiski*, no. 104 (1979): 59–90.

5. P. Vitiazev, *Chastnye izdatel'stva v Sovetskoi Rossii* (Petrograd: by the author, 1921); G. V. Zhirkov, "Istoriia Sovetskoi tsenzury: period diktata gosudarstvennogo izdatel'stva (1919–1921 gg.)," *Vestnik Sankt-Peterburgskogo universiteta*, ser. 2, Istoriia, iazykoznanie, literaturovedenie, 1995, no. 3: 78–81; Fitzpatrick, *Commissariat*, 133–34; E. L. Nemirovskii and V. I. Kharlamov, eds., *Istoriia knigi v SSSR, 1917–1921* (Moscow: Kniga, 1985), 2: 107–12; M. K. Svichenskaia, "Kooperativnoe knigoizdanie 1917–1930 gg," *Kniga: Issledovaniia i materialy* 72 (Moscow: Terra, 1996), 106–9.

6. Narkompros resolution on private publishers, 18 August 1921, *Pechat' i revoliutsiia*, no. 2 (August–October 1922): 235; Moscow soviet resolution on publishing, 26 August 1921, in *Izdatel'skoe delo v pervye gody Sovetskoi vlasti (1917–1922). Sbornik dokumentov i materialov*, ed. E. A. Dinershtein (Moscow: Kniga, 1972), 180; Sovnarkom resolution on private publishers, 12 December 1921, *Pechat' i revoliutsiia*, no. 4 (1) (January–February 1922): 342–43; E. A. Dinershtein, "Reforma izdatel'skogo dela 1921 goda," *Kniga: Issledovaniia i materialy* 20 (Moscow: Kniga, 1970), 71–86; A. I. Podgornova, *Sovetskoe knigoizdanie v 20-e gody. Istoriko-pravovoe issledovanie* (Moscow: Nauka, 1984), 10–16.

7. Lunacharskii, "Svoboda knigi," 3–9.

8. On the period of Gosizdat "dictatorship" see Zhirkov, "Istoriia Sovetskoi tsenzury," 78–85.

9. Vitiazev, *Chastnye izdatel'stva*, 2–5.

10. These letters were printed ibid., 57–63. In addition to rallying his fellow publishers, Vitiazev also lobbied Gorky for help (Primochkina, Nikitin, and Ostrovskaia, "Gor'kii v bor'be za sokhranenie kul'tury," 63–66).

11. E. Zamiatin, "Ia boius'," *Dom iskusstv*, no. 1 (1921): 43–45.

12. A. Lunacharskii, review of *Dom Iskusstv*, in *Pechat' i revoliutsiia*, no. 2 (August–October 1921): 225.

13. A. Voronskii, "Ob otshel'nikakh, bezumtsakh i buntariakh," *Krasnaia nov'*, 1921, no. 1 (June): 292–95. See also Konstantin Fedin's caustic review in *Kniga i revoliutsiia* 1, nos. 8–9 (1921): 85–86.

14. "Ozhog: K istorii nevyshedshii 'Literaturnoi gazety' 1921 goda," *Literaturnoe obozrenie*, 1991, no. 2: 95–97; E. I. Zamiatin to L. N. Zamiatina, 25 June 1921, in *Rukopisnoe nasledie Evgeniia Ivanovicha Zamiatina*, 2 vols., Rukopisnye pamiatniki, no. 3 (St. Petersburg: Rossiiskaia natsional'naia biblioteka, 1997), 1: 237; Iurii Annenkov, *Dnevnik moikh vstrech* (New York: Inter-Language Literary Associates, 1966), 1: 252; and Vladislav Khodasevich, "Melochi," *Vozrozhdenie*, 7 September 1933, 3.

15. Dokladnaia zapiska Soiuza Petrogradskikh Kooperativnykh Izdatel'stv (Petrograd, 1921), in GARF f.2306, op.1, d.696, l.78–86.

16. The physiologist Ivan Pavlov and the philosopher E. L. Radlov also joined Vitiazev's defense of private publishing (Sorokin to Vitiazev, [1921], RGALI f.106, op.1, d.157, l.34–35; and "Neizvestnye avtografy I. P. Pavlova, E. L. Radlova, P. A. Sorokina," *Russkaia literatura*, 1990, no. 3: 165–66).

17. D. Lutokhin, "Sovetskaia tsenzura. (Po lichnym vospominaniiam)," *Arkhiv russkoi revoliutsii* (Berlin) 12 (1923): 157–58.

18. N. L. Meshcheriakov, "O rabote gosudarstvennogo izdatel'stva v novykh usloviiakh," *Pechat' i revoliutsiia,* no. 4 (1) (January–March 1922): 166.

19. Excerpt from Politburo protocols, 18 November 1921, RGASPI f.17, op.60, d.271, l.1; Michael S. Fox [David-Fox], "Glavlit, Censorship and the Problem of Party Policy in Cultural Affairs, 1922–28," *Soviet Studies* 44, no. 6 (1992): 1053; Zhirkov, "Istoriia sovetskoi tsenzury," 78–86; and Blium, *Za kulisami,* 49–54.

20. Gosizdat instructions to its regional branches, January–February 1922, Tsentral'nyi gosudarstvennyi arkhjv literatury i iskusstva Sankt-Peterburga (henceforth TsGALI SPb) f.31, op.1, d.2, l.1–5. Meshcheriakov complained that the Cheka military censors often forbade materials that the Politotdel had approved (Podgornova, *Sovetskoe Knigoizdanie,* 40; Izmozik, *Glaza i ushi,* 48–50; and Blium, *Za kulisami,* 44–46).

21. A. Evgen'ev [A. E. Kaufman], "O Vol'nykh izdatel'stvakh," *Vestnik literatury,* 1921, nos. 4–5 (April–May): 11; Evgen'ev [Kaufman], "'Byt' ili ne byt" vol'nym izdatel'stvam?" *Vestnik literatury,* 1921, nos. 6–7 (June–July): 10–11; "Svoboda i nezavisimost'," *Letopis' doma literatorov,* no. 4 (20 December 1921): 1; "Staryi god," *Letopis' doma literatorov,* nos. 5–6 (1–2) (15 January 1922): 1–2; "Peterburg, 1-oe fevralia," *Letopis' doma literatorov,* no. 7 (1 February 1922): 1.

22. Board of the All-Russian Union of Writers to Commissar of Enlightenment A. V. Lunacharskii, 30 December 1921, GARF f.2306, op.1, d.1164, l.10–11ob. (published in Blium, *Za kulisami,* 274–77).

23. Gosizdat Politotdel to Commissar of Enlightenment Lunacharskii, 16 January 1922, GARF f.2306, op.1, d.1164, l.7–9 (published in Blium, *Za kulisami,* 277–80).

24. Protocols of the Narkompros troika, 8 February 1922, GARF f.2306, op.1, d.1164, l.1.

25. N. Meshcheriakov as chief of Gosizdat Politotdel to Lunacharskii, 25 January 1922, GARF f.2306, op.1, d.456, l.66–66ob.; also see P. Lebedev-Polianskii to Lunacharskii, 28 January 1922, GARF f.2306, op.1, d.456, l.69, and Podgornova, *Sovetskoe Knigoizdanie,* 37–38.

26. Lebedev-Polianskii to Lunacharskii, 28 April 1922, ARAN f.597, op.3, d.11, l.1–2ob.; A. V. Blium, ed., "Iz perepiski A.V. Lunacharskogo i P.I. Lebedev-Polianskogo," *De Visu,* 1993, no. 10 (11): 16–23; Fox, "Glavlit," 1050–51, 1060–62.

27. Excerpts from Politburo protocols, 13 February 1922, in *Vlast' i khudozhestvennaia intelligentsiia. Dokumenty RKP(b)-VKP(b), VChK-OGPU-NKVD o kul'turnoi politike. 1917–1953 gg.,* comp. Andrei Artizov and Oleg Naumov (Moscow: Mezhdunarodnyi fond "Demokratiia," 1999), 35.

28. N. L. Meshcheriakov, "O chastnykh izdatel'stvakh," *Pechat' i revoliutsiia,* no. 6 (July–August 1922): 128–34.

29. Lenin to N. P. Gorbunov, 6 February 1922, *PSS,* 54: 155–56. Meshcheriakov responded the next day by outlining current Politotdel procedures (ibid., 609–10; Dinershtein, "Reforma," 84).

30. Agitprop protocols, 21 February 1922, RGASPI f.17, op.60, d.141, l.16.

31. Ibid., l.16–17. See also Gosizdat protocols, 28 February 1922, GARF f.395, op.9, d.195, l.47–48.

32. See Pethybridge, "Concern," 445.

33. "Pis'mo tov. L.D. Trotskogo," *Pod znamenem marksizma,* 1922, nos. 1–2 (January–February): 5–7 (quotes from 6). This issue actually appeared in March, after the aforementioned Agitprop resolutions.

34. Agitprop protocols, 23 February 1922, RGASPI f.17, op.60, d.141, l.18–19ob.; Orgburo protocols, 27 February 1922, RGASPI f.17, op.112, d.293, l.2.

35. Head of Gosizdat Politotdel N. Meshcheriakov to Orgburo, 2 March 1922, and Orgburo protocols, 3 March 1922, RGASPI f.17, op.112, d.295, l.27–27ob., 2; Petrograd Gosizdat Politotdel to *Vestnik literatury* editorial board, [8 March 1922], RO IRLI f.592, op.1, d.411, l.1; Lutokhin, "Sovetskaia tsenzura," 159.

36. Agitprop protocols, 21 March 1922, RGASPI f.17, op.60, d.141, l.20–21; Politburo protocols, 22 March 1922, RGASPI f.17, op.3, d.284, l.3. A commission consisting of Unshlikht, Lunacharskii, and Rykov was assigned to work out the details of this newly formed body in charge of censorship.

37. "Utrennee zasedanie 1-go aprelia. Sodoklad tov. Iakovleva," *Pravda,* 2 April 1922, 3.

38. S. L. Frank, *Ocherk metodologii obshchestvennykh nauk* (Moscow: Bereg, 1922); N. O. Losskii, *Logika* (Petrograd: Nauka i shkola, 1922); L. Karsavin, *Noctes Petropolitanae* (Petrograd: [A. S. Kagan], 1922). Academia and Nauka i Shkola were associated with a number of eminent philosophers, historians, and literary critics, whereas Semën Frank and others had founded Bereg.

39. V. Nevskii, "Nostradamusy XX-go veka," *Pod znamenem marksizma,* 1922, no. 4 (April): 95–100; Nevskii, "Restavratsiia idealizma i bor'ba s 'novoi' burzhuaziei," *Pod znamenem marksizma,* 1922, nos. 7–8 (July–August): 121–31; I. Borichevskii, "Neskol'ko slov o tak nazyvaemoi 'russkoi filosofii'" and "Dogmaticheskoe bogoslovie pod pokrovom filosofii," *Kniga i revoliutsiia* 2, no. 3 (15) (1922): 31–36; V. Bystrianskii, "Pokushenie s negodnymi sredstvami," *Kniga i revoliutsiia* 2, no. 7 (19) (1922): 1–8. On the campaign against idealism, see also Pethybridge, "Concern," and Fediukin, *Bor'ba,* 36–39.

40. A Russian translation did not appear until late 1922; what was available was the German original of volume 1 and excerpts from volume 2 ("Predislovie," *Osval'd Shpengler i Zakat Evropy* [Moscow: Bereg, 1922], 3).

41. Stepun, *Byvshee,* 2: 275–79; A. Lavretskii, "Iz auditorii. Zakat Evropy. (Lektsiia F. A. Stepuna)," *Narodnoe prosveshchenie* (weekly), no. 92 (10 December 1921), 13.

42. H. Stuart Hughes, *Oswald Spengler: A Critical Estimate,* rev. ed. (New York: Charles Scribner's Sons, 1962).

43. S. L. Frank, "*De Profundis,*" 219–34; Boobbyer, *S. L. Frank,* 117–19. See also Izgoev's essay in Woehrlin, *Out of the Depths,* "Socialism, Culture, and Bolshevism," 125–44.

44. Spengler reserved for Russia a special place outside European civilization. *The Decline of the West* had much in common with and may have even been partially influenced both by the Pan-Slavist Nikolai Danilevskii's *Russia and Europe* and by the conservative romantic Konstantin Leont'ev's *Byzantium and Slavdom.* Spengler, although horrified by Bolshevism, did give it credit for clearing away the artificial imperial edifice (Hughes, *Spengler,* 44–50, 53–54, 147–49; Andrzej Walicki, *The Slavophile Controversy: History of a Conservative Utopia in Nineteenth-Century Russian Thought,* trans. Hilda Andrews-Rusiecka [Oxford: Clarendon Press, 1975], 503–8, 513–30).

45. Nikolai Berdiaev, "Predsmertnye mysli Fausta," in *Osval'd Shpengler,* 71–72.

46. Fëdor Stepun, "Osval'd Shpengler i Zakat Evropy," in *Osval'd Shpengler*, 5–7, 12–16, 26, 30–31.

47. S. L. Frank, "Krizis zapadnoi kul'tury," in *Osval'd Shpengler*, 35–41, 49–54 (quote on 40). See also Boobbyer, *S. L. Frank*, 113–14.

48. See, e.g., P. F. Preobrazhenskii, "Osval'd Shpengler i krushenie istiny. (Stranitsy iz istorii gibeli odnoi kul'tury)," *Pechat' i revoliutsiia*, no. 4 (1) (January–February 1922): 58–65. The author, a fellow-traveler professor of ancient history at MGU, was sympathetic to Spengler's portrait of decaying bourgeois Europe and of its "universal" truths but criticized his unremitting hostility to socialism.

49. Lenin to Gorbunov, 5 March 1922, *PSS*, 54: 198.

50. Karl Grasis, "Vekhisty o Shpenglere," *Krasnaia nov'*, 1922, no. 2 (6) (March–April): 196–211; Sergei Bobrov, "Kontuzhennyi razum," *Krasnaia nov'*, 1922, no. 2 (6) (March–April): 231–41; and P. Preobrazhenskii, review of *Osval'd Shpengler. Zakat Evropy*, by N. A. Berdiaev et al., *Pechat' i revoliutsiia*, no. 5 (April–June 1922): 307–9.

51. G. Piatakov, "Filosofiia sovremennogo imperializma. (Etiud o Shpenglere)," *Krasnaia nov'*, 1922, no. 3 (7) (May): 182–97. (Piatakov wrote in response to an inadequately critical article by V. Bazarov, "O. Shpengler i ego kritiki," *Krasnaia nov'*, 1922, no. 2 [6] [March–April]: 211–31.) V. Vaganian, "Nashi rossiiskie shpengleristy," *Pod znamenem marksizma*, 1922, nos. 1–2 (January–February): 28–33.

52. In his 5 March 1922 letter to Gorbunov (see n. 49), Lenin mentioned that he was going to have a talk about the Russian Spengler book with Unshlikht, as will be discussed in chapter 7.

53. We have already seen Frank's and Berdiaev's disappointment with this. See also Boris Vysheslavtsev, "Zakat Evropy (Ob Osval'de Shpenglere)," *Feniks* (Moscow), no. 1 (1922): 114–21.

54. The literary evenings and jubilees are discussed in chapter 4. On the commemoration of Pushkin, see Robert P. Hughes, "Pushkin in Petrograd, February 1921," in *Cultural Mythologies of Russian Modernism: From the Golden Age to the Silver Age*, ed. Boris Gasparov et al. (Berkeley: University of California Press, 1992), 204–13. On Blok see, inter alia, "Velikaia utrata. A. A. Blok skonchalsia 7-go avgusta," *Vestnik literatury*, 1921, no. 8 (August): 9–12; "Uvekovechenie pamiati A. A. Bloka," *Vestnik literatury*, 1921, no. 9 (September): 13; Iul'ii Aikhenval'd, *Poety i poetessy* (Moscow: Severnye dni, 1922), 7–30; *Ob Aleksandre Bloke. Sbornik statei* (Petrograd: Kartonnyi domik, 1921); P. Guber, "Poet i Revoliutsiia," *Letopis' doma literatorov*, no. 1 (1 November 1921): 1–2; K. I. Chukovskii, "Stikhotvornye poslaniia Bloka," *Letopis' doma literatorov*, no. 2 (15 November 1921): 6; and A. Belyi, "Vospominaniia ob Aleksandre Bloke," *Literaturnye zapiski*, 1922, no. 2 (June 23): 23–30. On Korolenko see, inter alia, V. A. Miakotin, ed., *Pamiati Vl. G. Korolenko* (Moscow: Zadruga, 1922); A. B. Petrishchev, ed., *V. G. Korolenko: zhizn' i tvorchestvo. Sbornik statei* (Petersburg: Mysl', 1922); S. Shvetsov, "Iz rannikh vstrech s. V. G. Korolenko," *Vestnik literatury*, 1922, nos. 2–3 (February–March): 11–13; A. V. Peshekhonov, "Iz pis'ma," *Letopis' doma literatorov*, no. 7 (1 February 1922): 2; A. Petrishchev, "Iz vospominanii o V. G. Korolenko," *Letopis' doma literatorov*, no. 7 (1 February 1922): 3; S. D. Protopopov, "Materialy dlia biografii V. G. Korolenko," *Utrenniki* 1 (1922): 85–90. Both Blok and Korolenko were celebrated in official publications as well.

55. The heralding of Dostoevsky as prophet began with Vladimir Solov'ev's "Three Speeches" soon after the author's death and was furthered by D. S. Merezhkovskii's 1906 essay "Prophet of the Revolution." Merezhkovskii's appraisal of the revolutionary ethos (and his interpretation of Dostoevsky's depiction of it) was not nearly as negative as much later Dostoevsky commentary—including Merezhkovskii's own post-1917 writings. (See Vladimir Seduro, *Dostoyevski in Russian Literary Criticism, 1846–1956* [New York: Octagon Books, 1969], 29, 39–46, 127–28, 310–11n.)

56. Nikolai Aleksandrovich Berdiaev, "Specters of the Russian Revolution," in Woehrlin, *Out of the Depths*, 41. He made a similar assertion in his 1921 volume, *Dostoevsky's Worldview:* "In the most exact sense of the word, he was the prophet of the revolution: it took place in the way he said it would; he revealed its inner dialectic and gave it form, grasping its nature in the depth of the spirit's evolution" (Nicholas Berdyaev, *Dostoevsky*, trans. Donald Attwater [London: Sheed and Ward, 1934], 133–34).

57. Both this book and his "End of the Renaissance," also prohibited by the Politotdel, were prepared for publication by the Petrograd-based Epokha, an enterprise launched by Zamiatin and Chukovskii in 1921 (*Bibliographie des oeuvres de Nicolas Berdiaev*, comp. Tamara Klépinine [Paris: YMCA, 1978], 31; "Izdatel'stvo 'Epokha,'" *Novaia russkaia kniga*, 1922, no. 1 [January]: 35). The volume was published in Prague in 1923 and translated into eight languages. The Politotdel's prohibition of this book was protested in the December 1921 letter from the All-Russia Union of Writers to Lunacharskii (see n. 22).

58. Berdyaev, *Dostoevsky*, 133–59 (quotes on 135, 136, and 137).

59. Ibid., 151.

60. Iu. I. Aikhenval'd, "Osoboe mnenie. (K 100-l. rozhdeniia F. M. Dostoevskogo)," *Vestnik literatury*, 1921, no. 10 (October): 1–2.

61. N. Losskii, "O prirode sataninskoi. (Po Dostoevskomu)," *F. M. Dostoevskii: Stat'i i materialy*, vol. 1, ed. A. S. Dolinin (Petrograd: Mysl', 1922), 67–92.

62. L. P. Karsavin, "Fëdor Mikhailovich Dostoevskii. (30 okt. 1821–28 ianv. 1881)," *Artel'noe delo*, 1921, nos. 17–20: 2–4; reprinted in *Lepta*, 1993, no. 5: 124–27 (quote on 125).

63. P. Sorokin, "Zavety Dostoevskogo," *Artel'noe delo*, 1921, nos. 17–20: 4–7, italics in original.

64. V. Bonch-Bruevich, *Vospominaniia* (Moscow: Khudozhestvennaia literatura, 1968), 23; Robert Louis Jackson, "In the Interests of Social Pedagogy: Gorky's Polemic against the Staging of *The Devils* in 1913 and the Aftermath in 1917," in his *Dialogues with Dostoevsky: The Overwhelming Questions* (Stanford: Stanford University Press, 1993), 121–33; Marc Slonim, "Dostoevsky under the Soviets," *Russian Review* 10, no. 2 (April 1951): 118–30; and Seduro, *Dostoyevski*, 72, 85–93. Shortly after Gorky's condemnation of the stage production of *The Demons*, Lenin referred to a novel by the Ukrainian writer V. K. Vinnichenko as "an arch-awful imitation of the arch-awful Dostoevsky" (Lenin to I. F. Armand, June 1914 [not later than 5 June], *PSS*, 48: 295).

65. K., "V zhurnal'nom mire. III. Dostoevskii i revoliutsiia," *Krasnaia nov'*, 1922, no. 1 (5) (January–February): 289–91. Similarly critical of the idealist interpretation of Dostoevsky was D. Blagoi, review of *Dostoevskii. Stat'i i materialy pod redaktsiei A. S. Dolinina*, in *Pechat' i revoliutsiia*, no. 8 (November–December 1922): 213–15.

66. V. Pereverzev, "Dostoevskii i revoliutsiia. (K stoletiiu so dnia rozhdeniia)," *Pechat' i revoliutsiia,* no. 3 (November–December 1921): 3–10. See also Slonim, "Dostoevsky," 124–25, and Seduro, *Dostoyevski,* 128–33.

67. A. V. Lunacharskii, "Dostoevskii, kak khudozhnik i myslitel', " *Krasnaia nov',* 1921, no. 4 (November–December): 204–11 (quote on 211). See also Seduro, *Dostoyevski,* 193–95.

68. V. Friche, "F.M. Dostoevskii. (1821–1921)," *Narodnoe prosveshchenie,* no. 91 (25 November 1921): 6–7.

69. Ch. Betrinskii, "Dni Dostoevskogo. (Pis'mo iz Moskvy)," *Vestnik literatury,* 1921, no. 12 (December): 9.

70. V. Pereverzev, *Tvorchestvo Dostoevskogo* (Moscow: Gosizdat, 1922). For a thorough catalog of Dostoevskiana during this period, see N. A. Sokolov, "Materialy dlia bibliografii F. M. Dostoevskogo, 1903–1923 g.g.," appendix to *F. M. Dostoevskii. Stat'i i materially,* vol. 2, ed. A. S. Dolinin (Moscow: Mysl', 1924).

71. Seduro, *Dostoyevski,* 132–33, 139.

72. See Hilde Hardeman's excellent *Coming to Terms with the Soviet Regime: The "Changing Signposts" Movement among Russian Emigrés in the Early 1920s* (Dekalb: Northern Illinois University Press, 1994); and also Mikhail Agursky, *The Third Rome: National Bolshevism in the USSR* (Boulder, Colo.: Westview Press, 1987).

73. Robert C. Williams, "'Changing Landmarks' in Russian Berlin, 1922–1924," *Slavic Review* 27, no. 4 (December 1968): 581–93 (quote on 581).

74. I. L. [Ia. B. Livshits], "Disput o 'smene vekh,'" *Put',* 9, 10, 13, 14, 15, 16, 17, 18, and 20 December 1921; Ia. Livshits, "Novye i starye vekhi. (Dva sobesedovaniia v Dome Literatorov o sbornike 'Smena vekh')," *Letopis' doma literatorov,* no. 3 (1 December 1921): 11; Hardeman, *Coming to Terms,* 104–6.

75. Ia. Livshits, "'Vekhi' i 'Smena vekh.' (Disput v Dome Literatorov)," *Letopis' doma literatorov,* nos. 5–6 (15 January 1922), 10–11; "V Dome Literatorov," *Letopis' doma literatorov,* nos. 8–9 (25 February 1922): 8.

76. Sorokin, "'Smena vekh,'" 1–3; Hardeman, *Coming to Terms,* 103–4.

77. A. S. Izgoev, "Vlast' i lichnost'," 3. Sorokin's formulation of the "Anglo-Saxon position" and Izgoev's critique of this conception are discussed in the introduction.

78. A. S. Izgoev, "'Vekhi' i 'Smena vekh,'" in Izgoev et al., *O smene vekh* (Petrograd: Izdatel'stvo "Logos" pri dome literatorov, 1922), 9, 18, 21–24. See also Hardeman, *Coming to Terms,* 93, 106.

79. A. B. Petrishchev, "Chuzhie zemliaki," in Izgoev et al., *O smene vekh,* 70–80. See also Hardeman, *Coming to Terms,* 106–7.

80. J. Clemens, "Novye vekhi i Russkaia gosudarstvennost'," in Izgoev et al., *O smene vekh,* 25–27, 33–51, italics in original. On Brusilov, see Hardeman, *Coming to Terms,* 6–7.

81. Livshits, "'Vekhi' i 'Smena vekh,'" 11.

82. A. Voronskii, "Literaturnye otkliki," *Krasnaia nov',* 1922, no. 2 (6) (March–April): 262–63.

83. E. Preobrazhenskii, "Oblomki staroi Rossii," *Pod znamenem marksizma,* 1922, nos. 1–2 (January–February): 33–35.

84. The Cheka also included the "counterrevolutionary collection 'O *smene vekh*'" in its reasons for deporting Viktor Iretskii, a key figure in the House of Litterateurs. Kleinman, whom the Cheka knew only by his pseudonym, Clemens, was "not located"

during the arrests and not expelled (List of Anti-Soviet Intellectuals, TsA FSB f.1, op.6, d.160E, l.76, and List of Anti-Soviet Intellectuals [annotated by Iagoda], RGASPI f.2, op.2, d.1245, l.7).

85. Hardeman, *Coming to Terms*, 177–79.

86. For a latter-day articulation of this differentiation between the usefulness of the *smenovekhovtsy* and the irreconcilability of "staunch counterrevolutionaries," see Fediukin, *Bor'ba*, 298–300.

87. V. M. Shtein edited *Ekonomicheskoe vozrozhdenie*. *Artel'noe delo* was the organ of the Petrograd Craft-Artel Cooperative Union (*Severokustar'*); its editor, V. S. Miroliubov, fancied making it a general publicistic journal. A number of its contributors were expelled, and Miroliubov was replaced in 1923 (S. I. Subbotin, "'Takie chistye liudi . . .' Viktor Sergeevich Miroliubov: redaktorskaia deiatel'nost' v 1917–1923 godakh," *Lepta*, 1993, no. 5: 117–24).

88. Sorokin uses the English neologism in the original.

89. Pitirim Sorokin, "Nachalo velikoi revizii," *Vestnik literatury*, 1922, nos. 2–3 (February–March): 1–3.

90. P. A. Sorokin, "Voina i militarizatsiia obshchestva," *Artel'noe delo*, 1922, nos. 1–4 (January–February): 3–10.

91. P. A. Sorokin, "Vliianie voiny na sostav naseleniia, ego svoistva i obshchestvennuiu organizatsiiu," *Ekonomist*, 1922, no. 1: 77–107 (esp. 90–97, 101–7), italics in original; Sorokin, "Voina i militarizatsiia," 9–10.

92. Sorokin, *Leaves*, 282–91.

93. Elena Sorokin, prologue to Pitirim A. Sorokin, *Hunger as a Factor in Human Affairs*, trans. Elena Sorokin, ed. T. Lynn Smith (Gainesville: University Presses of Florida, 1975), xxix–xxxvi. Sorokin and his wife managed to smuggle the manuscript out of Russia, but it was published only posthumously.

94. P. A. Sorokin, "Vliianie goloda na sotsial'no-ekonomicheskogo organizatsiiu obshchestva," *Ekonomist*, 1922, no. 2: 23–53.

95. P. A. Sorokin, "Golod i ideologiia obshchestva," *Ekonomist*, 1922, nos. 4–5: 3–5, italics in original.

96. "'Veruiu, Gospodi! Pomogi Moemu Neveriiu,' (neizdannaia stat'ia Pitirima Sorokina)," *Otechestvennye arkhivy*, 1992, no. 2: 47–53, italics and ellipses in original. The page proofs of this piece are in Lutokhin's collection, RO IRLI f.592, op.1, d.380.

97. B. D. Brutskus, "Problemy narodnogo khoziaistva." After his expulsion, it was published in Berlin with the addition of several passages that had been eliminated by the censor (Brutskus, *Sotsialisticheskoe khoziaistvo. Teoreticheskie mysli po povodu russkogo opyta* [Berlin: Tritemis, 1923]; Brutzkus, *Economic Planning in Soviet Russia*, trans. Gilbert Gardiner [London: George Routledge and Sons, 1935]).

98. Brutzkus, *Economic Planning*, xv; cited in John Howard Wilhelm, "The Soviet Economic Failure: Brutzkus Revisited," *Europe-Asia Studies* 45, no. 2 (1993): 344.

99. A pseudonymous article by Izgoev entitled "An Assessment of the Economic State of Contemporary Russia," intended for publication in *Ekonomist*, was banned by the censors. (Page proofs are in RO IRLI f.592, op.1, d.320.)

100. Brutskus, "Problemy narodnogo khoziaistva," no. 1: 52–60, no. 2: 163–73, no. 3: 54–62, 69–72; Wilhelm, "Brutzkus Revisited," 346–49.

101. Lenin, "O znachenii," 11–12.

102. A. Bubnov, "Vozrozhdenie burzhuaznoi ideologii i zadachi agitpropraboty," *Pravda,* 27 July 1922, 2; also in *Kommunisticheskaia revoliutsiia,* 1922, no. 8 (1 August): 4–5. See also R. Arskii, "Reaktsiia. (Neskol'ko zamechanii o No 2 'Ekonomista')," *Petrogradskaia pravda,* 6 April 1922, 2–3.

103. Kedr-Livanskii, "Ob ekonomistakh iz 'Ekonomista' i intelligentsii za granitsei," *Kniga i revoliutsiia* 2, no. 7 (19) (1922): 13; Nevskii, "Restavratsiia idealizma," 128–29; and V. Motylev, "Ob osnovnykh problemakh ekonomicheskoi teorii sotsializma," *Krasnaia nov',* 1922, no. 4 (July–August): 193–206.

104. P. Mesiatsev, "Agrarnyi vopros i agrarnaia politika," *Pod znamenem marksizma,* 1922, no. 3 (March): 104–14. Mesiatsev was critiquing Brutskus's recent book calling for the reprivatization of land (B. D. Brutskus, *Agrarnyi vopros i agrarnaia revoliutsiia* [Petrograd: Pravo, 1922]).

105. "Rech' tov. Lenina na fraktsii Vserossiiskogo s"ezda metallistov," *Pravda,* 8 March 1922, 1–2; "Rezoliutsiia XI s"ezda R.K.P. o pechati i propagande," *Vestnik agitatsii i propagandy,* 1922, nos. 4–5 (15 June): 74–78.

106. Draft report on anti-Soviet groupings among the intelligentsia, sent by Ia. Agranov to GPU chair Dzerzhinskii, 1 June 1922, RGASPI f.17, op.86, d.17, l.55–59.

107. Politburo protocols of 8 June 1922, RGASPI f.17, op.3, d.296, l.2–3, 7, with Unshlikht's Draft Resolution, RGASPI f.17, op.163, d.279, l.11–12.

108. Glavlit would replace the Gosizdat Politotdel a month later.

109. "Illiuzii kontr-revoliutsionnoi 'demokratii,'" *Pravda,* 17 May 1922, 1; and O. [L. D. Trotskii], "Diktatura, gde tvoi khlyst?" *Pravda,* 2 June 1922, 1. The originals of this article, with Trotsky's handwritten corrections, are at www.rusarchives.ru/evants/exhibitions/phliner_doc.shtml.

110. A. Bubnov, "Vozrozhdenie," *Pravda,* 2–3, and *Kommunisticheskaia revoliutsiia,* 3–19. Bubnov's role in editing Zinoviev's speech can be seen in the drafts in RGASPI f.17, op.60, d.154, l.50–53ob., 54–57.

111. Zinov'ev, *Ob antisovetskikh,* 3–47.

112. Ibid., 9–32, 40–41 (quotes on 17, 31). Zinoviev asserted that in using repression, "it is necessary only that the Soviet regime knows when, whom, where, and under what conditions to conduct shootings" (ibid., 42).

113. Stenogram of the Twelfth All-Russian Conference of the RCP(b), RGASPI f.49, op.1, d.3, l.279–81; *Vserossiiskaia konferentsiia R.K.P. (bol'shevikov). Biulleten',* no. 3 (8 August 1922): 3.

114. Zinov'ev, *Ob antisovetskikh,* 48–55. Other Bolshevik leaders present included Kamenev, Bukharin, and Iaroslavskii.

115. "Soveshchanie po voprosam agit-propagandy," *Kommunisticheskaia revoliutsiia,* 1922, nos. 9–10 (1 September): 129–34; N.N., "Partiinoe soveshchanie o pechati," *Zhurnalist,* no. 1 (September 1922): 59–60; A. S. Bubnov, "The Press in the New Conditions," speech to press workers' section, October 1922, RGASPI f.17, op.60, d.154, l.33–37; "Nash plenum. Pechat' v novykh usloviiakh," *Zhurnalist,* no. 2 (1922): 48–49; Mikh. Kol'tsov, "V nastuplenie," *Pravda,* 4 October 1922, 1.

116. *Tretii Vserossiiskii S"ezd politprosvetov R.S.F.S.R. Biulleten',* no. 1 (29 November 1922): 3.

117. Ibid., 7–11. See also Bubnov, "Politicheskie illiuzii NEP'a na ushcherbe," *Kommunisticheskaia revoliutsiia,* 1922, no. 15: 3 (reprinted in *Burzhuaznoe restavratorstvo na vtorom godu NEP'a* [Petrograd: Priboi, 1923], 34).

118. V. Pletnev, "Na ideologicheskom fronte," *Pravda*, 27 September 1922, 2–3; Iakov Iakovlev, "O 'proletarskoi kul'ture' i Proletkul'te," *Pravda*, 24, 25 October 1922, 2–3; B. Frezinskii, "Utopii i real'nosti. (N. I. Bukharin o kul'ture)," in *Revoliutsiia i kul'tura. Stat'i i vystupleniia 1923–1936 godov*, by Nikolai Bukharin (Moscow: Fond imeni N. I. Bukharina, 1993), 9–10; and Mally, *Culture of the Future*, 221–25. Bukharin agreed with Lenin on the need to use *spetsy* but worried about the possible effects on the proletariat (see, inter alia, "Problema kul'tury v epokhu rabochei revoliutsii," *Pravda*, 11 October 1922, 3; and N. Bukharin, "Burzhuaznaia revoliutsiia i revoliutsiia proletarskaia," *Pod znamenem marksizma*, 1922, nos. 7–8 [July–August]: 61–82).

119. Resolutions of Petrograd Agitprop Conference, based on report of A. Bubnov, 17 November 1922, RGASPI f.17, op.60, d.154, l.44, 47–47ob.

120. Orgburo protocols, 1 January 1923, RGASPI f.17, op.112, d.400, l.2.

121. Bubnov, "Politicheskie illiuzii," 3–7, and A. Bubnov, "Ideologiia burzhuaznoi restavratsii v pervonachal'nyi period NEP'a," in his *Na ideologicheskom fronte*, 22–23, 26, 28–29.

122. Sergei B—oi [N. Alekseev], "Formy razvitiia," 82–83.

123. Lutokhin, "Sovetskaia tsenzura," 158, 163–64.

124. By Dzerzhinskii's proposal, Politburo members were to spend at least two to three hours a week perusing "Whiteguard" publications. GPU military censors and Glavlit handled the circulation of these materials, access to which was tightly circumscribed (Orgburo protocols, 10 February 1922; Unshlikht to the Orgburo, 3 March 1922; Unshlikht to Stalin and the CC, 18 May 1922; and Orgburo protocols, 22 May 1922, all in RGASPI f.17, op.112, d.332, l.33–35ob., 2–3; Politburo protocols, 26 May 1922, RGASPI f.17, op.3, d.294, l.3; Secretariat protocols, 9 June 1922, RGASPI f.17, op.112, d.339, l.3, 9; Politburo protocols, 10 August 1922, RGASPI f.17, op.3, d.307, l.3; Secretariat protocols, 29 September 1922, RGASPI f.17, op.112, d.372, l.3–4; and Fox, "Glavlit," 1056).

125. Lenin to Dzerzhinskii, 19 May 1922, *PSS*, 54: 265–66, italics in original; and Lenin to Stalin, 17 July 1922, passed on to Dzerzhinskii, RGASPI f.2, op.2, d.1338, l.1 (also in Koenker and Bachman, *Revelations from the Russian Archives*, 232).

126. A photocopy of Lenin's marked copy of *Utrenniki* is in RGASPI f.2, op.1, d.23245.

127. Lenin to Dzerzhinskii, 19 May 1922, *PSS*, 54: 265–66, italics in original; Politburo protocols, 26 May 1922, RGASPI f.17, op.3, d.294, l.2; Politburo protocols, 1 June 1922, RGASPI f.17, op.3, d.295, l.3. The initial decision to abolish *Novaia Rossiia* is in the Petrogubispolkom protocols, 13 May 1922, TsGALI SPb f.31, op.1, d.2, l.35.

128. The Petrograd GPU censors chided the Politotdel for allowing the publication of the first volume of *Utrenniki* without their having had a chance to examine it (Petrograd military censorship to Gosizdat Politotdel, 9 May 1922, TsGALI SPb f.31, op.1, d.5, l.2).

129. Lutokhin, "Sovetskaia tsenzura," 159–60.

130. Several were closed by order of the Politotdel, others by the Politburo commission on deportations (protocols of the Politburo commission [Unshlikht, chair, Kamenev, Kurskii, Iagoda, and Agranov present], TsA FSB f.1, op.6, d.160E, l.77; Deputy Chair of Petrograd Gosizdat Politotdel to Editorial Board of *Ekonomist*, memo, 11 July 1922, RO IRLI f.592, op.1, d.399; Lutokhin, "Sovetskaia tsenzura," 165).

131. Board of the cooperative publisher Zadruga to Glavlit requesting reconsideration, [not before 28 October] 1922, RGALI f.608, op.2, d.16, l.1–2ob.; Ia. V. Leont'ev, "Kooperativnoe izdatel'stvo 'Zadruga,'" *Kooperatsiia. Stranitsy istorii* 3 (1993): 117. Zadruga board members expelled included Mel'gunov, Kizevetter, V. M. Kudriavtsev, and V. S. Ozeretskovskii ("Iavochnyi list chlenov pravleniia izdatel'stva 'Zadruga,'" RGALI f.305, op.1, d.1309). The GPU forestalled an attempt by former Zadruga leaders to coalesce around a new publishing society called Sredi knig the following year ("Proekt postanovleniia 12-go otdeleniia SO GPU ob izdatel'stvakh 'Zadruga' i 'Sredi knig,'" [March 1922], in Makarov and Khristoforov, *Vysylka vmesto rasstrela*, 180–81).

132. Zubashev and Pumpianskii were both on the board of *Ekonomist.* L. M. Pumpianskii should not be confused with L. V. Pumpianskii, who was active in *Vol'fila* at the same time.

133. List of Anti-Soviet Intellectuals in Petrograd, TsA FSB f.1, op.6, d.160E, l.73.

134. Lutokhin, diary entry for 4–5 February 1923, RO IRLI f.592, op.1, d.3, l.11, emphasis in original. (A slightly abbreviated version of this story is in his "Sovetskaia tsenzura," 166.)

135. The decree establishing Glavlit is in *Izvestiia*, 23 June 1922. See also M. Shchelkunov, "Zakonodatel'stvo o pechati za piat' let," *Pechat' i revoliutsiia*, no. 7 (4) (September–October 1922): 172–88; Blium, *Za kulisami*, 82–85, 105–12; and Brian Kassof, "The Knowledge Front: Politics, Ideology, and Economics in the Soviet Book Publishing Industry, 1925–1935" (Ph.D. diss., University of California, Berkeley, 2000), chap. 4.

136. Protocols of the second meeting of censorship representatives (Ia. Iakovlev, chair), 23 October 1922, and protocols of the Communist Party Secretariat, 10 November 1922, RGASPI f.17, op.112, d.385, l.100, 4.

137. Glavlit circular to its *Oblast'* branches, [before 24 November 1922], TsGALI SPb f.31, op.1, d.2, l.52.

138. Glavlit instructions, signed by Lebedev-Polianskii, to its local organs, [before 29 November 1922], TsGALI SPb f.31, op.1, d.2, l.53–55. Standard forms for evaluating and cataloging book publishers and periodicals were issued, as were the "visas," to be given as a mark of permission (TsGALI SPb f.31, op.1, d.2, l.64–64ob., 65–65ob., 68, 69).

139. Glavlit circular to its *Oblast'* branches, 18 December 1922, TsGALI SPb f.31, op.1, d.2, l.99; cited in Blium, *Za kulisami*, 141; see also Fox, "Glavlit," 1058–59.

140. Unshlikht contended that the extensive dissemination of counterrevolutionary literature made the rapid formation of Glavlit critical (Unshlikht to Stalin and the CC, 1 September 1922, RGASPI f.17, op.112, d.372, l.81).

141. Narkompros instructions, signed by Pokrovskii, on the required registration of publications in the RSFSR and on their supply to state book depositories, 6 May 1922, TsGALI SPb f.31, op.1, d.2, l.7–8ob.

142. Bulletin no. 1, Orgburo Commission on private book market surveillance, "top secret," 10 September [1922], RGASPI f.17, op.60, d.178, l.3–13; Orgburo protocols, 7 December 1922; Meeting of Agitprop Department Heads, 5 December 1922; and Lebedev-Polianskii [with Bubnov's handwritten approval] to Orgburo, "top secret," 28 November 1922, RGASPI f.17, op.112, d.395, l.4, 152, 153.

143. Glavlit Bulletin no. 1, January 1923, RGASPI f.17, op.84, d.309, l.148–211; Glavlit Bulletins no. 2, March 1923, and no. 3, May 1923, TsGALI SPb f.31, op.1, d.13, l.3–138. Copies (marked "top secret") were sent to Lenin, Trotsky, Stalin, Kamenev, Bubnov, Lunacharskii, Unshlikht, and the Petrograd and Kharkov Glavlit branches.

144. Glavlit circular to all regional and provincial organs on examining foreign nonperiodical press, 7 July 1923, and Glavlit top secret circular to all regional and provincial organs, 17 August 1923, TsGALI SPb f.31, op.1, d.9, l.74–75, 130–33; Blium, *Za kulisami,* 86–87, 233–34. Several of Pil'niak's stories were even read in the Politburo after Lunacharskii and Lebedev-Polianskii openly clashed over whether to censor them (Politburo protocols, 10 and 17 August 1922, RGASPI f.17, op.3, d.307, l.2, and d.308, l.5; Blium, *Za kulisami,* 119–20).

145. For instance, of 562 domestically produced manuscripts received in December 1922, 13 (2.3 percent) were forbidden, and 106 others (19 percent) were permitted with corrections. Percentages were higher for private publishers—for the same month, 12 of 155 manuscripts (8 percent) were banned, and 58 others (37 percent) were permitted with corrections. For the same month, the import of 35 of 87 Russian-language books (40 percent) published abroad was prohibited, including all 9 on politics and all 6 on philosophy; of foreign-language books, 78 of 113 (69 percent) were denied permission. Figures were similar for the following months (Glavlit Bulletin no. 2, TsGALI SPb f.31, op.1, d.13, l.6, 60–61).

146. Michael David-Fox has noted that Glavlit was based on the principle that "regulation and control must triumph over other considerations such as compromise with the intelligentsia" (Fox, "Glavlit," 1060).

147. Trotsky to the Politburo, memo, 30 June 1922, RGASPI f.17, op.3, d.302, l.7–8 (published in "'Eta podderzhka vyrazhalas' v forme gonorara,'" *Istochnik,* 1995, no. 6: 132); Blium, *Za kulisami,* 87.

148. Glavlit directed that all bookstores and libraries be checked for materials that had not received a visa (circular to all regional and provincial organs, 17 March 1923, TsGALI SPb f.31, op.1, d.9, l.17).

149. "Literatura i NEP," *Literaturnye zapiski,* 1922, no. 2 (June 23): 1–2.

150. S. Ingulov, "Mysli o s"ezde," *Zhurnalist,* no. 5 (1923): 3–10; cited in Matthew Lenoe, *Closer to the Masses: Stalinist Culture, Social Revolution, and Soviet Newspapers* (Cambridge: Harvard University Press, 2004), 22.

151. As Katerina Clark has noted, during NEP "the majority of private publishing houses existed in little more than name, and costs and increasingly heavy taxation ensured that they progressively dwindled in numbers and were effectively eliminated well before plan years" ("Quiet Revolution," 210–11; see also Blium, *Za kulisami,* 134).

Chapter 6. The Deportations, Part I: Precedents and Planning

Epigraph: "Ob antisovetskikh techeniiakh," *Petrogradskaia Pravda,* 5 September 1922, 2.

1. Zinov'ev, *Ob antisovetskikh,* 9.

2. As A. L. Litvin notes, "In contrast to the VChK, which was seen as a commission created in an extraordinary time for the defense of the revolution, the GPU . . . occupied a principal place in the protection of the totalitarian state" (*Krasnyi i belyi terror v Rossii: 1918–1922 gg.* [Kazan': Tatarskoe gazetno-zhurnal'noe izdatel'stvo, 1995], 301–2). See also A. M. Plekhanov, *VChK-OGPU. 1921–1928 gg.* (Moscow: Izdatel'stvo "X-History," 2003), 98–108; L. A. Boeva, *Deiatel'nost' VChK-OGPU po formirovaniiu loial'nosti grazhdan politicheskomu rezhimu (1921–1924 gg.)* (Moscow: "Kompaniia Sputnik+," 2003), 39–64; S. V. Leonov, "Reorganizatsiia VChK v

GPU," in *Istoricheskie chteniia na Lubianke, 1999 god: Otechestvennye spetssluzhby v 1920–1930-kh godakh* (Moscow and Novgorod: Federal'naia sluzhba bezopasnosti RF/Novgorod State University, 2000), 36–42; and Leggett, *Cheka,* 346–50.

3. The discursive constitution of enemies is the subject of Donald J. Raleigh, "Languages of Power: How the Saratov Bolsheviks Imagined Their Enemies," *Slavic Review* 57, no. 2 (Summer 1998): 320–49

4. See Krasil'nikov, "Vysylka i ssylka," 28–44; and Leggett, *Cheka,* 339–52.

5. Lenin's centrality is emphasized in A. M. Gak et al., "Deportatsiia inakomysliashchikh," 75–89.

6. Frank Golder, an ARA official and historian, observed: "The Bolsheviks are very human and very parvenu and very eager to stand well in the eyes of their neighbors" (Golder to Christian Herter, 16 October 1922, in Golder, *War, Revolution, and Peace in Russia: The Passages of Frank Golder,* comp. and ed. Terence Emmons and Bertrand M. Patenaude [Stanford: Hoover Institution Press, 1992], 233).

7. Jacques Rossi, *The Gulag Handbook: An Encyclopedia Dictionary of Soviet Penitentiary Institutions and Terms Related to the Forced Labor Camps,* trans. William A. Burhans (New York: Paragon House, 1989), 70, 425.

8. See Krasil'nikov, "Vysylka i ssylka," 27–28.

9. CC Secretary Molotov and VChK chair Dzerzhinskii, memo, "secret," [not before 17 February] 1921, RGASPI f.17, op.84, d.228, l.52.

10. Fëdor Dan, *Dva goda skitanii (1919–1921)* (Berlin: Russische Bucherzentrale "Obrasowanije," 1922), 236.

11. VChK Deputy Chair Unshlikht to Politburo, 4 June 1921, in "Stsenarii 'do-likvidatsii.' Planovost' v rabote VChK-GPU," *Nezavisimaia gazeta,* 8 May 1992, 5. Cheka leaders warned that the SRs and Mensheviks would use NEP to corrupt workers and peasants (VChK Chair Dzerzhinskii et al. to all regional chekas, September 1921, RGASPI f.17, op.84, d.227, l.55–56ob.).

12. Political prisoners to VTsIK, declarations, 28 April and 7 May 1921, in *Men'sheviki v 1921–1922 gg.,* ed. Z. Galili and A. Nenarokov (Moscow: Rosspen, 2002), 213–15, 229–31; Boris Dvinov, *Ot legal'nosti k podpol'iu (1921–1922)* (Stanford: Hoover Institution, 1968), 45–46; Broido, *Lenin and the Mensheviks,* 125–26; André Liebich, *From the Other Shore: Russian Social Democracy after 1921* (Cambridge: Harvard University Press, 1997), 93. Striking workers and political opponents were sent to provincial prisons on several additional occasions in 1921.

13. Dan, *Dva goda,* 233; GPU report on the work of members of anti-Soviet parties among the youth, signed by Unshlikht, n.d. [1922], RGASPI f.17, op.84, d.231, l.33–36.

14. Dvinov, *Ot legal'nosti,* 72; and Iu. O. Martov to P. B. Aksel'rod, 3 December 1922, in *Men'sheviki v 1921–1922 gg.,* 383. On the deportation of the leaders of the famine relief committee, see chapter 1.

15. RSDLP Moscow Committee, declaration, December 1921, in *Men'sheviki v 1921–1922 gg.,* 394. See also protest of RSDLP CC to VTsIK, 8 December 1922, ibid., 387–88; Dvinov, *Ot legal'nosti,* 77–78.

16. Politburo protocols, 14 December 1921, RGASPI f.17, op.3, d.244, l.3; Krasil'nikov, "Vysylka i ssylka," 29–30.

17. The committee to purge Mensheviks and SRs from public organizations, created in late 1921, is mentioned in, inter alia, Politburo protocols, 20 March 1922, RGASPI, f.17, op.3, d.283, l.114.

18. Social-Democratic prisoners in Butyrka to VTsIK, declaration, 2–4 January 1921, in *Men'sheviki v 1921–1922 gg.*, 398–401; Deputy Chair of VChK Unshlikht to Lenin and the Politburo, 7 January 1922, with VChK resolution on the deportations, RGASPI f.5, op.2, d.46, l.9–10; Dan, *Dva goda*, 236–50; Politburo protocols, 5 January 1922, RGASPI f.17, op.3, d.249, l.6–7; Dvinov, *Ot legal'nosti*, 82–83.

19. The Bolsheviks, Dan claimed, were "afraid of the Mensheviks, as of fire" and wanted them gone before Moscow soviet elections. Their haste met logistical obstacles, as it would later in the year, in this case problems with Latvian and German visas (Dan, *Dva goda*, 253–64; Dvinov, *Ot legal'nosti*, 84; Gak, "Deportatsiia inakomysliashchikh," 78; *Sotsialisticheskii vestnik*, 23 February 1922, 11).

20. Dan, *Dva goda*, 267, ellipses in original.

21. Dvinov, *Ot legal'nosti*, 85.

22. The Menshevik organ *Sotsialisticheskii vestnik* declared that "the date marked by the banishment of social-democrats from Russia is one of the most disgraceful dates in the history of the decay and growth of the Bolshevik dictatorship" ("Izgnanie iz kommunisticheskogo raiia," *Sotsialisticheskii vestnik*, 3 February 1922, 14).

23. Mensheviks often felt that they could rely on the sympathies of certain Bolshevik leaders to soften punishment (Liebich, *From the Other Shore*, 91–92; Broido, *Lenin and the Mensheviks*, 51).

24. Lenin to Molotov for members of the Politburo, 30 January 1922, and Lenin to Unshlikht, 31 January 1922, in *PSS*, 54: 148–49.

25. Politburo protocols, 20 April 1922, RGASPI f.17, op.3, d.289; l.4; T. I. Til,' "Sotsial-demokraticheskoe dvizhenie molodezhi 1920–kh godov," *Pamiat': istoricheskii sbornik* 3 (New York: YMCA Press, 1980 [Moscow, 1978]), 189–90, 198–200; Liebich, *From the Other Shore*, 127. The group remained active despite these arrests, continuing to put out its illegal journal, *Iunii proletarii*, and it therefore remained a frequent target of GPU attentions into the mid-1920s. (See also Broido, *Lenin and the Mensheviks*, 102–3.)

26. P. A. Podbolotov and L. M. Spirin, *Krakh men'shevizma v sovetskoi Rossii* (Leningrad: Lenizdat, 1988), 196; Dvinov, *Ot legal'nosti*, 140. Similar deportations had occurred or were to occur from other cities as well, including Kharkov (Dvinov, *Ot legal'nosti*, 152).

27. Dvinov, *Ot legal'nosti*, 142–47; S. Wolin, *Men'shevizm v pervye gody NEPa* (New York: Inter-University Project on the History of the Menshevik Movement, 1961), 75.

28. Liebich notes that Menshevik leaders quickly understood the role the epithet *Menshevism* was coming to play (*From the Other Shore*, 125, 378nn8–9).

29. Litvin, *Krasnyi i belyi terror*, 301–2; Leonov, "Reorganizatsiia VChK v GPU," 36–42; Boeva, *Deiatel'nost' VChK-OGPU*, 39–64; Plekhanov, *VChK-OGPU*, 98–108; Leggett, *Cheka*, 339–52.

30. Secret Department circular to local GPU organs, 25 April 1922, in "V. I. Lenin: 'Khoroshii kommunist v to zhe vremia est' i khoroshii chekist,'" *Istochnik*, 1996, no. 1: 116–17.

31. Lenin to D. I. Kurskii, 20 February 1922, "On the tasks of Narkomiust under NEP," *PSS*, 44: 396–97, italics in original; and Lenin, "Supplement to draft of RSFSR criminal code" and letter to D. I. Kurskii, 17 May 1922, *PSS*, 45: 190–91. On his meeting with Kurskii see ibid., 45: 549.

32. Izmozik, *Glaza i ushi*, 110–18, 133–34; Holquist, "Information," 432–43; Terry Martin, "Obzory OGPU i Sovetskie istoriki," in *"Sovershenno sekretno": Lubianka—*

Stalinu o polozhenii v strane (1922–1934 gg.), vol. 1 (1922–1923), ed. G. N. Sevost'ianov et al. (Moscow: Institut rossiiskoi istorii RAN, 2001), 21–26; Nicolas Werth, "A State against Its People: Violence, Repression, and Terror in the Soviet Union," in *The Black Book of Communism: Crimes, Terror, Repression*, ed. Stéphane Courtois et al., trans. Jonathan Murphy and Mark Kramer (Cambridge: Harvard University Press, 1999), 134–35.

33. Politburo protocols, 20 March 1922, RGASPI, f.17, op.3, d.283, l.114. On the activities of the Bureaus of Assistance in VUZy, see Krasil'nikov, "Politbiuro, GPU i intelligentsiia," 52–53.

34. Unshlikht, resolution on Bureaus of Assistance, confirmed by the Politburo, 22 March 1922, RGASPI f.17, op.3, d.284, l.4, 10–11; "V. I. Lenin: 'Khoroshii kommunist,'" 115–16.

35. Iagoda and Samsonov, circular, 22 April 1922, in "V. I. Lenin: 'Khoroshii kommunist,'" 117–19.

36. N. Krupskaia, "Obstanovka, v kotoroi pisalas' stat'ia Lenina 'O znachenii voinstvuiushchego materializma,'" *Pod znamenem marksizma*, 1933, no. 1: 148–49.

37. See, inter alia, John Shelton Curtiss, *The Russian Church and the Soviet State, 1917–1950* (Boston: Little, Brown, 1953), 106–28.

38. Jonathan W. Daly, "'Storming the Last Citadel': The Bolshevik Assault on the Church, 1922," in *The Bolsheviks in Russian Society: The Revolution and the Civil Wars*, ed. Vladimir N. Brovkin (New Haven: Yale University Press, 1997), 239–40; and N. A. Krivova, *Vlast' i Tserkov' v 1922–1925 gg. Politbiuro i GPU v bor'be za tserkovnye tsennosti i politicheskoe podchinenie dukhovenstva* (Moscow: AIRO-XX, 1997), 35–36.

39. Daly, "Bolshevik Assault," 244–45; Krivova, *Vlast' i Tserkov'*, 36–41, 53–62.

40. V. I. Lenin to V. M. Molotov for members of the Politburo, 19 March 1922, in "Iz arkhivov partii," *Izvestiia TsK KPSS*, no. 4 (1990), 190–93; cited in Daly, "Bolshevik Assault," 245, and Krivova, *Vlast' i Tserkov'*, 63–65.

41. Politburo protocols, 20 March 1922, RGASPI f.17, op.3, d.283, l.6–7 (published in "Iz arkhivov," 194–95); "Supplement" to Politburo protocols, 22 March 1922, RGASPI f.17, op.3, d.284, l.9; Krivova, *Vlast' i Tserkov'*, 66–69; Daly, "Bolshevik Assault," 246; Trotsky to the Politburo on measures to seize church valuables, accepted by the Politburo, 23 March 1922, in *Politbiuro i Tserkov', 1922–1925 gg.*, vols. 1–2 of *Arkhivy Kremlia*, ed. N. N. Pokrovskii and S. G. Petrov (Moscow: Rosspen, 1997–98), 1: 154.

42. Daly, "Bolshevik Assault," 248–50; Curtiss, *Russian Church*, 114–15.

43. GPU report to the Politburo on the activities of clergymen in connection with the seizure of church valuables, 20 March 1922, in *Politbiuro i Tserkov'*, 1: 149–50.

44. Krivova, *Vlast' i Tserkov'*, 52. This was accompanied by the creation of the sixth branch of the GPU Secret Department, to which was designated jurisdiction over church matters (ibid., 83).

45. See Curtiss, *Russian Church*, 119–20. For a detailed account of the Moscow process and its aftermath, see Krivova, *Vlast' i Tserkov,'* 125–43.

46. This despite Tikhon's having explicitly disavowed the émigré calls for the restoration of the monarchy and denying any intention of calling believers to rise up against the Soviet regime (Patriarch Tikhon to the GPU, declaration, 5 April 1922, in *Politbiuro i Tserkov'*, 2: 145).

47. Quoted in Curtiss, *Russian Church*, 120.

48. Kamenev, Tomskii, Rykov, and on occasion Kalinin preferred more lenient sentences; Lenin, Zinoviev, Stalin, Trotsky, and Molotov usually favored harsher punishment. Kamenev's proposal to commute the sentences of several Moscow clergymen was accepted as the basis for a deal with the renovationists in which they would issue a declaration openly supporting the regime and denouncing the patriarch and Synod leaders (Krivova, *Vlast' i Tserkov'*, 137–42; Daly, "Bolshevik Assault," 252–53; notes on the results of the Politburo voting on Kamenev's suggestion, [8 May 1922], in *Politbiuro i Tserkov'*, 1: 213–14).

49. Krivova, *Vlast' i Tserkov'*, 137–39. This declaration was printed in *Izvestiia* on 13 May 1922.

50. Krivova, *Vlast' i Tserkov'*, 147–50; Daly, "Bolshevik Assault," 255–58.

51. The events outlined in Semenov's piece, particularly the supposed SR involvement in Fania Kaplan's August 1918 assassination attempt on Lenin, were to form the basis of the charges against the SR leaders tried in summer 1922 (Marc Jansen, *A Show Trial under Lenin: The Trial of the Socialist Revolutionaries, Moscow, 1922*, trans. Jean Sanders [The Hague: Martinus Nijhoff, 1982], 23–25; S. A. Krasil'nikov and K. N. Morozov, "Predislovie," in *Sudebnyi protsess nad sotsialistami-revoliutsionerami [iun'–avgust 1922 g.]*, comp. Krasil'nikov, Morozov, and I. V. Chubykin [Moscow: Rosspen, 2002], 20–26).

52. Unshlikht's proposal concerning Semenov to Politburo, 23 March 1922, RGASPI f.17, op.3, d.285, l.7.

53. On the Cheka's instructions concerning the need to combat SR and Menshevik influence among peasants and workers, see n. 11, above.

54. Unshlikht et al.,GPU digest on the internal political position in the RSFSR, March 1922, RGASPI f.17, op.84, d.296, l.11.

55. Lenin to Kurskii, 20 February 1922, "On the tasks of Narkomiust under NEP," *PSS*, 44: 396–97.

56. Cited in Jansen, *Show Trial under Lenin*, 107.

57. Preobrazhenskii warned the Politburo that it had lost the case against the SRs in the court of international opinion, and that "the death penalty would be an enormous political mistake" (Preobrazhenskii to Politburo, 26 July 1922, in Krasil'nikov, Morozov, and Chubykin, *Sudebnyi protsess*, 309; see also L. S. Sosnovskii to Trotsky, 22 July 1922, and G. Ia. Sokol'nikov to the CC RCP, 31 July 1922, ibid., 304–5, 315–16).

58. Jansen, *Show Trial under Lenin*, 164–66. Lenin noted that though Gorky's letter had been "vile," the attacks in response had perhaps been excessive (Lenin to Bukharin, 7 September 1922, RGASPI f.2, op.1, d.24803, l.1).

59. As will be discussed in chapter 7.

60. Krasil'nikov and Morozov, "Predislovie," 27–28, 43–51; Jansen, *Show Trial under Lenin*, 47.

61. A. Lunacharskii, *Byvshie liudi: Ocherk istorii partii es-erov* (Moscow: Gosizdat, 1922), 79–80.

62. Jansen, *Show Trial under Lenin*, 134–35.

63. Dzerzhinskii to Samsonov, n.d. [late August 1922], RGASPI f.76, op.3, d.399, l.6.

64. Jansen, *Show Trial under Lenin*, 174–75.

65. GPU deputy chair Unshlikht et al., GPU report on the political-economic condition of the Republic for October 1922, n.d. [November 1922], RGASPI f.17, op.84, d.296, l.60–61.

66. Jansen, *Show Trial under Lenin,* 176–77; A. I. Iur'ev, "Poslednie stranitsy istorii partii sotsialistov-revoliutsionerov," *Otechestvennaia istoriia,* 2001, no. 6 (November–December): 129–35.

67. Not all Bolsheviks believed that these conversions were genuine. Although Dzerzhinskii calmly noted that SRs mistakenly released from prison could easily be rearrested (Iur'ev, "Poslednie stranitsy," 131), past sins often proved dangerous later on, when the search for enemies became even more relentless.

68. Lenin to N. P. Gorbunov, 5 March 1922, *PSS,* 54: 198.

69. See chapter 5.

70. Lenin, "O mezhdunarodnom i vnutrennem polozhenii sovetskoi respubliki. Rech' na zasedanii kommunisticheskoi fraktsii vserossiiskogo s"ezda metallistov," 6 March 1922, *PSS,* 45: 9, italics in original.

71. Lenin, "O znachenii voinstvuiushchego materializma," 12.

72. Lenin, speeches at the Eleventh Party Congress, 27–28 March 1922, *PSS,* 45: 89, 121.

73. Politburo protocols, 27 April 1922, RGASPI f.17, op.3, d.290, l.4. Shortly after her expulsion, Kuskova received a letter from Gorky claiming that he had been told of the impending deportation of all of the members of the famine relief committee in April (Gorky to Kuskova, 30 June 1922, GARF f.5865, op.1, d.389, l.9). In Germany and out of favor, he was powerless to intervene.

74. "Sud'ba i raboty Russkikh pisatelei, uchenykh i zhurnalistov za 1918–1922 g.," *Novaia russkaia kniga,* 1922, no. 4: 35; Tsekipros to VChK, 10 February 1922, and Unshlikht for VChK Secret Department to Tsekipros, [February 1922], GARF f.5462, op.4, d.110, l.11–12. Local Bolsheviks accused Kuskova of instigating provocative speeches at a January 1922 regional cooperators' congress. Prokopovich initially taught at the Vologda Institute of Education until this was brought to the attention of the State Academic Council (GUS) political section (excerpts from State Academic Council scientific-political section protocols, 14 April 1922, GARF f.298, op.2, d.64, l.37).

75. E. D. Kuskova to S. P. Mel'gunov, 26 April 1922, RGALI f.305, op.1, d.460, l.17ob.–18; also Kuskova to E. P. Peshkova, 20 March and 4 May 1922, Institut mirovoi literatury Arkhiv A. M. Gor'kogo [Arkhiv Gor'kogo] FEP-kr. 36–19–10 and 36–19–2. She complained of her inability to acquire materials and write in Kashin, where she had been sent "without having committed any crime" (Kuskova to D. A. Lutokhin, 9 May 1922, RO IRLI f.592, op.1, d.169, l.1–2ob.).

76. E. D. Kuskova to D. A. Lutokhin, 27 May 1922, GARF f.636, op.1, d.99, l.8, and Kuskova to Lutokhin, n.d., GARF f.636, op.1, d.99, l.6–7.

77. E. D. Kuskova to P. E. Mel'gunova, 4 June 1922, RGALI f.305, op.1, d.1356, l.1–2ob.

78. Unshlikht to Stalin, 10 May 1922, in *Lubianka. Stalin i VChK-GPU-OGPU-NKVD, Ianvar' 1922–dekabr' 1936,* ed. A. N. Iakovlev, comp. V. N. Khaustov et al. (Moscow: Mezhdunarodnyi fond "Demokratiia," 2003), 28. See also Unshlikht to Stalin, 23 May 1922, ibid., 29; and Krasil'nikov, "Vysylka i ssylka," 28–29.

79. Krasil'nikov, "Vysylka i ssylka," 29.

80. Lenin, additions to draft of RSFSR criminal code and letter to Kurskii, 15 May 1922, *PSS,* 45: 189.

81. "Postanovlenie Vserossiiskogo Tsentral'nogo Ispolnitel'nogo Komiteta. O vvedenii v deistvii Ugolovnogo Kodeksa RSFSR," and "Ugolovnyi Kodeks RSFSR," *SUR*, 1922, art. 153, pp. 202–39.

82. Article 57 reads, "Any attempt to overthrow the victorious proletarian revolution, the worker-peasant Soviet regime, and the worker-peasant government . . . , and any attempt to aid that part of the international bourgeoisie, that . . . strives to overthrow it by means of intervention, blockade, spying, financing the press, etc., is to be considered counterrevolutionary" ("Ugolovnyi Kodeks," 209).

83. Lenin to Kurskii, 15 May 1922, *PSS*, 45: 189, italics in original. Other Bolsheviks echoed this rhetoric, stressing the ties between internal and external enemies, and the language was incorporated into Article 57.

84. Lenin, additions to draft of RSFSR criminal code and letter to Kurskii, 17 May 1922, *PSS*, 45: 190–91, italics in original.

85. Exile is explicitly mentioned as an appropriate punishment in Article 70 only for "propaganda and agitation in the direction of aiding the international bourgeoisie" ("Ugolovnyi kodeks," 211).

86. Lenin to Dzerzhinskii, 19 May 1922, *PSS*, 53: 265–66, italics in original.

87. Lenin's handwritten notes for his letter to Dzerzhinskii emphasize that it was particularly critical for Politburo members to read Whiteguard literature diligently (RGASPI f.2, op.1, d.23229, l.1).

88. Semashko to Lenin and all Politburo members, 21 May 1922, RGASPI f.2, op.1, d.23224, l.1. The underlining is Lenin's (cited in Krasil'nikov, "Politbiuro, GPU i intelligentsiia," 34–35).

89. Lenin, *PSS*, 45: 270; Krasil'nikov, "Politbiuro, GPU i intelligentsiia," 35; Politburo protocols, polled over the telephone, 24 May 1922, RGASPI f.17, op.3, d.294, l.5.

90. Politburo protocols, 26 May 1922, RGASPI f.17, op.3, d.294, l.3.

91. This document is also discussed in chapter 5.

92. Agranov, "Report," RGASPI f.17, op.86, d.17, l.55–56.

93. Ibid., l.57–59.

94. Werth, "A State against Its People," 134–35; Martin, "Obzory OGPU i Sovetskie istoriki," 21–26; Izmozik, *Glaza i ushi*, 110–18, 129–34.

95. [Trotskii], "Diktatura, gde tvoi khlyst?"

96. Tomskii opposed specifically the excessive involvement of the GPU in controlling *spets* organizations (Tomskii to CC commission on *spets* unions and to Stalin, memo, June 1922, RGASPI f.17, op.86, d.17, l.71).

97. This resolution is also described briefly in chapter 5.

98. Politburo protocols, 8 June 1922, RGASPI f.17, op.3, d.296, l.2–3. When this standing body was created, as will be discussed below, it fell within the competence of the NKVD; Narkomiust had only an advisory role.

99. Ibid., l.2–3, 7. See also Unshlikht's complete "Draft resolution" in Politburo protocols, 8 June 1922, with materials to the protocols, 2–8 June 1922, RGASPI f.17, op.163, d.279, l.11–12.

100. Agranov wrote a second memo dealing specifically with the doctors' congress and outlining what measures should be taken in response (Agranov, report on the physicians' congress to the GPU presidium, 5 June 1922, in Makarov and Khristoforov, *Vysylka vmesto rasstrela*, 78–81).

101. Politburo protocols, 8 and 22 June 1922, RGASPI f.17, op.3, d.296, l.3, and d.299, l.3–4; Unshlikht to Politburo on deportation of physicians, 21 June 1922, in Makarov and Khristoforov, *Vysylka vmesto rasstrela,* 84.

102. Central Bureau of Vsemediksantrud Physicians' Sections (TsB) protocols, 29 June and 27 July 1922, TsB Expanded Plenum protocols, 10 September 1922, GARF f.5465, op.4, d.287, l.33–33ob., 38–38ob., 50–50ob.

103. TsB protocols, 6 July 1922, GARF f.5465, op.4, d.287, l.34.

104. TsB protocols, 12 and 27 July 1922, with response from GPU contained in protocols of 20 July 1922, GARF f.5465, op.4, d.287, l.35, 36, 38–38ob.

105. TsB protocols, 27 July 1922, GARF f.5465, op.4, d.287, l.38; Kiev regional GPU to Ukrainian GPU in Kharkov, telegram, 17 July 1922, in Makarov and Khristoforov, *Vysylka vmesto rasstrela,* 87. The regime implied that the arrests took place because of links to the Menshevik Party and called the physicians' congress "objectively" Menshevik, but only three of those arrested were in fact Social Democrats. Of those at the May congress, eighty-five were nonparty, six were Mensheviks, one was an SR, and two were Bolsheviks. When Zinoviev spoke of "objective Menshevism," however, he made clear that he meant a shared agenda, and not actual party membership (TsB protocols, 12 July 1922, GARF f.5465, op.4, d.287, l.35; Zinov'ev, *Ob antisovetskikh,* 15; Ia. Kats, "II Vserossiiskii s"ezd vrachebnykh sektsii," *Meditsinskii rabotnik,* 1922, no. 5 [1 July]: 5. The doctors' party affiliation is from GARF f.5465, op.4, d.286a, l.114–324).

106. These physicians were Z. I. Izrail'son of Orel, N. V. Falin of Vologda, a certain Rozanov of Saratov, and eight Petrograders—A. E. Gutkin, E. S. Kantsel,' D. S. Zbarskii, Iu. N. Saltykova, I. E. Bronshtein, P. P. Pavlov, N. K. Kargens, and E. B. Soloveichik (Politburo Commission protocols [Unshlikht, chair; Kamenev, Kurskii, Iagoda, and Agranov present], 31 July 1922, TsA FSB f.1, op.6, d.160E, l.77).

107. This was not the first time the regime targeted students. The exile of Menshevik youth, a number of whom were MGU students, is described near the beginning of this chapter. In December 1921 a handful of students at Moscow's Petrovskii Agricultural Academy were to be deported to provincial locations until this was protested by student groups and Narkomzem. Another group was arrested in February 1922 when the Cheka claimed to find SR materials (Deputy Commissar of Agriculture Teodorovich et al. to Unshlikht, [early January 1922], and Petrovskii Academy student council representatives to Lunacharskii, 2 January 1922, GARF f.1565, op.18, d.3, l.44–46; Unshlikht, GPU report on anti-Soviet party work among the youth, [not before July 1922], RGASPI f.17, op.84, d.231, l.36–37).

108. It is not clear from the GPU report how many students were involved and whether the political labels in this case were related to actual party affiliation or were more loosely applied (Unshlikht, GPU report on anti-Soviet party work among the youth, RGASPI f.17, op.84, d.231, l.32–39).

109. Iakovleva to MVTU Rector Lukin, telegram, 3 July 1922, TsMAM f.1992, op.1, d.163, l.240.

110. "These organizations," Iakovleva asserted, "formed exclusively for academic and collective aid for the studentry, did not understand their direct tasks and took upon themselves political functions that did not belong to them" (Glavprofobr Chair V. Iakovleva to MVTU board, 28 June 1922, and MVTU board, declaration, 30 June 1922, TsMAM f.1992, op.1, d.163, l.248, and d.152, l.77).

111. Academic Sections to the MVTU board, 19 June 1922, and protocols of MVTU student body assembly, 18 February 1922, TsMAM f.1992, op.1, d.163, l.53ob.

112. Wives and relatives of students arrested by the GPU to the MVTU Board, declaration, 18 July 1922, TsMAM f.1992, op.1, d.163, l.262.

113. Rector M. Lukin et al. to Glavprofobr Chair Iakovleva, 11 November 1922; Lukin et al. to Iakovleva, 23 November 1922; A. Tsiurupa et al. for VTsIK department on individual amnesties to MVTU, 17 January 1923, TsMAM f.1992, op.1, d.159, l.174, l.192, 223.

114. Although I was not allowed to see the originals of the GPU Collegium protocols at the TsA FSB, I was given a set of excerpts, "Protokoly Kollegii OGPU po adm. vysylke. NN 154–257, 1.7–31.10.1922." GPU materials relating to preparations for the arrests (not including the Collegium protocols themselves) are in Makarov and Khristoforov, *Vysylka vmesto rasstrela*, 89–103.

115. Kamenev attempted to protect his reputation as a moderate by claiming that he had not known about the deportations until after the arrests. The American historian and ARA official Frank Golder, among others, rightly suspected that Kamenev was not telling the truth (Golder, *War, Revolution, and Peace*, 214).

116. Rozanov, Vigdorchik, and Magula were prominent members of the Vsemediksantrud doctors' section.

117. S. L. Frank's *Essay on the Methodology of Social Sciences* was published by Bereg in 1922.

118. Lenin to Stalin, 17 July 1922, sent to Dzerzhinskii and returned, RGASPI f.2, op.2, d.1338, l.1, italics in original (published in English in Koenker and Bachman, *Revelations from the Russian Archives*, 232).

119. Lenin's role is emphasized in many of the recent Russian articles on the deportations. See in particular Gak et al., "Deportatsiia inakomysliashchikh."

120. Politburo protocols, 20 July 1922, RGASPI f.17, op.3, d.304, l.3, published in Iakovlev, *Lubianka: Ianvar' 1922–dekabr' 1936*, 39.

121. Dzerzhinskii to Unshlikht, 5 September 1922, RGASPI, f.76., op.3, d.303, l.1–3.

122. Dzerzhinskii's note, which followed a meeting with Lenin at his convalescent home, laid out a methodology for doing this. Gak ("Deportatsiia inakomysliashchikh," 87) emphasizes the tie between Lenin's directives to Dzerzhinskii and the latter's memo.

123. Commission on administrative exile, list of active anti-Soviet intellectuals (professoriat), [late July 1922], TsA FSB f.1, op.6, d.160E, l.61–71. For a list of those intellectuals who were expelled between May 1922 and March 1923, see the appendix.

124. List of litterateurs discussed at a 22 July 1922 GPU meeting (Unshlikht, chair, comrades Iu. M. Steklova, Znamenskii, Ionov, and Lebedev-Polianskii present); and list of Petrograd anti-Soviet intellectuals, TsA FSB f.1, op.6, d.160E, l.68–71, 72–76.

125. Lists of anti-Soviet intellectuals, TsA FSB f.1, op.6, d.160E, l.67, 68, 70–71, 76

126. Ibid., l.61–71. Iakovleva had been a member of the Vecheka Collegium and chair of the Petrograd Cheka in 1918–19 (B. I. Berezhkov, *Piterskie prokuratory. Rukovoditeli VChK-MGB, 1918–1954* [St. Petersburg: Russko-Baltiiskii informatsionnyi tsentr BLITs, 1998], 53–60; Leggett, *Cheka*, 450). It is unclear whether Iakovleva or any of the other consultants voiced opposition to the expulsion of any professors who are therefore not mentioned on these lists.

127. Zinoviev and Lunacharskii became involved in a quarrel serious enough to be brought before the Politburo (Politburo protocols, 20 and 27 July 1922, RGASPI f.17,

op.3, d.304, l.4, and d.305, l.5). Lunacharskii's relation to the deportations will be discussed in greater detail in chapter 7.

128. Lists of anti-Soviet intellectuals, TsA FSB f.1, op.6, d.160E, l.61–62.

129. Ibid., l.65, 68, 72, 73.

130. The GPU's efforts to arrest the nonexistent Chaadaev are described in chapter 5.

131. The use of such a tool was not a peculiarly Bolshevik device; it had been perfected by all sides during the Civil War as a method for vilifying the other side and making its total destruction that much more necessary. See Holquist, "State Violence as Technique," and Raleigh, "Languages of Power."

132. Unshlikht to Stalin, 20 July 1922, in Iakovlev, *Lubianka: Ianvar' 1922–1936*, 40.

133. Politburo protocols, 27 July 1922, RGASPI f.17, op.3, d.305, l.3.

134. Interdepartmental Politburo commission protocols, 31 July 1922, TsA FSB f.1, op.6, d.160E, l.77.

135. Unshlikht to Enukidze, with draft decree on administrative exile, 31 July 1922, GARF f.1235, op.39, d.53, l.26–27; Unshlikht to Stalin, 2 August 1922, in Iakovlev, *Lubianka: Ianvar' 1922—dekabr' 1936*, 42.

136. This assumption is present in a number of the memoirs cited here—e.g., Losskii, *Vospominaniia*, 237.

137. Politburo protocols, 10 August 1922, RGASPI f.17, op.3, d.307, l.2.

138. GPU Collegium protocols (Unshlikht, chair), 13 August 1922, GARF f.1235, op.39, d.57, l.126.

139. VTsIK made sure to get extensive input from the NKVD and Narkomiust before confirming the decree (VTsIK Presidium protocols, 3 August 1922, GARF f.1235, op.39, d.86, l.274–81; Kurskii to Enukidze with draft resolutions, and excerpt from VTsIK Presidium protocols, 10 August 1922, GARF f.1235, op.39, d.53, l.19–25).

140. "Dekret Vserossiiskogo Tsentral'nogo Ispolnitel'nogo Komiteta Ob administrativnoi vysylke" (10 August 1922), *SUR*, 1922, art. 646, pp. 813–14. Unshlikht's draft is in GARF f.1235, op.39, d.53, l.26–27.

141. After their separation in fall 1923, the NKVD RSFSR and the OGPU came into conflict on a number of issues, especially jurisdiction over administrative exile (George Lin, "Fighting in Vain: The NKVD RSFSR in the 1920's" [Ph.D. diss., Stanford University, 1997], chaps. 1–3).

142. A point made in, inter alia, Iu. Goland, "Politika i ekonomika (ocherki obshchestvennoi bor'by 20-x godov)," *Znamia*, 1990, no. 3: 126.

Chapter 7. The Deportations, Part II: Arrest, Negotiation, and Expulsion

Epigraph: Golder, *War, Revolution, and Peace*, 211–15 (entries for 22 and 26 August 1922).

1. Ibid., 208 (entry for 10 August 1922).

2. Head of GPU Secret Department Samsonov and head of the fourth division of GPU Secret Department Reshetov, report on state of operation to expel anti-Soviet intellectuals, 23 August 1922, sent to Unshlikht and forwarded to Lenin; report on the state of the operation to expel anti-Soviet intellectuals, 26 August 1922, with note from Ezerskaia to Lenin, 27 August 1922, RGASPI f.5, op.1, d.2603, l.3–14. (A number of the archival documents cited in this chapter have also been recently

published in Makarov and Khristoforov, *Vysylka vmesto rasstrela.*) On the arrests, see also S. I. Levin, "Beseda s Miakotinym," *Rul'*, 1 October 1922, 5.

3. Lenin to Unshlikht, 17 September 1922, and Iagoda to Lenin, 18 September 1922, with annotated "Lists of Anti-Soviet Intellectuals," RGASPI f.2, op.2, d.1245, l.1–7 (published in Koenker and Bachman, *Revelations from the Russian Archives*, 233–39).

4. N. Losskii, *Vospominaniia*, 238; B. N. Losskii, "K 'izgnaniiu liudei mysli' v 1922 godu," *Stupeni*, 1992, no. 1 (4): 65; V. A. Reshchikova, "Vysylka iz RSFSR," *Minuvshee: istoricheskii al'manakh* 11 (1992): 200–202; Levin, "Beseda s Miakotinym," 5; "Protocols of Interrogation of V. A. Miakotin," [August 1922], in Makarov and Khristoforov, *Vysylka vmesto rasstrela*, 295–96; "Podpiska V. A. Miakotina GPU s obiazatel'stvom vyekhat' iz Sovetskoi Rossii," 19 August 1922, in *Rossiia. XX vek. Dokumenty*, 2002, no. 8, doc. 22 (http://idf.dn.ru/12/22.shtml); Stepun, *Byvshee*, 2: 414–15; "Protocols of Interrogation of F. A. Stepun," 22 September 1922, and "Resolution of the GPU Secret Department Regarding F. A. Stepun," 3 November 1922, in Makarov and Khristoforov, *Vysylka vmesto rasstrela*, 336–37.

5. Nikolai Berdiaev, *Samopoznanie, sochineniia* (Moscow: EKSMO-Press, 1997), 489.

6. M. Osorgin, "Kak nas uekhali," *Poslednie novosti*, 28 August 1932, 4; and Osorgin, *Vremena*, 144–49.

7. Sorokin, *Leaves*, 299–303.

8. V. V. Stratonov, "Po volnam zhizni," GARF f.5881, op.2, d.669, l.276ob.–79 (pp. 538–43), ellipses in original.

9. Novikov, *Ot Moskvy*, 323–24.

10. Stratonov, "Po volnam zhizni," l.279ob. (p. 544); Trubetskoi, *Minuvshee*, 316.

11. See, e.g., Losskii, *Vospominaniia*, 238, and Izgoev, "Piat' let," 6.

12. Excerpts of GPU Collegium protocols on administrative exile, 3 August 1922, provided by TsA FSB. Mel'gunov had been arrested multiple times. D. M. Shchepkin and S. M. Leont'ev, who, like Mel'gunov, had been accused in the Tactical Center case, were also sentenced at this time but in the end were not allowed to leave Russia.

13. Mel'gunov, *Vospominaniia*, 2: 86, and P. E. Mel'gunova, "Prodolzhenie," ibid., 81. Mel'gunov was not aware for some time that he was to be allowed to go abroad (Frank Golder to Archibald Cary Coolidge, 13 and 28 August 1922, in Golder, *War, Revolution, and Peace*, 218, 218n).

14. Preobrazhenskii, the former head of Glavprofobr, was a logical choice to join this new troika.

15. Politburo protocols, 10 August 1922, RGASPI f.17, op.3, d.307, l.3; "Nastroenie studenchestva," *Dni*, 15 November 1922, 3; N. N. Il'kevich, *Akademik Gavril Goretskii: Pervoe stolknovenie s GPU. K istorii vysylki za granitsu otechestvennoi intelligentsii v 1922 godu: Dokumental'nyi ocherk* (Smolensk: Posokh, 1998), 13, 31–36; and excerpts of GPU Collegium materials, 7 September 1922, from materials given to me at TsA FSB.

16. See, e.g., Frank Golder to Christian Herter, 18 and 22 August 1922, in Golder, *War, Revolution, and Peace*, 211–12. See also Golder, "Partial and Unofficial List of 'Administrative Exiles' from Moscow," Hoover Archives, Frank Golder Collection. My thanks to Bert Patenaude for alerting me to this document.

17. The London *Times* reported the arrests on 23 August 1922, and the *New York Times* and several Russian émigré newspapers carried the story a day later.

18. Frank Golder to Christian Herter, 22 August 1922, 11 P.M., and Golder to Professor Ephraim Adams, 26 August 1922, in Golder, *War, Revolution, and Peace,* 214–15; *New York Times,* 27 August 1922, 3.

19. *Izvestiia,* 30 August 1922, 1; *New York Times,* 27 August 1922, 1, 3; Golder, *War, Revolution, and Peace,* 217. Those present at the interview included the American fellow travelers Louise Bryant and Anna Louise Strong.

20. "Doklad tov. Zinov'eva," *Petrogradskaia pravda,* 30 August 1922, 3; and "Ob antisovetskikh techeniiakh," *Petrogradskaia pravda,* 5 September 1922, 2–3. The full stenograms, including a lengthy speech by Zinoviev's right-hand man, G. I. Safarov, are in TsGA SPb f.1000, op.6, d.276, l.27–54.

21. "Pervoe predosterezhenie," *Pravda,* 31 August 1922, 1. It is likely that the article's author was E. A. Preobrazhenskii, one of *Pravda*'s editors, who was in close touch with the GPU (Unshlikht to Preobrazhenskii, 29 August 1922, TsA FSB f.1, op.6, d.160E, l.59).

22. Quoted in "Stalin preduprezhdaet o novoi polose krasnogo terrora," *Segodnia,* 16 September 1922, 1.

23. Excerpts from many of the individual files, which are held in the FSB archive, have now been published in Makarov and Khristoforov, *Vysylka vmesto rasstrela,* 203–397. See also V. G. Makarov, "Arkhivnye tainy: intelligentsiia i vlast'," *Voprosy filosofii,* 2002, no. 10: 108–55; Kogan, "Vyslat' za granitsu," 70–79; A. V. Velidov, "Nikolai Berdiaev—arest i vysylka," *Sovershenno sekretno,* 1991, no. 8: 2–3; L. Polikovskaia, "M. A. Osorgin v sobstvennykh rasskazakh i dokumentakh GPU," *Minuvshee; istoricheskii al'manakh* 19 (1996): 199–209; I. A. Il'in, *Sobranie sochinenii,* ed. Iu. T. Lisitsa, supp. vol. 1, *Dnevnik, Pis'ma, Dokumenty (1903–1938)* (Moscow: Russkaia kinga, 1999), 429–38; L. G. Barsova, "Ivan Ivanovich Lapshin: Zhizn' i trudy," *Zvezda,* 1997, no. 10: 189–92; G. Faiman, "'I vsadili ego v temnitsu . . .' Zamiatin v 1919, v 1922–1924 gg.," in *Novoe o Zamiatine: Sbornik materialov,* ed. Leonid Geller (Moscow: Izd-vo "MIK," 1997), 82–83; Il'kevich, *Akademik Gavril Goretskii,* 13–15.

24. A question on this form concerning relatives living in other cities caused a great deal of anxiety. Stratonov, for instance, agonized over naming his adult daughter in Odessa but feared the consequences of lying to the GPU (Stratonov, "Po volnam zhizni," l.280 [p. 545]).

25. "Protocols of Interrogation of M. A. Osorgin," [August 1922], in Makarov and Khristoforov, *Vysylka vmesto rasstrela,* 304–5; Polikovskaia, "Osorgin," 203–4; Velidov, "Nikolai Berdiaev," 3; "Pokazaniia A. A. Kizevetter GPU," 22 August 1922, in *Rossiia. XX vek. Dokumenty,* 2002, no. 8, doc. 24 (http://idf.dn.ru/12/24.shtml).

26. Stratonov, "Po volnam zhizni," l.286ob. (p. 558). The recently published protocols of his interrogation confirm that his response was indeed along these lines (Makarov and Khristoforov, *Vysylka vmesto rasstrela,* 340–42).

27. Faiman, "Zamiatin," 82. Zamiatin was utterly baffled to be considered a counterrevolutionary (Zamiatin to A. K. Voronskii, 21 September 1922, in A. Iu. Galushkin, ed., "E. I. Zamiatin, Pis'mo A K. Voronskomu: K istorii aresta i nesostoiavsheisia vysylki E. I. Zamiatina v 1922–1923 gg.," *De Visu,* no. 0 [1992]: 14).

28. Il'in, *Dnevnik, Pis'ma, Dokumenty,* 433–34; Velidov, "Nikolai Berdiaev," 2; "Protocols of Interrogation of S. E. Trubetskoi," 18 August 1922, in Makarov and Khristoforov, *Vysylka vmesto rasstrela,* 365–66; Trubetskoi, *Minuvshee,* 316; Stepun, *Byvshee,* 2: 417–18. Stepun apparently succeeded in his efforts not to offend

his interrogator, who, he recalled, was pleased with his answers and even asked for a copy of his latest book.

29. Il'in, *Dnevnik, Pis'ma, Dokumenty,* 433–34; Faiman, "Zamiatin," 82.

30. Sergei Trubetskoi was an exception (Makarov and Khristoforov, *Vysylka vmesto rasstrela,* 365–66).

31. Velidov, "Nikolai Berdiaev," 2–3; Polikovskaia, "Osorgin," 207.

32. Excerpts from these GPU Collegium protocols are in Makarov and Khristoforov, *Vysylka vmesto rasstrela.* See also Polikovskaia, "Osorgin," 204; Il'in, *Dnevnik, Pis'ma, Dokumenty,* 429–38; Velidov, "Nikolai Berdiaev," 3; Levin, "Beseda s Miakotinym," 5.

33. Osorgin, "Kak nas uekhali," 4–5; Polikovskaia, "Osorgin," 200–206; Stratonov, "Po volnam zhizni," l.286ob.–87 (pp. 558–59).

34. Osorgin, "Kak nas uekhali," 5.

35. Stratonov, "Po volnam zhizni," l.287ob.–88 (pp. 560–61). Sakharov was eventually allowed to stay in Russia.

36. See, e.g., Trubetskoi, *Minuvshee,* 319–20.

37. Losskii, *Vospominaniia,* 239–40.

38. Stratonov, "Po volnam zhizni," l.292 (p. 569); Sorokin, *Leaves,* 305–6; Losskii, *Vospominaniia,* 321–22.

39. Losskii, *Vospominaniia,* 240; Reshchikova, "Vysylka," 203; Stratonov, "Po volnam zhizni," l.292–94ob. (pp. 569–74); Novikov, *Ot Moskvy,* 326; Sorokin, *Leaves,* 301; Osorgin, "Kak nas uekhali," 5; Trubetskoi, *Minuvshee,* 318–19.

40. Stratonov, "Po volnam zhizni," l.294 (p. 573); Osorgin, "Kak nas uekhali," 5. Iasinskii, officially KUBU's vice-chairman, was its de facto leader and was also the chairman of its Moscow branch.

41. Stratonov, "Po volnam zhizni," l.293–95ob. (pp. 571–76). The petitioning to change some of the sentences of expulsion will be discussed below.

42. Osorgin, "Kak nas uekhali," 5; Sorokin, *Leaves,* 304; Stratonov, "Po volnam zhizni," l.295ob. (p. 576).

43. Osorgin, "Kak nas uekhali," 5.

44. Sorokin gives his account in *Leaves,* 307–8.

45. Stratonov, "Po volnam zhizni," l.297ob.–98 (pp. 580–81); Osorgin, "Kak nas uekhali," 5; Trubetskoi, *Minuvshee,* 324. Both Stratonov and Trubetskoi note that the mother never once fed the "baby" during the long journey to Petrograd. Trubetskoi claims to have seen her lean it against a chair at a station stop en route while she spoke with a *chekist.*

46. Trubetskoi, *Minuvshee,* 323.

47. Osorgin, "Kak nas uekhali," 5. Complaints like Osorgin's were common, if not always fair. Stratonov related how, after a meeting of the Math-Physics Faculty, Novikov returned grousing bitterly that no one spoke on their behalf (Stratonov, "Po volnam zhizni," l.297 [p. 579]). In fact, however, the faculty did express its "deep gratitude to Dean V. V. Stratonov for his selfless execution of the duties of dean in a most difficult time for the faculty" and hoped that he might "as soon as possible be among us once again" (protocols of the Physics-Math Faculty of Moscow State University, 13 September 1922, TsMAM f.1609, op.1, d.587, l.14–15). Stratonov implied that Novikov's real irritation was with the fact that he, the former rector, did not receive a similar expression of gratitude. On the other hand, Novikov did not discuss this episode in his own memoirs.

48. Novikov, *Ot Moskvy,* 328.

49. Sorokin, *Leaves,* 308.

50. Cited in Boobbyer, *S. L. Frank,* 115.

51. Stratonov, "Po volnam zhizni," l.298 (p. 581).

52. Reshchikova, "Vysylka," 203; Sorokin, *Leaves,* 308.

53. P. E. Mel'gunova, "Prodolzhenie," 82.

54. Stratonov, "Po volnam zhizni," l.300 (p. 585).

55. Trubetskoi, *Minuvshee,* 325.

56. Stratonov, "Po volnam zhizni," l.301–2ob. (pp. 587–90); Novikov, *Ot Moskvy,* 330–31; Reshchikova, "Vysylka," 204–5; Boobbyer, *S. L. Frank,* 116.

57. Boris Khariton, "K istorii nashei vysylki," *Dni,* 13 February 1923, 2; B. N. Losskii, "Nasha sem'ia na poru likholetiia, 1914–1922 godov," *Minuvshee: istoricheskii al'manakh* 12 (1991): 129–32; Izgoev, "Piat' let," 11. Viktor Iretskii, for example, was in prison from 6 September to 23 October. He received his German visa on 11 November and left several weeks after the rest of his colleagues (Iretskii's GPU *udostverenie,* RGALI f.2227, op.1, d.207, l.1, and German visa, ibid., d.208, l.1–2ob.).

58. An invitation to this evening is in RO RGB f.163, op.1, d.317, l.96.

59. B. N. Losskii, "Nasha sem'ia," 134–35.

60. Izgoev, "Piat' let," 10. After a thorough customs search, nothing in the end was taken (ibid., 10–11).

61. Novikov, *Ot Moskvy,* 327; Golder, *War, Revolution, and Peace,* 215.

62. Sorokin, *Leaves,* 307.

63. Order 553/s [secret], NKID, 1 November 1922. A transcription of this document, located at the Ministry of Foreign Affairs archive, was kindly shown to me by M. E. Khlopaeva.

64. Stepun, *Byvshee,* 2: 425–26.

65. Reshchikova, "Vysylka," 203.

66. Sorokin to Vitiazev, 22 September [1922], RGALI f.106, op.1, d.157, l.33–33ob.

67. "Zapisi pod chertoi," 272.

68. A few additional deportees, as will also be mentioned in the epilogue, returned after World War II.

69. M. E. Khlopaeva, who has worked in the regional archives, has indicated that several provincial cities, including Nizhnii Novgorod, planned the deportations of one or two professors.

70. Malysheva, "Kazanskie professora," 53–60. Ovchinnikov, the former rector of Kazan University and a leader of the struggle against VUZ reforms, tried to intercede on behalf of the others before he himself was arrested.

71. *Poslednie novosti,* 24 September 1922. These three were the first intellectuals actually to leave Soviet territory as part of the deportation campaigns.

72. D. V. Omel'chuk and S. B. Filimonov, "Sledstvennoe Delo S.N. Bulgakova (1922)," in *Arkheograficheskii ezhegodnik za 1995 god* (Moscow: Nauka, 1997), 320–22; S. N. Bulgakov, "Iz 'Dnevnika,' 18 (31) Dekabria 1922 g.," in *Tikhie dumy,* ed. V. V. Sapov (Moscow: Respublika, 1996), 351.

73. Bulgakov, "Iz 'Dnevnika,'" 352.

74. The GPU Collegium did not confirm his expulsion until October (excerpts of the GPU Collegium protocols, TsA FSB). See also Stepun, *Byvshee,* 2: 426.

75. Khariton, "K istorii," 2. Iretskii arrived in Stettin on 17 December (RGALI f.2227, op.1, d.208, l.1ob.), while his wife remained with their son in Russia and set about plying the proper channels to allow him to return (E. V. Antipova to Iretskii, 31 December 1922 and 7 January 1923, RGALI f.2227, op.1, d.121, l.1–4ob.).

76. D. A. Lutokhin, "Dnevnik za 1923 g," RO IRLI (Pushkinskii Dom), f.592, op.1, d.3, l.2, 11–13ob. He went from Tallinn to Stettin aboard the same steamship, the *Preussen,* and arrived in Berlin on 17 February.

77. Politburo protocols, 18 January 1923, RGASPI f.17, op.3, d.330, l.1; and V. F. Bulgakov, "Kak prozhita zhizn'," part 11, "Poslednie gody zhizni v Moskvy," RGALI f.2226, op.1, d.60, l.114–15. According to a note in Bulgakov's archival materials, VTsIK approved his exile on 10 February 1923 (RGALI f.2226, op.1, d.115, l.7).

78. V. Bulgakov, "Kak prozhita zhizn'," part 11, l.99–111.

79. Ibid., l.113–18.

80. Speeches at a farewell gathering on the occasion of V. F. Bulgakov's departure for Czechoslovakia, 5 March 1923, RGALI f.2226, op.1, d.115, l.1, 4, 11.

81. V. Bulgakov, "Kak prozhita zhizn'," l.137. Bulgakov and his family returned to Russia in 1948, as will be mentioned in the epilogue.

82. Such sentiments were already present in the discussions of the interdepartmental Politburo commission in July 1922, particularly regarding whether to deport Zamiatin (TsA FSB f.1, op.6, d.160E).

83. According to one émigré newspaper, Unshlikht and L. M. Karakhan, the assistant Foreign Affairs commissar, were upbraided at a Sovnarkom meeting after the expulsions for having allowed Sorokin, Kuskova, and other intellectuals to go abroad ("Nepredusmotritel'nost' chekistov," *Dni,* 30 November 1922, 3; cited in Sorokin, *Leaves,* 309). I have not uncovered any archival confirmation of this rumor.

84. Sorokin, *Leaves,* 309.

85. Protocols of the CC of the Ukrainian Communist Party, 23 June 1922, RGASPI f.17, op.84, d.358, l.14.

86. As discussed in chapter 2.

87. Chairman of Ukrainian GPU [V. N. Mantsev] et al., list of anti-Soviet VUZ professors, instructors, and public figures subject to internal deportation or expulsion, Kharkov, 3 August 1922, RGASPI f.5, op.1, d.2603, l.3–4.

88. Ibid., l.4, 6–10.

89. Ukrainian Politburo protocols, 1 November 1922, RGASPI f.17, op.112, d.388, l.83–83ob.; GPU Deputy Chair Unshlikht to Orgburo, "top secret," 13 November 1922, ibid., l.81–81ob.; Secretariat protocols, 16 November 1922, RGASPI f.17, op.112, d.387, l.3; Orgburo protocols, 20 November 1922, RGASPI f.17, op.112, d.388, l.3.; and Ukrainian Politburo protocols, 24 November 1922, RGASPI f.17, op.84, d.358, l.62.

90. Unshlikht to Politburo, 12 and 19 December 1922, in Makarov and Khristoforov, *Vysylka vmesto rasstrela,* 167–68, 170–71; Unshlikht to Stalin and the Politburo, "top secret," 5 January 1923, from materials given to me at TsA FSB: transcription of AP RF f.3, op.58, d.175, l.107; Politburo protocols, 11 January 1923, RGASPI f.17, op.3, d.329, l.2; GPU Deputy Chair Unshlikht and Secret Dept. Deputy Head Andreeva to CC RCP, 15 December 1922, RGASPI f.17, op.112, d.400, l.41; Ukrainian Politburo protocols, 10 January 1923, RGASPI f.17, op.84, d. 358, l.70–70ob.; and protocols of Politburo Commission on the Ukrainian Intelligentsia, 1 February 1923, from materials given to me at TsA FSB: transcription of AP RF f.3, op.58, d.175, l.113–15.

91. Radek's articles in *Pravda* appeared on 16 and 20 July 1922.

92. "Vse—na pisatelei," *Golos Rossii,* 16 September 1922; V. Khodasevich, "Gor'kii," *Sovremennye zapiski* (Paris) 70 (1940): 142.

93. "Pis'mo Gor'kogo," *Nakanune,* 21 September 1922, 3.

94. "Pechat'," *Rul'*, 23 September 1922, 2; Aleksandr Iablonskii, "Maksim Milostivyi!" *Rul'*, 29 September 1922, 2; and A. Iu. Galushkin, "Eshche raz o pis'me Gor'kogo v gazetu 'Nakanune,'" in *Gor'kii i ego epokha: Issledovaniia i materialy* (Moscow: Nauka, 1989), 2: 256–61. Galushkin contends that the letter in *Nakanune* should be considered a "hidden protest" by Gorky against the deportations (ibid., 260).

95. A. V. Lunacharskii, "Tretii front," *Izvestiia,* 26 August 1922, 1. These remarks can be interpreted as a plea by Lunacharskii that he be more involved in cultural policy.

96. Lunacharskii to GPU Presidium, 19 October 1922, in Barsova, "Lapshin," 190.

97. "Nauka i shkola. Tov. Lunacharskogo u studentov," *Izvestiia,* 12 October 1922, 5.

98. Lunacharskii to Kamenev, 28 November 1922, in *Rossiia. XX vek. Dokumenty,* 2002, no. 8, doc. 36 (http://idf.dn.ru/12/36.shtml).

99. *Tretii Vserossiiskii S"ezd politprosvetov RSFSR. Biulleten'*, no. 1 (29 November 1922): 3–4.

100. There is little record of correspondence between petitioners and the Politburo (those most likely to have been petitioned were later purged and thus have smaller archival collections). Although I did not find petitions from the arrested intellectuals addressed to Kamenev, there is a substantial collection of other appeals to him from this time (GARF f.5446, op.72, d.338), and it is he who is most often mentioned in memoirs. Press reports indicate that it was to Kamenev and Rykov that relatives of the imprisoned SRs and their lawyers turned with pleas for clemency and for information (see, e.g., "Exiled Russians to Leave This Week," *New York Times,* 28 August 1922, 13).

101. Politburo protocols, 24 August 1922, RGASPI f.17, op.3, d.309, l.3.

102. See chapter 6.

103. Goland, "Politika i ekonomika," 136; Bailes, *Technology and Society,* 64–66, 77–78.

104. This change was probably made to allow Iakovleva to unify command over the administration of VUZy and to permit Volgin to concentrate on running MGU.

105. Moscow State University, signed Rector Volgin et al., to the Glavprofobr Council on VUZ Affairs, 22 August 1922, TsMAM f.1609, op.4, d.2a, l.1–1ob.

106. Head of Glavprofobr Iakovleva to the board of Moscow University, telegram, received 30 August 1922, TsMAM f.1609, op.4, d.2a, l.7.

107. Petrograd Technology Institute, signed by Rector N. Bartel's et al., to KUBU, 17 August 1922, TsGA SPB f.2995, op.3, d.8, l.10.

108. These letters include support for the direct appeal of Emilia Brutskus, the wife of Boris, as well as those of PGU, PTI, and other VUZy (TsGA SPb f.2995, op.3, d.8, l.5–7, 27, 28, 37, 41, 47, 48, 51).

109. See also the letters from PGU on behalf of Karsavin, Desnitskii-Stroev, Lapshin, Selivanov, Odintsov, and Losskii (TsGA SPb f.7240, op.14, d.127, l.52, 54, and TsGA SPb f.2995, op.3, d.8, l.24, 36). Though the Political Red Cross was also used (see, for example, the appeal of N. R. Brilling's wife in GARF f.8409, op.1, d.5, l.1–1ob.), it was at just this moment that Peshkova's organization was temporarily disbanded. Frank Golder went so far as to say that "with the closing of this organization, comes to an end, so far as I am able to learn, the last nonofficial organization in Russia, the ARA

excepted. Everything else is in the hands of the Soviet. It is the most thoroughly centralized government in the world" (Golder to Ephraim Adams, 26 August 1922, in Golder, *War, Revolution, and Peace,* 217).

110. On Krasin, see Timothy Edward O'Connor, *The Engineer of Revolution: L. B. Krasin and the Bolsheviks, 1870–1926* (Boulder, Colo.: Westview Press, 1992).

111. Petrograd Technology Institute, signed by Rector Bartel's et al., to Commissar of Foreign Trade Leonid Borisovich Krasin, telegram, 25 August 1922, TsGA SPb, f.3025, op.1, d.2614, l.22.

112. Petrograd Technology Institute, signed by Rector Bartel's et al., to Comrade Iakovleva, Glavprofobr, 6 September 1922, TsGA SPb, f.3025, op.1, d.2614, l.24–24ob.

113. The Moscow Higher Technical School (MVTU) appealed on behalf of a number of professors, with a fair degree of success (Engineering-Construction Faculty to MVTU board, 23 August 1922, Mechanical Faculty to the rector, 23 August 1922, and protocols of the MVTU board, 23 August 1922, TsMAM f.1992, op.1, d.163, l.281, 292–93).

114. Khariton, "K istorii," 2; excerpts from protocols of Dzerzhinskii Commission on reexamination of appeals for rescinding sentence of exile, 31 August 1922, RGASPI f.5, op.1, d.2603, l.15.

115. Jansen, *Show Trial under Lenin,* 18, 75, 78; Krasil'nikov and Morozov, "Predislovie," 80, 94; "Exiled Russians," *New York Times,* 28 August 1922, 13; VTsIK Presidium protocols, 7 December 1922, GARF f.1235, op.39, d.86, l.27–30; Politburo protocols, 21 June 1923, RGASPI f.17, op.3, d.361; Dzerzhinskii Commission protocols, 31 August 1922, RGASPI f.5, op.1, d.2603, l.15; and R. M. Iangirov, ed., "Pis'ma A. V. Chaianov," *Minuvshee: istoricheskii al'manakh* 18 (1995): 498.

116. Bogdanov, for instance, had explicitly condoned the expulsions of Parshin and Kukolevskii, and Glavprofobr that of Kukolevskii and other professors on whose behalf it now appealed (TsA FSB f.1, op.6, d.160E, l.62, 67).

117. Dzerzhinskii Commission protocols, 31 August 1922, RGASPI f.5, op.1, d.2603, l.15–16.

118. Iagoda to Lenin, 18 September 1922, with annotated lists of intellectuals, RGASPI f.2, op.2, d.1245, l.3–7.

119. Grigorii Kaminskii and Boris Kushner to Dzerzhinskii, 20 September 1922, RGASPI f.17, op.112, d.374, l.313, emphasis in original. As noted in chapter 3, Osinskii had argued in vain for a more conciliatory line toward the cooperatives at the recent Party Conference.

120. Protocols of Secretariat, 27 September 1922, RGASPI f.17, op.112, d.374, l.9. (Molotov's opinion is scrawled on the copy of the letter to Dzerzhinskii passed along to the Politburo.) On the Bolsheviks' anxieties concerning SRs in prominent agricultural positions, see Heinzen, "'Alien' Personnel," 84–86, 93–96.

121. Survey of Politburo members, 3 October 1923, RGASPI f.17, op.3, d.385.

122. On the efforts of Narkomzem to hold on to *spetsy,* see Heinzen, "'Alien' Personnel," 73–100.

123. GPU to Glavprofobr, 18 November 1922, and MGU Rector Volgin to Iakovleva, 21 November 1922, GARF f.1565, op.18, d.3, l.16, 11; Deputy CC Secretary Nazaretian (for Stalin) to Unshlikht and Samsonov, 14 December 1922, RGASPI f.17, op.84, d.397, l.119; GPU (Unshlikht and Samsonov) to the CC, 19 December 1922, transcription from AP RF by M. E. Khlopaeva. Oganovskii was one of the few MGU

professors arrested in August 1922 who was allowed to continue teaching (see *Otchet 1-go Moskovskogo gosudarstvennogo universiteta za 1924 g.* [Moscow: Izdanie 1-go Moskovskogo Gosudarstvennogo Universiteta, 1925], 7). Like other agronomists working in Soviet institutions, he would again come under fire at the end of the decade.

124. Galushkin, "Zamiatin," 17; Politburo protocols, 7 and 14 December 1922, RGASPI f.17, op.3, d.311, l.4 and d.326, l.3, 7. Though it was the intervention of well-connected allies that "rescued" Zamiatin, his removal from the list was in line with the original recommendation of the interdepartmental troika, which, after hearing the opinions of the "literary" experts, had noted that "upon deportation abroad he would become a dangerous leader. He needs to be sent either to Novgorod or Kursk, but not in any circumstance abroad" (TsA FSB f.1, op.6, d.160E, l.73).

125. See chapter 6. On Voronskii and *Krasnaia nov'*, see Maguire, *Red Virgin Soil*, esp. chaps. 1 and 3.

126. Voronskii to Zamiatin, n.d. [after 21 September 1922], in Galushkin, "Zamiatin," 17. The manuscript for *We* had recently been completed and was circulating in Bolshevik and non-Bolshevik intellectual circles

127. Zamiatin to Voronskii, [21 September 1922], ibid., 14.

128. Pil'niak to Zamiatin, 20 November 1922, ibid., 17; Annenkov, *Dnevnik*, 265–66.

129. Galushkin, "Zamiatin," 18–19. Zamiatin may also have met with Trotsky. At one point he even received his visa to leave, but this permission was later rescinded.

130. Staff Professor Vladimir Ivanovich Charnolusskii to the Dean of the Faculty of Social Sciences of MGU [N. Lukin], 15 November 1922, GARF f.1565, op.18, d.3, l.13–14ob.

131. MGU board, signed by Volgin as rector, to Glavprofobr, 21 November 1922, GARF f.1565, op.18, d.3, l.12.

132. This deduced from her scrawl at the top of Charnolusskii's appeal to Lukin (see n. 130, above).

133. GPU Deputy Chair Unshlikht and Head of Secret Branch Samsonov to Head of Glavprofobr Iakovleva, "top secret," 1 December 1922, GARF f.1565, op.18, d.3, l.15. The interdepartmental troika had initiated his case over the summer, which then received the approval of the newly operating NKVD special commission on 4 November.

134. It is unclear whether Dzerzhinskii supported or opposed Charnolusskii's appeal (Politburo protocols, 18 January 1923, RGASPI f.17, op.3, d.330, l.1).

135. Oleg Volobuev and Nikolai Simonov, eds., "Stan'te diktatorom, Vladimir Il'ich!" *Rodina*, 1991, nos. 11–12: 30–31; S. V. Zhuravlev, ed., "'Ne mogu molchat' . . .' (pis'ma N.A. Rozhkova V.I. Leninu 1919, 1921 gg.)," in *Arkheograficheskii ezhegodnik za 1991 god* (Moscow: Nauka, 1994), 302–3; and Oleg Volobuev, ed., "'Bez grazhdanskoi voiny nigde ne oboitis','" *Rodina*, 1992, no. 3: 49.

136. See A. P. Kupaigorodskaia, *Vysshaia shkola Leningrada*, 158; and V. V. Mavrodin, ed., *Istoriia Leningradskogo Universiteta. Ocherki, 1819–1969* (Leningrad: Izdatel'stvo Leningradskogo Universiteta, 1969), 244–53.

137. Lenin to Stalin, 17 July 1922, RGASPI f.2, op.2, d.1338, l.1; Zhuravlev, "'Ne mogu,'" 300–301.

138. Rozhkov to Iakovleva, 1 December [28 November], 1922, GARF f.1565, op.18, d.3, l.9. The fact that Rozhkov was present at a meeting of the Council on VUZ Affairs on 15 August 1922, two days before the arrests, is further indication of Iakovleva's trust in him.

139. The Bolsheviks sponsored "movements" of former SRs and Mensheviks for propaganda purposes; this, among other things, was the basis of the SR trial (Liebich, *From the Other Shore*, 79–80, 125; and Jansen, *Show Trial under Lenin*, esp. 16–17).

140. Politburo protocols, 19 and 26 October 1922, RGASPI f.17, op.3, d.318, l.3, and d.319, l.1. .

141. The summary of this meeting is in *PSS*, 54: 669.

142. Lenin to Stalin, dictated over telephone, 8 December 1922, *PSS*, 54: 320.

143. Lenin to Zinoviev, 7 or 8 December 1922, *PSS*, 54: 319–20, italics in original.

144. Lenin to Stalin, dictated over telephone, 13 December 1922, RGASPI f.2, op.2, d.1344, l.1, published in Volobuev, "Bez grazhdanskoi," 49.

145. On the repentance of former SRs and Mensheviks, see, inter alia, Jansen, *Show Trial under Lenin*, 176–77.

146. Politburo protocols, 14 December 1922, 9 February 1923, and poll by telephone of 26 February 1923, RGASPI f.17, op.3, d.326, l.3; d.335, l.2, and d.338, l.36.

147. Ia. M. Bukshpan to MGU rector [V. P. Volgin], 9 September 1923, GARF f.1565, op.18, d.21, l.26.

148. Z. Grinberg, Narkompros Commission on Foreign Purchases, to Deputy Commissar of Enlightenment V. N. Iakovleva, 10 September 1923, with handwritten notes by Iakovleva; and Iakovleva to Grinberg, 4 October 1923, GARF f.1565, op.18, d.21, l.25, 24; *Otchet MGU za 1924 g.*, 9.

149. The GPU even declared that Pëtr Velikhov, the former dean of MVTU's Engineering-Construction Faculty, was unfit to teach because he was insane—perhaps the first use of this infamous label against a political enemy (GPU Deputy Chair Unshlikht and Head of the KRO Artuzov to V. N. Iakovleva, "top secret," 12 May 1923, GARF f.1565, op.18, d.3, l.6, and Unshlikht and Artuzov to Iakovleva, 23 May 1923, GARF f.1565, op.18, d.15, l.42).

150. *Obzor* for October 1922 by GPU data, RGASPI f.17, op.84, d.296, l.23–24; and GPU Deputy Chair Unshlikht et al., brief *obzor* of Politico-Economic Situation of the RSFSR for December 1922, RGASPI f.17, op.84, d.296, l.121. The December report nonetheless cautioned that the only sign of life among Mensheviks and SRs was in a particularly crucial area: work among the youth.

151. Proposal of Unshlikht to the Politburo, 14 December 1922, and Politburo Protocols, 14 December 1922, RGASPI f.17, op.3, d.326, l.7 and l.3. The Politburo removed some of Unshlikht's strictest suggestions (including punishing party members who petitioned on behalf of arrested Mensheviks) before setting the proposal in motion.

152. S. A. Krasil'nikov, "Ssylka v 1920-e gody," *Minuvshee: istoricheskii al'manakh* 21 (1997): 184–85n; correspondence between various branches of the NKVD and GPU, 1922–23, GARF f.393, op.43, d.82; and GPU directive forming a Special Bureau on the Deportation of "Anti-Soviet Elements of the Intelligentsia," 2 November 1922, in *Lubianka: Organy VChK-OGPU-NKVD-NKGB-MGB-MVD-KGB. 1917–1991. Spravochnik*, ed. A. N. Iakovlev, comp. A. I. Kokurin and N. V. Petrov (Moscow: Mezhdunarodnyi fond "Demokratiia," 2003), 439–40.

153. VTsIK Presidium protocols, 12 and 16 October and 20 November 1922 (with "clarification," signed by Enukidze, 25 November 1922), GARF f.1235, op.39, d.86, l.57–58, 127, 134–40; Krasil'nikov, "Ssylka v 1920-e gody," 184.

154. Politburo protocols, 10 August 1922, RGASPI f.17, op.3, d.307, l.3; M. E. Khlopaeva kindly showed me her transcription of a document listing the deported Georgian Mensheviks, from the Ministry of Foreign Affairs archive.

155. N. B. Bogdanova, *Moi otets byl—Men'shevik* (St. Petersburg: Memorial, 1994), 90–92; Dvinov, *Ot legal'nosti*, 155–56; Krasil'nikov, "Ssylka v 1920-e gody," 176–78. Bogdanov spent the rest of the decade in various states of exile, forced labor, and arrest.

156. Although the materials available at GARF on administrative exile make it appear that recidivists made up the majority of those exiled after the beginning of 1923, it is likely that most materials on political exiles ended up in the FSB archive, where they were not accessible to me at the time of my research.

157. Although, as Solzhenitsyn has stressed, socialist politicals, White counterrevolutionaries, and common criminals were sharply differentiated within the camps, those sentenced by the NKVD commission were all deemed socially dangerous. In particular, politicals and counterrevolutionaries were often lumped together under Article 57.

Epilogue: The Deportees in Emigration

Epigraph: Mikh. Osorgin, "Tem zhe morem," *Sovremennye zapiski*, no. 13 (7 December 1922): 217, ellipses in original.

1. Berdiaev, *Dream and Reality*, 244–45. Chamberlain offers a thorough explication of the deportees in emigration in *Philosophy Steamer*, 173–262.

2. "At first we remained a united group of 'deported citizens,'" Osorgin recalled, "and then we scattered. At first we 'knew more than the others,' and then we knew just as little. At first we were 'people of a special psychological makeup,' and then the majority settled into obligatory émigré activities" (Osorgin, "Kak nas uekhali," 5).

3. I. A. Il'in, "Rech' pered russkimi professorami-izgnannikami," 14 November 1922, in Il'in, *Sobranie sochinenii*, vols. 9–10: 233; "Berlinskaia zhizn'. Vecher v chest' vyslannykh," *Dni*, 17 November 1922, 6; and Robert C. Williams, *Culture in Exile: Russian Emigrés in Germany, 1881–1941* (Ithaca: Cornell University Press, 1972), 249.

4. "Priezd vyslannykh iz Sov. Rossii," *Rul'*, [21] November 1922, 6; "Berlinskaia zhizn'. Sobranie vyslannykh," *Dni*, 29 November 1922, 5; "Russkaia literaturnaia i nauchnaia zhizn' za rubezhom," *Novaia Russkaia kniga*, 1922, nos. 11–12 (November–December): 27; "Vecher vyslannykh," *Dni*, 7 January 1923, 9; Lutokhin, diary entry for 21 February 1923, RO IRLI f.592, op.1, d.3, l.15. Lutokhin later complained that the Committee of the Deported seemed to exist only so that Iasinskii could be its chair (diary entry for 14 April 1923, RO IRLI f.592, op.1, d.3, l.29ob.).

5. It is Marc Raeff's argument that the emigration, despite its political bickering, was successful in creating an alternative Russia and preserving its cultural heritage (Raeff, *Russia Abroad: A Cultural History of the Russian Emigration, 1919–1939* [New York: Oxford University Press, 1990], esp. 3–5).

6. It was renamed the Russian Academic Union in Germany, and Iasinskii and Karsavin were elected its leaders ("Reorganizatsiia berlinskoi akademicheskoi gruppy," *Dni*, 3 December 1922, 7; "Khronika. Reorganizatsiia berlinskoi akademicheskoi gruppy," *Poslednie novosti*, 8 December 1922, 3; and Raeff, *Russia Abroad*, 60–61).

7. Frank, Aikhenval'd, Losskii, and Karsavin were also active in this academy ("Russkaia religiozno-filosofskaia akademiia pri Amerikanskom Khristianskom Soiuze

Molodykh liudei," *Dni*, 16 November 1922, 4; "Russkaia literaturnaia i nauchnaia zhizn' za rubezhom," *Novaia Russkaia kniga*, 1922, nos. 11–12 [November–December]: 27; Berdiaev, *Dream and Reality*, 247–48; Boobbyer, *S. L. Frank*, 123–25; and Williams, *Culture in Exile*, 249–52).

8. Osorgin, Aikhenval'd, and Berdiaev were involved in forming the Writers' Club, and Volkovyskii, Khariton, and Mel'gunov were active in the Union of Journalists and Litterateurs ("Russkaia nauchnaia i literaturnaia zhizn' za rubezhom," *Novaia russkaia kniga*, 1922, no. 10 [October]: 26, and 1923, no. 2 [February]: 40; Williams, *Culture in Exile*, 131; and Thomas R. Beyer, "The House of the Arts and the Writers' Club. Berlin 1921–1923," in *Russische Autoren und Verlage in Berlin nach dem Ersten Weltkrieg*, ed. Thomas R. Beyer, Gottfried Kratz, and Xenia Werner [Berlin: Berlin Verlag A. Spitz, 1987], 31–33).

9. Raeff, *Russia Abroad*, 73; "Literatura i kul'tura. O knigoizdatel'stve 'Zadruga,'" *Dni*, 5 November 1922, 16.

10. Williams, *Culture in Exile*, 131–32.

11. D. A. Lutokhin, "Zarubezhnye pastyri," *Minuvshee: Istoricheskii al'manakh* 22 (1997): 77; Robert H. Johnston, *New Mecca, New Babylon: Paris and the Russian Exiles, 1920–1945* (Montreal: McGill-Queen's University Press, 1988), 27; Raeff, *Russia Abroad*, 91–92; Boobbyer, *S. L. Frank*, 125; V. Bulgakov, "Kak prozhita," RGALI f.2226, op.1, d.61, l.117–70; S. P. Postnikov, *Russkie v Prage, 1918–1928* (Prague: [Volia Rossii], 1928), 141–43; and N. Losskii, *Vospominaniia*, 249.

12. "Russkaia literaturnaia i nauchnaia zhizn' za rubezhom," *Novaia russkaia kniga*, 1923, no. 1 (January): 36, and 1923, no. 2 (February): 39; Williams, *Culture in Exile*, 130–31; Raeff, *Russia Abroad*, 61–64; Postnikov, *Russkie v Prage*, 36–41, 54–58, 69–100; Novikov, *Ot moskvy*, 329–64; and *Czechoslovak Help to the Russian and Ukraine Emigration* (Prague: [Czechoslovak] Ministry of Foreign Affairs, 1924).

13. Aleksei Tolstoi, "Otkrytoe pis'mo N. V. Chaikovskomu," *Nakanune*, 14 April 1922.

14. Valentin Bulgakov recalled that "in those days the chasm separating the motherland and the emigration was not yet so deep. The division had not been made final." Most émigrés still believed that they would return to Russia in the near future (Bulgakov, "Kak prozhita," RGALI f.2226, op.1, d.61, l.54–55). GARF contains much documentation, in addition, on the return of White Army officers and other Civil War foes via several amnesties during 1922–23.

15. The Orgburo ordered the infiltration of émigré student groups in early 1922. In late December, the GPU sent Communist students from Moscow to a left-student congress in Berlin to lobby for reconciliation with Soviet Russia (addendum to Orgburo protocols, 10 February 1922, RGASPI f.17, op.60, d.137, l.33; commission for work among Russian émigré studentry protocols, 20 May 1922, RGASPI f.17, op.112, d.339, l.117; report, "The Russian Studentry Abroad," First Conference of Russian Student Organizations Abroad, Berlin, 27–30 December 1922, and theses on report, "Cultural Tasks of the Studentry," RGASPI f.17, op.84, d.309, l.243–46ob., 247; M. Glebov, Bureau of Communist Students, report on émigré studentry to the CC RCP, 13 February 1923, RGASPI f.17, op.84, d.309, l.241–42; see also Hardeman, *Coming to Terms*, 164–65).

16. This, of course, furthered the suspicions of far right émigrés that they were actually Soviet spies. On the legal status of Russian émigrés, see Z. S. Bocharova, comp.,

Russkie bezhentsy: Problemy rasseleniia, vozvrashcheniia na Rodinu, uregilirovaniia pravovogo polozheniia (1920–1930-e gody) (Moscow: Rosspen, 2004).

17. Krestinskii to Unshlikht, copies to Stalin, Kamenev, et al., 21 October 1922, RGASPI f.17, op.112, d.385, l.116; protocols of the Secretariat of the CC RCP, 10 November 1922, RGASPI f.17, op.112, d.385, l.4; Unshlikht et al. to I. V. Stalin, memo, 4 December 1922, in Iakovlev, *Lubianka. Stalin i VChK-GPU-OGPU-NKVD*, 69–70; and Politburo protocols, 14 December 1922, RGASPI f.17, op.3, d.326, l.5.

18. Bor. Or., "'Raznoglasiia v russkom voprose.' (Doklad E. D. Kuskovoi)," *Rul'*, 24 August 1922; "'Umerla li Rossiia?' 2-oi doklad E. D. Kuskovoi," *Poslednie Novosti*, 2 August 1922; E. Kuskova, "Bol'sheviki—nashi deti," *Poslednie novosti*, 13 and 14 September 1922; M. Mironov, "Rossiia, Emigratsiia, i nashi zadachi. (Doklad E. D. Kuskovoi)," *Poslednie Novosti*, 5 October 1922; E. Kuskova, "Bor'ba za vlast'," *Dni*, 6 February 1923; Kuskova, "Pis'mo iz Berlina," *Poslednie Novosti*, 1, 8, 18, 22, and 28 April 1923, and 18 May 1923; and Kuskova, "Zhiteiskoe," *Dni*, 28 April 1923.

19. E. Kuskova to V. A. Maklakov, 7 and 21 February 1923, Vasilii A. Maklakov Papers, box 9, folder 14, Hoover Institution Archives. I thank Jason Antevil for sharing his research on this correspondence.

20. P. Sorokin, "Nravstvennoe i umstvennoe sostoianie sovremennoi Rossii," *Volia Rossii*, 1922, no. 4 (1 November): 25–33, and no. 5 (15 November): 21–33 (quote from no. 4, p. 33). These ideas were developed in Sorokin, *Sovremennoe sostoianie Rossii* (Prague: Vl. A. Vinnichuk, 1922); Sorokin, "To, chto chasto zabyvaetsiia," *Krestianskaia Rossiia*, 1923, nos. 2–3: 14–31; and Sorokin, "Rossiia posle nepa," *Krestianskaia Rossiia*, 1923, no. 4: 140–59. Kuskova rebutted Sorokin's claims concerning this demoralization and degeneration in Ek. Kuskova, "A chto vnutri?" *Volia Rossii*, 1922, no. 6 (34) (1 December): 28–37, and no. 7 (35) (15 December): 31–42; Sorokin responded with "Eshche raz o moral'nom sostoianii Rossii (otvet E. D. Kuskovoi)," *Volia Rossii*, 1923, no. 1 (15 January): 32–39.

21. A. A. Kizevetter to V. A. Maklakov, 1 December 1923, in "'Bol'shevizm est' neschast'e, no neschast'e zasluzhennoe.' Perepiska V. A. Maklakova i A. A. Kizevettera," *Istochnik*, 1996, no. 2: 9, italics in original. Kizevetter was one of the few who quickly understood that few of the émigrés would be returning any time soon (ibid., 10).

22. Osorgin wrote to Berdiaev, who shared much of his disdain, that "people here are comical. They believe that they are not rotten [*tukhlye*] émigrés. Perhaps it is true that they aren't rotten and only accidentally smell bad" (Osorgin to Berdiaev, 11 December 1923, Berdiaev Collection, Bakhmeteff Archive, Columbia University, New York).

23. A. Petrishchev, "O narodnoi nravstvennosti," *Dni*, 12 December 1922, 1; Petrishchev, "Eshche o nravstvennosti i o revoliutsii," *Dni*, 21 December 1922, 1–2; Petrishchev, "Bol'shevizm krasnyi i belyi," *Dni*, 20 January 1923, 1–2; Petrishchev, "Kul'tura i politika," *Dni*, 11 February 1923, 1–2.

24. Fëdor Stepun, "Mysli o Rossii," *Sovremennye Zapiski*, no. 17 (1923): 351–75.

25. Mikh. Osorgin, "Priiatie Rossii," *Dni*, 4 February 1923, 1; Osorgin, "Italianskoe pis'mo," *Volia Rossii*, 1923, no. 15 (15 September): 44. On his views of the emigration, see also Donald M. Fiene, "The Life and Works of M. A. Osorgin, 1878–1942" (Ph.D. diss., Indiana University, 1973), 89–103.

26. As Kuskova wrote to B. A. Bakhmeteff, Peshekhonov's contentions "left far behind the provocative tone of my first papers. The essence is the same, but going even further" (Kuskova to Bakhmeteff, 2 April 1923, Bakhmeteff Collection, Bakhmeteff

Archive, Columbia University, New York; cited in Antevil, "Politics of Russian Populism," 612).

27. Peshekhonov, *Pochemu ia ne emigriroval?* (Berlin: Obelisk, 1923); and Peshekhonov, "Rodina i emigratsiia," *Volia Rossii,* 1925, nos. 7–8: 102–28; nos. 9–10: 94–115; no. 11: 60–99. See also Antevil, "Politics of Russian Populism," 612–17. As Antevil notes, Peshekhonov (as well as Kuskova, Osorgin, and other "returnists") remained committed to democratic socialism, had no ties to the Soviet state, and thus should not be confused with the *smenovekhovtsy.*

28. S. Mel'gunov, "My i oni," *Poslednie novosti,* 27 July 1923; and Antevil, "Politics of Russian Populism," 618–25. On Mel'gunov's rightward political evolution, see Iu. N. Emel'ianov, *S. P. Mel'gunov: v Rossii i emigratsii* (Moscow: Editorial URSS, 1998), 67–70, and P. N. Miliukov, *Emigratsiia na pereput'e* (Paris: Resp.-Dem. Ob"ed., 1926), 82–89.

29. Miliukov, who was consistently more sympathetic toward Kuskova and Peshekhonov than most, provides a detailed account of "returnism" and the publicistic battles concerning it in *Emigratsiia na pereput'e,* 70–122.

30. Kuskova acknowledged this point in a response to Miliukov ("Mysli vslukh," *Poslednie novosti,* 5 November 1925, 2). Even Petrishchev, who had been critical of the emigration, distanced himself from Peshekhonov ("Na chistotu," *Dni,* 11 October 1925, 2).

31. Ek. Kuskova, "Mysli vslukh," *Poslednie novosti,* 25 October 1925, 2; M. A. Osorgin, "Trebuetsia lantset," *Poslednie novosti,* 28 October 1925, 2, Also Osorgin, "O srokakh bytiia," *Dni,* 3 October 1925, 2.

32. Mikh. Osorgin, "Razgovor s dukhom rodstvennika," and A. Kerenskii, "Vskryvsheesia nedorazumenie," *Dni,* 11 November 1925, 2. (Both articles are in Mikhail A. Osorgin, *Selected Stories, Reminiscences, and Essays,* ed. and trans. Donald M. Fiene [Ann Arbor: Ardis, 1982], 84–92.) Kerensky eventually invited Osorgin to contribute and even to edit the literary page of the resurrected Paris version of *Dni* (Fiene, "Aftermath," ibid., 93–94).

33. Peshekhonov, "Rodina i emigratsiia," nos. 7–8: 104; cited in Antevil, "Politics of Russian Populism," 646.

34. Antevil, "Politics of Russian Populism," 663–66; excerpts from Politburo protocols, 24 April 1924 and 4 June 1925, in "'Poruchit' motivirovat' otkaz,'" *Istochnik,* 2000, no. 5: 68; A. V. Peshekhonov to Soviet plenipotentiary in Czechoslovakia, declaration, 16 May 1925; Peshekhonov to Krasin, 26 May 1925; Krasin to Peshekhonov, 9 June 1925; Soviet plenipotentiary in Czechoslovakia to Peshekhonov, 24 July 1925; and Figner to Peshekhonov, 21 November 1925, Rukopisnyi otdel Rossiiskoi natsional'noi biblioteki (henceforth RO RNB), f.581, op.1, d.4, l.3, 5; d.36, l.1; d.50, l.1; and d.55, l.1.

35. While working in Riga, Peshekhonov was allowed to return to Russia several times on short visits, and he was buried in Leningrad in 1933 (Antevil, "Politics of Russian Populism," 673–82).

36. In 1924 Lutokhin wrote, "They are so used to portraying Soviet Russia in black colors alone that any objective word calls forth mistrust: some thought, '*smenovekhovets,* Communist, Soviet agent'" ("Sem' toshchikh let. [Mezhdu Vladivostokom i Pragoi]. Iz vospominanii," RO RNB f.445, op.1, d.4, l.11).

37. "Let those who really want to return to Russia," Sorokin wrote in irritation. "As far as I am concerned, I despise (not even hate, but despise) the current bunglers—that

is, rulers—of Russia, and in spite of a limitless love for Russia . . . and readiness to return and work for her in the most difficult conditions, at the current time my return is useless" (Sorokin to Lutokhin, 1 February 1925, in "Dve sud'by. (Pitirim Sorokin i Dalmat Lutokhin)," *Vazhskaia oblast'*, 1992, no. 6: 17–31). Also on their falling out, see Lutokhin, "Zarubezhnye pastyri," 33–46.

38. D. Lutokhin, "Russkaia zhizn'. Rossiia i emigratsiia," *Volia Rossii* 1923, no. 11 (15 June): 77–84.

39. "[Peshekhonov] was the single public figure [in the emigration], with whom I felt a solidarity," Lutokhin wrote in "Zarubezhnye pastyri," 76–85.

40. A. P. Lutokhin to the chairman of VTsIK, 5 May 1927, RO IRLI f.592, op.1, d.289, l.1–10b.; Pil'niak to Lutokhin, 1 January 1924, 2 March 1925, and 19 May 1927, in "Pis'ma Boris Pil'niaka V. S. Miroliubovu i D. A. Lutokhinu," *Russkaia literatura*, 1989, no. 2: 231–34. Gorky's letters to Lutokhin are in Maksim Gor'kii, *Neizdannaia perepiska*, vol. 14 of *Arkhiv A. M. Gor'kogo* (Moscow: Nauka, 1976), 378–443. (Gorky's assistance in Lutokhin's return is referred to in, inter alia, his letter of 22 January 1927 [p. 423].) After his return, Lutokhin's attempts to publish were routinely rejected (Iu. I. Kombolina, introduction to Lutokhin, "Zarubezhnye Pastyri," 10–11). He was arrested in Leningrad as a "socially dangerous element" in 1935, but Gorky's intervention again saved him from deportation or worse, and he lived without further hindrance until his death during the blockade in 1942.

41. S. L. Frank, *Biografiia P. B. Struve* (New York: Chekhov Publishing House, 1956), 131–32.

42. Il'in's extensive correspondence with Struve after his deportation is in Il'in, *Sobranie sochinenii*, suppl. vol. 2, *Dnevnik. Pis'ma. Dokumenty (1903–1938)*, 115–209. Despite his conservative views, Il'in was one of the first to advise Struve to disassociate himself from *Vozrozhdenie* as it became openly reactionary (Richard Pipes, *Struve: Liberal on the Right, 1905–1944* [Cambridge: Harvard University Press, 1980], 390–91).

43. On the polemics around Il'in's ideas, see N. Poltoratskii, *I. A. Il'in i polemika vokrug ego idei o soprotivlenii zlu siloi* (London, Ont.: Zaria, 1975); Poltoratskii, *Ivan Aleksandrovich Il'in: zhizn', trudy, mirovozzrenie. Sbornik statei* (Tenafly, N.J.: Hermitage, 1989), 120–31. The many articles constituting this debate are published as "O soprotivlenii zlu siloi: Pro et contra. Polemika vokrug idei I. A. Il'ina," in Il'in, *Sobranie sochinenii*, vol. 5, 289–556.

44. I. Il'in, *O soprotivlenii zlu siloiu* (Berlin: [Tipografiia Ob-va "Presse"], 1925).

45. Frank, *Struve*, 131–32. Berdiaev, *Dream and Reality*, 245.

46. Nikolai Berdiaev, "Koshmar zlogo dobra. (O knige I. Il'ina 'O soprotivlenii zlu siloiu')," *Put'*, 1926, no. 4 (June–July): 78. Losskii was far more sympathetic to Il'in's views than was Berdiaev (N. O. Lossky, *History of Russian Philosophy* [New York: International University Press, 1951], 387–89).

47. Berdiaev, *Dream and Reality*, 245–46. Whereas the returnists suggested day-to-day principled social activity, Berdiaev referred to a "painful process of inner purification" ("Dukhovnye zadachi Russkoi emigratsii," *Put'*, 1925, no. 1 [September]: 3–7).

48. Boobbyer, *S. L. Frank*, 134–37; Frank, *Struve*, 123–47; Nikolaj Plotnikov, "Revolution and the Counter-Revolution: The Conflict over Meaning between P. B. Struve and S. L. Frank in 1922," *Studies in East European Thought* 46 (1994): 187–96; and "Ispytanie revoliutsii i kontrrevoliutsii: Perepiska P. B. Struve i S. L. Franka (1922–1925)," *Voprosy filosofii*, 1993, no. 2: 115–39.

49. Fëdor Stepun, "Mysli o Rossii. (O 'Vozrozhdenii' i vozvrashchenstve)," *Sovremennye zapiski*, no. 28 (1926): 365–92.

50. Florovskii's correspondence with Leningrad historians in the 1950s–60s is at the Slovanska Knihovna in Prague.

51. After twenty-five years in exile, Bulgakov resumed his post as head of the Tolstoy Museum in Moscow, which he had founded shortly before his deportation.

Conclusion: The Intelligentsia in Soviet Russia

Epigraph: Nikolai Ognev, *The Diary of a Communist Undergraduate*, trans. Alexander Werth (New York: Payson and Clarke, 1929), 62–67, cited in part in Halfin, *Darkness to Light*, 198.

1. G. Zinov'ev, "Doklad na Vserossiiskom s"ezde nauchnykh rabotnikov 23-go noiabria 1923 g.," in *Sud'by russkoi intelligentsii: Materialy diskussii, 1923–1925 gg., ed.* V. L. Soskin (Novosibirsk: Nauka, 1991), 137–58.

2. L. Trotskii, "K pervomu vser. s"ezdu nauchnykh rabotnikov," *Pravda*, 24 November 1923, 1.

3. "Zakliuchitel'noe slovo t. Bubnova," *Tretii Vserossiiskii S"ezd politprosvetov RSFSR. Biulleten'*, no. 1 (29 November 1922): 16. Daniel Todes has called Pavlov a "prosperous dissident," noting that his fame and the Bolsheviks' desire to establish Soviet science caused them to tolerate his consistent criticism through the 1920s (Daniel Todes, "Pavlov and the Bolsheviks," *History and Philosophy of the Life Sciences* 17 [1995]: 379–418).

4. Lunacharskii and Bukharin argued against cultural maximalism at, inter alia, a public discussion on the question of the intelligentsia in March 1925 ("Sud'by sovremennoi intelligentsii, 1925 g. Doklad A. B. Lunacharskogo, vystupleniia P. N. Sakulina, N. I. Bukharina, Iu. V. Kliuchnikova," in Soskin, *Sud'by*, 18–54; see also Leon Trotsky, *Literature and Revolution*, trans. Rose Strunsky [New York: International Publishers, 1925]).

5. "Sud'by sovremennoi," 35–36. Hellbeck examines Bukharin's remarks in *Revolution on My Mind*, 133, 140.

6. On the negative portrayal of the intelligentsia throughout the 1920s, see Halfin, *Darkness to Light*, 196–98.

7. Hardeman, *Coming to Terms*, 180–82; Iagoda to Molotov, report on the journal *Rossiia*, and CC resolution on the journal *Novaia Rossiia*, in *Khrestomatiia po otechestvennoi istorii (1914–1945 gg.)*, ed. A. F. Kiselev and E. M. Shchagin (Moscow: VLADOS, 1996), 737–41; OGPU documents on expulsion of Lezhnev, in Makarov and Khristoforov, *Vysylka vmesto rasstrela*, 265–68; and Kassof, "The Knowledge Front," 306–7. Lezhnev, strangely enough, was allowed to return to the Soviet Union in 1930 and even joined the party at Stalin's own invitation. That he was expelled at the midpoint of NEP and returned at the climactic moment of the "cultural revolution" is yet another example of inconsistencies in the traditional periodization of the waves of cultural struggle.

8. This point is made in Amir Weiner, "Nature, Nurture, and Memory in a Socialist Utopia: Delineating the Soviet Socio-Ethnic Body in the Age of Socialism," *American Historical Review* 104, no. 4 (October 1999): 1121.

9. Pit. Sorokin, "Sovremennaia intelligentsiia," *Dni*, 21 November 1922.

10. Mikh. Osorgin, "Novaia intelligentsiia," *Dni*, 6 December 1922.

11. Hellbeck details how one intellectual, Zinaida Denisevskaya, gradually came to accept this role in *Revolution on My Mind*, 115–64.

12. Douglas R. Weiner, *A Little Corner of Freedom: Russian Nature Protection from Stalin to Gorbachev* (Berkeley: University of California Press, 1999). Weiner notes that most field naturalists attempted to delimit their activities to the realm of *nauchnaia obshchestvennost'* (scientific public opinion) rather than *obshchestvennost'* in the larger sense (30–31).

Index

Italicized page numbers indicate the names of the deportees listed in the index.